THE CRITICAL TURN

Kritik: German Literary Theory and Cultural Studies
Liliane Weissberg, *Editor*

BOOKS IN THIS SERIES

MICHAEL MORTON

THE CRITICAL TURN

STUDIES IN

KANT, HERDER, WITTGENSTEIN,

AND CONTEMPORARY THEORY

Wayne State University Press   Detroit

COPYRIGHT © 1993 | BY WAYNE STATE UNIVERSITY PRESS

Detroit, Michigan 48202. All rights are reserved.

No part of this book may be reproduced without formal permission.

Manufactured in the United States of America.

99 98 97 96 95 94 93   5 4 3 2 1

LIBRARY OF CONGRESS | CATALOGING IN PUBLICATION DATA

Morton, Michael.

The critical turn : studies in Kant, Herder, Wittgenstein, and

contemporary theory / Michael Morton.

p.   cm.—(Kritik)

Includes bibliographical references and index.

ISBN 0-8143-2376-6 (alk. paper)

1. Literature—Philosophy.   2. Skepticism in literature.

3. Dogmatism in literature.   4. Kant, Immanuel, 1724–1804.

5. Herder, Johann Gottfried, 1744–1803.   6. Wittgenstein, Ludwig,

1889–1951.   I. Title.   II. Series.

PN49.M67   1993

801—dc20   92-13153

DESIGNER | S. R. TENENBAUM

FOR DANNY

AND ALL HIS BROTHERS

There is a massive central core of human thinking which has no history . . . : there are categories and concepts which, in their most fundamental character, change not at all. Obviously these are not the specialties of the most refined thinking. They are the commonplaces of the least refined thinking; and are yet the indispensable core of the conceptual equipment of the most sophisticated human beings. It is with these, their interconnexions, and the structure that they form, that a descriptive metaphysics will be primarily concerned.

P. F. Strawson, *Individuals: An Essay in Descriptive Metaphysics*

CONTENTS

ABBREVIATIONS

AR	*The Autonomy of Reason*
CIS	*Contingency, Irony, and Solidarity*
CP	*Consequences of Pragmatism*
CTH	*The Critical Theory of Jürgen Habermas*
CV	*Contingencies of Value*
DWN	*Doing What Comes Naturally*
HL	"History and Literature"
ITC	*Is There a Text in This Class?*
KMA	*Kant's Theory of Mental Activity*
KTI	*Kant's Transcendental Idealism*
OC	*On Certainty*
PI	*Philosophical Investigations*
PMC	*The Postmodern Condition*
PMN	*Philosophy and the Mirror of Nature*
RC	"A Reply to my Critics"
SSR	*The Structure of Scientific Revolutions*
SWS	Herder's *Sämtliche Werke*
TLP	*Tractatus Logico-Philosophicus*
UP	"What Is Universal Pragmatics?"
Z	*Zettel*

INTRODUCTION

AMONG THE MOST SALIENT DEVELOPMENTS IN RECENT YEARS IN the field of literary studies is the much discussed, analyzed, commented upon, and argued over ascendancy of "theory." The kinds of things that those active in the field today are inclined to say about the objects of their professional concern have come to be informed by "philosophical" considerations of one sort or another, both to an extent and in a fashion seldom if ever discernible in the work of their counterparts of as recently as a generation ago. Efforts to determine the distinctive nature of literary texts and the procedures one ought to follow in interpreting them—efforts that have figured prominently in discussions among critics for almost as long as there has been something recognizable as literature in existence at all—have been largely either supplanted by or assimilated to inquiries regarding the status of knowledge claims in general and the possibility, or lack thereof, of such claims ever being secured. The latter sort of reflection looms large in contemporary critical deliberations in a way that, so far as I can tell, was not the case (or rarely so) prior to about the early-to-mid-1960s. Questions of what we can plausibly claim to be able to say about the meanings of literary works have been "reinscribed" within a context of radical interrogation of the possibility of saying, or meaning, anything about, or by, anything; and this "recontextualization" has in turn furthered, at the same time that it has been furthered by, the tendency to question the legitimacy of distinguishing in any fundamental way between specifically literary texts and any other kind at all. What, if anything, can we know? And how? By what criteria? How do we even understand these questions? And assuming that we do understand them in some way, what answers, if any, can we reasonably hope to find for them? It has, I think, become all but impossible—and perhaps not even "all but" anymore—for anyone in literary studies who does not at least take cognizance of such questions as these and of the various issues that they raise, whether or not one seeks to engage such questions and issues directly oneself, to claim for one's work the serious attention of others in the field. And to the limited extent that I am in a position to assess recent developments in other areas of the humanities and social sciences, much the same seems increasingly to hold true there as well.

The starting point for the reflections on these and related matters that I offer here is a twofold conviction: first, the dominant tenor of critical studies today is, as it has been for at least a decade and a half now, one of prevailing *skepticism* regarding the possibility of securing knowledge claims; second, this skeptical outlook nonetheless represents, as skepticism always has done, a wholly untenable position. A claim this sweeping, of course, already demands at least some elaboration and qualification. Two particularly important points requiring attention are the following. First, the term *skepticism* covers a considerable amount of not entirely uniform philosophical ground. In its long history, it has been employed by friend and foe alike to refer to a number of broadly similar, but also distinguishable, attitudes toward the nature of reality and the relationships to it capable of being entered into by the human mind.[1] Whatever the differences in detail, however, skepticism always comes down eventually to either an outright denial or something that entails a denial that anyone ever has definitive knowledge of objective reality. And it is in this sense that I use the term throughout the discussion here. It is particularly important, I think, to insist on the term *ever* in this connection. The notion of a partial or qualified skepticism, understood as a skepticism applying only to certain phenomenal domains but not to others, or within a given domain only to a certain extent but no further, strikes me as simply an oxymoron; for it would also concede, at least tacitly, that there is after all something out there, or in us, of which we can in the end be truly certain. To take an often-used example, this is rather like being only a little pregnant. There is, of course, a perfectly standard nontechnical use of *skeptical* in which the term expresses nothing more than doubt or suspicion regarding some knowledge claim or claims in particular. To characterize oneself as "skeptical" in this sense is merely to indicate a desire not to be overly credulous. This is, however, no more to adopt *skepticism* as a philosophical position in the sense of that notion relevant to the discussion here—the sense to which in particular, as I shall argue, the skeptical strain of contemporary criticism is committed—than it would be to adopt pacifism if one were to impose on oneself the restriction of fighting only in just wars.

Second, although at least some critics today actually do seem to profess a more or less undiluted form of skepticism in the sense of the term just given, one of the more striking features of the contemporary scene is the way in which many other critics seek in effect to combine a basic penchant for skepticism with one form or another of metaphysical dogmatism, drawing on now the one, now the other, standpoint as the occasion demands, but with little apparent sense for the fundamental self-contradiction to which in so doing they commit themselves.[2] One principal reason, indeed, that it has often proved so difficult to develop a coherent synoptic view of the contemporary critical scene is precisely the extraordinary number of different ways in which individual critics somehow manage to preserve in their own thinking this coexistence of the mutually exclusive. At the same time, however, there is also a certain fairly definite chronology to be noted here. The mixture of dogmatism and skepticism did not happen all at once. Rather, it was only *after* primarily skeptical modes of thought had gained a more or less substantial degree of acceptance in their own right that various dogmatic strains then began to be grafted on to them. And, partly for this reason, I want provisionally to hold the two positions apart and continue for the moment to treat skepticism by itself.

To put, then, what I take to be the key point with regard to skepticism in slightly different terms: the skeptical outlook *denies* that such things as *facts* about the world are knowable with *certainty* by human beings. The principal reason for expressing this view as a matter of *denial* is to block in advance a move by which many contemporary skeptics believe they can rescue their position. This is the contention that they are not actually "asserting" anything; rather they are, for example, merely "trying to change the subject" or "proposing a new way of looking at things not bound to notions of 'truth' or 'falsehood' at all" or something of the sort. As Donald Davidson observes, however, to be accounted "skeptical," a theory need not "make reality unknowable"; it is sufficient that it "reduce reality to so much less than we believe there is."[3] This finely nuanced distinction is, I think, ideally suited to capturing much of what is most characteristically skeptical in contemporary theory. It applies perfectly, for example, to the conflation of text and opinion-about-text that is among the most prominent features of literary criticism today and of which we will consider some specific instances later. The expression "what we believe there is," by the way, does not refer in Davidson's idiom to mere opinion or supposition. As we shall see, one of Davidson's most important insights, central to his version of what I will be calling the *critical* standpoint, is the recognition that belief is inherently, in his word, "veridical."

In place of facts and our knowledge of them, the skeptical outlook posits such things as contexts of belief, differential perspectives, ideological colorings, culturally determined matrices of perception, and the both various and variable interpretations that from time to time a given individual or group may happen to adopt (contingently, as it is sometimes put) on the basis of these contexts, perspectives, and the rest. The vocabulary of belief contexts, interpretations, contingency, and the like, in addition to being familiar to virtually everyone in criticism today as a result of the work of some of the currently most influential figures in the field, is at the same time, however, also one to which no avowed skeptic of the past, from Pyrrho to Mauthner, would have felt the slightest difficulty assenting. It is worth noting this, I think, to remind ourselves once again of both the ancient lineage and the essential continuity of the skeptical tradition from antiquity to the present. Though it is surely too much to characterize the history of philosophy, with Whitehead, as merely "a series of footnotes to Plato," it would by the same token also be difficult to deny that philosophers have frequently overestimated by a wide margin the degree of originality actually represented by their works. For examples of such overestimation one certainly need look no further than to many skeptically inclined thinkers of the late twentieth century. Repeatedly in their writings one finds, whether expressly or only tacitly, the same fundamental conviction that what they are saying really is being said for the very first time in the whole long history of thought. And given this belief, it is then not surprising, of course, that we also regularly find the same writers confidently predicting the imminent dawn of a new era in human history, now that the old dogmatisms, positivisms, and other superstitions of that ilk that had held the human race in thrall for so long have at last been overthrown and put behind us once and for all.

As suggested, skeptical doctrine in one form or another has by now to a considerable extent acquired the status of a virtual orthodoxy in much of contemporary criticism. That *reality* is merely a kind of fiction, *truth* a species of metaphor, and *understanding* a form of error or incomprehension are today, for many, things that literally go without saying. In characterizing this view as nonetheless untenable, its widespread acceptance notwithstanding, I do not mean simply that I think skepticism is mistaken; against that charge the skeptic will always have ready the standard response: "How do you know?" I mean that skepticism is incoherent, that there is no way of even enunciating it as a position one might consider adopting that does not at once collapse of its own unintelligibility. The skeptic's "How do you know?" is in this way preempted and undermined in advance by the other of the two basic questions to which, it has been alleged, all philosophical inquiry sooner or later comes down, namely: "What do you mean by that?" Not merely the burden of proof, but the logically prior task of showing that he has even succeeded in making sense, thus remains squarely on the shoulders of the skeptic. But it lies in the very nature of what he is trying to assert that this is also an obligation he is never able to discharge.

In the Preface to the second edition of the *Critique of Pure Reason* Kant characterizes his philosophical enterprise as, in the first instance, a "negative" one.[4] In the second edition of his *Fragments on Recent German Literature* (written, incidentally, more than a decade before even the first edition of the first *Critique*), Herder outlines his vision for a similarly conceived, but in this case linguistically-based, "negative philosophy."[5] And both in the *Tractatus* and in the *Philosophical Investigations*, as well as elsewhere in the post-1929 writings, Wittgenstein, too, indicates that he sees the primary task of philosophy as, in a sense fundamentally similar to those of Kant and Herder, a "negative" one: the purpose of doing philosophy is not to propound positive doctrine;[6] rather it is to clear away confusion,[7] and in that way to help people reach a point at which they can carry on with their lives in a manner at least unencumbered by the kinds of pseudo-problems that arise from a misapprehension of the grammar of ordinary language.[8] Kant, Herder, and Wittgenstein together provide the principal sources of inspiration for this book. And in the same spirit as I take theirs to have been, I see its purpose as also primarily a negative one.

Criticism today, it seems to me, finds itself to a large extent in a position analogous to the one of which Wittgenstein speaks in the *Investigations* when he says: "A *picture* held us captive. And we could not get outside of it, for it lay in our language and language seemed to repeat it to us inexorably" (*PI*, § 115). The "picture" in question—not the one to which Wittgenstein is referring, but the one that seems to have captivated much of contemporary critical theory—is a "negative" one in its own right, though in a sense of the term quite different from Kant's, Herder's, Wittgenstein's, and a fortiori my own. Its characteristic vocabulary is that of *in*determinacy, *de*-centering, *anti*-foundationalism, *dis*placement, and so on through a by now generally familiar list. In a word it is, again, the standpoint of radical *denial* that I suggested a moment ago has been the defining mark of skepticism in all ages.[9] Once trapped within this "prison-house of theory," as it were, one may easily end up going through much the same sort of quasi-ritualistic motions that Wittgenstein in the *Investigations* describes as having characterized an earlier stage of his own career. Referring to *TLP,* 4.5 ("The general form of a proposition is: This is how things are"), he says: "This is the kind of proposition that one repeats to oneself countless times. One thinks that one is tracing the outline of the thing's nature over and over again, and one is merely tracing round the frame through which we look at it" (*PI,* § 114).[10] Similarly, but in the opposite direction, if one has once been persuaded of the inevitability of the assumptions underlying the skeptical position, it will not be surprising if one then finds the conclusions regarding the supposed indeterminacy of meaning and nonexistence of objective factuality in which these assumptions issue (the manifestly counterintuitive character of these conclusions notwithstanding) wholly compelling as well. One continues "tracing . . . over and over again" what might be called "the general form of how things are not" and fails to recognize that in so doing one is in fact "merely tracing round the frame" that "holds one captive."

The impressive degree of acceptance enjoyed by skeptical outlooks today is to a large extent a reflection of the enormously powerful influence of Nietzsche. One supposes that in adopting a broadly skeptical standpoint with regard to matters of fact or meaning one is in effect merely being a good Nietzschean—that one is, for example, simply realizing the full implications of a notion such as the "death of God." Yet I think contemporary skeptics have on the whole been a bit hasty (at best) in concluding that they have actually assimilated all that Nietzsche had in mind with that message.[11] Just as Friedrich Schlegel foresaw that an inability to take seriously any longer the aesthetics of the beautiful would not in itself entail the end of aesthetics per se, but would instead merely give rise in time to what he called an "aesthetics of the ugly" (a prediction that, it seems scarcely necessary to add, has been more than amply borne out in the present day[12]), so Nietzsche recognized that the news of the "death of God" would not in itself automatically produce a general liberation from dependence on god-surrogates of all sorts. Nor would it be necessary that to perform their function such surrogates have an overtly positive or substantive nature. At the conclusion of *On the Genealogy of Morals* he states, in a formulation that goes to the heart of his analysis of the phenomenon of nihilism, "Man would rather will *nothing,* than *not* will"—or, as the passage has also been translated, somewhat less literally, but in a manner that may nonetheless bring out its relevance in the present connection even more clearly, "Man would sooner have the void for his purpose than be void of purpose."[13] What follows the era of *theology,* of domination by images of *God,* is by no means necessarily a time freed of dependence on such images altogether. It can equally well be one dominated by images of God-in-His-absence, the *deus absconditus,* and so, concomitantly, by the sort of negative theology that devotion to such images requires.

Arthur Danto notes that what "the final aphorism of the *Genealogy* . . . does is [to] restate the instinct of *ressentiment:* man would rather his suffering be meaningful, hence would rather will meaning into it, than acquiesce in the meaninglessness of it."[14] And he observes further, with respect specifically to the "announce[ment of] the death of God," that "[i]t is plain that [for Nietzsche] God did not die that something else should take His place"; the idea was "rather [that] the place [should] die with the occupant." Things, however, have not quite worked out that way:

> The genius of the third essay of the *Genealogy* lies in its inventory of the disguises the ascetic ideal takes, so that positions which define themselves as contrary to asceticism only exemplify it. As a class, these occupants of the position vacated by God impose on their subscribers a network of interpretation of suffering and project a kind of utopian redemption: science, politics, art, and certainly much that passes for psychological therapy, only change the name of the game.[15]

Danto lists here instances of positive, or substantive, surrogates adopted to fill the place of the now vanished, though not yet vanquished, God. But, as suggested a moment ago, there are also *negative,* or *privative,* versions of the same thing, and since about the mid-1960s, this is increasingly the form that the quest for god-surrogates has assumed in critical theory. One could look long and hard, I think, without finding a better capsule characterization of the psychology of contemporary skepticism than as an unwillingness to "acquiesce in the meaninglessness" of precisely that which one believes one has exposed as meaningless. A truly consistent deconstructionist, for example, would withdraw into a silence of Cratylan impenetrability.[16] But in fact, of course, that never happens. Instead, this sort of skeptic insists that even the (presumed) condition of "meaninglessness" somehow "be [made] meaningful" in its own right. And thus he "will[s] meaning into it," if only in negative and purportedly self-cancelling fashion—as he puts it, "under erasure."

Robert Scholes characterizes Derrida's "presentation of the history of writing," in the "Science and the Name of Man" section of *Of*

Grammatology, as the development, heavily influenced by André Leroi-Gourhan's *Le Geste et la parole,* of "a myth of lost linguistic plenitude." And he continues:

> Derrida extends this mythic nostalgia for a lost plenitude of language in a predictably linear and circular way to the present moment . . . , in which he himself functions as the precursor of a revived mythogrammatic culture, destined to emerge from the now decadent evil empire of linearity. . . . Because Derrida sees language as essentially differential—as the product of a purely divisive force that has shaped consciousness in its own image—he must find in history some actual language that corresponds to his view. And this is exactly what he finds, only it is situated in a mythic past, the inconceivable "before" of the mythogram, and in an equally mythic future, which is nevertheless at hand.[17]

In this same vein, consider Lyotard's distinction between what he terms "modern" and "postmodern" aesthetics:

> If it is true that modernity takes place in the withdrawal of the real and according to the sublime relation between the presentable and the conceivable, it is possible, within this relation, to distinguish two modes. . . . The emphasis can be placed on the powerlessness of the faculty of presentation, on the nostalgia for presence felt by the human subject. . . . The emphasis can also be placed on the increase of being and the jubilation which result from the invention of new rules of the game, be it pictorial, artistic, or any other. . . . [M]odern aesthetics is an aesthetic of the sublime, though a nostalgic one. It allows the unpresentable to be put forward only as the missing contents; but the form, because of its recognizable consistency, continues to offer to the reader or viewer matter for solace and pleasure. . . . The postmodern would be that which, in the modern, puts forward the unpresentable in presentation itself; that which denies itself the solace of good forms, the consensus of taste which would make it possible to share collectively the nostalgia for the unattainable.[18]

One aspect of the fundamentally flawed character of Lyotard's model here emerges in the examples (or one of them at any rate) that he proposes for his two tendencies in aesthetics: "It seems to me that the essay (Montaigne) is postmodern, while the fragment (*The Athaeneum [sic]*) is modern."[19] To suggest that the contributors to the *Athenäum,* and in particular the author of the *Athenäums-Fragmente,* Friedrich Schlegel, were somehow animated by "nostalgia" is either to misapprehend in a very fundamental way the nature of German Idealism or, if not that, then certainly at any rate to overlook its central importance for Jena Romanticism. (The situation with respect to "nostalgia" is, of course, rather different in the case of the Heidelberg Romantics.) What I am more concerned to emphasize at the moment, however, is that Lyotard has got his categories skewed with regard to the present as well. For as we have already seen to some extent, it is precisely what he represents as the postmodernists' reveling in unconstrained innovation that is in fact dominated throughout by a rigidly maintained "consensus" regarding "the missing contents." And it is, accordingly, also precisely in the— by now, virtually canonical—liturgy of nonpresence that one finds the "solace" that comes from "shar[ing] collectively [with one's fellow postmodernists] the nostalgia for the unattainable." Again, however, Nietzsche had already anticipated the point over a century ago. As Bernd Magnus notes,

> One way of reading Nietzsche's famous conclusion in the section of *Twilight of the Idols* called "How the 'True World' Finally Became a Fable" . . . is to argue that the cheerful acceptance of the collapse of the appearance/reality binary hierarchical opposition is phony, incomplete, and self-deceptive. It is to argue that the asymmetrical binary oppositions which are deeply characteristic of Western intellectual history, morality, and culture do not evaporate or collapse; rather the terms of the binary opposition merely change, offices are vacated and new incumbents take their place. . . . Incomplete nihilism, passive nihilism triumphs with the devaluation of the highest values.[20]

By the same token, it seems to be the case that every great thinker, at one time or another, also says things that those who admire him would probably just as soon he had not said. And this may be truer of Nietzsche than of almost any other important philosopher in our tradition. Certainly his writings are replete with utterances that, if meant seriously (with Nietzsche, of course, not always something that can be taken for granted), are difficult not to regard as embarrassments or worse. Familiar examples include his attempt to construct an argument showing that the eternal recurrence of the same is in fact a metaphysical-cosmological necessity—surely one of the worst arguments ever produced by a philosopher of genius[21]—as well as many of his justly notorious remarks regarding women. One statement not ordinarily viewed in a similarly dubious light, but which I would nevertheless urge deserves to be, is his famous profession of concern that we should not be rid of the idea of God so long as we continued to believe in grammar.[22] This passage is, of course, frequently cited today in wholly approving tones; yet it raises a number of very considerable difficulties, some of which will occupy us at much greater length in the discussion to follow. For the moment it is perhaps sufficient to note that if Nietzsche were actually correct in his diagnosis, the result would be to make of theism itself an entirely noncontroversial, even trivial, matter. For it is clearly no more possible *not* to "believe" in "grammar" (if by *grammar* is meant something like logical syntax) than it would be not to "believe" that one were suffering a headache at the moment of experiencing its pain.[23] Just as the experience itself and the awareness of the object of experience are in the case of a headache *identical*, so the very attempt to express one's "disbelief" in "grammar" ineluctably involves the one making the attempt in what is sometimes called "performative contradiction."

Both belief and disbelief are propositional attitudes. But propositions are not even conceivable apart from logical syntax. And valid propositions, accordingly, are impossible unless that syntax, too, is valid. From this, however, it follows that one cannot *truly*, or even *coherently*, express (or seek to express) one's disbelief in grammar—one cannot, that is, utter the statement "I do not believe in grammar" and intend it as true—without in the same breath tacitly acknowledging the validity of the very thing one is attempting to deny.[24] But what can in principle never be doubted cannot be an object of belief either; the two states of mind are conceptually linked in such a way that the possibility or impossibility of the one necessarily entails the corresponding condition in the case of the other. On the other hand, of course, it is obviously perfectly possible either to believe or to disbelieve in God. And thus it turns out that the linkage to which Nietzsche means to point is not there after all. But if "believing" in "grammar" does not commit one in any sense to a belief in God, the same cannot be said of belief in (for example) grammatology. The metaphysics of deconstruction—and the same holds true mutatis mutandis for all other forms of contemporary skepticism—is simply a kind of negative image of what Nietzsche appears to have been trying to refer to with his evocation of a grammatically entailed theism. It is, in other words, the "void" that one is henceforth prepared to take for "purpose," in the belief that all substantive candidates for the role of purpose have now been exposed as irredeemably fraudulent or self-deceptive. It is the "negative theology," as the theory of deconstruction in particular has frequently been termed,[25] created by an age not yet capable of doing without the form of the idea of God but also unable to sustain any longer the belief in a divine substance.[26] Just as a photographic negative does not cease to be an image of the thing represented in it, so negative foundationalism—which is structurally what skepticism always amounts to, in its contemporary no less than its traditional variants—continues to be precisely as metaphysically foundational in character as the "onto-theological" position against which it purports to set itself. And for that reason, too, it is today, just as at every similar juncture in the past, once again mistaken in supposing that it has finally succeeded in overcoming that position.

PART ONE

CONTEMPORARY SKEPTICISM IN

CRITICAL PERSPECTIVE

My aim is: to teach you to pass from a piece of disguised nonsense to something that is patent nonsense.

Ludwig Wittgenstein,
Philosophical Investigations

TWO WAYS TOO MANY,
ONE WAY TOO FEW

THERE IS TODAY A WIDELY ACCEPTED VIEW THAT, IN RICHARD Rorty's words, "[t]here . . . are two ways of thinking about various things." As Rorty puts it, "[I]t is the difference between regarding truth, goodness, and beauty as eternal objects which we try to locate and reveal, and regarding them as artifacts whose fundamental design we often have to alter."[1] Haskell Fain similarly asks, "Does history present us with an untold story, the task of the narrative historian being to *discover* the story? . . . Or do the historian and the philosopher of history invent the stories?"[2] Thomas Kuhn notes, "Observation and experience can and must drastically restrict the range of admissible scientific belief, else there would be no science. But they cannot alone determine a particular body of such belief. An apparently arbitrary element, compounded of personal and historical accident, is always a formative ingredient of the beliefs espoused by a given scientific community at any given time."[3] And it turns out that the latter element, as reflected in the various "paradigms" that have historically been "constitutive of science," is also, in as literal a sense of the term *nature* as can be given a coherent interpretation at all, "constitutive of nature as well."[4] Paul Feyerabend expresses a basically similar view of the relationship between science and reality, though in a manner characteristically both more blunt and rather more polemical than Kuhn: "The entities postulated by science are not found, and they do not constitute an 'objective' stage for all cultures and all of history. They are shaped by special groups, cultures, civilizations; and they are shaped from a material which, depending on its treatment, provides us with gods, spirits, a nature that is a partner of humans rather than a laboratory for their experiments, or with quarks, fields, molecules, tectonic plates. Social monotony implies cosmic monotony—or 'objectivity', as the latter is called today."[5] Once again, the choice implicitly envisioned as primary is the same. It is between, on the one hand, a conception of reality as *already* simply *there*, waiting for us to be either right or wrong about it, and, on the other, a view that sees what we are sometimes pleased to call "reality" in any set of circumstances in particular as actually nothing more than an "interpretation," one that is at bottom a product of (themselves ultimately contingent) decisions taken relative to those circumstances and therefore also always revisable or exchangeable for any other interpretation we may later come to prefer to it for whatever reason.[6]

Fredric Jameson speaks of the "crisis [in efforts to provide a philosophically adequate legitimation of science's implicit claim to reveal the truth about things] . . . of which the historical theories of Kuhn or Feyerabend stand as crucial symptoms." He in turn locates this phenomenon in the broader context of "the so-called crisis of representation." At issue is the clash between "an essentially realistic epistemology, which conceives of representation as the reproduction, for subjectivity, of an objectivity that lies outside it—[thereby] project[ing] a mirror theory of knowledge and art, whose fundamental evaluative categories are those of adequacy, accuracy, and Truth itself," and a "non- or postrepresentational 'epistemology' " opposed to this view in all the respects mentioned.[7] Lyotard, from the Foreword to whose influential *The Postmodern Condition*, discussed briefly above, the foregoing is taken, speaks similarly of a contemporary "crisis of narratives" growing out of the battle between modern and postmodern sensibility. It is the battle between the quest for epistemic legitimation through "reference to a metadiscourse . . . making an explicit appeal to some grand narrative" on the one hand and an attitude of "incredulity toward metanarratives" on the other.[8] In Lyotard's view, the tide clearly favors the latter: "This is what the postmodern world is all about. Most people have lost the nostalgia for the lost narrative" (*PMC*, p. 41). "The [meta]-narrative function," he contends, "is being dispersed in clouds of narrative language elements. . . . Conveyed within each cloud are pragmatic valences specific to its kind. Each of us lives at the intersection of many of these. However, we do not necessarily establish stable language combinations, and the properties of the ones we do establish are not necessarily communicable" (*PMC*, p. xxiv). For Lyotard, too, as in one way or another for most of the other writers cited thus far in this chapter, there is a primary and fundamental "right to *decide* what is true" (emphasis added), one that he sees as bound up intimately with "the right to decide what is just" (*PMC*, p. 8). It follows for him that "there is a strict interlinkage between the kind of language called science and the kind called ethics and politics" (*PMC*, p. 8). Echoing Foucault, Lyotard maintains that "knowledge and power are simply two sides of the same question" (*PMC*, pp. 8–9). And thus he asserts as "the first principle underlying our method" the thesis that "to speak is to fight" and that "speech acts," accordingly, "fall within the domain of a general agonistics" (*PMC*, p. 10).

The same assumption that it is necessary to choose between the two (and only two) alternatives of "what there *is*, independently of what we say" and "what we *say*, regardless of what (if anything) there 'really' is," is central as well to the critical theories of Barbara Herrnstein Smith and Stanley Fish. As is well known, both Smith and Fish opt for the latter standpoint, and both display what is, if anything, an even more pronounced tendency than Lyotard to interpret that position in "agonistic" terms. In *Contingencies of Value*, Smith, citing Hume's contention that "the same Homer who pleased at Athens and Rome two thousand years ago is still admired at Paris and London," responds with the demurrer that "we have reason to wonder if it is indeed quite 'the same' Homer."[9] Smith is evidently uncomfortable with the idea that the *Iliad* and the *Odyssey* just *are* what they are and have always been so, independent of anything external to them—including, in particular, readers (an idea with which, *thus stated*, I agree that one has good reason to be uncomfortable). She is, however, also evidently unable to see any way of avoiding that view of the Homeric epics, so long as one continues to adhere to the (apparently commonsensical) belief that they have in fact not changed one iota since the time, centuries ago, that they were given their definitive form. In this circumstance, the commonsensical view ends up being sacrificed. No "properties of literary works," she asserts, can serve as points of reference enabling us to speak of them as persisting unchanged (indeed, unchangeable) throughout their history. For "those properties are themselves among the variables of literary value" (*CV*, p. 15), and how works are evaluated obviously changes all the time.[10]

The result of this argument is to posit a fundamental link between the very *existence* of the work and the history of its critical reception.[11] That result has been achieved, however, only at what seems the rather steep price of emptying the concept of "existence" itself of anything recognizable as ontological content. For it is clearly not the case that, on the view in question, the multitude of different "Iliads" and "Odysseys" to whose "existence" (in some sense) we are now apparently committed are thought of as existing *in the same way* as were the *one Iliad* and *one Odyssey* that we formerly took to be the things referred to by the expression "the Homeric epics." The whole point of introducing the new theory was precisely not to expand the inventory of "objects" *as formerly conceived* by a factor equal to the number of their readers; it was to get away from that old notion of "existence" altogether. Yet it is also clear that the theory provides us with no *other* notion of "existence" to which to turn in default of that earlier one. To put it another way: The theory takes aim at the view that the *one Iliad* and *one Odyssey* possess an objectively invariant existence *in the sense of being wholly independent of what anyone might think or say about them or even whether anyone happens to be aware of them at all.* It is *this* way of conceiving objective existence that we have now been assured is delusory, reflective of nothing more than a confused ideal of epistemic integrity. But since the theory has available to it no other way of conceiving objective existence than this one, in throwing this conception overboard it perforce abandons objectivity itself altogether. I agree that the specific notion of objectivity rejected by the theory is indeed an unsustainable one. But it is, if anything, a still greater error to suppose that one can get along with no notion of objectivity whatsoever. In practice, of course, no one ever does, for what seems the very good reason that no one ever could. [12] (It is worth noting, I think, that if one were to remove from works of contemporary anti-objectivist or anti-realist or anti-foundationalist critical theory all propositions asserting that something is in fact, or always, or necessarily, or inescapably the case, these would in most instances be reduced by a rather significant fraction of their length.) Yet such a renunciation of objectivity is, in effect, precisely what is being contemplated here, as if it really were a genuine option. With the dispersal of "existence" across a vast array of different loci of evaluation, the same opposition that we have now encountered several times in the writings of a number of other contemporary critics and theoreticians between "what there (independently) *is*" and "what gets (interpretively) *said*" is once again inscribed as exhaustively descriptive of logical space, with the nod also once again going to the latter alternative. Yet, to repeat, what has not yet been found here is some way of analyzing the existence of epistemic objects that would be capable of relating them in essential fashion to the human subjects for whom they have the status of such objects, but which in so doing would not at the same time so relativize them that it becomes no longer possible to speak of them as *objects* at all. Instead the theory leaves us with no alternative to regarding them as merely different ways of talking about, or otherwise responding to, whatever it is—in any case, by hypothesis, *not* objects—that is supposed to be providing the stimulus for such talk or response in the first place.

A similar epistemological dualism, fraught with essentially the same difficulties, also underlies, as suggested a moment ago, the "antifoundationalist" position of Stanley Fish. Here again we find the same key assumption that a single pair of alternatives constitutes the ineluctably given starting point of critical reflection. At the beginning of the Preface to *Is There a Text in This Class?*, for example, Fish declares, "There isn't a text in this or any other class if one means by text what E. D. Hirsch and others mean by it, 'an entity which always remains the same from one moment to the next' (*Validity in Interpretation*, p. 46); but there is a text in this and every class if one means by text the structure of meanings that is obvious and inescapable from the perspective of whatever interpretive assumptions happen to be in force."[13] The possibility that these two alternatives might not be the *only* ways in which the concept of "text" can be construed is never considered. Rather it is simply taken for granted that unless one is prepared to adopt the latter view, one is necessarily committed to regarding a text as a kind of ontologically free-floating *ens realissima*. Finding that a difficult position to sustain, however (as, again, one surely ought to find it), Fish, like Smith, opts instead to conflate texts themselves with what people say about texts and with predictably similar results. The former notion is subsumed entirely to the latter, thereby draining it of any substantively distinct content in its own right. In consequence, it becomes no longer even *conceptually* possible to distinguish between, on the one hand, the considerable range of opinions that have been expressed regarding (for example) Goethe's novel *Die Leiden des jungen Werther* and, on the other, the text of the novel itself. With the completion of the revisions for the second edition of 1787, however, the latter was in fact effectively set in stone. It *could* have been subsequently revised still further, of course—historically there have certainly been few more inveterate revisers of their works than Goethe—but as a matter of fact it was not; and after March 22, 1832, it no longer could have been even in principle.

As Fish himself in effect acknowledges, this positing of the "what there (independently) *is*/what gets (interpretively) *said*"-dichotomy as the necessary starting point for reflection, and the subsequent collapsing of the former pole into the latter, which he sees in view of that starting point as the only defensible course to take, have together become the *idée maîtresse* informing all his critical work, whatever the particular questions or issues with which he happens to be engaged on a given occasion. As he says in the Preface to his most recent collection of essays, "[E]very essay in this book is the same; no matter what its putative topic each chapter finally reduces to an argument in which the troubles and benefits of interpretive theory are made to disappear in the solvent of an enriched notion of practice."[14] This basic conceptual scheme, developed initially as an organon for the interpretation of literary texts, has now grown into a set of principles admitting of perfectly general application, synchronically as well as diachronically, on both the micro- and the macro-scale, capable both of being inserted into any specific field of inquiry in particular and of representing the fundamental structure of the history of thought at large. It embraces what Fish calls "three basic oppositions:

> first, between a truth that exists independently of all perspectives and points of view and the many truths that emerge and seem perspicuous when a particular perspective or point of view has been established and is in force; second, an opposition between true knowledge, which is knowledge as it exists apart from any and all systems of belief, and the knowledge, which because it flows from some or other system of belief, is incomplete and partial (in the sense of biased); and third, an opposition between a self or consciousness that is turned outward in an effort to apprehend and attach itself to truth and true knowledge and a self or consciousness that is turned inward in the direction of its own prejudices, which, far from being transcended, continue to inform its every word and action. Each of these oppositions is attached in turn to an opposition between two kinds of language: on the one hand, language that faithfully reflects or reports on matters of fact uncolored by any personal or partisan agenda or desire; and on the other hand, language that is infected by partisan agendas and desires, and therefore colors and distorts the facts which it purports to reflect.[15]

All these oppositions are, of course, at bottom ultimately one and the same. Fish employs different names at different times for the two opposed poles. In the essay from which the foregoing is taken, they are denominated the "philosophical" (or "foundational" or "serious") standpoint and its "rhetorical" opposite number, respectively.[16] For him, these exhaust between them the range of possible options: "The history of Western thought," he maintains, "could be written as the history of th[e] quarrel" between the two. That history (and that quarrel), moreover, are far from having been concluded; rather "the debate continues to this very day and . . . its terms are exactly those one finds in the dialogues of Plato and the orations of the sophists."[17] Intellectual history thus turns out to be in some ways a remarkably simple and straightforward matter. Its basic categories number only two, and they always have. For these coincide essentially with the beginnings of critical thought itself in our tradition.

The epistemology of Fish's scheme thus accords in all essential respects with that of Smith. For her as well, the bête noire is what she calls "the traditional telegraphic model of discourse in which communication is seen as the *duplicative transmission* of a code-wrapped message from one consciousness to another, [and] 'truth-value' is seen as a measure of the extent to which such a message, when properly unwrapped, accurately and adequately reflects, represents, or corresponds with some independently determinate fact, reality, or state of affairs" (*CV*, p. 94). For both Smith and Fish, the alternative to this model is an understanding of, in Smith's words, "[v]erbal transactions" as "structurally adversarial" (*CV*, p. 108). On this view, differences of opinion are reducible ultimately to "battles" over "evaluative authority . . . fought out in social arenas and along lines of authority and power defined by social, institutional, and economic categories: age and gender, class and political status, teacher versus student, censor versus citizen, bureaucrat versus artist, art producer versus art distributor versus art consumer, and so forth" (*CV*, p. 72).[18] Fish expresses essentially the same view on numerous occasions, if not always in quite such bellicose terms. For example, he describes "the anti-foundationalist claim" as asserting that

> whatever foundations there are (and there always are some) have been established by persuasion, that is, in the course of argument and counter-argument on the basis of examples and evidence that are themselves cultural and contextual. Anti-foundationalism, then, is a thesis about how foundations emerge, and in contradistinction to the assumptions that foundations do not emerge but simply *are*, anchoring the universe and thought from a point above history and culture, it says that foundations are local and temporal phenomena, and are always vulnerable to challenges from other localities and other times.[19]

If there is any point of difference between Fish and Smith in this regard, it would appear to be the comparatively minor one that, in Smith's view, an alternative to "the traditional telegraphic model" has not yet actually been worked out in the requisite comprehensive fashion. Although, she maintains, "that model of discourse, along with the entire structure of

conceptions, epistemological and other, in which it is embedded, is now
felt in many places to be theoretically unworkable,"

> [i]t has not . . . been replaced by any other widely appropriated
> model. There have been, of course, throughout the century, so-
> phisticated demonstrations of precisely that unworkability, ...
> but for the moment . . . an alternate account of our commerce
> with the universe *and* our commerce with each other is not yet
> available. In the meantime, the telegraphic model of communica-
> tion, along with its associated conception of truth as correspon-
> dence to an independently determinate reality, continues to
> dominate theoretical discourse. (*CV*, pp. 94–95)

For Fish, however, as we saw a moment ago, the desired "alternate account" has been available since antiquity; indeed, it came into being
virtually simultaneously with the position to which both he and Smith
are opposed.

Although I think Fish is clearly correct in his assessment as far as it
goes, it would not in the end make much difference if he were not. The
question of whether this "alternate account" has long been part of the
intellectual landscape in one form or another or is only now really beginning to be worked out in satisfactory fashion is itself finally moot. The
crucial point here is that neither Fish nor Smith recognizes the possibility of a *third* alternative. In the idiom that I have adopted for purposes of the present discussion, for both of them it is *either* dogmatism
or skepticism, *tertium non datur*. Another way in which this basic point
can be seen, and one that at the same time helps prepare the ground for
some key elements of the argument to follow, is by looking at Smith's
and Fish's common rejection of Habermas's theory of communicative rationality and the basically similar reasons they offer for that rejection.

Smith writes that "in defining genuine communication as something
altogether uncontaminated by strategic or instrumental action," but
rather "as occurring only when and insofar as the participants' actions
are 'oriented' toward an 'agreement' that presupposes the mutual recognition by both parties of 'corresponding validity claims of comprehensibility, truth, truthfulness . . . , and rightness,' "[20] Habermas "has
secured a category that is . . . quite empty." For "having thus disqual-
ified and bracketed out what is, in effect, the entire motivational structure of verbal transactions, he is left with an altogether bootstrap
operation or magic reciprocality, in which the only thing that generates,
sustains, and controls the actions of speakers and listeners is *the gratuitous mutuality of their presuppositions*" (*CV*, p. 110; emphasis added).
It seems scarcely to follow, however, that unless one accepts the "structurally adversarial" model of discourse favored by Smith, one is *eo ipso*

ignoring altogether for purposes of one's theory "the entire motivational structure of verbal transactions." I think Habermas would surely regard with some incredulity the suggestion to that effect as far as his own theory is concerned. That consideration aside, however, I am at the moment more concerned with what strikes me as the somewhat curious phrase with which the passage last cited concludes. It appears from the context that two distinct claims are actually being made here: first, the fact that people agree as much as they do in their beliefs must itself be regarded as something of a miracle (or, at any rate, would have to be so regarded, if there were not shared "motivational structure[s]" to which we could look for the explanation); and, second, even if, for the sake of argument, the possibility of the miracle is granted, any theory essentially dependent on the assumption of it (as, for example, Habermas's is alleged to be) is for that very reason still unable to develop an adequate, comprehensive account of "verbal transactions" among human beings.

Theories such as Smith's and Fish's have an evident problem with the phenomenon of basic, widespread, and persistent agreement. In some ways, it would be much more convenient for these theories if the human condition actually were a Babel-like scene of mutual incomprehension among radically distinct linguistic communities. We would all, on this view, regularly find ourselves in a position like that of the Square in *Flatland*, who, having been granted a visit to the Third Dimension (being transformed into a Cube for the duration of his stay there), upon his return home seeks in vain to convince his fellow Flatlanders of the existence of that realm, unable as he is even to make the notion of a "third" dimension intelligible to two-dimensional creatures.[21] It is a principal thesis of the present study, however, that this in fact never happens because it is logically impossible that it should happen. The notion of massive and permanent unintelligibility (and a fortiori disagreement) between or among human beings is itself unintelligible. The argument for this claim has yet to be made here, of course. For the moment, however, the ball is still in Smith's and Fish's court. Basic, widespread, and persistent agreement on innumerable aspects of experience evidently must be dealt with in some way by their theories. It is obviously no use denying the reality of the phenomenon itself. Rather, as we have seen, what is denied is the existence of enduring *objects* of experience in which such agreement might be thought to converge. Returning to her earlier example of "the 'properties' of a [literary] work" (with the term *properties* now set in scare-quotes), including such things as "its 'structure,' 'features,' 'qualities,' and of course its 'meanings' " (with these terms similarly set off), Smith asserts again that these "properties" "are not fixed, given, or inherent in the work 'itself' but are at every point the variable products of particular *subjects'* interactions with it" (*CV*, p. 48). With *it*?, we want to ask. But what is *it* here? In the context, this certainly looks very much like a classic Kantian *Ding an sich*. Whatever *it* may be, however, it is in any case, as we have seen, "never 'the *same* Homer' " (*CV*, p. 48).

If we ask then why, at least with respect to the basic "features" and "qualities" of the texts, it generally looks like the same Homer to everyone who takes a look, the answer we receive is that "[t]his is not to deny that some aspect, or perhaps many aspects, of a work may be constituted in similar ways by numerous different subjects" (*CV*, p. 48). Perhaps many, indeed, one may be inclined to respond. To characterize this as an understatement seems scarcely to do the remark justice. A minimal list of such "similarly constituted aspects" would include every word in the text of any given edition of the work in question (or, for those who do not know the language of the particular edition, and who thus may not always be in a position to recognize individual words as discrete entities, at least the configuration of the marks on the page);[22] the exact order in which these words occur; the syntactic units into which they are grouped; the larger divisions of the text (where such exist) into books, chapters, acts, scenes, cantos, strophes, or whatever it may be; and so on and on in this vein. Smith maintains, however, that "to the extent that this duplication occurs," it is not as a result of anything in the work itself; rather it is merely "because the subjects who do the constituting are themselves similar" (*CV*, p. 48). There follows a brief gloss of the notion of "similarity" invoked here: ". . . similar, not only or simply in being human creatures (and thereby, as it is commonly supposed, 'sharing an underlying humanity' and so on) but in occupying a particular universe that may be, for them, in many respects recurrent or relatively continuous and stable, and/or in inheriting from one another, through mechanisms of cultural transmission, certain ways of interacting with texts and 'works of literature' " (*CV*, p. 48). This is in several respects an intriguing passage. Perhaps the first question to which it gives rise is just how we are to understand the reference to " 'sharing an underlying humanity.' " On the one hand, it may seem that Smith actually is prepared to accept this as a legitimate way of speaking. For the locution "similar, not only or simply in being human creatures," which immediately precedes the reference to " 'sharing an underlying humanity,' " might certainly be taken as establishing a context in which a belief in the notion of a common humanity is held to be valid. On the other hand, though, there is the consideration that the expression is placed in scare-quotes. And this may suggest that the notion of an " 'underlying humanity' " is really being treated here in the same slightly mocking and ultimately dismissive way that we earlier saw in the case of the concepts of " 'properties,' " " 'structure,' " " 'features,' " and the like. This latter suggestion also seems to accord somewhat better with the reference, cited above, to the "gratuitous mutuality" of different people's various "presuppositions."

The question remains, then: is *any* credence to be accorded, on the terms of Smith's theory, to the notion of our being in important respects "similar . . . simply in [virtue of] being human creatures"? The answer, I think, is finally a qualified "yes and no." Mostly no; but for certain purposes, where the theory requires it, at least partly yes. The reference in this same passage to "mechanisms of cultural transmission" reminds us that Smith frequently appears to be in no doubt whatsoever about the possibility of identifying with complete certainty objectively real properties of both persons and institutions. We recall, for example, in connection with the earlier elaboration of the ways in which "[v]erbal transactions" are supposedly reducible to "battles" over "evaluative authority," that the "social arenas" in which these "battles" are waged and the various "lines of authority and power defined by [the] social, institutional, and economic categories" in which the combatants are arrayed were themselves spoken of in epistemically wholly unqualified terms. And this is merely one example among many. Indeed, the bulk of Smith's exposition consists precisely of one such apodictically asserted claim after another. In itself, of course, this does not (yet) constitute grounds for reproach. One can hardly be criticized for following a practice to which in the nature of the case there is no alternative. And as we noted earlier, making assertions as to what is and is not objectively the case is not a dispensable option, insofar as one is engaged in discourse at all. What I am questioning is rather the *selective* use to which, without argument or explanation, that discursive mode is being put here. For what is it, after all, about properties of persons such as "age and gender," or "lines of authority and power defined by . . . class and political status," or "mechanisms of cultural transmission" by which "certain ways of interacting with texts" are "inherit[ed]," that enables us to speak of them as entirely real in and of themselves, while on the other hand " 'works of literature' " and their " 'properties' " are held to be mere "evaluative" projections? The question is never discussed (or, so far as I can tell, even raised) in Smith's argument.

The point of raising it here is not (or not in every case at least) to impugn that tacit ascription of reality to things other than literary works and their properties. The force of the question runs the other way. Such things as age and gender, for example, are obvious realities. But works of literature, and thus a fortiori their various constitutive properties, are surely no less obviously real. In the case of a notion such as "class," to be sure, it is necessary to proceed more cautiously and with somewhat greater attention to relevant distinctions. If by that term is meant simply a particular set of persons defined in accordance with socioeconomic parameters such as income, employment, housing, family circumstances, and the like, then it seems to me perfectly obvious that there are classes, too. Thus understood, the notion is not only philosophically unexceptionable; employed judiciously, in the hands of a skillful investigator, it can be of considerable value in illuminating important aspects of society. There is, however, also another common sense of the term *class*. In this usage it is intended to denote a supraindividual entity, one possessing its *own* characteristic properties independent of anything that may or may not be true of any of its members in particular. The terms of its definition are thus neither derivable from nor disconfirmable by what, from this point of view, are merely local and contingent features, incidental to the nature of the concept itself. Among the properties typically posited for this entity are *consciousness* and *interest*. On this view, there is, for example, a uniquely specifiable *working-class consciousness*, which embodies the essential standpoint peculiar to *workers*, regardless of what in any given case happen to be the views and outlooks of any actual workers. Nor is this sort of positing of collective entities and their properties restricted to the socioeconomic sphere. Essentially the same move can equally well be made in the case of such things as gender and race, and it is, of course, far from unusual today to see that done as well. The roots of theories of this sort, at least in their modern form, may be traceable ultimately to Rousseau. The pivotal distinction in *The Social Contract* between the "general will" and the "will of all," with priority in the determination of social policy accorded to the former, provides the basis on which, for example, the seeming absurdity that a person can be "forced to be free" is not only not absurd but is in fact deducible in accordance with strict logic.[23] This distinction is, I think, the proximate ancestor (anticipations of it can be discerned at least as far back as Plato) of such contemporary notions as "false consciousness," as well as its remedy, "consciousness-raising." Armed with the view in question, if one should find that the actual beliefs and goals of a given individual (say, a worker, or a woman, or a black person) do not happen to coincide with the consciousness and interest that have been postulated for the relevant class, gender, or race, respectively, then the latter notions will not be the ones felt in need of adjustment. Rather the individual in question must be, if not "compelled," then at the very least certainly urged vigorously, "to be free" by adopting the outlook that, by hypothesis, ideally reflects that person's essential nature.

A commitment to the existence of quasi-personalized but nonetheless wholly supraindividual entities is among the hallmarks of much contemporary critical discourse.[24] To profess a view neither derived from experience nor refutable by it is, however, essentially a definition of dogmatic metaphysics.[25] And it seems to me that (for example) the notion of "class" just considered clearly fits that definition. My reason for going on at some length on this matter is not to now read everything just said about the metaphysical sense of *class* back into Smith's use of the term. At the same time, however, I do not see any way to square that use with the simpler and more straightforward sense of *class* that I gave initially, in which the term denotes merely a group of individuals defined in accordance with a property or properties that they verifiably possess, and who are therefore counted as members of the group only and precisely to the extent that those defining marks are actually present. I think there is no getting around the recognition, not merely of an *objectivist* component to Smith's argument—something that, as I have been urging, is inescapable in any event—but, at least in part, a *metaphysically dogmatic* one as well. Nor would it be difficult to cite other, and perhaps even more telling, examples tending in the same direction, as we shall see below. Smith's argument can thus, in sum, be taken as exemplary of the mixture of dogmatic and skeptical tendencies that, I am suggesting, in one version or another informs much contemporary critical theory. And one consequence of this mixture in Smith's case in particular is that her critique of Habermas (to return to the point from which this excursus began) ends up going wide of the mark on both sides at once. Habermas's project, or at least the part of it with which Smith is concerned, can be fairly described as what she herself, interestingly enough, terms a "neo-Kantian transcendental analysis" (*CV*, p. 113) of the conditions of *intelligibility*. I say interestingly, because although she adopts what seems to me the right vocabulary for talking about what Habermas is trying to do, her criticism of his theory nonetheless includes no reference to what a transcendental analysis itself actually is. Specifically, it takes no account of how (if successful) such an analysis yields a position that is *neither* dogmatic *nor* skeptical in its epistemology, but rather a third thing altogether (which I will later term *critical realism*). Firmly situated as she is within a (pre-critical) dogmatic-skeptical matrix, she is obliged to draw any weapons that she wishes to bring to bear against Habermas from one or the other of those two sources. But since, as it turns out, neither of them will quite do the job by itself, she is in the end left with no alternative but, in effect, to continue moving back and forth between them, drawing on now the one, now the other, as the needs of the argument appear to dictate.

Smith contends "that what neo-Kantian transcendental analysis describes as the 'presuppositions' of speech are *redescribable* as the recurrent tendencies of verbal agents, human or otherwise, as the products of the differentially effective consequences of their prior interactions" (*CV*, p. 113). And her position is that we should in fact adopt such a redescription. (The reason for the qualification "human or otherwise" in the passage just cited becomes clear in a moment.) Now, in order that this sort of "economic accounting" (*CV*, p. 112), as she terms it, even be possible (much less true), we must obviously be in a position to say something specific about "the dynamics of economy" (*CV*, p. 112) as they apply to speech situations. And Smith is clearly convinced that we are in fact so positioned. She is certain, for example, of the fact that "[w]e engage in verbal transactions because. . . . it is often the best way to affect the beliefs and behaviors of other people in ways that serve our interests, desires, or goals" (*CV*, p. 107), and she is no less certain of what those "interests, desires, and goals" typically are, how they are most likely to be realized, and with what "costs and benefits" (*CV*, p. 111) to ourselves. The "structurally adversarial" character of "[v]erbal transactions" (*CV*, p. 108) alluded to earlier figures prominently in such calculations as these:

> For, given the dynamics and constraints of reciprocality just described, it will tend to be in the *speaker's* interests to provide only as much "information" as is required to affect the listener's behavior in the ways he himself desires and *no* "information" that it may be to his general *dis*advantage that she know or believe;[26] at the same time, it will tend to be in the *listener's* interest to learn *whatever* it may be useful or interesting for her to know, whether or not her knowing it happens also to be required or desired by the speaker. Thus, to describe what is presupposed by all communication is to describe the conditions not only for mutually effective interactions but also *and simultaneously* for mutual mis-"understanding," deceit, and exploitation; and although the more extravagant reaches of these latter possibilites are no doubt commonly limited by their ultimately negative consequences for those who hazard them too often or indiscriminately, the converse possibilities remain radically excluded: specifically, the kinds of equivalences, symmetries, duplications, and gratuitous mutualities that are commonly posited as normally achieved in verbal transactions or as defining "communication." (*CV*, p. 108)

Now, apart from the rather unattractive view of human relations apparently assumed here as more or less the norm in our dealings with one another (and also apart from the explicit acknowledgment that it is indeed possible for us to *know* certain things, in the sense of apprehending correctly what is *truly* the case), this passage reflects a very basic confusion with regard to the nature of language itself, one that goes to the heart of what is ultimately untenable in Smith's theory.

As Wittgenstein notes in the *Investigations*, "Lying is a language-game that needs to be learned like any other one" (*PI*, § 249). As with all other uses of language, it, too, requires a shared context of mutual intelligibility and communicability to occur at all. It is as impossible to lie to someone who does not already understand perfectly well what the utterance intended to deceive or mislead *means* as it would be, for example, to fool someone blind from birth about the color of an object. In order that anyone be fooled about anything, it is necessary that the intended victim first have the *concept* of whatever it is that is to be concealed from him. (The point becomes clearer still, perhaps, when we consider that it is equally impossible to communicate to someone blind from birth the *true* color of an object. One can, of course, always speak the words "Snow is white" to the person, but *communication* will no more take place in such a case than it would if one were to say "Schnee ist weiß" to a nonspeaker of German.) What Smith believes to be "radically excluded" from the realm of human discourse can thus be seen to be in fact radically *necessary*, if any such discourse is to take place at all (including even the sort of semiotic *bellum omnium contra omnes* that she appears to regard as the normal state of things). What she refers to as "the gratuitous mutuality of [different speakers'] presuppositions" is in fact what Wittgenstein terms the common "form of life" of those speakers, that which constitutes them as (among other things) a *linguistic* community in the first place. Failing to recognize this, Smith commits the non sequitur of supposing that because error and deception are always possibilities, they might also be (indeed, actually are) permanent, universal realities. It does not follow, however, from the fact that in any given set of circumstances a certain state of affairs may obtain that the same state of affairs could therefore obtain always and everywhere. Indeed, phenomena—that is, actual events or conditions—depend for their very logical possibility precisely on the fact that they are not always the case. Wittgenstein illustrates the point by means of the example of counterfeit money; it requires only a little reflection to see both that and why not all money could be counterfeit, even in principle. (The same considerations also enable us to see why logical truths, which do hold always and everywhere, are themselves not strictly speaking facts at all, but rather what might be thought of as schemata of facts.) Error and deception are in this sense phenomena. They occur, and can occur, only within an already established discursive framework. And from this it obviously follows that they cannot themselves be conditions of the possibility of that framework's operation.

Confusion on this basic point readily leads to such a claim as Smith's that in fact "there is *no* 'communication' in the sense either of a *making common* of something (for example, 'knowledge') that was previously the possession of only one party or in the sense of a *transferral or transmission of the same* (information, feelings, beliefs, and so on) from one to the other" (*CV*, p. 109). Rather, "[i]t is inevitable that there will be disparities between what is 'transmitted' and what is 'received' in any exchange simply by virtue of the different states and circumstances of the 'sender' and 'receiver,' including what will always be the differences—sometimes quite significant ones—produced by their inevitably different life-histories as verbal creatures" (*CV*, p. 109). Similar distortions, it is maintained, are inevitably occasioned by "the structure of interests that motivates and governs all verbal interaction" (*CV*, p. 109): what one interlocutor is determined to hear, or to find out, is never exactly the same as what the other is trying to say, or is prepared to divulge. On this view, indeed, the ordinary tendency if anything is rather toward greater divergence than convergence. It is not difficult to see underlying claims such as these the deep-seated misconception regarding the actual working of language that Wittgenstein analyzes in the section of the *Investigations* often referred to as the "private-language argument." (It is worth noting, by the way, that the passage from the *Investigations* cited above regarding the presuppositions of lying occurs in the context of precisely this analysis.) Perhaps the best-known portion of that argument involves the famous image of the "beetle-in-the-box." Wittgenstein constructs a kind of thought-experiment designed to aid us in seeing what is wrong with the (at first glance, apparently both commonsensical and unproblematic) assumption that the meanings of words as used—in this case, specifically terms for sensations such as pain or the perception of colors; the point, however, is a general one, applicable to all instances of language use—are referrable ultimately to the "private" experience or understanding of the particular individual using them on a given occasion:

> Now someone tells me that *he* knows what pain is only from his own case!—Suppose everyone had a box with something in it: we call it a "beetle". No one can look into anyone else's box, and everyone says he knows what a beetle is only by looking at *his* beetle.—Here it would be quite possible for everyone to have something different in his box. One might even imagine such a

thing constantly changing.—But suppose the word "beetle" had a use in these people's language?—If so it would not be used as the name of a thing. The thing in the box has no place in the language-game at all; not even as a *something:* for the box might even be empty.—No, one can 'divide through' by the thing in the box; it cancels out, whatever it is. That is to say: if we construe the grammar of the expression of sensation on the model of 'object and designation' the object drops out of consideration as irrelevant. (*PI*, § 293)

The assumption that *only I* really and completely know what I mean by a given expression—and this is obviously the key assumption underlying Smith's denial of the reality of "communication"—can thus be seen to rest on a failure to have considered adequately the inherently *public* and *social* character of language.

A slightly different, and in some ways even better, view of what Wittgenstein is getting at with the "private-language argument," as Anthony Kenny notes, can be had by looking at a somewhat earlier section of the text. Here again Wittgenstein proposes a thought-experiment:

Let us imagine the following case. I want to keep a diary about the recurrence of a certain sensation. To this end I associate it with the sign "S" and write this sign in a calendar for every day on which I have the sensation.—I will remark first of all that a definition of the sign cannot be formulated.—But still I can give myself a kind of ostensive definition.—How? Can I point to the sensation? Not in the ordinary sense. But I speak, or write the sign down, and at the same time I concentrate my attention on the sensation—and so, as it were, point to it inwardly.—But what is this ceremony for? for that is all it seems to be! A definition surely serves to establish the meaning of a sign.—Well, that is done precisely by the concentrating of my attention; for in this way I impress on myself the connexion between the sign and the sensation.—But "I impress it on myself" can only mean: this process brings it about that I remember the connexion *right* in the future. *But in the present case I have no criterion of correctness.* One would like to say: whatever is going to seem right to me is right. And that only means that here we can't talk about 'right'. (*PI*, § 258; second emphasis added)

As Kenny notes, this passage is liable to be misunderstood: "Wittgenstein is not arguing 'When next I call something "S" how will I know it really is S?' He is arguing 'When next I call something "S" how will I know what I *mean* by "S"?' " (emphasis added).[27] The really fundamental objection to the notion that language is ultimately "private" to the individual using it is not even so much that that assumption gives us no way of distinguishing between when we get things right and when we get them wrong (not even when what we are talking about is our own inner experience). To be sure, that would be bad enough. At a still deeper level, however, this assumption deprives us of any assurance that when we use a given term on occasions subsequent to our first use of it, we even *mean* the same thing by it that we formerly meant. If each of our "languages" really were "private" to each of us individually, in other words, not only would we be unable in principle to tell the difference between our correct and our mistaken judgments (again, even those that we make with regard to our own experience); we would quite literally not even know what we were saying from one moment to the next. We could not be certain even of our *own* discursive intentions. Wittgenstein provides a further explanation of why this is so a few sections later:

> Let us imagine a table (something like a dictionary) that exists only in our imagination. A dictionary can be used to justify the trans- lation of a word X by a word Y. But are we also to call it a justifi- cation if such a table is to be looked up only in the imagination?— "Well, yes; then it is a subjective justification."—But justification consists in appealing to something independent.—"But surely I can appeal from one memory to another. For example, I don't know if I have remembered the time of departure of a train right and to check it I call to mind how a page of the time-table looked. Isn't it the same here?"—No; for this process has got to produce a memory which is actually *correct*. If the mental image of the time- table could not itself be *tested* for correctness, how could it con- firm the correctness of the first memory? (As if someone were to buy several copies of the morning paper to assure himself that what it said was true.) (*PI*, § 265)

As Kenny notes, the flaw in the procedure proposed by Wittgenstein's imaginary interlocutor is this:

> We are supposing that I wish to justify my calling a private sen- sation 'S' by appealing to a mental table in which memory-samples of private objects of various kinds are listed in correlation with symbols. . . . To make use of such a table one must call up the right memory-sample: e.g. I must make sure to call up the memory-sample that belongs alongside 'S' and not the one which belongs to 'T'. But as this table exists only in the imagination, there can be no real looking up to see which sample goes with 'S'. All there can be is *remembering* which sample goes with 'S', i.e.

remembering what 'S' means. But this is precisely what the table
was supposed to confirm. In other words, the memory of the
meaning of 'S' is being used to confirm itself. (pp. 192–93)

I have thought it worthwhile to devote this much space to an examination of the "private-language argument" (and there is a great deal
more to that argument that it has not been possible to consider at all
here) because the confusion that Wittgenstein seeks to address by
means of it is so persistently prevalent. It is, moreover, a confusion that
seems to know no boundaries of method or school. I have at one time or
another been assured by colleagues of virtually every methodological
stripe, from the most traditional "humanist" to the most obsessively
postmodernist, that "of course, we can never *really* know what another
person is thinking or feeling, or what that other person *really* means by
what he or she says." Some critics appear to believe that support can be
derived from this (presumed) truth for the thesis that the meaning of
literary texts in particular is inherently indeterminate. Even if we could
inquire directly of the author as to his intended meaning—so this argument runs—we would be no better off than we are now, simply confronting his text alone. For we would still have to interpret whatever
response we might receive, and in that effort we would be as fatally
hampered as before by the same ineradicable residue of uncertainty. We
will return to this issue again and again, from a number of different vantage points, in the course of the discussion here. But I hope that this
consideration of the "private-language argument," however brief, has
nevertheless gone at least some way toward showing why the view in
question is not merely mistaken but, indeed, strictly incoherent. As
Wittgenstein remarks succinctly elsewhere in the *Investigations*, "I can
know what *someone else* is thinking, not what I am thinking. It is correct
to say 'I know what you are thinking', and wrong to say 'I know what I
am thinking.' (A whole cloud of philosophy condensed into a drop of
grammar.)" (*PI*, II, p. 222; emphasis added).[28]

Wittgenstein is intent on developing a *transcendental* analysis of experience primarily in *linguistic* terms. It is "[g]rammar," he says, that
"tells what kind of object anything is" (*PI*, § 373); indeed, he goes so far
as to maintain (in almost Heideggerian fashion) that "*[e]ssence* is expressed by grammar" (*PI*, § 371). And, as noted earlier, Habermas, too,
is intent on constructing a transcendental argument of basically the
same sort. As we also observed, however, there appears to be a major
blind spot in Smith's theory for what this type of analysis and argumentation actually consists in. And thus, in the end, her intended critique of Habermas does not really engage his position at all. As she sees

it, Habermas is merely invoking an "imagin[ary] . . . superlunary universe" (*CV*, p. 111) in place of the "*sublunary*" (*CV*, p. 112) one we actually inhabit:

> The image of a type of communication that excludes all strategy, instrumentality, (self-)interest, and, above all, the profit motive, reflects what appears to be a more general recurrent impulse to dream an escape from economy, to imagine some special type, realm, or mode of value that is beyond economic accounting, to create by invocation some place apart from the marketplace—a kingdom, garden, or island, perhaps, or a plane of consciousness, form of social relationship, or stage of human development— where the dynamics of economy are, or once were, or some day will be, altogether suspended, abolished, or reversed. (*CV*, p. 112)

This view of Habermas as, in effect, trying by a kind of philosophical legerdemain to replace the more or less messy, rough-and-tumble conditions under which we are obliged to live with a vision of an ideal, zero-friction world is, however, to misconstrue his intention in a very fundamental way. To be sure, one is perhaps justified in feeling that Habermas's own terminology, with its characteristic references to such things as the "ideal speech situation," does not always do all that it might to reduce the likelihood of such confusion. And I think it is probably also fair to say that Habermas does sometimes tend to run together his analysis of how verbal exchange *actually* functions—that is, the disclosure of the transcendental presuppositions of the possibility of human discourse in any form—with somewhat more specific recommendations of how he would *like* to see people comport themselves in their discursive dealings with one another. The passage from generalized theoretical analysis to particular political and social program is often fairly fluid in his writings. Nonetheless, at the most basic level, as we shall see at greater length below, Habermas, like Kant, Herder, and Wittgenstein before him, is seeking simply to describe what must be the case in order that distinctively human experience, linguistic and otherwise, be possible at all.

What I have just termed Smith's blind spot for the nature of specifically transcendental analysis appears in what I think can only be called somewhat striking fashion in connection with her attempt to escape the charge of self-referential inconsistency, which all skeptical theories sooner or later invite. She writes that

> when someone (an objectivist, for example) insists that I make truth-claims when I speak, he merely reasserts his inability to en-

tertain any alternate structure of conceptions of what he calls "truth." . . . According to the analysis of language that maintains that I make truth-claims in the very act of opening my mouth ("to communicate" or "to assert" as distinguished from just yawning), my dog likewise makes truth-claims in the very act of opening his. Indeed, in accord with a transcendental analysis of language, our mutual interactions (that is, mine with my dog) flourish only because of our mutual presuppositions of truth and sincerity: my dog assumes that when I call "Here, Fido, dinner!" his dinner is really there, and I assume that when he barks at my arrival home, he is sincerely happy to see me. (Of course, we could just be trying to manipulate each other.) (CV, p. 113)

It is difficult to know exactly what to make of this rather breezy anthropomorphism of the canine. How a commitment to such a view is supposed to follow from a "transcendental analysis of language" is in any case, to say the least, not made wholly clear here. And in point of fact, as the Wittgensteinian notion of "form of life" helps remind us, precisely the opposite is true. In a well-known and often-cited passage from the *Investigations*, Wittgenstein observes: "If a lion could talk, we could not understand him" (*PI*, II, p. 223). For, as he notes elsewhere in the same work, it is "only of a living human being and what resembles (behaves like) a living human being" that one can say that it has human or humanlike properties, for example, that "it has sensations; it sees; is blind; hears; is deaf; is conscious or unconscious" (*PI*, § 281)—or, as in the case at hand, that it engages in discursive communication.

In saying this, of course, Wittgenstein is not endorsing anything like the Cartesian view that because animals do not have souls, they must therefore be regarded as mere insentient mechanisms; he is not denying that animals have sensations at all. His point is that because the only notions available to us of such things as sense, consciousness, and language itself are formed in accordance with our specifically human experience, it is only of humans, or of creatures that in the relevant respects sufficiently resemble humans, that it can even make sense for us to predicate these things. For example, "Only of what behaves like a human being can one say that it *has* pains" (*PI*, § 283). And in the particular case of pain, of course, the degree of resemblance between humans and animals—that is, the similarity between the pain behavior of a suffering person and, say, a suffering dog—is ordinarily more than enough to make the ascription of a sensation of pain to the latter not only permissible but, indeed, in most cases impossible to avoid. This relative isomorphism of experience does not extend indefinitely, however. As we approach the so-called "higher" faculties, the extent of the overlap

between humans and increasing numbers of animal species becomes
ever more attenuated, as the gulf between respective "forms of life"
grows ever wider. (This is, in Wittgenstein's view, why we would not be
able to "understand" even a linguistically articulate lion. There is just
too little that humans and lions have in common in the ways they live
their lives to provide a sufficient basis for mutual comprehension.) We
have no trouble acknowledging that a dog can feel pain. But, Wittgenstein asks, "Why can't a dog simulate pain? Is he too honest? Could one
teach a dog to simulate pain? Perhaps it is possible to teach him to howl
on particular occasions as if he were in pain, even when he is not. But
*the surroundings which are necessary for this behavior to be real sim-
ulation* are missing" (*PI*, § 250; emphasis added). One might as well, for
example, call the changes in color by which a chameleon appears to
blend into its surroundings tactics of simulation. Actually, as is now
known, the chameleon's change of color has nothing at all to do with the
color of its surroundings, being caused rather by such things as fear or
anger, changes in air temperature, and the degree of the animal's exposure to light. But even if the commonly held belief regarding the chameleon's camouflaging of itself were true, *instinctual* behavior would
still not be properly regarded as simulation, at least not in the (more or
less) distinctively human sense of pretense. Like lying, to which it is obviously closely related, pretense is a human language-game requiring
the prior acquisition of an extensive array of more basic concepts in order that one be able to "play" it at all. As Wittgenstein observes: "A
child has much to learn before it can pretend. (A dog cannot be a hyp-
ocrite, but neither can he be sincere.)" (*PI*, II, p. 229).

In the passage at hand, to be sure, Smith does not actually express in
so many words a commitment to the version of the pathetic fallacy, not
uncommon among pet owners, according to which some animals really
are held to be capable of experiencing virtually the entire range of human attitudes, intentions, and desires, and also of articulating these
states of mind in identifiable fashion. And given that fact, I certainly do
not wish to impute such a belief to her. Regardless of how one may be
inclined to construe the interactions between humans and their pets,
the point I am chiefly concerned to make here is another one altogether.
It is that the moral to which Smith evidently believes her dog example
points, namely "that what neo-Kantian transcendental analysis describes as the 'presuppositions' of speech are *redescribable* as the recurrent tendencies of verbal agents, human or otherwise, as the
products of the differentially effective consequences of their prior interactions" (*CV*, p. 113), is at bottom nothing more than a form of category mistake. The possibility of "redescription" of one thing in terms of

another that is being asserted here actually conflates the transcendental with the empirical level of analysis. The *structures* of *possible* discourse, in other words, are being treated as if they were themselves *objects* of a *particular* discourse. And thus the putative "redescription" in fact does not even reach the level of addressing (much less refuting) the arguments of those who, like Habermas and Wittgenstein, are seeking to elucidate the *former*. The emergence of any objects of discourse whatsoever within the horizon of human experience—whether these be "recurrent tendencies of verbal agents," "products of the differentially effective consequences of their prior interactions," or anything else—presupposes precisely the structures of discourse that transcendental analysis of the type engaged in by (among others) Wittgenstein and Habermas seeks to disclose. And, that being so, it plainly makes no sense to try to account for the workings of these structures themselves in terms of such objects. That is, however, precisely what the (alleged) possibility of "redescription" appealed to by Smith in effect tries to do. (It is roughly as if one were to try to explain the fact that dogs do not feign affection by "redescribing" them as possessed of too much innate integrity to do so.)

Complicating matters still further, at the same time that Smith invokes the elements of her presumed redescription against the legitimacy of a transcendental analysis of language in the manner of Habermas (or, by extension, Wittgenstein), she nevertheless also continues to insist, against the charge of self-referential inconsistency, that "[w]hat [she is] offering here is neither an 'assertion' of some *p* nor a 'denial' of assertion-in-itself or truth-in-itself, but an *alternate description* of what is *otherwise described* as 'assertion,' 'denial,' and 'truth' " (*CV*, p. 113). Indeed, the two sets of claims are made in virtually the same breath. Yet it remains obscure how *any* description, whether purportedly "alternate" or not, can help being an " 'assertion' of some *p*," simply by virtue of being, precisely, a description in the first place. (Indeed, it is difficult to see how a sentence that begins with the words "What I am offering here is" can itself be anything other than such an assertion.) If certain phenomena are "redescribable as the recurrent *tendencies* of verbal agents," and if, moreover, those "tendencies" can be explained as "the *products* of the differentially effective *consequences* of [those agents'] prior interactions" (emphasis added), then surely it must be the case that both those tendencies themselves and the various causal mechanisms assumed to have produced them truly exist. What else would be the point of using the term *(re)description* in this connection at all? The logic of discourse implicit in such notions as "description" and "redescription" is not something that one can simply alter at will. As we saw in connection with the "private-language argument," it is not even logically possible to say, with Humpty Dumpty, that "[w]hen *I* use a word, . . . it means just what I choose it to mean—neither more nor less."[29]

Of course, not everything that anyone ever says is a description or assertion; there are many other uses besides these to which language is put. And this consideration may appear, at least momentarily, to provide Smith with a way by which she can continue to reject the transcendental standpoint, and do so cogently, while nevertheless at the same time also avoiding the trap of self-refutation into which actually coming out and positing something as a fact would clearly propel her. The appearance, however, is fleeting at best. To urge the reader to accept that there are no objective facts, but only various strategic, value-driven interactions among verbal agents, is in itself, strictly speaking, not yet (quite) to make an assertion. The grammar of exhortation is not that of assertion. *Neither*, however, is an exhortation such as this (yet) a *description* (whether "alternate" or not) at all. To the extent that Smith is *merely*, as she puts it, "exhibit[ing] . . . for sale" a particular "verbal/conceptual construct" (*CV*, p. 113)—that is, encouraging the acceptance by the reader of her way of viewing things—she is not yet open to the charge of self-referential inconsistency; but neither does she yet have *anything* for the reader actually to accept or reject. As soon as the discursive space that is being held for the moment by the expression "verbal/conceptual construct" is filled in, however, which is to say, as soon as Smith specifies exactly what her view of things in particular *is*, she is in the realm of description, and is thus also ineluctably asserting that some things truly are the case and others not. Unable to ground such assertion in transcendental (or critical realist) terms, however, as we have seen, she has no alternative but simply to *posit* her "dynamics of economy" as, without benefit of further argument, simply the way things are. And thus, as already noted, her theory in the end merely reinstates in a new idiom the peculiar combination, so characteristic of contemporary theory, in which a skeptical denial of objective fact is mounted on the basis of a metaphysically dogmatic postulation of the ultimate nature of reality.

APORIAS OF ANTI-FOUNDATIONALISM

CHAPTER TWO

GIVEN WHAT WE HAVE SEEN OF THE OVERALL SIMILARITY IN outlook between Smith and Fish, it is not surprising to find them in substantial agreement with regard to Habermas in particular, both as far as the rejection of his views itself is concerned as well as, to a considerable extent, in the particular reasons they give for that rejection. And thus it is also not surprising to find many of the same problems that we encountered in Smith's theory reappearing in Fish's, often in nearly identical form. To begin with, just as we saw in the case of Smith's specification of the principles underlying her anti-objectivism, so Fish, too, lays out the foundations of his anti-foundationalism in straightforwardly dogmatic fashion. The "presence" of "anti-foundationalist arguments," he states, "in whatever form . . . is signaled by such assertions as 'there are no unmediated facts,' 'all activity is irremediably interpretive,' 'there is no such thing as a neutral observation language,' 'there is no escaping politics,' 'all descriptions are from a perspective,' etc."[1] (By 'dogmatic,' again, I mean that these claims are presented in such a way that they simply have to be taken on faith if they are to be taken at all. No actual *argument* is ever presented that would *demonstrate* the truth of any of them. And for reasons that we have to some extent already touched on, but which I want to consider again in a moment as they pertain to Fish's position in particular, it is difficult to see how one ever could be presented that would not at once undo itself in the very process of being formulated.) Also like Smith, Fish takes advantage to some extent of Habermas's occasional (perhaps more than occasional) failure to distinguish as sharply as he might between the properly *transcendental* and the more specifically *programmatic* aspects of his theory—that is, again, between the effort to show what is *logically* presupposed by *all* discourse (including even attempts, such as Fish's, to deny the reality of those presuppositions), on the one hand, and the case for certain *particular modes* of discourse that, in view of the ineluctability of those presuppositions, it would make *pragmatically* good sense for us to adopt, on the other. As we saw, Smith's argument simply conflates these two aspects, subsuming the transcendental to the programmatic without remainder; as a result, her argument never actually engages the really fundamental part of Habermas's theory of language and communication at all. Fish, however, is on the whole rather more attentive to the distinction between these two levels of analysis. And thus he is able to construct an argument that does address Habermas's transcendental standpoint itself, and which, accordingly, requires somewhat more in the way of response. I believe, of course, that such a response is possible. Before turning directly to that task, however, I want to look more closely at the various assertions just cited that he adduces as representative of the anti-foundationalist position.

Perhaps the first thing to note about these claims is that although Fish evidently regards them as more or less equivalent, in fact they are not. For not all of them are true, but neither are all of them (necessarily) false. And when the truth values of different statements diverge, obviously they cannot all be saying the same thing. Two of these statements seem to me beyond rescue on any plausible reading of them, while another two, and perhaps a third, can be viewed in a way (albeit not Fish's) that renders them not only unexceptionable but indeed demonstrably true. Consider what is probably the easiest case first: both logical and empirical difficulties arise in connection with the positing of what might be called the ubiquity of the political. Etymology, history, and common usage agree in associating the concept of "politics," in the first instance, with the various activities and decisions involved in the governance of society (the *polis*), the organization and functioning of its public institutions, and the establishment of policy on matters of public concern. That is a broad enough definition, to be sure, to include (among other things) the pursuit of virtually any partisan agenda by any interested individual or group as it relates to the allocation of power and resources in the polity at large or in any of its subunits. By analogy with this basic sense of the term certain forms of activity that take place in the context of what can be thought of as quasi-polities, or polities-in-miniature (school elections, for example, or at least some labor-management negotiations), as well as efforts to order and regulate relations among different polities themselves on the international scale, are naturally spoken of as political as well. What does not follow from this primary sense, however, at least not with any logical force (notwithstanding that it has become an increasingly popular rhetorical move in recent years), is the essentially metaphorical extension of the notion of politics to all situations without exception in which conflicting views or interests may be involved and where, for whatever reason, it may be felt that some resolution or accommodation needs to be reached.

The problem with this sort of blanket metaphoricization of the political is that it tends to ignore the distinctive features of the particular context in which a given activity, now designated simply and without differentiation as political, may be occurring. One may in this way come to speak, for example, of the "politics" of the family or of the university. The danger here is one to which Wittgenstein is constantly trying to alert us, namely that of removing a term or concept from the context in which it is actually at home, and where accordingly it functions in cogently identifiable fashion, and attempting to employ it in a setting so different from that first one that no real application is possible and where, in consequence, only confusion or worse results. To pursue the examples just given, in order for talk of family or university politics to be in place at all, it would first have to be shown that a family or a university, properly understood, is in the relevant respects sufficiently *like* a body politic. In point of fact, however, I think that no such showing is possible in either case. What can very easily happen, however, as Wittgenstein, Nietzsche, Bacon, and many other thinkers have long pointed out, is that one can end up being seduced by one's own metaphor. And in the cases at hand, the effect can easily take the form of a self-fulfilling prophecy. One may begin treating the family or the university *as if it were* a polity. Convinced by the force of the political metaphor, and not recognizing that one has simply accepted the applicability of that metaphor unreflectively, never thinking to subject the question of that applicability to critical examination in its own right, one may find oneself viewing the relations among family members or members of a university community on the model of competing interest groups, with each of these understood to be simply seeking for itself the maximum degree of power over the whole that it can attain. And once enough members of the entities in question have become so convinced, and have, in consequence, themselves begun behaving in ways consonant with that conviction, it will in time become true that activities within these contexts indeed *are* properly characterized as political. The common non sequitur at the end of this chain of events, then, is the conclusion that the very state of affairs one has brought about oneself, in a process legitimated by nothing more than the arbitrary imposition of a metaphor, was actually inevitable all along; one supposes this to be merely a natural outgrowth of features inherent in the underlying reality of the situation itself.

Apart from specific examples such as these, however, other, more purely conceptual, considerations tell against not merely the validity, but indeed the coherence, of the contention that "there is no escaping politics." Considerations similar to these, moreover, can be brought to bear as well against the still more sweeping claim that "all activity is irremediably interpretive." However widely the conceptual net may be cast, almost any understanding of the political is going to include among its central elements such notions as "intention," "desire," "choice," "value," and the like. Indeed, one might seek to defend the thesis of the ubiquity of the political by extending this line of thought and simply stipulating that the concept of politics is to be understood as *coextensive* with our notions of intentionality, evaluation, and the rest. That would entail some obvious violence to ordinary usage, of course, and would also result in what strikes me as a rather needless impoverishment of our conceptual vocabulary; for if *politics* just *means* "whatever anybody wants to do, have, be, or otherwise feels a predilection for," then it is not clear what is supposed to be the point of holding on to the vocabulary of politics and the political as a specific idiom in its own right. Nevertheless, although apparently both arbitrary and confusing, such a move might still be made. And in fact, if it is not made, there would appear to be left open by default at least some avenue by which one could after all "escape politics."[2] Yet not even measures this extreme suffice to yield the desired universalization of the political. For beyond what seems to be the inherent implausibility of seeing all our thoughts and deeds against the backdrop of some partisan agenda, it is not even the case that everything that anyone ever says or does can intelligibly be regarded as a matter of intentionality, evaluation, or choice to begin with. And in seeing why this is so, we are better able to recognize the flaw in the claim that "all activity is irremediably interpretive" as well.

"The absent-minded man who at the order 'Right turn!' turns left, and then, clutching his forehead, says 'Oh! right turn' and does a right turn.—What has struck him? An interpretation?" (*PI*, § 506). "If I give anyone an order I feel it to be *quite enough* to give him signs. And I should never say: this is only words, and I have got to get behind the words. Equally, when I have asked someone something and he gives me an answer (i.e. a sign) I am content—that was what I expected—and I don't raise the objection: but that's a mere answer" (*PI*, § 503). "What this shews is that there is a way of grasping a rule which is *not* an *interpretation*, but which is exhibited in what we call 'obeying the rule' and 'going against it' in actual cases" (*PI*, § 201). "When I obey a rule, I do not choose" (*PI*, § 219). " 'But how can a rule shew me what I have to do at *this* point? Whatever I do is, on some interpretation, in accord with the rule.'—That is not what we ought to say, but rather: any interpretation still hangs in the air along with what it interprets, and cannot give it any support. Interpretations by themselves do not determine meaning" (*PI*, § 198). "Does it *follow* from the sense-impressions which I get that there is a chair over there?—How can a *proposition* follow from sense-impressions? Well, does it follow from the propositions which describe the sense-impressions? No.—But don't I infer that a chair is there from impressions, from sense-data?—I make no inference!" (*PI*, § 486). "To interpret is to think, to do something; seeing is a state" (*PI*, II, p. 212). "I shall get burnt if I put my hand in the fire: that is certainty. That is to say: here we see the meaning of certainty. (What it amounts to, not just the meaning of the word 'certainty.')" (*PI*, § 474). "Does man think . . . because he has found that thinking pays?—Because he thinks it advantageous to think? (Does he bring his children up because he has found it pays?)" (*PI*, § 467). "Look on the language-game as the *primary* thing. And look on the feelings, etc., as you look on a way of regarding the language-game, as interpretation" (*PI*, § 656). "Justification by experience comes to an end. If it did not it would not be justification" (*PI*, § 485; cf. § 1: "Explanations come to an end somewhere"; also §§ 29, 217, and 326, and II, p. 180). "[A]n explanation may indeed rest on another one that has been given, but none stands in need of another—unless *we* require it to prevent a misunderstanding. One might say: an explanation serves to remove or to avert a misunderstanding—one, that is, that would occur but for the explanation; not every one that I can imagine" (*PI*, § 87). "What has to be accepted, the given, is—so one could say—*forms of life*" (*PI*, II, p. 226). "Following a rule is analogous to obeying an order. We are trained to do so; we react to an order in a particular way. But what if one person reacts in one way and another in another to the order and the training? Which one is right? Suppose you came as an explorer into an unknown country with a language quite strange to you. In what circumstances would you say that the people gave orders, understood them, obeyed them, rebelled against them, and so on? The *common behavior of mankind* is the system of reference by which we interpret an unknown language" (*PI*, § 206; emphasis added).

It would not be difficult to go on multiplying examples of this sort at virtually whatever length one might choose. The point that Wittgenstein is trying to bring home here—in keeping with the method of the *Investigations* as described in the Preface, from as many different directions and by means of as many different concrete illustrations as possible—though central to his philosophy, is nevertheless one that seems to be overlooked by many contemporary critics and theoreticians who would enlist him in support of their views. There has now been repeated innumerable times in the literature the claim that whereas the "early" Wittgenstein (of the *Tractatus*) was still in thrall to the ancient, misguided idea of an Absolute Truth capable of being stated definitively once and for all, the "later" (post-1929) Wittgenstein, having awoken from his dogmatic slumbers, came to recognize in good nominalist fashion that there really is only a constantly shifting, endlessly variable array of not merely different, but indeed frequently incompatible, "language-games." In terms of the idiom I have been employing here, he is seen as having moved from a belief in the reality (and discoverability) of "what there *is*" to an acceptance of the fact that there is nothing beyond, or beneath, or otherwise more fundamental than "what(ever) gets *said.*" In other words, he trades in his former, hard-edged, hyper-austere metaphysical dogmatism for a more easy-going version of skeptical relativism. That is not the most usual way in which the view in question tends to be expressed, of course. One speaks rather, for example, of a shift from the paradigm of logic to that of rhetoric, from timelessness to history, from the presumption of an Archimedean vantage point to an acceptance of radical situatedness and contextuality, from universality to particularity, from necessity to contingency, and so forth. Whatever the particular terms favored by a given commentator, however, the basic picture remains essentially the same. In it, precisely two alternatives are envisaged, between which only a stark, either/or choice is possible. In the course of his career, Wittgenstein is seen as having opted first for the former member of each pair just mentioned and then, at a later point, having seen the error of his youthful ways, for the latter.

The principal problem with this persistent dichotomizing of Wittgenstein is that it leaves him effectively mired in the very pre-critical, dogmatic-skeptical context of thought that, beginning already with his earliest work in philosophy, he seems to have been concerned above (almost) anything else to find a way of overcoming. Of the many respects in which his philosophical career is fundamentally continuous from beginning to end, this is arguably the most important. There is some danger of getting ahead of the argument here, but the point must be made at least briefly to indicate the relevance of the series of passages from the

Investigations cited a moment ago to the task of showing exactly what has gone wrong in Fish's postulation of the ubiquity of the political and the interpretive. To begin with, then, Wittgenstein is, so far as I can tell, unwavering in his recognition of the reality of objective fact. From the opening proposition of the *Tractatus*, "The world is all that is the case" (*TLP*, 1), which he glosses immediately as "The world is the totality of facts, not of things" (*TLP*, 1.1), to the late remarks collected posthumously under the title *On Certainty*,[3] I think it is probably safe to say that there is no more consistent theme in his writings than this. The differences between the *Tractatus* and *On Certainty* in this regard—such differences as there are—are best viewed, I think, as reflective merely of a basic difference of emphasis in the two works: what in the *Tractatus* is dealt with through an analysis of the logic of *description* is approached in *On Certainty* from the opposite direction, by means of an investigation of the logic of *doubt*.[4] If the *Tractatus* is concerned to reveal the nature of the substantive constitution of factuality, *On Certainty* represents a logical complement to that analysis: in the course of an argument more privative than substantive in tenor, it relentlessly undermines even the intelligibility of the supposition that the world of factuality might *not* be as objectively real as (virtually) everyone takes it to be as a matter of common sense. In neither case, however (and, so far as I am aware, in none of the writings that fall between these two endpoints in his career either), does Wittgenstein understand factuality in metaphysically dogmatic terms. Indeed, if the development in his thinking over the years were to be summed up in a single phrase, I think it might well be this: an increasingly clear recognition, and, in proportion, ever more explicit articulation, of the principle that objective factuality (and one needs to underscore the term *objective* here) is inseparable from the human beings for whom the facts are what they are. As Donald Davidson articulates essentially the same insight: "Nothing in the world, no object or event, would be true or false if there were not thinking creatures."[5]

Now, if *this* is all that one means to say with statements such as "there are no unmediated facts," or "all descriptions are from a perspective" (or even "there is no such thing as a neutral observation language")—and I confess I can see no other way in which these statements can be understood as coherent claims at all—then it seems to me perfectly clear that there are indeed "no unmediated facts." This is simply the view that I call critical realism. But it is surely no less clear that this is not what Fish means to say. For, in his view, there are not actually any *facts* at all; rather, there are *only* "mediations," or "perspectival judgments"—or "interpretations" and "politically motivated choices and decisions." And for this reason he is able to regard the five "assertions" we have been considering here, all of which, he has declared, "signal" the "presence" of "anti-foundationalist arguments," as essentially equivalent. Fish's denial of objective factuality follows naturally from his prior acceptance, noted earlier, of the bipartite scheme of "what there (independently) *is*—what gets (interpretively) *said.*" He sees no way to conceive of facts as objective, determinate, fixed, unalterable (once in the past), and all the rest of the attributes that we normally—indeed, in most ordinary circumstances, automatically—associate with the notion of factuality, except at the price of simultaneously conceiving of them as ontologically independent entities, existing prior to and so unaffected by our knowledge of them. Once that latter alternative has been rejected (again, sensibly enough, as far as it goes), the underlying epistemological dualism that ultimately determines all of Fish's reflections on these matters leaves him with no recourse but to posit the ubiquity of interpretation, perspective, politics, and the rest of the now familiar set of categories.

In addition to the unreflected assumption that factuality can be understood, if at all, *only* as a matter of ontological independence, there is a further, and no less uncritically accepted, assumption operative here. It is that something like an interpretation would even be conceivable, much less possible, in the absence of an enabling context—consisting of, among other things, objective facts—already in place. Precisely this confusion gives rise to the assumption that Wittgenstein is trying to get us to recognize in the passages from the *Investigations* cited above, as well as in many others that could be cited, some of which we shall have occasion to see in a moment. Once this key point has been recognized, however, the temptation to invoke "interpretation" (or any of its cognates) as itself the *condition* of factuality effectively dissolves. For clearly no x can be analyzed as a function of a y different from it, if y already presupposes the prior existence of x in order that it exist at all. In accordance with common usage, as I take Wittgenstein to be urging as well, I think it makes most sense to regard interpretations as examples of what might be called second-order phenomena, supervenient on factuality. Specifically, I think interpretations are in general best understood as particular ways of *reacting to* facts—more specifically still, as proposals stating what a given set of facts, in the view of the interpreter, signifies or betokens or reveals about other facts.

Whether this particular way of viewing interpretation is found congenial or not, however, the more basic point that interpretation can in any case not be foundational of phenomenal reality can be seen from at least two other directions as well. Let us adopt, for the sake of argument, the contrary hypothesis. Let us grant the anti-foundationalist's contention that it all really is just "interpretation" (we will come back to this *really* in a moment). *Everything* that anybody thinks or says is merely an "interpretation" of some sort; and all "interpretations" are, of necessity, on an equal footing with one another, there being, by hypothesis, no objective reality anywhere that could serve as a standard by which the relative cogency or plausibility of different interpretations could be assessed. With everything he has been insisting on having thus apparently been conceded him, however, the anti-foundationalist now finds that the bottom drops out of his argument of its own weight. For if he is now asked to explain what specific conceptual work the notion of "interpretation" itself is performing here, he is evidently at a loss for an answer. Nor is it at all surprising that that should be so. Universal predication is, in the nature of the case, vacuous. When we encounter it, we simply perform the same operation seen above in connection with Wittgenstein's private-language argument: we "divide through"—here, by "interpretation"—and are then left with nothing other than the same old down-to-earth, garden-variety assertions of what is and is not the case that we have always had, some of which will turn out on examination to be true, while others will not.

The doctrine of ubiquitous interpretation catches up with and undermines itself in yet another way. (This is the point at which the check written a moment ago with the term *really* would have to be cashed, but where it in fact bounces. And seeing why this is so affords us at the same time one of many possible vantage points from which to note both how and why Fish's attempt to rescue his theory from the charge of self-referential inconsistency or perfomative contradiction necessarily fails.) It is obvious that the thesis that "all activity is irremediably interpretive" cannot, on pain of manifest self-contradiction, be intended as a statement of objective fact in its own right. Rather it, too, must be understood as in some sense an "interpretation" (of just what remains mysterious, of course—as we saw above in connection with Smith, so Fish's theory as well appears to entail a kind of tacit rehabilitation of the *Ding an sich*). But it is also clear that this neither is nor can be the end of the matter. For there is now the question of our *understanding* of the proposition (or, perhaps better, quasi-proposition) itself—that is, the *meaning* of the statement constituted by the words *all, activity, is, irremediably,* and *interpretive,* linked together and uttered in that order. How do we know if we have grasped that meaning correctly? But, of course, on the terms of the theory itself, the question cannot even be asked. For, again, by hypothesis, there is no objective fact of the matter—in this case, no determinate, unequivocal meaning of the statement—to be recovered at all. Apparently, therefore, we are committed to an infinite regress of interpretations, with no resting place—and so no final answer—possible even in principle. This is surely bad enough news for Fish's theory. For it entails that we quite literally can never know for certain even what that theory *is*. But, on the other hand, as just seen, precisely that conclusion is entailed by nothing other than the statement of the theory itself, which we must, accordingly, have been able to "understand" at least well enough to follow out the directions implicit in it. It thus turns out, in other words, that if we understand the theory, we can never understand it; and, alternatively, if we do not understand the theory, well, then once again we obviously just don't understand it.

But the difficulties are not over yet. For have we not after all simply been taking for granted in all this that we *know* what an interpretation itself is, and therefore that we can recognize with unimpeachable certainty when we are engaged in that activity and when not? (Again, there must be *some* difference between when one is doing interpretation and when not, if we are to avoid the vacuousness of universal predication. *Interpretation* cannot simply be a name for whatever anyone and everyone may happen to be doing, whenever and wherever it may happen to be.) But this merely reintroduces at the next level up the problem encountered in the paragraph just preceding. For if interpretations can be identified apodictically as such, if we can in any circumstances say with absolute certainty that anyone (e.g., ourselves) is performing an act of interpretation, then clearly there are at least that many objective facts in the world. But, as we have seen, it is precisely the reality of objective factuality that the anti-foundationalist position is intent on denying. And so, again, we apparently find ourselves committed to an infinite regress, this time of a kind of meta-order. For if previously we were constrained, on pain of self-contradiction, to see ourselves, as it were, as a race of semiotic Flying Dutchmen, unable ever to come to rest in a once-and-for-all definitive reading of the thesis that "all activity is irremediably interpretive," we are now evidently unable even to get on board the ship in the first place (or, at any rate, to identify our location with sufficient reliability to say for certain that that is in fact where we are). Either we are condemned to continue our interpretive wanderings indefinitely, or we are not yet able even to embark on the journey.

There is, of course, no lack of critics and theoreticians today ready to claim that the prospect of an infinite regress of interpretation holds no philosophical terrors whatever for them. Apart from anything else that may be said against this claim, the really fundamental confusion embodied in it is simply the belief that it is possible to make coherent sense of the notion of such an infinite regress at all. Gary Shapiro distinguishes usefully between Derrida and Peirce in this regard. He notes that

> Derrida is a skeptic about meaning who thinks that if there were to
> be any meaning at all it would require the inclusion of an infinite
> number of moments at the "beginning" and the "end" of the pro-
> cess of meaning. But . . . all presumed ends or beginnings dis-
> solve into endless ranges of prior and posterior nodes of meaning.
> Anything with such indeterminate boundaries can hardly be that
> full, present, and defined thing which we are wont to think of as
> meaning. Therefore there is no meaning, although there is, in its
> place, an ultimately plural and diffuse web of *écriture*. From a
> Peircean point of view this is to confuse intensive and extensive
> infinity. It is to suppose that that which has an internal complexity
> of the highest degree must necessarily lack all definition and
> boundary.[6]

In other words, where for Derrida "all writing refers back to an earlier
writing and so on *ad infinitum*," Peirce "makes a crucial distinction between the continuity of the sign-process and its indefinite or infinite extension." In his view,

> the sign-process is continuous in that it has no absolute first or last
> term. But there are many cases of continuous series which are not
> indefinitely or infinitely extended—such as a line segment. We
> can consistently conceive of a sign-process beginning (or ending) at
> some point in time, even though it makes no sense to talk of the
> absolutely first (or last) sign in the series.[7]

Wittgenstein, too, makes essentially the same point (as, indeed, does
Herder already in the eighteenth century).[8] On numerous occasions,
Wittgenstein returns to what is clearly for him the pivotal observation
that explanations, interpretations, justifications, and other similar operations "come to an end somewhere" (indeed, that, in the nature of the
case, they must do so). So far as I know, he first expresses the point in
just this way in the opening section of the *Philosophical Investigations*,
cited above, and as we shall see to some extent in what follows, it is re-
asserted with particular frequency in *On Certainty*. Whether formulated in precisely these terms or not, however, the theme, as with
virtually all the centrally important themes in his philosophizing, runs
like a continuous thread through his writings from beginning to end. It
is already implicit, for example, in the following passage from the *Tractatus*: "The meanings of primitive signs can be explained by means of
elucidations. Elucidations are propositions that contain the primitive
signs. So they can only be understood if the meanings of those signs
are already known" (*TLP*, 3.263). There is no circularity, vicious or

otherwise, in this state of affairs. For, as Wittgenstein makes ever more explicit in his later writings, but as he clearly already recognizes in his first work as well, we are always able, as the court of last resort, to look past merely verbal exchange to the concrete level of what actually gets *done:* "What signs fail to express, their application shows. What signs slur over, their application says clearly" (*TLP,* 3.262). Similarly in *The Blue Book,* with the principal difference merely that both the specific vocabulary and overall philosophical demeanor are now those of Wittgenstein ca. 1933, rather than ca. 1920:

> there is the idea that if an order is understood and obeyed there must be a reason for our obeying it as we do; and, in fact, a chain of reasons reaching back to infinity. This is as if one said: "Wherever you are, you must have got there from somewhere else, and to that previous place from another place; and so on *ad infinitum.*" (If, on the other hand, you had said, "wherever you are, you *could* have got there from another place ten yards away; and to that other place from a third, ten yards further away, and so on *ad infinitum,*" if you had said this you would have stressed the infinite *possibility* of making a step. Thus the idea of an infinite chain of reasons arises out of a confusion similar to this: that a line of a certain length consists of an infinite number of parts because it is infinitely divisible; i.e., because there is no end to the possibility of dividing it.) If on the other hand you realize that the chain of *actual* reasons has a beginning, you will no longer be revolted by the idea of a case in which there is *no* reason for the way you obey the order.[9]

It is, however, in *Zettel* that Wittgenstein brings out perhaps most clearly exactly what is logically amiss in positing an infinite regress of (for example) interpretations: "The reasoning that leads to an infinite regress is to be given up not 'because in this way we can never reach the goal', but because *here there is no goal;* so it *makes no sense to say* 'we can never reach it'. We readily think that we must run through a few steps of the regress and then so to speak give it up in despair. Whereas its aimlessness (the lack of a goal in the calculus) can be derived from the starting position" (emphasis added).[10]

Wittgenstein's crucial insight, expressed in different ways in these passages from various stages of his career, is, I take it, the following. There is an inclination to regard explanations (or justifications or interpretations) assumed to be endless as instances of what might be called explanation (and the rest) in progress. So regarded, they seem in all essential respects indistinguishable from explanations generally, merely with the difference (itself assumed to be incidental) that here the process just happens to go on forever. Wittgenstein's point, however, is that this assumption represents a fundamental confusion, one made possible (as usual in such cases) by our having forgotten the basic conceptual grammar of the terms we are employing. An explanation (or justification or interpretation) that, by hypothesis, never comes to an end, or ever could do so, is not simply something that is permanently underway toward being a completed explanation. It is not an *explanation* to begin with, anymore than a door that could never be closed (or, for that matter, opened) would be a door at all. The man who says, "The door to my office is always open," if he is speaking the literal truth, does not yet have a door to his office. Rather he has, at most, a kind of decorative adornment at the entrance to his office that happens to be in the shape of a door. In like manner, one could not be said to have a clock (not even a malfunctioning one), if no matter what one did, the dial of the ostensible timepiece always moved along with the hands. I want to return to this point at greater length in a moment, with particular attention to why, for Wittgenstein, the fact that explanation *does* come to an end somewhere is not to be confused with its being arbitrarily brought to an end wherever one likes. Before doing so, however, I want to draw out some of the implications of what we have now seen for Fish's attempt to save his theory from the charge of self-referential inconsistency.

In the Introduction to *Doing What Comes Naturally*, that attempt takes the following form. Fish contends that the charge of self-referential inconsistency

mistakes the nature of the anti-foundationalist claim, which is not that there are no foundations, but that whatever foundations there are (and there always are some) have been established by persuasion, that is, in the course of argument and counter-argument on the basis of examples and evidence that are themselves cultural and contextual. Anti-foundationalism, then, is a thesis about how foundations emerge, and in contradistinction to the assumptions that foundations do not emerge but simply *are*, anchoring the universe and thought from a point above history and culture, it says that foundations are local and temporal phenomena, and are always vulnerable to challenges from other localities and other times. This vulnerability also extends, of course, to the anti-foundationalist thesis itself, and that is why its assertion does not involve a contradiction, as it would if what was being asserted was the impossibility of foundational assertion; but since what is being asserted is that assertions—about foundations or anything else—have to make their way against objections and counter-examples, anti-foundationalism can without contradiction include itself under its own scope and await the objections one might make to it; and so long as those objections are successfully met and turned back by those who preach anti-foundationalism (a preaching and a turning back I am performing at this very moment), anti-foundationalism can be asserted as absolutely true since (at least for the time being) there is no argument that holds the field against it. (*DWN*, pp. 29–30)

I have thought it worthwhile to cite the passage at some length, inasmuch as this represents, to my knowledge, Fish's best effort anywhere in his writings to avoid the charge in question. In seeing why that effort nonetheless fails, we thus gain at the same time an especially good view of what is fundamentally untenable about anti-foundationalism at large, regardless of the particular form it may assume in any given context.

It is easy, I think, to come to the end of this passage, with its confident, if unilateral, declaration of victory, experiencing an uncomfortably mixed feeling. On the one hand, it seems clear on the face of it that somewhere along the line a bit of conceptual sleight of hand must have been performed to give the conclusion reached here even the appearance of plausibility. For, after all, can one simply make it so by saying so that "there is no argument that holds the field against" one's position? Is that not rather to engage in a more or less unvarnished form of question begging? (Development of effective argumentation in support of our beliefs would certainly be a far less onerous task than, for the most part, it actually is if this were a move generally available to all.) And what of the notion of a theory's being "absolutely true . . . for the time being"? Can that locution be given a coherent sense at all? Or is it not rather like saying of some state of affairs that it is always and everywhere the case, but only for now? On the other hand, the conjuring trick—if that is what it is—has apparently been performed so artfully that one may find it difficult, at least initially, to identify the precise point at which it occurred. And in this circumstance one may be unable to shake completely the nagging suspicion that this effort on Fish's part to keep his theory at bay from itself might not after all have to be accounted a success. To see why in point of fact it does not, we need to look back to two earlier key junctures in the passage. Fish says that "what is being asserted [with "the anti-foundationalist thesis"] is that assertions—about foundations or anything else—have to make their way against objections and counter-examples." By itself, of course, this does not exactly distinguish his position from any of a host of others that might be adopted. It is surely safe to say that there are few, if any, people who do *not* believe that "assertions," if they are to command our assent, must show themselves capable of holding up in the face of "objections and counter-examples." What gives this—in itself, rather uncontroversial—thesis its specifically anti-foundationalist spin is the additional claim that the process of "argument and counter-argument" by which "whatever foundations there are" are "established" occurs always "on the basis of examples and evidence that are themselves *cultural* and *contextual*," and hence that these "foundations" (such as they are) remain of necessity always merely "*local* and *temporal* phenomena, . . . always *vulnerable* to challenge from other localities and other times" (emphasis added).

Let us again for the sake of argument grant the anti-foundationalist everything he seems to be asking here. Let us assume with him that there really is *nothing* of which we can legitimately claim to be *certain*—not merely to *feel* certain, but actually to *be* it—no assertion whatsoever that we might make, no matter how apparently well secured, that is not sooner or later "vulnerable to challenge" from some other quarter. (In fact, of course, for reasons that we have to some extent seen already, and as Wittgenstein observes repeatedly, in particular in *On Certainty*, a vast amount of what we take to be the case is *effectively* beyond challenge, for the reason that it cannot be questioned at all without at the same time draining the very concepts of belief, questioning, and the like of meaning in their own right. Thomas McCarthy, in his critical study of Habermas, notes that "certain basic elements of scientific thought" are in fact "historically and culturally universal." These include "the fundamental principles of logic, some elementary mathematical concepts and inductive procedures, certain general structures of sensory experience"[11]—and I think surely more than a little besides that he might have mentioned as well. Fish, of course, does not regard the fact of universal agreement as telling at all against his theory. As we noted above in connection with Smith, his theory, too, would obviously collapse at once if he were to do so. We shall return to this point below for a closer examination of some of the issues that it raises.) In granting all this, have we now conceded "the field" to the anti-foundationalist position? Indeed, we have not. And it is precisely by declining to bring against that position any of the more usual objections to it, all of which the sophisticated anti-foundationalist has by now become quite adroit at parrying, that we are better able to see how anti-foundationalism actually denies the field to itself. Precisely in attempting to avoid the charge of self-refutation by "includ[ing] itself under its own scope and

await[ing] the objections one might make to it," anti-foundationalism has
already brought against itself an objection that, in the very nature of the
case it wants to make, it is unable ever to overcome.

Despite its best efforts, the anti-foundationalist attempt to go completely historicist, as formulated here by Fish, has nevertheless allowed
one thing to slip through the net. That is the notion of "argument" itself,
along with the correlative notions of "example" and "evidence." Actually, "*allowed* to slip through" is the wrong way to put it, insofar as that
way of expressing the matter might imply carelessness or oversight. For
nothing could ever have been done to prevent this outcome. The attempt to go completely historicist—and the point can easily be shown to
apply mutatis mutandis to all the various other calls for radical "historicization" so much in evidence today, not merely to Fish's version in particular—confronts an insuperable dilemma. Either it is the case that the
notion of "argument" and all that accompanies it represents a historical
constant, or it is not. There may, of course, be all sorts of different ways
in which the conceptual space defined by the term *argument* is filled in
different cultural contexts. Regardless, however, of what, as a contingent matter, may be held locally and temporally to constitute the criteria of a good or persuasive argument—what particular standards of
evidence, what rules of inference, and the like—in other words, regardless of what specific content the concept of "argument" may happen to
be given in any set of circumstances in particular, it must be the case
either that that conceptual space itself persists over time as a constant
feature of the human condition, or that there just is no such conceptual
space at all. (We are, of course, not obliged to construe this "space" in
rigidly essentialist terms in its own right. Wittgenstein's notion of "family resemblance" serves equally well—indeed, I think, rather better—
in enabling us to deal with it.) To opt for the former alternative,
however, is obviously to recognize the existence of at least one supra-
historically foundational entity, not, of course, in the sense of something
outside of history (where would *that* be?), but something that, while always historically realized in the concrete terms of some context in particular, is also always and everywhere present as a *formal* dimension of
our being.[12] Such an acknowledgment is tantamount to an admission
that after all not everything can be relativized without remainder to
discrete contexts and is thus plainly fatal to the anti-foundationalist
thesis. Yet if one declines to take this step, opting instead for the latter
alternative, then the anti-foundationalist thesis cannot even be formulated. The universalist claim that "foundations" are "always" a function
of culturally and contextually determined "argument" is in this case
emptied of content; for whatever the term *argument* may now be taken

to mean, it can at any rate, by hypothesis, not be the *same* meaning from one instance of foundation-establishment to the next. But if that is so, then the claim is no more informative with regard to "foundations" and how they come into being than saying "all crows are black" would be with regard to crows if the reference of the term *black* itself were constantly changing.

Thus, even if one is prepared to find no contradiction in the assertion that anti-foundationalism is both "absolutely true" (even if only "for the time being") and yet also "always vulnerable to challenges"—and, though I have bracketed this issue for the moment to pursue the argument in another direction, it seems to me clear that each of these characterizations in fact necessarily excludes the other—the very *possibility* of claiming *intelligibly* that "there is no argument that holds the field against" anti-foundationalism is itself already fatal to the anti-foundationalist program. That is, if it is so much as assumed that that proposition has a coherent sense—and inasmuch as having a sense is a minimal condition of a proposition's being either true or false, that assumption is tacitly made in asserting the proposition at all—then, given the particular content of the anti-foundationalist thesis, the claim that "no argument holds the field against it" must be false. The very *making* of that claim already constitutes all the argument necessary to drive it from the field. For, again, the claim depends decisively on the notion of "argumentation" itself having a sense. But, as McCarthy notes in his discussion of Habermas's conception of the "ideal speech situation," "if argumentation is not to lose its sense," certain "supposition[s]" must be made (*CTH*, p. 310). And all of these (as we shall continue to see in the next chapter as well) are fatal to anti-foundationalism as Fish describes it. It appears to lie in the nature of conceptualization itself that the very formulation, or attempted formulation, of a thoroughgoingly historicist outlook will always be incapable of enclosing itself entirely within itself. (This point was already recognized over two centuries ago, not coincidentally by one of the foremost early advocates of an incorporation of historical perspectives in our thinking generally, namely Herder.) Rather it inevitably leaves at least one loose end hanging, as we have seen Fish's version do here in the form of the notion of "argumentation." And once we begin pulling on that thread, it is not long before the entire anti-foundationalist fabric begins to unravel. For considerations like those that we have introduced in connection with the concept of "argument" apply in equal measure to others among the central notions on which anti-foundationalism must depend even for its articulation.

In the course of criticizing an argument of Stephen Toulmin's,[13] Fish speaks of the "dilemma . . . [that] awaits anyone who first acknowledges the essential historicity of all human endeavor but then seeks a place or a moment in which the pressure of that historicity can be escaped. For Toulmin (as for so many others) that space is named rationality, and the moment is the one in which the mind, now armed with an awareness of its tendency to bias, turns its back on bias and moves into what Toulmin calls elsewhere the 'courts of rationality' " (*DWN*, p. 438).[14] " '[T]he operative question' " in Toulmin's view, Fish notes, " 'is, which of our positions [equivalent for Fish, as he indicates at this point, to our "interpretive standpoints"] are rationally warranted, reasonable or defensible—that is, well-founded rather than groundless opinions' " by virtue of having been produced in accordance with an " 'impartial rational standpoint' " (*DWN*, p. 438).[15] To this Fish responds, "My question is, from what position is this question about our positions to be asked?" (*DWN*, p. 438). For, he continues, "the specification of what is and is not an 'impartial manner' [of reasoning, weighing evidence, and the like] is itself an *'interested'* act, that is, an act performed within a *set of assumptions*—concerning what is and is not evidence and what are and are not criteria for judgment—that is, constitutive of and inseparable from some *partial* view of the world" (*DWN*, p. 439; first two emphases added). With this statement of what he terms "the strong thesis of anti-foundationalist or interpretivist thought" (*DWN*, p. 439), Fish believes that he has deprived Toulmin of any way of answering the question that he has just put to him that would not at once destroy the latter's own position.[16] As my emphases in the passage are intended to suggest, however, it seems to me that Fish has in fact stopped at least one question too soon here. *My* question is: how were we able to develop these "interests" and formulate these "assumptions" in the first place?

Fish's argument depends throughout, notwithstanding that he is frequently at some pains to deny the fact, on the sort of radically decisionist model of human intellection that both Wittgenstein and Habermas, among others, show to be unsustainable. His central claim that human "behavior . . . is possible and intelligible only within the context of some interested, non-neutral vision," and hence that even "[w]hen we act impartially . . . we do so 'by our lights,' which means that we act within and as an extension of an interpretive and therefore partial notion of what being impartial means" (*DWN*, p. 439), founders on an analysis of the concepts of "interestedness" and "interpretation" themselves. For these concepts, too, have their foundations. *Their* intelligibility depends on presuppositions—though that is at least a potentially misleading term for it—whose roots extend more deeply still into the linguistic-existential fabric of our being. And thus, purely on conceptual grounds, we are already able to see that they cannot possibly be the points of ultimate reference Fish takes them to be. To put it another way, Fish traps himself in a dilemma precisely analogous to the one in which he rightly sees Toulmin caught, the one that "awaits anyone who first acknowledges the essential historicity of all human endeavor but then seeks a place or a moment in which the pressure of that historicity can be escaped." If "[f]or Toulmin that space is named rationality," for Fish it is named "anti-foundationalism." The tenets of the "anti-foundationalist thesis" play precisely the same structural role in his thinking that is played by the fundamental postulates in any metaphysically dogmatic system. The only thing that may to some extent obscure this fact is simply that Fish's dogmatism (like Smith's, discussed earlier) is—however initially paradoxical the formulation may appear—the dogmatism of skepticism. The choice that confronts all of us, Fish no less than anyone else, is *not* between a consistent, unblinking "acknowledg[ment of] the essential historicity of all human endeavor," on the one hand, and the search for "a place or a moment in which the pressure of that historicity can be escaped," on the other. For, as we have now seen, there is no coherent way in which the supposed "*essential* historicity of *all* human endeavor" can be "acknowledg[ed]" at all, inasmuch as the very attempt to do so ineluctably places one conceptually in a position that neither is nor can be itself captured by the thesis on which one is intent. And because *this* position, moreover, is one that we cannot avoid occupying in any case, no matter what we do, the choice is rather between possible ways of construing it. And these essentially reduce to two: either *precritical* (and so metaphysically dogmatic) or *critical*.

PRE-CRITICAL AND CRITICAL:
FISH AND HABERMAS

CHAPTER THREE

I

AS I HAVE INDICATED SEVERAL TIMES NOW, FISH STANDS ON
one side of the *pre-critical-critical* divide, Habermas (and, behind him,
Wittgenstein, Kant, and Herder) on the other. And it is for this reason
at bottom that Fish's critique of Habermas, though more penetrating
than Smith's, nevertheless like hers also ultimately fails even to find its
target, much less to score a hit on it. Indeed, as we shall see, this attempted critique comes to grief on precisely "the problem on which"
Fish maintains Habermas's "critical project repeatedly founders, the
problem of beginning or taking the first step" (*DWN*, p. 452). Fish explains what he means by this. He notes that "Habermas acknowledges
th[at] many others . . . have set for themselves . . . the goal of specifying the most basic and abstract level of [linguistic] competence." Yet
these "predecessors," Habermas feels,

> "do not generalize radically enough and do not push through the
> level of accidental contexts to general and unavoidable presuppo-
> sitions" (p. 8).[1] That is, they do not transcend but remain within
> the "prevailing realm of purposes" because "they start from the
> model of the isolated, purposive-rational actor" (p. 12). Having
> said this, Habermas is now obligated to explain how it is possible
> to do anything *but* "start from the model of the . . . purposive-
> rational actor." (*DWN*, pp. 452–53)

70

The beginnings of what becomes something of a pattern in Fish's treatment of Habermas are already discernible here. He implies that Habermas has in effect placed on himself an obligation which it is nevertheless inherently impossible to discharge. Yet if we look more closely, it turns out that what Fish represents Habermas as "[h]aving said" is in fact, in a small but pivotally important respect, not what the latter says at all. In citing Habermas's text the second time, as just seen, Fish omits the word "isolated"; the ellipsis in the passage from *DWN* just given is Fish's. This is, however, by no means a merely incidental omission. On the contrary, consulting the larger context in which the passage in question occurs reveals that the point on which Habermas is intent at this juncture turns precisely on that particular word. He is criticizing those theoreticians of language who, he says, in "start[ing] from the model of the *isolated,* purposive-rational actor," "thereby fail . . . to reconstruct in an appropriate way the specific moment of *mutuality* in the understanding of identical meanings or in the acknowledgment of *intersubjective* validity claims" (emphasis added).[2] It is precisely on the notions of mutuality and intersubjectivity, however, that Habermas's (like Wittgenstein's) *transcendental* analysis of the structures of human experience decisively depends. Operating as he is exclusively within a pre-critical context of thought, however, Fish consistently misses this central point.

In large part for this reason, I think, he professes puzzlement at Habermas's explicit endorsement in "What Is Universal Pragmatics?" of "[t]he use theory of meaning developed from the work of Wittgenstein," which asserts "that the meaning of linguistic expressions can be identified only with reference to situations of possible employment" (*UP,* p. 30). For, as Fish reads him, Habermas "nevertheless persists in positing meanings 'determined by formal properties of speech situations in general, and not by particular situations of use' " (*DWN,* p. 454; although Fish does not provide the page reference here, the passage cited appears on page 31 of *UP*). Now, if this really were all there were to Habermas's view, Fish would certainly seem to be correct in noting a fundamental inconsistency in it. Surely, however, the logical error is *too* blatant not to arouse our suspicions. Can Habermas really have been that oblivious to the structure of his own argument? And in fact all that is necessary to dissolve the appearance of contradiction is to relocate the apparently offending passages in the larger context of Habermas's text. Following the reference to Wittgenstein cited above, Habermas does allow that "[t]he analysis of general structures of speech can indeed begin with general sentence structures." "However," he continues in the sentence immediately following, "it is directed to formal properties of sentences only from the perspective of the possibility of *using sentences* as elements of speech, that is, for representational, expressive, and inter-personal functions" (*UP*, p. 31; Habermas's emphasis). Further along on the same page he elaborates: "[T]he meanings of linguistic expressions are relevant [to the concerns of "universal pragmatics"] *only insofar as* they contribute to speech acts that satisfy the validity claims of truth, truthfulness, and normative rightness" (*UP*, p. 31). Only having said *this* does Habermas then add that "universal pragmatics is distinguished from empirical pragmatics, e.g., sociolinguistics, in that the meaning of linguistic expressions comes under consideration only insofar as it is de-termined by *formal properties of speech situations in general,* and not by particular situations of use" (*UP*, p. 31).

The broader context makes clear, I think, that there is no contradic-tion at all between Habermas's characterization of the aims of "universal pragmatics" and his earlier profession of adherence to Wittgenstein's "use theory of meaning." Quite the contrary—as Habermas conceives it the program of "universal pragmatics" consists precisely in an elabora-tion and systematic articulation of Wittgenstein's general theoretical principle. To consider "the meaning of linguistic expressions" from the vantage point of how that meaning "is determined by *formal properties of speech situations in general*" (emphasis added) just *is* to base one's analysis on the injunction implicit in the Wittgensteinian view (as stated by Habermas) that if "the meaning of linguistic expressions" is to be grasped at all, it must be in terms of "*situations of possible employment*" (emphasis added). It is precisely *not* to say that the meaning of a par-ticular utterance is, or ever could be, determined *solely* by "formal properties of speech situations in general." The expression "only insofar as" in the passage cited at the conclusion of the preceding paragraph (an expression Fish does not include in his citation of Habermas) clearly re-fers in the context to the particular *nature* of the role played by such "formal properties" in determining meaning, the particular *extent* of the contribution to the production of meaning stemming from that quarter. It neither asserts nor implies that these properties are or could be the *exclusive* factors *exhaustively* determining linguistic meaning in any given concrete case in particular. Indeed, if this were not Habermas's view, there would clearly be no point to the distinction that he explicitly draws in this passage between two sorts of semantic analysis, which he terms "universal" and "empirical pragmatics," respectively; for in that case "universal pragmatics" would be able to do the entire job by itself, without even adverting to concrete particulars as they occur at the "em-pirical" level. This does, indeed, seem to be Fish's understanding of the aims (and claims) of "universal pragmatics"; but, as we have now seen, it is just as clearly not Habermas's.

It is thus to misrepresent Habermas's position in a very fundamental way to say, as Fish does in the passage cited above, that he "persists in *positing* meanings 'determined by formal properties of speech situations in general, and not by particular situations of use' " (emphasis added). For this is precisely what he does not do. Neither Hahermas nor Wittgenstein supposes that there is such a thing as a free-floating, use-independent linguistic meaning, exhaustively describable in terms of the purely *formal* properties of the utterance in which that meaning is contained. Later in *UP* Habermas makes the point again in, if anything, still more explicit fashion: "[A] consistent analysis of meaning is not possible without reference to some situations of possible use" (*UP*, p. 46). What both Wittgenstein and Habermas do recognize, however, is that it is possible to say a good deal about the *rules* governing the *conditions of possibility* of meaning, which is to say, to engage in a *transcendental* analysis of the dealings that human beings have with one another by means of language. Distinguishing between what he calls the "particular" and the "universal aspects of speech acts," Habermas states:

> The task of empirical pragmatics consists . . . in describing speech acts typical of a certain milieu, which can in turn be analyzed from sociological, ethnological, and psychological points of view. General pragmatic theory, on the other hand, is occupied with reconstructing the rule system that underlies the ability of a subject to utter sentences in any relevant situation. Universal pragmatics thereby raises the claim to reconstruct the ability of adult speakers to embed sentences in relations to reality in such a way that they can take on the general pragmatic functions of representation, expression, and establishing legitimate interpersonal relations. . . . The three general pragmatic functions—with the help of a sentence, to represent something in the world, to express the speaker's intentions, and to establish legitimate interpersonal relations—are the basis of all the particular functions that an utterance can assume in specific contexts. (*UP*, pp. 32–33)

To this Fish would presumably respond that "sociological, ethnological, and psychological" analysis is, in the nature of the case, all we are ever going to get, and hence all that it could ever make sense for us to seek. Yet this objection encounters a difficulty that we have already seen to be implicit in Fish's theory; and while Habermas evidently does not feel it necessary to make the point explicit at this juncture, it might have made for a slightly stronger presentation of his argument had he done so. It is the problem of accounting even for the intelligibility, much less the validity, of those very analyses themselves in a way that does not at the same time fatally undermine the thesis of universal particularism and partiality, in support of which Fish would want to appeal to them in the first place as (allegedly) the most fundamental levels of analysis available to us. Nor, by the way, is it necessary, to defend Habermas's view against Fish's criticism of it, that one commit oneself to absolutely every element in the entire architectonic of his system; in the case at hand, for example, one is not obliged to accept as definitive the specification of precisely *three* "general pragmatic functions" or precisely *these* three. As I have already indicated to some extent, I think there are points on which Habermas's theory is open to legitimate criticism, as well as others where, although basically on solid ground, he nevertheless needlessly leaves himself open to objections. In neither case, however—and this is the point I am chiefly concerned to make at the present juncture—is he vulnerable to the specific attack that Fish mounts against him. In general, a theory *critical* in conception, in the sense of that term in which I am using it here—and whatever else it may be, Habermas's theory of language is plainly that[3]—can never be undermined from a pre-critical perspective.

Fish's misrepresentation of Habermas becomes more serious yet when he states that "the only direction Habermas provides [in the search for "institutionally unbound speech acts," about which more in a moment] is to 'start with concrete speech acts embedded in specific contexts and then disregard all aspects these utterances owe to their pragmatic functions' " (*DWN*, p. 454; the passage cited is from *UP*, p. 31). If this actually were Habermas's intention, of course, one might well wonder why, then, he nevertheless continued to refer to his program of analysis precisely as "universal *pragmatics*." Once again, however, the larger context in which the passage cited appears clears up the confusion. In a paragraph headed "*Sentences versus Utterances*," Habermas writes: "*If* we start with concrete speech actions embedded in specific contexts and then disregard all aspects that these utterances owe to their pragmatic functions, we are left with *linguistic expressions*" (*UP*, p. 31; emphasis added). And he continues:

> Whereas the elementary unit of speech is the speech act, the elementary unit of language is the sentence. The demarcation is obtained by attending to conditions of validity—a grammatically well-formed sentence satisfies the claim to *comprehensibility*; a communicatively successful speech action requires, *beyond the comprehensibility of the linguistic expression*, that the participants in communication be prepared to reach an understanding, that they raise claims to *truth, truthfulness, and rightness* and re-

ciprocally impute their satisfaction. *Sentences are the object of linguistic analysis . . . , speech acts of pragmatic analysis. (UP,* pp. 31–32; emphasis added)

In other words, precisely what Fish represents as Habermas's proposed starting point for analysis is actually used by him to distinguish his own program from another sort of investigation altogether. The distinction Habermas has in view here clearly parallels the familiar one between the *locutionary* and *illocutionary* force of an utterance, and despite what one would conclude on the basis of Fish's account, it is explicitly the *latter*—that is, "speech actions [precisely *as*] embedded in specific contexts," and thus precisely *not* "disregard[ing] those aspects that these utterances owe to their pragmatic functions"—with which Habermas's theory of communicative competence is concerned: "We can . . . say that [it is] the illocutionary force of a speech action . . . [that] fix[es] the communicative function of the content uttered" (*UP,* p. 34).

As the passage just cited indicates, Habermas does adopt at least part of the standard terminology of speech-act theory. In *UP* the pragmatic-linguistic, speech act-sentence distinction just seen reappears a few pages later as that between the "*illocutionary*" and the "*propositional component*" (*UP,* p. 36) of any utterance.[4] The two components together constitute the "*double structure*" (*UP,* p. 41) of all speech. These "two components," Habermas maintains, "can vary independently of one another" (*UP,* p. 41); in particular, "the propositional content can be held invariant across changes in illocutionary potential" (*UP,* p. 36). Indeed, he insists, "this level of differentiation of speech is a precondition for an action's ability to take on representational functions, that is, to say something about the world, either directly in the form of a statement or indirectly through mentioning a propositional content in nonconstative speech acts. . . . [T]he propositional content *must already be known* to the participants if the expressed behavior is to be understandable" as the particular action that it is (*UP,* p. 37; emphasis added). In other words, unless the *locutionary* force of a given utterance has been grasped, it will not be possible to bring about either the *illocutionary* or the *perlocutionary* effect that the utterance is intended to produce at all. "The illocutionary act," Habermas says, "fixes the sense in which the propositional content [i.e., the locutionary component] is employed" (*UP,* p. 42). As McCarthy illustrates: "[I]n different situations the utterance of p may amount to 'I assert that p,' 'I promise that p,' 'I request that p'" (*CTH,* p. 426, n. 8), and, of course, much else besides. Accomplishing any of these speech-acts obviously presupposes, not merely that the interlocutors be able to distinguish between an assertion and (for example) a promise or a request, but also that they understand the meaning of *p* itself. Communication would be no less impossible if the *propositional sense* of "the door is open" could not be distinguished from that of (say) "the door is closed" or "the window is open" than it would be if *stating* that the door is open could not be distinguished from *promising* to open it oneself or *requesting* that someone else do so.

In saying all this, however, it may appear that we have given at least the possibility of new life to the really fundamental objection that Fish wants to bring against Habermas. For even if it can be shown (as we have now seen that it can) that Fish is in certain respects seriously mistaken with regard to how Habermas actually conceives the program of "universal pragmatics"—specifically, that there is no merit to the contention that the latter intentionally "disregard[s]" the "pragmatic functions" of speech-acts in the belief that "the meaning of linguistic expressions" can be "determined by formal properties of speech situations in general," independently of "particular situations of use"—the mere fact that Habermas is prepared to admit for purposes of analysis an abstract distinction between the "propositional" and "illocutionary" components of a speech-act may appear to give Fish all the leverage he needs to begin deconstructing the entire Habermasian edifice. Notwithstanding Habermas's repeated insistence that the four fundamental "validity claims" of comprehensibility, truth, truthfulness, and rightness (or appropriateness) are not raised in isolation from one another but are rather *conjointly* presupposed in the production of any speech-act, in Fish's view the mere assumption of a distinguishable and consistently redeemable claim to comprehensibility, which Habermas associates with the "propositional" component of the speech act, while the other three claims determine in one combination or another, depending on how they happen to be "thematized" in a given context, the "illocutionary" component, is already to give away too much in the direction of stable and determinate meaning. For Fish, in other words, comprehensibility itself, far from being an unavoidable *presupposition* of communicative action, is itself in principle (in a phrase that Rorty, with whom we earlier saw Fish to be in basic agreement, likes to use) always "up for grabs" and so in need of "interpretive" resolution in its own right.

I want to consider in a moment an example, one provided by Fish himself, of the lengths to which one can in practice be driven in the effort to hold on to this view. It is admittedly a somewhat extreme example, perhaps; *extremes* of implausibility, however, are after all precisely what we are trying to bring to light here. First, however, we must make a prefatory observation. One principal way in which, as noted earlier, Fish's critics have regularly set themselves up as easy targets for rebuttal is by attempting to produce at least one instance of perfectly determinate, yet also context-independent, linguistic meaning: an expression (typically a statement) whose sense could be exhaustively and unambiguously read off from nothing more than the meanings of the words of which it is composed and the syntactic links in accordance with which those elements are connected with one another. Fish is exceptionally ingenious at finding ways in which, through an appropriate modification of the circumstances in which the statement is presumed to have been uttered or a shift in the perspective from which it is understood to be regarded, even the seemingly most unequivocal formulations can plausibly be shown to admit of a number of different interpretations, all of them perfectly legitimate in light of the framing conditions posited for them. Such arguments—as Fish acknowledges, really so many variations on a single basic argument—take for granted, of course, that each of the multiple meanings thus produced is *itself* wholly stable and determinate. The *interpretive, context-relative production* of meaning, in other words, yields in each case a semantic-syntactic entity that is *itself shorn of all trace of ambiguity or indeterminacy.* The fact that Fish does not see in this a refutation, but rather, on the contrary, precisely the confirmation, of his theory brings us within sight of the crucial point at which anti-foundationalism, having come within an eyelash of the truth, nevertheless finally lapses into confusion and self-refutation. That is to say, Fish comes as close as, in all likelihood, it is possible to come to giving an adequate account of the relationship between human beings, language, and the world, while still remaining within a pre-critical context of thought. Not having made the "critical turn," however, notions of factual objectivity, semantic determinacy, universal structures of rationality, and the like continue to be construable for him *only* in metaphysically dogmatic terms—that is, as instances of "what there (independently) *is.*" Rejecting this option (at least in intention), he thus has open to him, as we have seen, only the other of the two pre-critical positions, namely the skeptical analysis of factuality, meaning, and the rest as merely so many manifestations of "what gets (interpretively) *said.*"

In another essay collected in *Doing What Comes Naturally,* Fish repeats his familiar "contention" that "explicit or literal meanings do [not] in fact exist," the reason being, again, that "[m]eanings only become perspicuous against a background of interpretive assumptions in the absence of which reading and understanding would be impossible. A meaning that seems to leap off the page, propelled by its own self-sufficiency, is a meaning that flows from *interpretive assumptions so deeply embedded that they have become invisible*" (emphasis added).[5] The notion of "invisible assumptions" is clearly indispensable to the anti-foundationalist argument. Indeed, I think it is not too much to say that it is *the* indispensable notion, the one on which the entire theory finally stands or falls. For on it depends the possibility of distinguishing between *really* objective facts and *really* determinate meanings, on the one hand, the existence of which Fish wants to deny, and, on the other hand, "an interpretation so firmly in place that it is impossible (at least for the time being) not to *take as* literal and unassailable the meaning it subtends" (*DWN*, p. 359; emphasis added), which Fish believes does properly describe the situation in which each of us always find himself or herself. On this point, anti-foundationalism can admit of no compromise: interpretation has to be seen as (to speak again with Rorty) "going all the way down." No matter how apparently objective the fact or unequivocal the meaning, all that we are ever (really) doing is *taking it to be so,* on the basis of mere *assumptions* (ultimately "invisible" ones) as to how things are and what they mean. If it can be shown—as I think it can without much difficulty—that the notion of "invisible assumptions" is itself incoherent, however, then the key distinction on which anti-foundationalism depends collapses, and we are well on our way to making the "critical turn."

Now to the example of which I spoke a moment ago. "Consider," says Fish,

> the stipulation in the Constitution that no one shall be eligible to be president "who shall not have attained to the age of thirty-five years"—a clause often cited wistfully by those who wish that the entire document had been written in the same absolutely explicit and precise language. But its explicitness and precision seem less certain the moment one pauses to ask an apparently nonsensical question: What did the writers mean by thirty-five years of age? The commonsensical answer is that by thirty-five years of age they meant thirty-five years of age; but thirty-five is a point on a scale, and the scale is a scale of something; in this case a scale of *maturity* as determined in relation to such matters as life expectancy, the course of education, the balance between vigor and wisdom, etc. When the framers chose to specify thirty-five as the minimal age of the president they did so against a background of concerns and cultural conditions within which "thirty-five" had a certain meaning; and one could argue (should there for some reason be an effort to "relax" the requirement in either direction) that since those conditions have changed—life expectancy is much higher, the period of vigor much longer, the course of education much extended—the meaning of thirty-five has changed too, and "thirty-five" now means "fifty." One might object that this argument . . .

could be made only by instituting special circumstances within
which "thirty-five" received a meaning other than its literal one;
but the circumstances within which the framers wrote and understood thirty-five were no less special; and therefore the literal
meaning thirty-five had for them was no less contextually produced than the literal meaning thirty-five might now have for
those who hear it within the assumption of contemporary political
and social conditions. (*DWN*, pp. 358–59)

Perhaps the first, though not necessarily most important, point to note
in response to this is simply by way of a reminder that here, as elsewhere, Fish, like contemporary skeptics generally, cannot even begin to
develop his argument without tacitly positing as both apodictically certain and definitively known a quite extensive body of theoretical, historical, psychological, and sociological *facts*.

More directly germane to present concerns, however, is the consideration that Fish's argument in this passage clearly depends, first, on a
conflation of the meaning of a term with the reason(s) for that term's
being employed by a particular group of language-users in a particular
context for a particular purpose, and, second, on a basic ambiguity with
regard even to the meaning itself that is in question: is it the number
thirty-five or the notion of being thirty-five years old that is at issue?
Once these two points are noted, however, the argument simply collapses. Let us assume for the moment that Fish's account of the framers'
reasons for choosing, specifically, thirty-five years of age as the minimum age of the president is essentially correct. Surely it is obvious that
that choice could not have been made at all, whether for these or for any
other reasons, if the framers had not already known what it is to *be*
thirty-five years old, as opposed to any other age, to begin with. And
that knowledge, in turn, although from one point of view extremely elementary, nevertheless (as Wittgenstein is constantly reminding us in
such situations) itself presupposes the possession of a not inconsiderable
amount of still more basic knowledge. In addition to the cardinality of
the number that is referred to in English by the term *thirty-five* (among
innumerable other possible ways of designating it), one must also know,
for example, what a year is, which in turn entails an already quite sophisticated grasp of notions of time and how its passage is reckoned.
Fish to the contrary notwithstanding, it is not the case that "thirty-five
is a point on a scale." Thirty-five *is* a natural number, one of the many
possible uses of which is *as* a point on a scale; that possibility, of course,
presupposes prior knowledge of what a scale itself is, which in turn depends on one's having the concept of measurement, and so once again it

goes in this vein. Thus, we can see that it is also not the case that the specification of "thirty-five as the minimal age of the president" occurred "against a background of concerns and cultural conditions within which 'thirty-five' had a certain meaning." The term *thirty-five* has the same meaning no matter what the "concerns and cultural conditions" may be; it names the *number* thirty-five. And analogous considerations hold for the expression *thirty-five years of age*. What *may* be understood differently, depending on differences in "concerns and cultural conditions," is the relationship between the requirements of the office of the presidency and the age by which as a rule one might be deemed up to fulfilling those requirements. To the extent that the considerations adduced by Fish in his argument make a case for anything, it is simply for amending the Constitution so as to change the minimum age at which one can be elected president. From the fact (if it is a fact) that what was an appropriate minimum age in 1787 no longer is and that another should be chosen in its stead, however, it no more follows that the meanings of the terms involved in that specification have themselves undergone a change than, from the fact (again, if it is a fact) that the presidency ought to be opened to foreign-born naturalized citizens, it would follow that the expression "natural born citizen . . . of the United States" (which appears in the same paragraph of Article II as the specification of the minimum age of the president) no longer *means* a person born in this country. Indeed, the very claim that Fish wants to make— that *within the specific context of Article II, Par. 4, thirty-five* might now plausibly be taken to mean fifty—can be asserted at all only if within the overall context of our language at large *thirty-five* and *fifty* do *not* mean the same thing. For otherwise the very distinction between the two ages, a distinction obviously presupposed in the argument for interpreting the constitutional requirement in question in a new way, itself vanishes; if *thirty-five already* means fifty, then an explicit argument urging that *thirty-five* be *reinterpreted* to mean fifty is clearly otiose. But surely it is a somewhat strange theory of language in which meaning-identity and meaning-difference are obliged to shift about in such antic fashion as this.

This exposure of the failure of one effort at meaning-destabilization in particular is readily generalizable to the anti-foundationalist program at large. Precisely what anti-foundationalism seeks to analyze as a *derivative* phenomenon, always produced by, and so relative to, some particular set of interests, purposes, and assumptions, is itself in every case ineluctably *presupposed* as the foundation, always already in place, in the absence of which that analysis itself could never even be initiated. To put it in slightly different fashion, Fish's contention that Habermas's argument "founders [on] the problem of beginning or taking the first step" (*DWN*, p. 452) depends on there actually *being* a "first step" that Habermas, along with everyone else, Fish included, has not *already* taken simply by virtue of entering into the community of human discourse at all. This, however, Fish can claim only by begging his own question against Habermas. "[H]ow," he asks,

> is one to know that a shared orientation between participants is a reflection of universal validity claims and not of the claims of a local or partisan project whose sway is (at least for the moment) unchallenged? How does one know, that is, whether the pragmatic and strategic components of speech have been set aside and bracketed or have merely been concealed by the force of "presupposed norms"? (*DWN*, p. 453)[6]

The locution "set aside and bracketed" already prejudices the case somewhat, of course, and in fact in two distinct ways. For, on the one hand, it effectively takes as given that in any speech act there always is *some* "strategic component" (in Habermas's sense of that term) that *needs* to be set aside and bracketed. And, on the other hand, we have already noted earlier the misunderstanding of Habermas's aims that is reflected in the suggestion that he *wants* to perform a corresponding operation in the case of the "pragmatic component" of speech, or that he even thinks such a thing would be possible while still talking about *speech* at all. More fundamental yet, however, is the consideration that if Fish is actually posing a (nonrhetorical) *question* here, then by that very fact there has also been presupposed an entire *logic of inquiry* by which that question might be answered along with all that such a logic entails: investigative procedures, marshalling and weighing of evidence, production and evaluation of arguments, and so forth. This much, to be sure, sounds very much like what we earlier saw to be Fish's own professed view, as expressed in his effort to defend his theory against the charge of self-referential inconsistency. Much the same problem that we saw that attempted defense encountering, however, arises in the present connection as well. For the presupposition of what I am here calling a logic of inquiry clearly entails that it be the *same* logic for all parties to the discussion. For, if not, it will no more be the case that a resolution of a question is being pursued as a collective enterprise than it would be that chess was being played if one of the (ostensible) players believed— and acted on the belief—that the opponent's pieces were taken by jumping them as in checkers. But unless participation in the discussion is to be limited in advance to only some parties, with others being excluded (which would at least seem to require a separate argument justifying such an exclusion), it follows that this logic of inquiry must therefore be the same for, and hence binding on, *everyone*.

A universalist conclusion of this sort plainly poses difficulties for anti-foundationalist theory. And thus it is not too surprising to find that Fish is not really posing a genuine question at all here. He is not, that is, framing a choice between two alternatives understood to be in principle equal candidates for adoption. Rather the answer has already been assumed as given. The passage just cited continues:

> It will do no good to respond by citing, as Habermas does, "clear cases in which the reactions of the subjects converge" (p. 19); for the clarity of those cases may itself be a function of the "epistemic presuppositions" (p. 29) of which they are supposedly independent. And even if it were possible to be sure that you had abstracted away from all "particular situations of use," what then would you be left with? The answer is "nothing." (*DWN*, p. 453)

Fish adds to this, in a passage that seems to me of pivotal importance both for understanding anti-foundationalism itself and for recognizing how close that theory actually comes to being a critical one while nevertheless remaining in the end within the pre-critical orbit: "I am not denying that there are clear cases or that they can serve to stabilize discourse, merely observing that the clarity they display is a function of the situations they supposedly transcend" (*DWN*, pp. 453–54). We need to see this claim against the backdrop of the Kantian distinction between the *transcendent* and the *transcendental*. The point of a critical argument, whether Kant's, Habermas's, Wittgenstein's, or whoever it may be, is precisely to show that it is *not* possible for us to "transcend" our situatedness. This is done by demonstrating, through a "transcendental" analysis of the conditions of possibility of *any* experience, that situatedness always and necessarily goes all the way to the horizon. The conditions of possibility thus disclosed describe the structure of that situatedness. The goal of a transcendental analysis, in short, is at once to establish the reality and to delineate the features of what might be called the Big Situation. One way of characterizing anti-foundationalism by contrast is precisely as the denial that there is any such thing as a Big Situation.[7]

The very possibility of that *denial*, however (and naturally also of the contrary *assertion* that all situatedness is instead local, particular, perspectival, and the rest), depends on certain presuppositions having been fulfilled. Denial and assertion are themselves (obviously) speech-acts, and the successful performance of any speech-act requires that certain conditions be met. (John Searle's analysis of the act of promising illustrates the point particularly well. Unless the conditions he identifies are fulfilled, no *promise* will in fact have been made, regardless of what words may have been uttered, or even how the person speaking those words may have intended that they be taken.[8]) A partial list of the relevant requirements in the case of denying/asserting would be the following. Before anything else, of course, it is necessary simply that the utterance by which the act is to be accomplished be understood by those to whom it is addressed; absent intelligibility, no discursive communication (or communication of any sort, for that matter) can take place. In addition, an utterance that is to function as a denial or an assertion must, by definition, make a statement as to what is or is not the case. Third, actual (as opposed to feigned) denial or assertion must, in order to *be* actual, be consciously intended as such. And finally, the surrounding circumstances must be such that a denial or assertion is in place. The mere uttering of a declarative sentence (or equivalent) in the form of an ostensible assertion or denial does not suffice. There must in addition be, for example, a competent interlocutor in a position to receive the communication, and there must also be something that needs communicating in the first place at the moment of the utterance. The assertion-schema (as we might think of it) "It's a nice day" will fail of effect—the speech-act of asserting will not actually have been accomplished—if spoken, for example, to a dog, to someone known to be a nonspeaker of English, to a deaf person, to oneself, or in one's sleep. Similarly (to borrow yet another Wittgensteinian example) if, sitting across from a person long known to me, I were suddenly to look up and say, "My name is Michael Morton," this would scarcely count as a proper assertion. Not that the statement could have no conceivable function, merely that whatever that function might be, it would in any case not be the one that we call making an assertion. Despite the similarity in form, none (or almost none) of the other conditions necessary for something to be an assertion would be present. In just the same way (borrowing again from Wittgenstein), although I can, of course, pass money from my right hand to my left, it could not be said, except perhaps as a kind of metaphorical joke, that my one hand had thereby given the other a gift.

As may already be evident to the reader, this list of prerequisites for the successful performance of an act of assertion or denial has not been chosen at random. What I have described here are simply the four "validity claims" of comprehensibility, truth, truthfulness (or sincerity), and rightness (or appropriateness) that Habermas maintains are raised in the performance of *every* speech-act. In other words, it appears that Fish cannot even undertake to disagree with Habermas without in the same moment performatively confirming him. This enables us, in turn, to recognize an additional respect in which Fish seems simply to have misunderstood the point on which Habermas is actually intent. The reader may, indeed, already have had the sense that there was something like a category mistake in Fish's earlier contrast between "a reflection of universal validity claims" on the one hand and "the claims of a local or partisan project whose sway is (at least for the moment) unchallenged" on the other, along with his contention (preliminary to the denial that anything can be made of the former notion at all) that there is no way in which the two could in practice ever be distinguished. By the latter sort of claim Fish appears to have in mind something *substantive* in nature— for example, the claim that a given expression means (determinately) thus-and-such in particular, or that thus-and-such hypothetical state of affairs in fact obtains in reality. "Universal validity claims," however, as Habermas understands that notion, are not of this sort at all. Although I think there is little denying that the choice of terminology is at least potentially misleading, I hope the discussion in the previous paragraph of how these "claims" actually function in practice has gone some way toward clearing up any confusion. A "universal validity claim," in Habermas's sense, is *not* a claim that thus-and-such statement (regarding meaning, factuality, or whatever) is universally valid; it is a type of "claim" that is *made universally* in the production of any statement or other speech-act whatsoever—that is, whenever anyone engages in linguistic communication at all. The "validity" in question refers to what Habermas calls the "redemption" of these claims, which is to say, to the tacit contention that they *are* redeemed (or redeemable). It says as yet nothing about the specifics of *how* that redemption occurs in any context in particular. The claim to comprehensibility, for example, says merely that one has spoken intelligibly; nothing whatever has yet been said about the content of that intelligibility, about how specifically one's utterance is to be understood. And so also with the claims to truth and contextual appropriateness. The former (again, tacit) claim is merely that one has (to put it in a kind of Gulliverese) said the thing that is the case (or, in speech acts other than statements, that one has correctly presupposed what is the case). The specifics of what actually *is*, or is held to be, the case do not yet figure in the deliberations at all at this point. Nor does the claim to appropriateness say anything whatsoever, either about what the circumstances in question actually are or about the specifics of the relational fit that is tacitly held to obtain between the utterance and its context—merely that there *are* such circumstances and such a relational fit.

The claim to truthfulness, or sincerity, seems to me to constitute something of an exception in this regard. Inasmuch as it would appear that there is only one way in which this claim can ever be "redeemed," one way in which the notion of being truthful or sincere can be cashed at all—namely, by meaning, or appearing to mean, what one says—it would seem that in this case the "validity claim" and its mode of "redemption" effectively coincide. This consideration points to a conclusion that I think is suggested on other grounds as well, notably by Wittgenstein's repeated insistence on the need of public criteria for inner states. It is that, of the four "validity claims" posited by Habermas, this one is in a certain sense largely dispensable from the analysis. The point I have in mind here was touched on earlier in connection with Smith's theory, where we noted the incoherence of supposing that permanent, universal dissimulation or concealment of one's "true" thoughts and feelings might actually be a genuine discursive possibility; and we shall return to the issue below in connection with Habermas's distinction between "communicative" and "strategic" action. At that time I will also attend to what may have struck the reader as a rather glaring loose end left hanging just a moment ago, in the form of what may have seemed a fairly casual blurring of the distinction between really meaning what one says and merely appearing to do so.

One extremely important implication of this analysis, I think, is that the "validity claim" of "truth" in particular is *independent* of how truth itself is conceived. Whether it be, for example, in historicist-interpretivist terms, as Fish's theory would have it, or instead, as I am obviously urging, as the epistemic counterpart of the ontological notion of objective reality, makes no difference to the *universality* of the claim itself. In other words, the making of this claim is not merely logically prior (as just seen) to what one happens to hold true in any set of circumstances in particular; it is prior as well even to what one thinks that *true* itself *means*. Precisely this consideration, however, represents an important link in the overall chain of analysis enabling us to see why, on conceptual grounds alone, the radical historicist-interpretivist thesis cannot be valid.

My reason for going on at some length on this matter is to make as clear as possible the central point that what Habermas means by "universal validity claims" are not claims at all in what is probably the most usual sense of that term, namely substantive assertions that thus-and-such is the case. Rather they embody *formal* conditions of the possibility of engaging in discourse at all. As McCarthy puts it, the "universal and necessary" character of these claims is a reflection of the fact that they represent *"precondition[s]* of the ability to make *distinction[s]*

fundamental to the definition of *any* speech situation" (*CTH*, p. 281;
emphasis added). There is, however, still further evidence that Fish
nonetheless continues to construe them in the substantively assertoric
terms just noted. He speaks of "the *establishment* of universal claims to
validity" (again, in contrast to the aims of "local and partisan efforts") as
the goal toward which the speech-acts with which Habermas is concerned are "oriented" (*DWN*, p. 453; emphasis added). By the same token, however, it must be acknowledged that Habermas himself is by no
means entirely free of blame for this confusion. As Fish notes, the analytical portion of "What Is Universal Pragmatics?" is prefaced "by
[Habermas's] performing an act of exclusion":

> "In what follows," [Habermas] declares, "I shall take into consid-
> eration only consensual speech actions," leaving aside both "stra-
> tegic" speech action and "the level of argumentative speech"
> (p. 4). By "consensual speech actions" Habermas means those that
> occur in "an idealized case of communicative action . . . in which
> participants share a tradition and their orientations are norma-
> tively integrated to such an extent that they start from the same
> definition of the situation and do not disagree about the claims to
> validity that they reciprocally raise" (pp. 208–9). (*DWN*, p. 453)

For two closely related reasons, this description of "consensual speech
actions" and the ostensible decision to focus for purposes of analysis on
these actions alone, taken together, are plainly fatal to Habermas's theory. Or they would be fatal to it, at any rate, if there were no other way
of understanding that theory except in accordance with the point of view
implicit in this description-cum-decision. Both the suggestion that universal validity claims are objects of possible agreement or disagreement
in their own right, rather than themselves the conditions, always already
in place, under which any such thing as agreement or disagreement (or
any other speech action) would be possible in the first place,[9] and the
concomitant sharp separation of speech actions into categorically distinct realms, which follows more or less naturally from that suggestion,
give Fish a more than adequate opening to develop his argument that
Habermas "can only proceed by assuming as already available the very
conditions (of freedom from the particular and the perspectival) whose
possibility he set out to establish" (*DWN*, p. 454).

Fortunately (at least from the standpoint of anyone who would like to
see Habermas able to avoid more or less obvious self-contradiction or
question-begging), there is also evidence that the view implicit in this
passage from "What Is Universal Pragmatics?"—and I think there is lit-

tle denying that it *is* implicit there, notwithstanding its rather disastrous consequences for the theory—nevertheless does not actually represent his best judgment regarding either the presuppositions of speech-acts in general or the various relationships between different categories of them. In his more recent "Reply to my Critics," Habermas explicitly rejects the criticism of his theory that maintains that "formal-pragmatic or transcendental-pragmatic grounding of the rationality-claims always involved in processes of consensus formation misleads us into losing sight of the moment of existential decision which is, in the final analysis, ungrounded." And in defense of that rejection he offers the following:

> Whenever speaking and acting subjects want to arrive purely by way of argument at a decision concerning contested validity-claims of norms or statements, they cannot avoid having recourse, intuitively, to foundations that can be explained with the help of the concept of communicative rationality. Participants in discourse do not have to come first to an agreement about this foundation; *indeed, a decision for the rationality inherent in linguistic understanding is not even possible.* In communicative rationality we are always already oriented to those validity-claims, on the intersubjective recognition of which possible consensus depends. (emphasis added)[10]

The term *validity-claims* is obviously being used in two distinct senses here. And while Habermas would doubtless have reduced somewhat his likelihood of being misunderstood, if he had merely varied his idiom a bit, nonetheless in light of what we have seen at earlier stages of the discussion here, I think his meaning is surely clear enough. The "contested validity-claims of norms or statements" referred to initially are specific, substantive assertions as to what is and is not the case or what should and should not be done in some given set of circumstances in particular. The very possibility of this (or any other) "contest[ing]," however, *presupposes* the existence of those "validity-claims" referred to at the end of the passage, to which "we are always already oriented" and which therefore function universally as the *formal* conditions making possible *any* communication.

But we are not quite out of the woods yet. There is still the matter of the division of speech-acts into different categories to be attended to. In a footnote to a passage at a later point in his "Reply," Habermas acknowledges that "a false impression is conveyed by the table in which [in "What Is Universal Pragmatics?"] I derive the analytic units for an analysis of speech-acts using idealising procedures, not from communicative acts but from social actions" (*RC*, p. 314, n. 67). The table referred to here, Habermas indicates, appears on page 40 of *UP.* For present purposes, the important thing about this table is that it represents "communicative actions" and "strategic actions" as categorically distinct types of "social actions." The elaboration of that distinction is then the concern of a table that appears in an extended note on page 209 of the same text. The latter table presents in schematic fashion the conceptual basis for the "act of exclusion" on which Fish fastens in the passage from *DWN* last cited. (Fish bases his argument in this passage in part on the text with which Habermas explains in discursive terms the "typology" [*UP*, p. 209] given in the table in question.) Habermas does not make clear in what exactly the "false impression . . . conveyed by th[is] table" is supposed to consist. One would hope, to be sure, that he was thinking of the implied gulf between the realms of the "communicative" and the "strategic." Yet if so, one's hopes would seem, at least initially, to be dashed. For on the same page of his "Reply" to which the footnote containing the mention of a "false impression" refers (i.e., *RC*, p. 264) we find repeated with very little change (and none that has any bearing on the discussion at the moment) the same table that appears on page 209 of *UP* with its division of the genus "social interactions" into separate "communicative" and "strategic" species. On the immediately preceding page, moreover, Habermas asserts flatly that "[t]he distinction between orientation to success and orientation to reaching understanding is decisive for the construction of my typology of action"; and as an additional table on this page makes explicit, "strategic action" falls in the former category, "communicative action" in the latter (*RC*, p. 263).[11]

But how then, it may be wondered, can the standpoint Habermas appears to be adopting here be reconciled with, for example, the longer passage from the same text cited a moment ago, in which, against theories that would interpret our relations to ourselves and others in ultimately decisionist terms, he invokes the structures of specifically *"communicative* rationality" as the necessarily prior conditions of *all* linguistic exchange? The issue is raised in, if anything, still more acute fashion by the way in which Habermas continues this passage. He notes that

> from the perspective of the life-world to which the actor belongs, the modes of action are not simply at one's disposal. The symbolic structures of a life-world are reproduced in forms of cultural tradition, social integration and socialisation; and . . . these processes *can* take place *only* through the medium of action orientated to reaching understanding. Thus for individuals who cannot acquire and maintain their identities otherwise than through carrying on

traditions, belonging to social groups, participating in socialising interactions, *the choice between communicative and strategic action is open only in an abstract sense.* . . . [C]ommunicative rationality, precisely as suppressed [as it is, at least in intention, in "strategic action"], is already embodied in the existing forms of interaction and does not first have to be postulated as something that ought to be. (*RC*, p. 227; last emphasis added)

Essentially the same standpoint is, indeed, already adopted in the opening paragraph of *UP.* Having specified "[t]he task of universal pragmatics" as that of "identify[ing] and reconstruct[ing] universal conditions of possible understanding," Habermas notes explicitly that "other forms of social action—for example, conflict, competition, *strategic action* in general—are derivatives of action oriented to reaching understanding" (*UP*, p. 1; emphasis added).

It would not be difficult to point to numerous other instances in Habermas's writings of this apparent vacillation between two different (indeed, incompatible) conceptions of the relationship between "communicative" and "strategic" action. What at first glance may appear to be a rather serious difficulty for his theory can, however, be resolved fairly easily if we simply recognize that, like the term *validity-claim*, so, too, the expression *communicative* action is employed in systematically ambiguous fashion in the exposition of that theory and, moreover, that its manner of discussion in fact precisely parallels the ambiguity in the use of *validity-claim* noted a moment ago. By *communicative action* Habermas often means action oriented toward the achievement of mutual understanding or consensus among linguistic actors. This is what we might call the substantive-assertoric sense of *communicative action*, analogous to the sense in which *validity-claim* refers to a claim that thus-and-such is the way things are as a matter of fact or the course that ought to be followed as a matter of right conduct. And in this sense communicative action does stand in opposition to strategic action, the defining mark of which is the effort to gain one's ends at the expense of others through deception, distortion, and manipulation (see again the tables in *UP*, p. 209, and *RC*, p. 264). At one point in *RC* Habermas takes this opposition even a step further, asserting that "[t]he typological distinction between communicative and strategic actions says nothing else than" that "to the degree that interactions cannot be coordinated through achieving understanding, the only alternative that remains is force exercised by one against the others (in a more or less refined, more or less latent manner)" (*RC*, p. 269). The parenthetical qualification is presumably intended to prevent the notion of "strategic action," thus characterized, from falling outside the orbit of language altogether. Precisely the fact that strategic action as conceived by Habermas *does* occur only in a *linguistic* medium, however, entails that, at a more fundamental level than the one envisaged in the contrast between "understanding" and "force," the goal of "achieving understanding" and the related one of thereby "coordinat[ing]" our "interactions" neither needs to be pursued nor even can be, because in the nature of the case it has always already been accomplished.

It is clearly fatal to Habermas's theory if the argument for it has to rely on an assumption of mutual candor and goodwill among all the parties to linguistic exchange. The only thing capable of withstanding the sort of counterarguments brought by Fish, Smith, and others is an analysis able to display a fundamental and ineluctable logic *common to all discourse*, the deceptive and the manipulative no less than that oriented toward mutual understanding (in the sense of substantive agreement openly and impartially arrived at). In other words, the distinction Habermas really needs to make more consistently explicit than, it seems to me, he does is between, on the one hand, the effort to "co-ordinate" or "harmonise" what is *not already* coordinated or harmonized, to achieve a consensual "understanding about something in the world" (*RC*, p. 265) that is *not already* in place, and, on the other hand, those things that must *always already* be *presupposed* with regard to the formal structures of our linguistic-existential "life-world" in order that such an effort (as well as any other involving language) be undertaken at all. In *UP* as suggested a moment ago, he goes at least part of the way in this direction. In particular, he at one point analyzes the difference between "communicative" and other types of linguistically performed actions as a matter of certain validity-claims being "suspended" in the latter. Specifically, in "strategic action," he contends, the claim to "truthfulness" is "suspended" (*UP*, p. 41). In a similar vein in *RC* he allows that it is "possible to construe strategic action as a *limit case* of communicative action by theoretically varying the (relevant) features.

> The model of strategic action remains if, starting from the case of communicative action, one thinks away step by step all the presuppositions of the use of language orientated to achieving understanding, if one abstracts, that is, from the consideration that the participants have regard for normative contexts, that they mean what they say, that they put forward the truth of propositions before others as a validity-claim. (*RC*, p. 267)

In both these cases, I think Habermas's point is perfectly correct as far as it goes. To speak without further qualification of "suspending" a par-

ticular "validity-claim" or of "abstracting" from the "presuppositions" of
ordinary speech, however, seems to me potentially misleading in at least
one respect. If the "suspension" of (for example) the claim to truthfulness is *overt*, then obviously the "strategy" being pursued by the one
doing the suspending will fail of effect. The difference between communicative action (in the substantive-assertoric sense) and strategic action can, in the nature of the case, be definitively ascertained only after
the fact—specifically, at such time as the individual engaged in the latter sort of action fails to "redeem" the claim to sincerity or trustworthi-
ness that was implicitly raised in the original speech-act. This does not
mean, of course, that every time we enter into a situation of linguistic
exchange we are automatically committing ourselves to limitless gullibil-
ity. There can be any number of good reasons for doubting at the moment of the performance of the speech-act itself that the claim to
sincerity is genuine. The point is simply that unless that claim (along
with the other three universal validity-claims) is *formally* made, no
speech act occurs at all. (This is the reason—to recall a point touched on
earlier—that the difference between truly meaning what one says and
only seeming to, though real enough in its own right, is nevertheless not
directly relevant to the formal analysis of speech-acts. For underlying
both these possibilities is a single structure of discourse, which they
both presuppose in precisely equal measure.[12]) More generally, to
"think away" or "abstract" from all the "presuppositions of the use of language orientated to achieving understanding," if by that is meant imagining as absent all the formal-structural dimensions of speech, is simply
to think away language itself. And thus, again, we are able to see—and,
to repeat, this is the point I think Habermas might well have made more
consistently explicit—that the structures of communicative action, understood in the formal (transcendental) sense of the term, are logically
prior to both communicative action in the substantive-assertoric sense
and strategic action.[13]

II

The analysis of strategic action as, in
effect, a deficient or privative mode of communicative action enables
us to see particularly well, I think, that one main objection brought by
Fish against Habermas's theory is in fact far more applicable to Fish's
own position. Fish contends that Habermas can proceed only by first

excluding from consideration all particular and concrete constituents of actual discourse (such things as specific interests, purposes, perspectives, and the like) and that his theory therefore depends from the outset on an act of abstraction it is never able to legitimate. As we have seen, Fish regards a version of strategic action as the paradigm of discursive exchange generally. For him, the irreducibly primitive units of analysis are a plurality of diverse, inherently partisan interests. On this view, the scene of language is at bottom merely an ongoing political-interpretive struggle for what has been called "the power to impose meaning."[14] What Fish overlooks, however, is that with everything about language other than partisan intent, including even the claim to "comprehensibility" itself (and a fortiori those to "truth" and normative "rightness"), thus relativized to a myriad of radically discrete strategically oriented centers of activity, there is no longer any way of accounting for either the conceptualization of these interests themselves or the degree of communicative reliability necessary to prosecute them in discursive fashion against one's opponents. To set the anti-foundationalist argument in motion at all, in other words, Fish has had to abstract from precisely the conditions of possible speech that that very argument cannot help at the same time presupposing as already in place.

We have noted that to a large extent Fish's criticism of Habermas stems simply from a misapprehension of what the latter is actually saying; and we have also noted that Habermas himself contributes his share to making this misapprehension possible. Essentially the same state of affairs is discernible as well in Fish's treatment (and, of course, rejection) of Habermas's notion of the "ideal speech situation." As Fish sees it, what Habermas means by this is "a situation consisting of perfectly symmetrical and reciprocal relationships between participants who neither dominate nor deceive one another" (*DWN*, p. 451). And, in his view, Habermas's intention in *UP* is "not only [to] rehearse the *desideratum* of the ideal speech situation, but [also to] tell us *how it can be brought about*" (*DWN*, p. 452; emphasis added). Nevertheless, Fish contends, for reasons that we have now seen several times, "however many times Habermas *describes* the ideal speech situation, it remains little more than the *expression of a fervent desire*, and we are still left without an answer to the question of how that desire is to be achieved" (*DWN*, p. 452; second emphasis added). Clearly Fish takes Habermas to be using *ideal* in the sense of a perfect (or as perfect as humanly possible) goal, an object or state that we strive to bring into being or at least approach as closely as possible. And, as far as that goes, I think there is little denying that Habermas often does employ the term in something like this sense. A decidedly utopian strain informs all of Habermas's thinking, and as I suggested earlier, the distinction between this political-programmatic aspect of his thought and its analytic-descriptive counterpart is not always drawn as sharply or clearly as one might wish. In a certain sense, of course, that distinction neither can nor should be drawn in absolute terms. When Habermas speaks, for example, of his "attempt to establish internal relations among reason, language, and society" (RC, p. 237), he in effect places himself in a tradition already represented in exemplary fashion by Herder, in which theoretical and practical considerations are understood to be ultimately and necessarily convergent. By the same token, however, as Habermas also recognizes, this convergence cannot be such that the distinction between the two sorts of consideration is obliterated altogether.[15] In particular, the theoretical cannot simply be reanalyzed *as* the practical, without leaving the entire program of analysis open to precisely the sort of objection from the side of Fish's anti-foundationalism that we are considering at the moment. Simply to assert, for example, that "linguistic communication is . . . by nature aimed at building consensus and not at influencing" would, taken by itself, appear arbitrary and dogmatic. And thus it would be vulnerable to Fish's charge that the whole theory of universal pragmatics rests finally on nothing more than large-scale question begging. It is necessary, accordingly, to add to such an assertion, as Habermas does at once, the further thesis "that the symbolic structures of the life-world *can* be reproduced *only* through the medium of action oriented to understanding" (RC, p. 237; emphasis added).

It is chiefly in the course of arguing for this latter thesis that Habermas invokes his notion of the "ideal speech situation." *Ideal*, employed in this connection, thus refers in the first instance *not* to an object or goal of our efforts. Rather it points in precisely the opposite direction, toward the theoretical conditions of possibility of undertaking a particular sort of activity—namely, the production of speech-acts—at all. The nearest (and by no means perfect) analogy I can think of to this sense of *ideal* is the notion of an ideal gas, as that notion is employed in chemistry to formulate laws describing the effects of variations in pressure, temperature, and volume on the behavior of gases. The fact that an "ideal gas," as defined in the kinetic-molecular theory of gases, neither exists in nature nor can even be produced artificially in the laboratory does not prevent us from using that notion in the construction of a scientific model that enables us to say quite a bit about the behavior of real gases. Similarly, the fact that the actual discourse of real people is never entirely uncluttered by factors extraneous (where not inimical) to the ideal (in the sense of goal) of dispassionate rationality, according to which the only admissible arbiter of disagreement is what Habermas calls "the unforced force of the better argument," constitutes no obstacle to the use of the abstract notion of the ideal speech situation as part of a rational reconstruction of the presuppositions unavoidably made by all speakers in the very act of entering into a situation of discursive exchange.[16] In Habermas's words,

> The ideal speech situation is neither an empirical phenomenon nor a mere construct, but rather an unavoidable supposition reciprocally made in discourse. This supposition can, but need not be, counterfactual; but even if it is made counterfactually, it is a fiction that is operatively effective in the process of communication. Therefore I prefer to speak of an anticipation of an ideal speech situation. . . . The normative foundation of agreement in language is thus both anticipated and—as an anticipated foundation—also effective. . . . The ideal speech situation would best be compared with a transcendental illusion were it not for the fact that . . . [in contrast to] the application of the categories of the understanding beyond experience, this illusion is also the constitutive condition of rational speech. The anticipation of the ideal speech situation has . . . the significance of a constitutive illusion which is at the same time the appearance of a form of life.[17]

The notion of the "ideal speech situation" can thus readily be seen to overlap with those of "universal validity-claims" and "communicative action," already discussed. In each case it is possible to discern a persistent ambiguity in Habermas's use of a key term—*ideal, validity,* and *communicative,* respectively—between what I have been calling a formal-transcendental and a substantive-assertoric sense.[18] In focusing for purposes of his criticism in each case only on the latter sense, Fish thus largely misses the point of what Habermas is actually trying to show by means of the theory of universal pragmatics. And, as we have also seen, he thereby fails in particular to recognize the extent to which his very criticism of that theory in fact constitutes in its own right a tacit, formal corroboration of it.

Habermas's suggestion at the end of the longer passage just cited, that the structures defining the ideal speech situation are in turn rooted in, and so expressive of, our "form of life," testifies all but explicitly, of course, to the ultimately Wittgensteinian provenance of that notion. We have already seen something of the very considerable extent to which, in part directly, and in part by way of Austin and Searle, Habermas derives his theory from an elaboration of insights and arguments formulated originally (at least in this century) by Wittgenstein. In a moment I want to turn directly to Wittgenstein to complete the demonstration of the point that, while coming at certain junctures extremely close to a statement of the basic insight of critical realism, Fish nevertheless in the end always lapses back into a version of (by definition, pre-critical) skepticism. And I want to make the transition from Habermas to Wittgenstein by way of a consideration of the former's distinction between "institutionally bound" and "unbound" speech-acts. Fish, as we have seen, denying that there is any such thing as the latter sort of speech-act at all, naturally finds the attempt to draw this distinction merely one more indication of how and why Habermas is never able even to get his theory off the ground. In reality, however, it appears that once again Fish has simply misunderstood what Habermas is actually intent on saying. As Fish sees it, the difference between institutionally bound and unbound speech-acts for Habermas is between "speech actions intelligible only within pregiven normative contexts" and those "that are intelligible without reference to any institutional context whatsoever" (DWN, p. 454). But, he continues, "it is the *existence* of institutionally unbound speech acts (and therefore of a linguistic space in which critical reflection can occur) that is the question, and the question is begged if it is answered simply by invoking the phrase 'institutionally unbound speech acts.' The problem is to *find* some" (DWN, p. 454).[19]

This interpretation of the distinction Habermas means to draw, with the concomitant suggestion that in so doing he has again succeeded merely in imposing on himself an inherently impossible task, parallels Fish's earlier contention that "the only direction Habermas provides is to 'start with concrete speech acts embedded in specific contexts and then disregard all aspects [that] these utterances owe to their pragmatic functions' " (DWN, p. 454; ref. to UP, p. 31). And, again, if Fish's way of representing Habermas's position really did provide an accurate rendering of the latter's views, it seems clear that here, too, he would indeed be guilty of question begging. As we have seen, however, Habermas does *not* propose to analyze speech-acts by "disregard[ing]" the properties that attach to them in virtue of their "pragmatic functions"; this process of abstraction yields not speech-acts at all, but rather "linguistic expressions," or, in other words, "sentence[s]" (UP, p. 31). Similarly, Habermas does not believe that we even could, much less ought to, analyze speech-acts by first taking care to avoid "reference to any institutional context whatsoever"; as he recognizes perfectly well, there are no such speech-acts. Although here, too, we are perhaps justified in questioning the wisdom of Habermas's choice of terminology—it is possible that he would have rendered himself somewhat less open to misinterpretation if he had opted to speak in terms other than those of "institutional unboundedness"—the point at which he is getting, if I have understood him correctly, is actually a quite straightforward and methodologically harmless one, by no means vulnerable to the objection that Fish sees it inviting.

Habermas introduces the distinction between the institutionally bound and unbound in this way. Speech-acts such as " 'betting,' 'christening,' 'appointing,' and so on," he says,

> are bound to a single institution (or to a narrowly circumscribed set of institutions). . . . The *institutional bond* of these speech acts can be seen in (among other things) the fact that the permissible propositional contents are narrowly limited by the normative meaning of betting, christening, appointing, marrying, and so on. One bets for stakes, christens with names, appoints to official positions, marries a partner, and so on. With institutionally bound speech acts, *specific* institutions are always involved. With institutionally unbound speech actions, only conditions of a *generalized* context must typically be met for a corresponding act to succeed. . . . [For example,] commands or advice or questions do not represent institutions but *types* of speech acts that can fit very different institutions. (*UP*, pp. 38–39; first emphasis Habermas's, subsequent emphasis added)

Again: "Institutionally unbound speech actions . . . are related to various aspects of *action norms in general;* they are not *essentially* fixed by *particular* institutions" (*UP*, p. 39; emphasis added). McCarthy captures exactly the key point at issue in this distinction by noting that whereas "the acceptability of ['institutionally bound'] speech acts is based on rules or norms that are *presuppositions of the type of act in question,*" " 'institutionally unbound' speech acts . . . do not presuppose particular institutions but can fit into a variety of institutional settings" (*CTH*, p. 283; first emphasis added).

Thus the "problem" that Fish sees arising in the effort even to "find" instances of institutionally unbound speech-acts vanishes. Indeed, once we are clear on just what Habermas means by the notion of "institutional unboundedness" (the potentially misleading vocabulary notwithstanding), it becomes difficult to imagine anyone getting through the day *without* both encountering and performing dozens, perhaps hundreds, of such acts. We recall that the specific examples given by Habermas are commanding, advising, and questioning. And it would certainly not be difficult to extend this list at much greater length. What Habermas has in view here, it seems to me, are what might be called action-schemas, in the sense of perennial, general forms of human behavior and interaction. Such forms are obviously capable of being instantiated in a host of different ways (in accordance, for example, with the specific features of a given historical or cultural context). Nevertheless they remain in general always recognizable, and so recoverable for analysis and "rational reconstruction," as just this or that action-schema in particular and no other. As Habermas puts it in *UP,*

> To the extent that universal-validity claims (the grammaticality of sentences, the consistency of propositions, the truth of hypotheses, the rightness of norms of action)[20] underlie intuitive evaluations, as in our examples, reconstructions relate to pretheoretical knowledge of a general sort, to *universal capabilities,* and not only to particular competences of individual groups (e.g., the ability to utter sentences in a Low-German dialect or to solve problems in quantum physics) or to the ability of particular individuals (e.g., to write an exemplary *Entwicklungsroman* in the middle of the twentieth century). When the pretheoretical knowledge to be reconstructed expresses a universal capability, a general cognitive, linguistic, or interactive competence (or subcompetence), then what begins as an explication of meaning aims at the reconstruction of *species competences.* (*UP,* p. 14; last emphasis added)

This, however, need not be regarded as merely an attempt to bring about a kind of backdoor rehabilitation of Platonism. Wittgenstein's analysis of the phenomenon of "family resemblance" (*PI,* § 67, passim) is surely enough to disabuse us of any lingering misapprehension to the effect that clarity of conceptual distinctions (to whatever degree of precision we may find necessary for a given purpose) entails a commitment to essentialism, and that the possibility of the former therefore stands or falls with the latter.[21] At an earlier point in the *Investigations,* in one of the sections leading up to the introduction of the notion of "family resemblance," Wittgenstein urges the reader to "[t]hink of how many different kinds of things are called [for example] 'description' "; in the same section, he implicitly warns us against even trying "to ask questions like: 'What is a question?' " (*PI,* § 24). The misapprehension that he is trying to get us to recognize here is the belief that, in principle, there must be a finite set of necessary and sufficient conditions that—if only we could find it—would enable us to determine in advance all and only those things properly regardable as questions.

In the immediately preceding section of the *Investigations,* the point is given a still more general formulation: "[H]ow many kinds of sentence are there? Say assertion, question, and command?—There are *countless* kinds; countless different kinds of use of what we call 'symbols', 'words', 'sentences'." By way of illustration, Wittgenstein suggests that we "[r]e-view the multiplicity of language-games in the following examples, and in others:

> Giving orders, and obeying them—
> Describing the appearance of an object, or giving its measurements—
> Constructing an object from a description (a drawing)—
> Reporting an event—
> Speculating about an event—
> Forming and testing a hypothesis—
> Presenting the results of an experiment in tables and diagrams—
> Making up a story; and reading it—
> Play-acting—
> Singing catches—
> Guessing riddles—
> Making a joke; telling it—
> Solving a problem in practical arithmetic—
> Translating from one language into another—
> Asking, thanking, cursing, greeting, praying. (*PI*, § 23)

Clearly some of these activities correspond, in Habermas's terminology, to "institutionally bound" and others to "institutionally unbound" speech-acts. In the former group would presumably go those that occur only within specific, more or less well-defined scientific, mathematical, linguistic—but also, for example, recreational—contexts; in the latter, those such as (once again) ordering, describing, or inquiring, all of which, as well as many others, can be instantiated in many different ways, depending on the particular context or situation, but which none-theless never cease to be, and to be recognizable precisely as, specific instances of a single basic type.[22]

The point is of some importance in view of something that Wittgen-stein says earlier in the same section of the *Investigations*. He notes that "this multiplicity [of language-uses] is not something fixed, given once and for all; but new types of language, new language-games, as we may say, come into existence, and others become obsolete and get forgot-ten." Without something like the distinction between institutionally bound and unbound speech-acts, one might perhaps be inclined to read Wittgenstein as expressing a radically historicist view of linguistic (and so also conceptual) change here. On this view, it would not be merely our specific, context-relative forms of activity that were thought to be capable of passing in and out of existence; the same would hold true even of the action-schemas reflective of what Habermas calls "universal capabilities" (themselves grounded, in turn, in general human "species competences"). That this is in fact *not* Wittgenstein's view, however, can be seen from the way in which he follows the very passage last cited. He notes that "[h]ere the term 'language-*game*' is meant to bring into prominence the fact that the *speaking* of language is part of an activity, or of a *form of life*" (last emphasis added). And two sections later (interestingly, once again in connection with the issue, seen earlier, of animals and language-use) he elaborates: "Commanding, questioning, recounting, chatting, are as much a part of our *natural history* as walking, eating, drinking, playing" (*PI*, § 25; emphasis added). That is, it would make no more sense to speak of *human beings* whose form of life did not include certain perennial linguistic-conceptual action-schemas (however variously realized in the concrete practice of everyday life) than it would to posit humans whose mode of existence included absolutely nothing characterizable as (for example) work, play, or taking nourishment.

Like many contemporary exponents of a basically skeptical position, however, Fish believes that actually his theory is substantially in accord with the views of the so-called "later" Wittgenstein. The following passage, selected more or less at random from one of Fish's earlier essays, can, I think, fairly be taken as representative in this regard:

> In large part, my argument follows from Wittgenstein's notion of a 'language-game' in which words are responsible *not to what is real* but to *what has been laid down as real* . . . by a set of constitutive rules; the players of the game are able to agree that they mean the same things by their words *not because they see the same things*, in some absolute phenomenal sense, but *because they are predisposed* by the fact of being in the game (of being parties to the *standard story*) to "*see them*." (emphasis added)[23]

Fish's commitment to the view that the two alternatives of "what there (independently) *is*" and "what gets (interpretively) *said*" exhaust between them the range of possible options appears here in particularly sharp outline.[24] And as we saw earlier in connection with his attempt to find a fundamental element of interpretivist indeterminacy in what was in fact a wholly straightforward and unambiguous passage from the U.S. Constitution, he is nothing if not determined to avoid any compromise with the former. That same adamancy—again, tacitly reflecting the recognition that no concession whatsoever can be made toward an acknowledgment of genuine objectivity without fatally undermining the entire

anti-foundationalist program—appears as well in the following passage
from a later section of *ITC*. Fish first allows that "[o]f course one might
want to argue that there is a bedrock level at which [for example] names
[written on a blackboard] constitute neither an assignment nor a poem
[as either of which, given certain circumstances, they might be re-
garded] but are merely a list. But," he maintains,

> that argument too falls because a list is no more a natural object—
> one that wears its meaning on its face and can be recognized by
> anyone—than an assignment or a poem. In order to see a list, one
> must already be equipped with the concepts of seriality, hierarchy,
> subordination, and so on, and while these are by no means eso-
> teric concepts and seem available to almost everyone, they are
> nonetheless learned, and if there were someone who had not
> learned them, he or she would not be able to see a list. The next
> recourse is to descend still lower (in the direction of atoms) and
> to claim objectivity for letters, paper, graphite, black marks on
> white spaces, and so on; but these entities too have palpability and
> shape only because of the *assumption* of some or other system of
> intelligibility, and they are therefore just as available to a decon-
> structive dissolution as are poems, assignments, and lists. (empha-
> sis added)

"The conclusion" to be drawn from this, Fish contends, "is that all objects are made and not found, and that they are made by the *interpretive
strategies* we set in motion" (emphasis added).[25]

The view that I am here calling "critical realism" consists in essence
in agreeing with the first half of this thesis and rejecting the second. In
this way it is able to do justice *both* to our commonsense intuition that
a great many things are, after all, objectively, definitively, and unalterably the case *and*, at the same time, to the recognition that there is nevertheless no such thing as (linguistically-conceptually) unmediated
factuality. The key step in the critical realist argument is the introduction of a fundamental distinction between the notions of "construct" and
"interpretation." Thus equipped, the critical realist is able to assert, on
the one hand, that it is not possible for us to speak of reality except insofar as it is constituted by the human beings whose reality it is, and yet,
on the other hand, that that reality is not diminished one whit in objectivity for being so produced. For we need to ask what, in the end,
objectivity itself actually means. As Kant recognized—this is, in a way,
the founding insight of the entire *kritische Philosophie*—the distinguishing marks of objectivity are simply universality and necessity of

judgment. That is all anyone has ever actually meant by *objectivity,* for the reason that it is all anyone ever *could* mean by it. The skeptic's error is to analyze objectivity not in this way but rather as inextricably bound to the notion of a universe of objects assumed to exist wholly independently of us and to which, accordingly, if we are to know them, we must somehow make our judgments correspond. The unfortunate result of this conflation, however, is that the rejection of the latter notion—in itself the right move to make, of course[26]—takes the former (i.e., objectivity) with it as well. What Kant, Herder, and Wittgenstein do, each in a somewhat different way, is instead to demonstrate the essential linkage of universality and necessity of judgment with basic forms of human life. Factuality can thus be understood as simultaneously a human *construct* and yet nevertheless still wholly *objective.* Another way to see this point—viewing it, as it were, from the opposite direction—is to note that the supposition that the world of our experience is *not* objectively real is not even intelligible (much less true) *except* on the assumption of a level of reality somehow *more* fundamental, and so more "real," than it; for otherwise, by hypothesis, the world as we actually experience it is quite literally as real as anything could be. That assumption, however, depends in turn on the very notion of "reality-as-independent-of-us" that even the skeptic agrees is incoherent. As we noted earlier, interpretation is one of many particular sorts of activity that take place *within* the world of experience. Specifically, as we indicated, it is probably most naturally understood as one way of reacting to facts, locating them in relation to one another in an overall context of explanation. It can in any case, however, not intelligibly be posited as the process or vehicle by which facts are *constituted* in the first place.

I have suggested more than once that Fish's theory comes extremely close to actually being a version of critical realism. That suggestion has been lingering in the background of the discussion for some time now as a kind of unredeemed promissory note, which the present juncture of the argument at last affords an opportunity to make good. This degree of theoretical proximity tends to make of anti-foundationalism a somewhat more interesting form of skepticism than many of the numerous other contemporary manifestations of that doctrine. At the same time, by concentrating on the comparatively small, but nonetheless pivotal, difference separating anti-foundationalism from critical realism, we are able to bring into especially sharp focus the really decisive respects in which skeptical and critical outlooks part company from one another. Fish, of course, recognizes the natural objection to which the adoption of a radically interpretivist standpoint appears to leave him open. But he believes he can avoid that objection in the following way. The longer passage last cited from *ITC* continues:

> This [i.e., the thesis that "objects are made . . . by . . . interpretive strategies"] does not, however, commit me to subjectivity because the means by which they are made are social and conventional. That is, the "you" who does the interpretative work that puts poems and assignments and lists into the world is a communal you and not an isolated individual. . . . [T]he mental operations we can perform are limited by the institutions in which we are *already* embedded. These institutions precede us, and it is only by inhabiting them, or being inhabited by them, that we have access to the public and conventional senses they make. Thus while it is true to say that we create poetry (and assignments and lists), we create it through interpretive strategies that are finally not our own but have their source in a publicly available system of intelligibility. (*ITC*, pp. 331–32)

From a critical realist point of view, this is almost unexceptionable. There is, however, one problem with it (apart, of course, from the reference again to "*interpretive* strategies"), and it is one that proves ultimately fatal to the position Fish is taking here. The problem concerns the two references to "conventional" determinations of reality.

Earlier we saw Fish refer parenthetically to what he termed "the standard story." And, as with the "communal," "institutional" determination of reality just noted, so this, too, is "a story in relation to which we are not tellers (and therefore free to approve or reject it) but characters, simultaneously enabled and limited by the ways of thinking and seeing it constrains" (*ITC*, p. 199). In any given case this "story" provides the content for the (in itself, purely formal) thesis that "all facts are discourse specific." Again, this appears, at least initially, to be not too far from critical realism. Once more, however, problems begin to make themselves manifest, both in Fish's development of the notion of "the standard story" and in his reading of its implications. These are, in fact, the same problems that arise in connection with the characterization of our determinations of reality as "conventional," merely expressed in a way that makes them somewhat more directly visible. Fish contends that "the standard story and the world it delivers rest on a bedrock of *belief*" (emphasis added). But

> [o]f course, not everyone believes the same thing or, to be more precise, not everyone's perceptions are a function of the same set

of beliefs, and so there will *not be one but many standard stories* in relation to which the world will be differently constituted, with different facts, values, ways of arguing, evidentiary procedures, and so on. . . . There are as many standard stories as there are systems of belief (and that is not as many as one might think), and the contests between them are not decided by shows of hands but by acts of persuasion. (*ITC*, pp. 199–200; emphasis added)

If "contests" between different systems of belief can occur at all, however, as they obviously both can and do, then equally obviously there must be some *common context* occupied by *both* parties to the dispute, in terms of which the disagreement between them is carried out. For, failing such a context, they would not be able to communicate anything whatsoever to each other and would therefore a fortiori be unable to engage in that particular form of communication known as registering disagreement. This consideration clearly sets definite limits to just how different different "standard stories" can be. Or rather, it lets us see that what Fish calls a "standard story," precisely to the extent that it *can* differ from other such "stories," cannot for any of us be exhaustively determinative of the world of our experience. For, underlying the particular "systems of belief" that provide both the foundation and the specific content of the "standard stories" that, by hypothesis, the parties in disagreement with one another do not share, there must in every such case be something still more fundamental that they do hold in common—or, as it might equally well be put, adopting Fish's own idiom, that holds them.

Since it is clear, moreover, that this must hold true for *any* set of interlocutors, drawn in whatever numbers and combinations one might wish from the entire range of humankind at large, past, present, and to come, it follows that Fish's parenthetical qualifier near the end of the passage last cited does not go quite far enough. Not merely is the number of bedrock "standard stories" and "systems of belief" not as great "as one might think"; it is not as great as Fish himself evidently thinks either.[27] There is, in fact, precisely *one* such "story." It then follows, however, that this cannot intelligibly be referred to as a "story" or "belief system" or "set of (interpretive) assumptions" or in any other way favored by Fish at all. For all these notions are already, in their very concepts, inherently *plural*. We can easily see this in the following way. If everyone always "believed," for example, precisely the same things, not only would we not speak of "beliefs" to begin with, we *could* not do so, even if, per impossibile, we were so inclined. Because nothing in our range of (so far as we could tell) possible or actual experience could be distinguished from anyone else's, there would quite literally be nothing for us to talk about. Fish himself, as I have suggested, on occasion comes at least very close to making precisely this point in his own right. He notes, for example, that "[o]ne cannot term the standard story a *pretense* without implying that there is another story that is not" (*ITC*, p. 243; emphasis added). As he recognizes, "words [such as] 'pretense,' 'serious,' and 'fictional' have *built into them* the absolute opposition . . . between language that is true to some extra-institutional reality and language that is not" (*ITC*, p. 243, emphasis added). To be sure, he also maintains that he has himself "been at pains to deny" (*ITC*, p. 243) this opposition. And yet, protestations to the contrary notwithstanding, it turns out that he cannot in practice dispense with it. On the immediately preceding page of the essay now under discussion he has already asserted flatly: " 'Shared pretense' is what enables us to talk about anything at all." And he glosses the notion of " 'shared pretense' " as follows: "When we communicate, it is because we are parties to a set of discourse *agreements* which are in effect *decisions as to what can be stipulated as fact*. It is these decisions and the agreement to abide by them, *rather than the availability of substance*, that makes it possible for us to refer" (*ITC*, p. 242; emphasis added). Again, the presumed inescapability of the (pre-critical) antinomy of "what there (independently) *is*" and "what gets (interpretively) *said*" is clearly visible as the underlying assumption here. And the same duality then reappears on the next page in the form of the "absolute opposition" that, as just seen, Fish rightly acknowledges is "built into" talk of "pretense" and other similar notions.

To be sure, one might try to find in the expedient of placing the expression *shared pretense* in scare quotes a possible way out of this bind. Perhaps, so this argument would go, Fish is thinking here of something like the Derridean gesture of writing "under erasure." But, if that is indeed his intention, he has sought help in a quarter from which none can be forthcoming. Derrida believes he can justify his procedure as a legitimate expository device on the grounds that certain locutions are, in the nature of the case, "inaccurate but necessary." Though unable ever to redeem the promise of integral, determinate signification that they implicitly make, they are nevertheless also the only resources that language places at our disposal. It is probably not too much to say that the basic incoherence of the entire Derridean project is epitomized in this notion of "inaccurate-but-necessary." For the question immediately arises: inaccurate with respect to what? If the question has an answer, then obviously the need to write "under erasure" vanishes. For in this case we simply derive from the elements of that answer itself (which, by hypothesis, are perfectly adequate) substitutes for the expressions that we thought somehow inadequate. Or, for that matter, we simply continue using those earlier expressions themselves, now with the understanding that they are to be analyzed in terms of the ones that we have just agreed are in no wise problematic. If, however, the question is inherently unanswerable, then again the need to write "under erasure" vanishes. For in this case we do not even have a cogent understanding of the thing that was supposed to require that sort of "writing" to begin with. To posit "inaccuracy," but at the same time to rule out in principle the possibility of a standard in relation to which that "inaccuracy" could be specified, makes no more sense than it would to say of someone moving toward an infinitely distant object that he had not yet gotten near enough to his destination. Basically the same point, moreover, can be made from a slightly different direction. If Derrida's analysis really did demonstrate the necessity of writing certain terms "under erasure," then plainly it would establish this necessity for *all* linguistic expressions. Not to admit (indeed, not to insist on) this extension of the "erasure"-principle to language at large would be to concede that at least *some* signification after all *is* literal rather than metaphorical, whole rather than partial, determinate rather than endlessly deferred—in short, all the things that Derrida maintains are impossible. But once universalized in this way, "erasure" is then open to one of Wittgenstein's favorite and most effective ways of dealing with conceptual or grammatical confusion. We simply "divide through" by "erasure," thereby eliminating it at a stroke from the linguistic field altogether. And in that way we are then left (again) with nothing more than language itself, just as intact and fundamentally unproblematic as we always knew it to be. The Wittgensteinian principle that whatever can be said at all can be said clearly remains as valid as ever (because actually an analytic proposition), as does the closely related principle that whatever we have no alternative but to express in a certain way is eo ipso literally as clear as can be. And to the extent that Fish's invocation of the notion of " 'shared pretense' " (with its echoes of Vaihinger's "Philosophie des 'als ob' ") might be thought to involve a tacit appeal to something like the Derridean figure of writing "under erasure," the moral is the same: belief in the possibility of employing language, as it were, with a permanent mental reservation—of meaning, but at the same time not quite meaning, what one says—simply reflects a basic confusion as to the nature of language, and so the limits of the conceivable, itself.[28]

As it turns out, however, this is not really the route that Fish wants to take in any case. Notwithstanding the fundamental difficulty noted a moment ago that doing so creates for his theory, he does in fact mean precisely what he says regarding the (supposedly) foundational character of "pretense" and "fictionality." Referring in the immediate context specifically to Searle's theory of speech-acts, but clearly with a more general application of the point in view as well, Fish contends that "[c]haracteristically [Searle's] arguments rest on a basic opposition: brute facts vs. institutional facts, regulative rules vs. constitutive rules, serious discourse vs. fictional discourse, the natural vs. the conventional." The common denominator here, as Fish sees it, is that "[i]n each case, the left-hand term stands for *something that is available outside of language,* something with which systems of discourse of whatever kind must touch base—*Reality,* the *Real World, Objective Fact*" (emphasis added). For Fish, on the other hand, as we have seen, such notions as these are simply empty. "What I am suggesting" against this, he says, "is that these *left-hand terms* are *merely disguised forms of the terms on the right,* that their content is not natural but made, that what we know is not the world but stories about the world, that no use of language matches reality but that all uses of language are interpretations of reality" (*ITC,* p. 243; emphasis added). For Fish, in other words, "to deny [the absolute opposition] between language that is true to some extra-institutional reality and language that is not" (*ITC,* p. 243) is not to show how these two seemingly irreconcilable positions can in fact be accommodated in a higher synthesis that preserves the really indispensable aspects of both. That task is the one to which critical realists, from Herder and Kant to Wittgenstein and down to the present day, have always been dedicated; this is just what it means to be a critical realist. Fish's move—as we have now seen repeatedly, the only one available to him within a pre-critical context of thought if he is to avoid metaphysical dogmatism[29]—is instead to deny altogether one pole of the antinomy and thereby seek to collapse it entirely into the other.

Fish, however, does not see this as creating any problems at all for his theory. Nothing of what he has said, he maintains,

> is . . . to deny that a standard of truth exists and that by invoking it we can distinguish between different kinds of discourse: it is just that the standard is not brute, but institutional, not natural, but made. *What is remarkable is how little this changes:* facts, consequences, responsibilities, they do not fall away, they proliferate and make the world—every world—alive with the significances our stories (standard and otherwise) create. (*ITC,* p. 243; emphasis added)

In fact, however (and *fact* seems to me precisely the apposite word here), "this" clearly changes everything. If that were not already evident, it would surely be so at the latest with Fish's reference to *"every world"* here. As Donald Davidson notes (gently, as is his wont, reminding the reader of the obvious), "there is at most one world."[30] And, as the "anthropic principle" (as it has come to be known in recent years among cosmologists) would seem to entail, there can be no fewer than one either.[31] For Fish, however, the notion of a—presumably, indefinitely large—plurality of "worlds" is evidently wholly unproblematic. Yet clearly this view cannot be maintained if one still understands the concept of "world" in its ordinary sense, as simply the sum total of what Wittgenstein at the beginning of the *Tractatus* terms "all that is the case" (*TLP*, 1). And, as we have seen, this is in fact not how Fish understands it. Because the notion of what *really* is the case—as he puts it (employing a technique that we might call, on analogy with the now familiar device of scare-quotes, scare-capitals), "Reality, the Real World, [and] Objective Fact"—is, in his view, inseparable from the assumption of a realm "outside of language," terms such as *world, fact, truth,* and other similar expressions can have no more than a kind of quasi-metaphorical status in his idiom. And thus, his assertion to the contrary notwithstanding, it turns out that anti-foundationalism does result in "facts, consequences, responsibilities," and much else besides "fall[ing] away," inasmuch as the terms by which we presume to designate them are now deprived of real reference. A "fact," as that notion is understood in the theory of anti-foundationalism, is no more an actually existent state of affairs than the concept of a perpetual motion machine is an actual repeal of the second law of thermodynamics.

Yet "actually existent state of affairs" is just what the word *fact* means. This is the sense in which everyone who becomes a competent speaker of English acquires the concept in the first place. And thus even should one reach the point of developing (or at any rate professing)[32] skeptical doubts about the validity of the concept—about the legitimacy of applying it to experience—that doubt is incapable of reaching back behind the *concept itself*. The sense "actually existent state of affairs" is ineluctably reflected in all uses of the word *fact* that can be understood at all, regardless of what one's views happen to be on the reality of "actually existent states of affairs." The collision between, on the one hand, Fish's recognition that no concession can be made to either genuine objectivity of fact or literalness of meaning without abandoning anti-foundationalism altogether and, on the other hand, the impossibility of *not* presupposing precisely what he is intent on denying if he is to take even the first step toward formulating that denial, appears in notably striking fashion at a point in the text currently under discussion just subsequent to the two longer passages last cited. Having first introduced the notions of what he calls the *"fiction"* of "intelligibility itself," the *"ideology"* of "meaning," and the *"assumption* of sense and of the possibility of its transmission," he goes on at once to say, without missing a beat: "Of course that assumption is *correct,"* adding in parentheses the acknowledgment (presumably already obvious to the reader) that he is at this very moment "depending on it[s]" correctness (pp. 243–44; emphasis added). But if the "assumption" in question is *not* incorrect (as Fish has just acknowledged it is not), then the (supposed) "fiction" and "ideology" to which he means to point are neither fictional nor ideological after all. For there is plainly no such thing as a "fiction" that is at the same time true or an "ideology" that is semantically value-neutral. Fish seeks to escape the dilemma that he has created for himself in the following way:

> [The "assumption" in question] is correct because as members of speech-act communities we are parties to rules that enforce it, rules that make sense rather than merely conform to it. Once sense is made it becomes possible to forget its origins, and when that happens the *myth of ordinary language* has established itself. (*ITC*, p. 244; emphasis added)

The reference to a supposed "myth" here reinstates the presumed fictionality of the "fiction" of "intelligibility" as well as the, also presumed, ideological character of the "ideology" of "meaning." But it also means that the "assumption," on which everything else finally depends here, is itself no longer "correct" in anything but a metaphorical sense. We are squarely back, in other words, in the world of "shared pretense," with all the ultimately fatal consequences for the entire anti-foundationalist project that, as we have seen, the introduction of that notion entails.

At the same time, however, this passage reminds us again of just how close Fish's position comes to critical realism. If he had simply *stopped* with the sentence that ends "make sense rather than merely conform to it," then (apart from his reference to an "assumption" having been made) a critical realist would find little if anything with which to quarrel. For this would be tantamount to severing the link between the notions of objective factuality and a realm "outside of language." The tacit assumption that this linkage is unbreakable is the foundation at the heart of anti-foundationalism. In abandoning that assumption, we open the way to critical realism by making two steps in particular possible. First, we are able to rid ourselves altogether of the very notion of a realm "outside of language" (in a way that, as just seen, Fish is not), having now recognized it as something of which we cannot even form a coherent conception. And, second (as it were, the flip side of this first move), we are able to reanalyze objective factuality precisely as a linguistic-existential construct, constituted in accordance with the rules that define (and, in *that* sense, determine) our form of life. For Fish, however, still bound to the assumption of an unbreakable linkage between the objective and the extra-linguistic, to speak of something as having been brought into being through the operation of "constitutive rules" is ineluctably to view it as "institutional," "conventional," and so, ultimately, "fictional." The problem that (as Fish himself acknowledges, at least temporarily) is "built into" "term[ing] the standard story a pretense" is thus inherently unsolvable within the framework of anti-foundationalist theory. For as long as we are obliged to characterize the most basic, bedrock elements of all our thinking and speaking as "stories" to begin with, we remain permanently trapped between the reality of "pretense" on the one hand and the delusion of "Reality" on the other.

This same, fundamental tension reappears in one guise after another, virtually wherever one looks in Fish's exposition of his theory. On the one hand, "[w]hen we communicate, it is because we are parties to a set of discourse *agreements* which are in effect *decisions* as to what can be *stipulated* as fact" (*ITC*, p. 242; emphasis added). And yet, at the same time, the "standard story" is one that "we are *not* . . . free to approve or reject," inasmuch as we are "*not* [its] tellers . . . but [rather ourselves] characters [in it], simultaneously enabled and limited by the ways of thinking and seeing it constrains" (*ITC*, p. 199; emphasis added). On the one hand, "sense is *made*," it has "*origins*," and thus presumably also makers and originators (*ITC*, p. 244; emphasis added). And yet, at the same time, *all* "the mental operations we can perform are limited by the [interpretive, sense-generating] institutions in which we are *already* embedded" (*ITC*, p. 331). On the one hand, "the standard story and the world it delivers rest on a bedrock of *belief*" (*ITC*, p. 199; emphasis added). And yet, at the same time, "what has been *laid down* as real," and which we are, accordingly, "*predisposed*" to " 'see' " in that way, has in every case been determined *in advance* by the "rules" of the "game" to which we are always already "parties" (*ITC*, p. 241; emphasis added). In short, anti-foundationalism cannot do without a basic element of decisionism in its very conception, but it is also wholly unable to accommodate such an element. Both the *consensualist* and the *contextualist* aspects of the theory are equally indispensable to it, but they are nevertheless also hopelessly at odds with one another. As Fish recognizes (and in this, it seems to me, he sees somewhat more clearly than do many other contemporary advocates of skeptical positions), the contextualist aspect is necessary if he is to avoid committing to a radically subjectivist (indeed, ultimately solipsistic) epistemological voluntarism. The consensualist aspect, however, is no less necessary, for otherwise there would be no reason not to regard the contextual determination of factuality and meaning as itself (in accordance with the central thesis of critical realism) the process by which the world of *objective reality* comes into being. Indeed, there would be no possibility of not doing so, which in turn means, however, that the notion of "context-relativity" it-self—as we saw earlier in the case of "belief"—would simply drop out, having ceased to do any conceptual work in its own right.

The anti-foundationalist picture of how "facts" and "meanings" are produced (in even the quasi-metaphorical sense of those terms that, as seen, is the closest the theory can allow itself to come to acknowledging literal reality) bears a considerable resemblance to the impossible situation already recognized by Herder in the *Treatise on the Origin of Language* in his analysis of the theory of linguistic conventionalism. Just as the conventionalist account of the origin of language cannot help pre-supposing the prior existence of the very thing whose emergence it pur-ports to explain, so something similar occurs in the case of anti-foundationalism. Here as well we have what is, by hypothesis, *basic, primary* "sense [being] *made*" by "speech-act communities" through the "constitutive rules" reflected in the various "standard stories" that they tell. Since there is nothing "natural" or inevitable about the par-ticular form that this process of origination takes in any given case, no "brute facts," for example, to determine its outcome, it must be sup-posed that a given community could, in principle, always have acted otherwise than it did, could have constituted itself and the "sense" pe-culiar to it in terms entirely different from the ones for which it actually opted. Given a different "partisan agenda," for instance, and thus a dif-ferent set of "interests" and "purposes" from the ones by which it was actually guided, what comes to be "stipulated" by the community in question as either fact or meaning presumably admits of virtually lim-itless variation. But precisely this possibility, which, as just seen, cannot *not* be admitted without reintroducing the very objectivist foundation-alism that anti-foundationalism is concerned above all to deny, has also been firmly ruled out by the very statement of the conditions from which the community-specific process of "making" (as opposed to merely "finding") "sense" is presumed to take its start. For, again, by hypothesis, prior to the initiation of that process (indeed, prior to its completion), the community is not yet in possession of—or, if one pre-fers, possessed by—anything recognizable as "sense" at all. And thus neither "interests" nor "purposes" nor anything else that presupposes conceptualization is even a possibility, much less a reality, for it.[33]

The irreducible tension in Fish's theory between what has to be done to bring "sense" into being in the first place and the "sense" that must already be presupposed if that process of "sense"-formation is to be undertaken at all is reflected in particularly pointed fashion in the oxymoronic notion of "invisible assumptions," which we saw introduced in a slightly different connection above, and which, at the time, I suggested holds the key to the ultimate incoherence of the anti-foundationalist argument. This notion is appealed to again (in effect, if not in quite so many words) in the same essay in which Fish undertakes his dispute with Habermas. He contends that *all* our thinking is "a function of the deeply *assumed* norms and standards that are the grounds of possibility of *any* moment [of intellection], including those named 'deliberation' or 'reflection' " (*DWN*, p. 441; first emphasis added). The claim, however, evidently does not extend to that "moment . . . named" "assumption" itself. And, indeed, it is clear that it cannot be so extended, without lapsing into an absurdity like that of the Fichtean self-positing Ego. Assumptions are things that we *make*. They reflect particular *choices* between alternative points of view. And they can, accordingly, prove right or wrong, correct or incorrect. All of this is simply part of what the term *assumption* means. As with the notion of "fact" discussed earlier, it is the form in which we acquired the concept in the first place. Clearly presupposed in all this making, choosing, and evaluating for correctness or incorrectness, however, is a prior context of intelligibility that is not itself (for reasons just adverted to, logically cannot be) the product of the assumption in question. And the same will obviously hold true for any additional assumption the anti-foundationalist might wish to invoke as the basis of this first one. The only thing that move accomplishes is the initiation of an infinite regress of "assumptions." But apart from the fact that, as noted earlier, in real life there are no infinite regresses—explanation, if it genuinely is explanation, always does end somewhere—an infinite regress is precisely what the anti-foundationalist in particular cannot afford. As we have seen, Fish insists that there is never a time at which there is not for each of us *some* foundation. There is always *something* on which we base everything else. Yet, even the acknowledgment that that something is in principle always subject to challenge does not make it possible to regard it simultaneously as *both* our foundation *and* itself founded on something still more fundamental. That is, however, precisely what it would have to be, if we were compelled to view it as merely one in an infinite series of candidates for foundational status, each one always referring us one step further back in the chain.

Once again, as seen earlier, Fish comes right to the edge of the critical recognition (in both senses of *critical* relevant to the present

discussion—crucially important and critical realist). On the immediately preceding page of the essay last cited, he notes that it is not possible for anyone actually to be a complete skeptic. The reason is that the
very ability to engage in skeptical doubting, questioning, and the like
"presuppose[s] some set of already-in-place distinctions, hierarchies,
values, definitions, which could not themselves be the object of 'skepticism' because they formed the taken-for-granted background against
and within which skepticism acquired its present shape." "Skepticism,"
he maintains, "is not a state, but an activity, something one performs,
and *one can perform it only within*—and not outside of—*the already
structured field* that is consciousness" (*DWN*, p. 440; emphasis added).
But that is to say that it is in fact not an activity one can perform at all.
For there is no possibility of ever attaining the sort of position outside
ourselves that would be necessary to question everything simultaneously. And yet unreserved skepticism, in the sense of an unqualified
denial of the reality of objective fact, is precisely the condition to which
anti-foundationalism aspires. It follows therefore, on its own showing,
that it can do so only by basing itself on a massive self-contradiction. For
the very decisionist, interpretivist analysis of knowledge-claims that is of
the essence of anti-foundationalism presupposes the possibility of occupying the sort of position outside of and prior to everything that, as just
seen, Fish himself recognizes is impossible.

The point emerges with particular clarity from a passage near the end
of the final essay in *DWN*. Posing "[t]he question [of] whether or not the
knowledge (the knowledge rhetoric offers us) that our convictions are
unsupported by anything external to themselves will operate to undermine those convictions" (emphasis added), Fish claims that it will not.
For "[w]henever we are asked to state what we take to be the case about
this or that, we will always respond in the context of what seems to us at
the time to be indisputably true, even if we *know, as a general truth,*
that everything can be disputed. *One who has learned the lesson of
rhetoricity does not thereby escape the condition it names*" (emphasis
added).[34] But the (supposed) "lesson of rhetoricity" is precisely that
there is no literal, objective "truth," much less that it could ever lay
claim to "general" (that is, presumably, permanent, universal, ahistorical) status. It follows, accordingly, that no such "lesson" can be
"learned" at all, no "knowledge" of any sort "offer[ed] us" by "rhetoric."
Precisely the inherent impossibility of such a "lesson" or such "knowledge" is the (purported) content of that very "lesson," that very "knowledge," itself. And thus it is not even the case that anti-foundationalism
must content itself with the comparatively modest status of being something that "seems to [its adherents] . . . to be indisputably true," even

as they recognize that it, too, like everything else, "can be disputed." As we saw earlier, this is basically the tack that Fish takes in an effort to avoid the charge of self-referential inconsistency. The reason why, as we noted at the time, that effort nevertheless fails reappears here in, if anything, still sharper outline. The very formulation of the anti-foundationalist thesis logically entails its own falsity. And that thesis can therefore become a candidate for possible adoption only to the extent that one fails to recognize this fact. Self-contradictory positions, however, neither need to be "disputed" nor, in a certain sense, even can be. For they have already—always already—undermined themselves from within far more thoroughly than could ever be done by any external criticism that might be brought against them.

PART TWO

NEOPRAGMATISM

MOSCOW (AP): E. Frenkel, one of the Soviet Union's growing number of psychic healers and mentalists, claimed he used his powers to stop bicycles, automobiles and streetcars.

He thought he was ready for something bigger, so he stepped in front of a freight train. It didn't work. The engineer of the train that ran Frenkel over said the psychic stepped onto the tracks with his arms raised, his head lowered and his body tensed.

The daily *Sovietskaya Rossiya* on Sunday said investigators looking into Frenkel's decision to jump in front of a train near the southern city of Astrakhan found the answer in the briefcase he left by the side of the track.

"First I stopped a bicycle, cars, and a streetcar," Frenkel wrote in notes that the investigators found. "Now I'm going to stop a train."

Durham Morning Herald, October 2, 1989

CRITERIA AND RATIONALITY

CHAPTER FOUR

I

JOHN SEARLE HAS OBSERVED OF DERRIDA THAT HE "HAS A distressing penchant for saying things that are obviously false."[1] The same can be said to some extent (to be sure, a significantly lesser extent than in the case of Derrida) of Richard Rorty. Rorty's tendency to do so, moreover, seems especially pronounced in connection with precisely those examples and analogies that he thinks most supportive of his position, but which in fact end up telling most strongly against the point he is intent on making. A passage that can stand for many similar ones in his writings in this respect is the following, from early in the opening chapter of *Philosophy and the Mirror of Nature*. Rorty has been discussing a number of what he sees as insuperable difficulties encountered by traditional attempts to draw a sharp distinction between the realm of the mental, on the one hand, and that of the material or physical, on the other; and he concludes on the basis of this discussion that the attempt itself should be abandoned. Summing up, he says:

> At this point we might want to say that we have dissolved the mind-body problem. For, roughly speaking, all that is needed to find this problem unintelligible is for us to be nominalists, to refuse firmly to hypostatize individual properties. Then we shall not be fooled by the notion that there are entities called pains

which, because phenomenal, cannot be physical. Following Wittgenstein, we shall treat the fact that there is no such thing as "a
misleading appearance of pain" not as a strange fact about a special
ontological genus called the mental, but just as a remark about a
language-game—the remark that we have the convention of taking
people's word for what they are feeling. *From this "language-
game" point of view, the fact that a man is feeling whatever he
thinks he's feeling has no more ontological significance than the
fact that the Constitution is what the Supreme Court thinks it is,
or that the ball is foul if the umpire thinks it is.* (emphasis added)[2]

As it turns out, neither side of the analogy that Rorty proposes here will
stand examination, and still less will the suggestion that the view underlying it is actually a Wittgensteinian one.[3] This is more immediately
apparent, to be sure, in the case of the references to the Constitution
and the game of baseball. It is so much more so, indeed, that a corresponding difficulty earlier in the passage, in the sentence-and-a-half
from "Following Wittgenstein" to "has no more ontological significance
than," which is supposed to provide the link between the ostensibly parallel cases of determining the presence of pain and either interpreting
the Constitution or umpiring a baseball game, is comparatively easy to
overlook. The problems at that earlier juncture, however, are no less
real than the ones that appear later, even if they do not announce themselves in quite the same overt fashion.

Probably the first thing to note in this regard is that Rorty actually
conflates two quite different things in his references to pain and the
ways in which we become aware of it: on the one hand, the incorrigibility of first-person reports of pain; on the other, our ability, as a rule,
to be entirely certain when someone else is in pain. The slippage comes
in the phrase "no such thing as 'a misleading appearance of pain.' " For
what remains unspecified in this is an answer to the question: appearance to whom? To the one actually experiencing the pain, or to the person observing someone else (apparently) in pain? The overall context
would appear to suggest that Rorty intends the latter. At the same time,
having associated this "no such thing," first with a "convention" that we
allegedly have "of taking [other] people's word for what they are feeling," and then with the (again, alleged) "fact that a man is feeling whatever he thinks he's feeling," he can surely not be said to have formulated
his position in wholly unambiguous fashion. The really fundamental difficulty with this part of the passage, however, lies at least one level
deeper. For whichever of the two possibilities we suppose Rorty to have
in mind, in neither case does our certainty of the presence of pain have
in general anything to do with anything that might properly be termed
a "convention."

Even at the risk of seeming to nitpick somewhat, it is worth recalling first of all that it has never been true of anyone that he *thinks* he is feeling (for example) pain.[4] What I can think is the case I can also, among other things, think is not the case; I can wonder whether it is the case and so also doubt that it is the case; it makes sense for me to inquire whether or not it is the case and thus also to gather evidence for its being (or not being) the case. Obviously, however, none of this is possible in connection with an experience such as being in pain. For here the phenomenon itself and the awareness of it on the part of the one having the experience are plainly identical.[5] But, it may be objected, isn't this sort of thing after all *just* nitpicking? I can imagine someone interjecting at this point with some impatience that whatever Rorty may have literally *said* in the passage at hand, it would of course never occur to him, any more than it would to anyone else, to *mean* to suggest that the two are somehow not identical. And what is the point of making such a federal case out of this anyway? The sentiment underlying this criticism is one I take seriously, even though I believe the criticism itself can be met. Notwithstanding the considerable advances achieved in this century by what is broadly known as "analytic philosophy," it is also true that an immense amount of time and energy has been wasted by many practitioners of that mode of philosophizing on the very sort of quibbling over minutiae in which my hypothetical critic sees me engaged here. In a memorable gibe, the late Walter Kaufmann once observed dryly that measured by the standards of the issues with which philosophy has traditionally been concerned, analytic philosophy often seems to manage "the rare feat of being frivolous and dull at once."[6]

Yet, having acknowledged all this, I think there is nonetheless no getting around the conclusion that Rorty's view is in the end not the same as, or even compatible with, the (for most people) eminently uncontroversial point regarding the experience of pain just noted. For it seems to me that there *is* a sense in which he is prepared to say—indeed, on the terms of his theory, is obliged to say—that one can (merely) "think" that one is feeling something. It is not, of course, as if he imagined that anyone might ever be wrong in so thinking. Although on one or two occasions he does at least come close to suggesting that he regards this as a genuine possibility, I doubt that such passages accurately reflect his considered view. But what he does appear to believe in this regard seems only marginally less implausible at best. It is that, however little there may ever be an *actual* discrepancy between what one thinks one is feeling and what one is truly feeling, there is nevertheless always what might be called a *logical* gap between the two. And thus, in the case of such things as pain, the phenomenon itself and the awareness of it on the part of the one experiencing it are after all *not* strictly identical. A central tenet of Rorty's neopragmatism says that our certainty, even of such things as our own individual pains, is ultimately dependent on, or in some sense a function of, what *other* people *happen* to say or do— with the emphasis falling equally on the locus of the determination and on its radical contingency. As he puts it at a later point in the text under discussion, "[T]he incorrigibility of first-person reports, like all matters concerning epistemic status, is a sociological rather than a metaphysical concern" (*PMN*, p. 219). There will be more to say later about this claim, the essence of which is repeated on numerous occasions through-out Rorty's writings. Of particular concern will be the *bipolar* scheme, expressed in the passage just cited in the form of an opposition between the "metaphysical" and the "sociological." This is the duality on which his overall argument ultimately depends, and I shall take the position that it is a principal reason why that argument in the end cannot help but fail.

The issues at stake here are thrown into still sharper relief in con-nection with our ability to be entirely certain that someone else is in pain (when that is in fact the case). No one, of course, would think of claiming that in our dealings with others there can literally be "*no such thing* as 'a misleading appearance of pain.' " As virtually any parent knows, the ability successfully to feign pain is one of the very early skills children tend to acquire; and there may be relatively few people who do not at one time or another make use of it later in life as well to accom-plish their ends. However that may be, though, it is clear there are also myriad circumstances in which the possibility of a misleading appear-ance of pain for all intents and purposes simply does not arise, even though it is someone else's pain that is at issue. Examples are not dif-ficult to find: a friend at the barbecue grill spattering himself with hot grease, or a child falling and skinning his knee, or (more dramatically) someone undergoing major surgery without anesthesia or lying in the road bleeding and with broken limbs after an automobile accident. In cases such as these, the possibility of feigned pain behavior is, in gen-eral, ruled out completely. For that possibility to be seriously enter-tained, we must assume the presence of some very special and unusual conditions: for example, someone playing an elaborate practical joke, or our having wandered inadvertently onto a movie set. Absent some such explanation as this, however, there is no question about the nature of the state of affairs: we know from what has happened to these people and how they are now behaving that they are in pain, period. Wittgenstein brings the point home in a way that he often finds useful in cutting through philosophical confusion. He suggests that we *try* to adopt the opposite standpoint—that is, to observe someone in a situation like those just described and to suppose at the same time that that person is none-theless *not* in pain—and note the consequences.[7] The extremes to which it is necessary to go to do this, in the form, for example, of the improb-able—in many cases, wildly improbable—explanatory hypotheses that have to be invoked, illustrate at least as well as could any formal argu-ment what might be called the existential grammar of pain for human beings (and, of course, not only for human beings but for sentient crea-tures generally, at least those with which we are thus far acquainted[8]).

What we see from all this, among other things, I think, is that it is no more correct to say that our certainty that someone else is in pain de-pends on a "convention of taking people's word for what they are feel-ing" than it would be to say this of our certainty that we are ourselves in pain. In the first place, as just noted and as virtually everyone knows as a matter of common sense anyway, in some situations people are in fact not feeling what they claim to be feeling, and it may be perfectly rea-sonable for us not to take them at their word. It will do no good, of course, for Rorty to try to rescue his claim by expanding it to something on the order of "we have the convention of taking people's word for what they are feeling just in case we know beyond a reasonable doubt that that is what they are feeling." For in this reformulation the alleged "con-vention" itself drops out, having ceased to contribute anything in its own right to accounting for our certainty as to what the people in question are feeling. (To borrow a well-known expression from William James, one of the founders of American pragmatism, its "cash value" has in this way been reduced to nil.) But it was precisely in order to provide the basis of such an account that this supposed "convention" was posited in the first place.

Nor, on the other hand, to approach the claim from another direction, are we essentially dependent for this certainty (when we have it) on "people's word." In many cases at least—I am inclined to think, prob-ably in most—we can know that someone is in pain without that person having to utter a sound. But, it may be objected, surely there must be at least some manifestation of the pain to indicate its presence—gritted teeth and contorted features, for example, or grasping of the injured area, writhing on the ground or the operating table, or something of the sort—and surely we can take this as, in an extended but still legitimate sense, that person's "word" to the effect that he is in pain (much as cer-tain forms of nonverbal expression have come to be regarded as pro-tected "speech" under the First Amendment to the Constitution). Once again, though, the rescue attempt fails. In a famous scene from the film *Lawrence of Arabia*, Lawrence extinguishes a lighted match by slowly pressing the lit end between his thumb and forefinger, not batting an

eye or otherwise changing expression as he does so. It strikes me as implausible to suppose that those witnessing this slightly bizarre ritual (apparently one to which the historical Lawrence was actually given) had to
wait upon an affirmative answer to their question as to whether this
didn't hurt—"Of course it hurts." "Then what's the trick?" "The trick is
not minding that it hurts."—in order to be entirely certain that at the
time of pressing out the match Lawrence was in fact in at least some
pain, no matter how well he was able to master and so conceal it. Similarly, it is, so far as I know, well-attested that in order to demonstrate
his capacity for endurance, Watergate burglar G. Gordon Liddy once
held his hand, palm open, over a candle flame long enough to inflict
severe burns on himself, remaining nevertheless silent and motionless
the whole time. Again, I think there is not the slightest doubt, regardless of what (if anything) Liddy may subsequently have said about the
experience one way or the other, that the pain was in fact excruciating.

The two points just seen can be summed up as follows. Our natural
(indeed, necessary) tendency to regard most people as telling the truth
most of the time, whether about what they are feeling or anything else,
is nonetheless not absolute. And, contrariwise, our certainty with regard specifically to what others are feeling (when we have such certainty) is not essentially dependent on hearing anything at all from
them; in many cases it is enough that we simply know the nature of the
experience itself that they are undergoing or have undergone. These
two considerations, taken together, point in turn to what seems to me
the heart of the difficulty with Rorty's position here. The really fundamental mistake, as already suggested, is to speak of a "convention" at all
in this regard, whether what is at issue is the incorrigibility of first-
person reports of feelings or the ability to be certain of what another
person is feeling. For it is of the essence of something's being a convention that it be *optional*. Conventions are things—preeminently, of
course, ways of speaking and acting—that are agreed upon in circumstances in which more than one course is possible. Whether that agreement be express or only tacit, accomplished all at once or only over a
period of time, makes no difference to the concept itself. To speak of
something as a "necessary (or unalterable) *convention*," in the sense of
a mode of behavior to the adoption or continued adherence to which
there was nevertheless understood to be *no alternative* whatsoever,
would be as incoherent as it would be to say of someone that he had only
one choice. Even a Hobson's choice (i.e., take it or leave it) does not
preclude acting in one way rather than another. We can no more conceive of a "necessary convention" or a "single choice" than we can conceive of a road going in only one direction.

Not that I mean to imply that Rorty doubts this. He knows what the word *convention* means, too. That is precisely the point. For this *is* the sense in which he intends that the word be taken in the passage we have been discussing. He believes, that is, that everything we say, even about such things as whether or not anyone (including ourselves) is in pain, really is ultimately optional. It is of the essence of his position that, as he often puts it, *all* discourses are *chosen*. There is, in other words, for him (to express the same position in the opposite way) no such thing as the truth or falsity of what we say about anything being *constrained by reality*. And thus, as seen, he also finds nothing amiss in asserting "that the Constitution is what the Supreme Court thinks it is, or that the ball is foul if the umpire thinks it is." The style of argumentation represented by this passage is very characteristic of Rorty's presentation of his views generally. In the particular case at hand, the idea is this: since it is supposedly clear to everyone that the right way to speak of the Constitution and of foul balls, respectively, is to say that the Supreme Court and the umpire determine what, or if, they are, as the case may be; and since the formal parallel to talk of pain (one's own or that of others) is presumably no less clear; the analogy should therefore help us to get over our traditional, but misconceived, ways of thinking about pain as well.

I think there is, indeed, a conclusion to be drawn from this analogy. It is, however, precisely the opposite conclusion from the one to which Rorty sees it pointing. For essentially the same basic considerations of which we have now reminded ourselves with respect to pain and our awareness of it, both in ourselves and in others, hold as well, and if anything even more clearly, in the case of the putatively supporting examples that Rorty cites. With respect to the former (and notwithstanding anything that Charles Evans Hughes may have said in an incautious moment), it is perfectly plain that what the Constitution is does not depend on what the Supreme Court or anyone else happens to think it is. The Constitution *is* the set of propositions beginning with the Preamble and running to the end of (as of this writing) the Twenty-Sixth Amendment. The historical evolution of our system of government has been such that the authority to determine the meaning of those propositions (where such determination is necessary) has come to be vested in the Supreme Court. That is, however, an entirely different matter, one having nothing even remotely to do with the ontological status of the text itself (and, as we shall see, not nearly as much as is sometimes supposed even with its interpretation and application). Similarly, the ball quite obviously *is* either in fair territory or in foul. It is well known that baseballs can sometimes be mysterious objects, especially when thrown by certain pitchers. Yet not even the great Sandy Koufax could get a ball to behave with the indeterminacy that quantum mechanics tells us is the nature of elementary particles to display (regardless of what some hitters may have believed to the contrary). And where the ball ends up once it has been hit is surely not to be thought less capable of unambiguous determination (at least in principle, if, for a variety of incidental reasons, not always in fact) than the location of a Koufax curve. The rules of baseball, of course, provide that the umpire makes the call as to whether the ball is fair or foul, and, moreover, that that call cannot ordinarily be overruled. It scarcely follows from this, however, that the umpire is infallible, nor even, with the now widespread availability of videotape instant replay, that there can be no conclusive demonstration that a given call was in fact erroneous.

One reason, I think, that the particular confusion reflected in Rorty's examples occurs as frequently as it does—and versions of it are, of course, to be found everywhere today in intellectual circles—is what Wittgenstein calls "a one-sided diet." By this he means the all-too-common tendency to rely for the development of one's theory on "only one kind of example" (*PI*, §593). To remain for the moment with the cases of foul balls and the Constitution, it will be natural, or at least much easier, to reach a conclusion such as Rorty's if one attends only to the difficult calls, those in which it is not immediately obvious to everyone how things are. But to do so is to overlook at least two important considerations: first, the situations in which such calls are required are precisely not the norm; and, second, there is not the slightest reason to suppose that the difference between these difficult situations and the ordinary ones with respect to relative ease of determination entails any difference whatsoever between the two with respect to things actually *being* one way or the other. What I think tends to happen, once these considerations are lost sight of, however, is that one begins to reason in the opposite direction. From the fact that some calls are difficult to make (which, of course, nobody denies), one concludes, first, that the nature of the case itself—that is, how things actually *are* in such situations—must itself be radically indeterminate; and second, that what is true in these cases must, by parity of reasoning, be true of all.

The best way to approach this confusion, I think, is also a Wittgensteinian one. The person caught up in it needs to be brought to see how much of the field (so to speak) he is overlooking in drawing the conclusion in question. The baseball case is the easier of the two to deal with, principally because the kinds of determination involved here (e.g., whether the ball is fair or foul) do not in any direct way involve a specifically linguistic component. Once these determinations have been made, of course, they must also be communicated to the players and the fans, but surely no one is going to find anything problematic in that. Or would Rorty want to maintain that the umpire has signaled "fair" only if someone else—the official scorer perhaps?—thinks he has? In that case, for whose word do we then wait before we "know" what the official scorer has done? And how, in turn, will that testimony be validated? And so it goes, once one has embarked on the path of radical skepticism. Consider, on the one hand, a ball hit so that it lands in the middle of center field, and, on the other, one popped back over the screen into the seats behind home plate. Is the first one foul, or the second one fair, "if the umpire thinks it is"? Merely to pose the question is to see the absurdity of the suggestion. Were an umpire actually to make such a call (and to insist on sticking by it even after being asked repeatedly what in the world he thought he was doing), he would be a prime candidate for anything from drug-testing to psychiatric evaluation. That the call itself would not be permitted to stand presumably goes without saying. But the situation is not for the most part essentially different in the case of the Constitution. And the one respect in which a significant difference does arise is not one from which Rorty can draw any support for his argument.

Consider, first, how comparatively few the sections of the Constitution are that ever figure in any way in the Supreme Court's deliberations as to what is and is not constitutional. We are all accustomed to seeing such phrases as "due process of law," "unreasonable search and seizure," "cruel and unusual punishment," and a number of others occupying prominent places in Court rulings. But when was the last time, for example, that a case before the Court turned on how the Twelfth Amendment was to be construed, or the Sixteenth, or, indeed, any of the amendments from Sixteen through Twenty-Six, not to speak of the bulk of the original seven Articles that is not even remotely controversial as to its meaning? Let us suppose, however, that a case actually were to center on one of these entirely straightforward passages, and let us suppose further that a majority of the Court were to declare that what the Constitution "meant" was precisely the opposite of what the passage manifestly said—that the First Amendment, for example, mandated the establishment of a state religion, or that the Eighteenth Amendment required the production, distribution, and consumption of alcoholic beverages, or that the Nineteenth Amendment prohibited women from ever voting. The Justices here would clearly be in a position at least as untenable as that of an umpire calling foul those balls hit to the outfield or fair those landing in the seats out of play.[9]

It can happen, of course, that from time to time the Supreme Court bases a ruling on nothing whatever in the Constitution. Well-known (and obviously controversial) recent examples are the majority opinions in *Griswold v. Connecticut* in 1965 and *Roe v. Wade* in 1973. That, however, has no bearing on the matter at hand here. A comparable instance in baseball might be one in which the umpire ejected a player for trying to steal the other team's signs on the grounds that, although nothing in the rules of baseball actually forbids this, there are, in the umpire's view, nevertheless certain "emanations" or "penumbras" implicit in those rules requiring that one refrain from such (again, in the umpire's view) unsportsmanlike conduct. No set of epistemological considerations is in itself in any position to prevent umpires or Supreme Court Justices or anyone else from acting irresponsibly, and the fact that irresponsible action is always a possibility is in turn no argument against epistemological conclusions. The fact that the Court ruled as it did in *Griswold* and *Roe* provides not the slightest support for the view that "the Constitution is what the Supreme Court thinks it is." It merely demonstrates that the Court (unfortunately) does not always limit itself to construing the Constitution.

The single important difference between the baseball and the judicial example stems, as suggested a moment ago, from the essential involvement of language in the latter. Specifically, it reflects the fact that it is never possible to remove from language (or natural language at any rate) absolutely every trace of ambiguity or other form of at least partially indeterminate meaning. Again, it cannot be emphasized too strongly that it does not follow from the fact that some expressions have to be interpreted that all of them do (i.e., for the community in whose language the expressions are cast; but who else, after all, are we talking about?), anymore than it follows from the fact that it is sometimes difficult to say whether the ball is fair or foul that it is not most of the time perfectly obvious to everyone in the ballpark which it is. But some expressions do after all call for interpretation, and in this respect the roles of the Supreme Court Justice and the umpire do differ significantly. At bottom, the umpire's job is simply to make the right call as often as humanly possible. That does not mean that he is supposed to get things merely as right as possible as often as possible; it means that he is supposed to get them right, period. Here there are no degrees of "rightness," only degrees to which it is recognized by inherently fallible human beings. As has been observed, the uncompromising embodiment of the discipline of reality is among the beauties of the national pastime in all its aspects. The ball *is* fair or foul, the pitch *is* a strike or a ball, the runner *is* safe or out; good umpires make the close calls correctly most of the time, the great ones almost always. Things, however, are not ordinarily so clear-cut in the case of the difficult calls that come before the Supreme Court.

What is or is not in a given case "due process" or an "unreasonable search" or "cruel and unusual punishment" can be extremely difficult to determine. That difficulty, moreover, tends to arise not so much from the facts of the cases, which at this level of jurisdiction are generally not in dispute. Rather it rests primarily with the concepts themselves that must be incorporated in these determinations. That is not to say, of course, that these and similar concepts are utterly lacking in clear meaning and still less that absolutely any interpretation anyone might want to give to them would be acceptable or even plausible. It *is* to say that what is or is not "due" or "reasonable" or "usual," unlike the alternatives fair/foul, strike/ball, or safe/out, is often a matter of degree, irreducibly so.

This is, however, a long way from being able to assert flatly that "the Constitution is what the Supreme Court thinks it is." In the first place, again, the *words* of the Fourteenth Amendment, with its "due process" clause, or the Fourth, prohibiting "unreasonable searches and seizures," or the Eighth, banning "cruel and unusual punishments," are just as unambiguously *there*—the *text* of these amendments is just as permanently *fixed* (until itself amended)—as are, for example, the words of the Sixteenth (permitting the levying of an income tax), the Eighteenth (Prohibition), or the Nineteenth (women's suffrage). That the Fourteenth, Fourth, and Eighth Amendments tend to receive somewhat more attention from the Court than do the Sixteenth, Eighteenth, and Nineteenth reflects (apart, obviously, from the fact that the Eighteenth was repealed by the Twenty-First) nothing more remarkable than the fact that applying some of their key terms in concrete situations is not always a cut-and-dried matter, but that nevertheless some application has to be made. Morality, like art, it has been said, consists in drawing the line somewhere. That is not, however, the same as saying that it can be drawn anywhere and still be either morality or art. It is not the case that every term must either have a single, univocal definition, unambiguously specifying all and only those things of which it is predicable (and that in every case the issue of its predicability must be a straight yes-or-no matter, just as a light switch is either on or off), or that it has no determinate meaning whatsoever and hence that any interpretation anyone might want to give it is necessarily as legitimate as any other. In my view, a strong candidate for most-underappreciated-important-insight on the part of a great philosopher is the one underlying Aristotle's theory of fourfold causation. Where Plato argues that the presence in the language of a given single term entails the existence of a single denotation of that term (if not on the phenomenal level, then in the realm of the Ideal), Aristotle is content to note that we in fact *use* certain terms—among them *cause (aitia)*—in a number of different ways, none of them necessarily reducible to any of the others, and to describe what those uses are. Thus the concept of causation can be—indeed, for Aristotle, is—manifold, without thereby ceasing to be a single concept.

The issue addressed in this way by Aristotle bears important similarities to the difficult calls that the Supreme Court is required to make. As competent speakers of English, the Justices have the concepts of such things as "due-ness," "reasonableness," "cruelty," and "usualness." By virtue of that linguistic competence, they are also aware, at least implicitly, that the range of application of these concepts is not the sort of thing that can be exhaustively determined a priori, if for no other reason than that it is not possible to specify in advance every sort of case in which the question of their applicability or inapplicability may arise. The human capacity to create unprecedentedly difficult cases for adjudication dwarfs the ability of even the most fertile imagination to envision such cases before they have actually arisen.[10] But the Justices also understand, finally—this is simply part of what it means to have the concepts in question—that not just anything can be accounted "due" or "reasonable" or any of the other terms on whose proper application the difficult cases tend to turn. As Aristotle's treatment of the notion of "cause" shows, it is entirely possible for a concept to be applicable to a number of different things, even quite different sorts of thing, without it following either that we therefore do not really have a single concept at all or on the other hand that its range of application is therefore in principle unlimited.[11] What the Justices do when they interpret the Constitution (again, those comparatively few passages in the Constitution whose meaning is not already perfectly clear and unambiguous) is thus to seek the best possible *fit* between, on the one hand, the sense that we already have of what is (for example) "reasonable" or "unreasonable," to this or that degree, in this or that set of circumstances, based in turn on our still broader notion of what it is to be reasonable or unreasonable in general, and, on the other hand, some new particular case or type of case for which a place has not yet been found on the reasonable-unreasonable scale. In a sense, it might almost be more appropriate to speak of the Supreme Court interpreting circumstances in light of the Constitution, rather than interpreting the Constitution itself at all. In the process, our notions of reasonableness and unreasonableness may themselves be modified to some extent. This will, however, appear either remarkable or otherwise possessed of deep philosophical significance only to someone who supposes that the requirement of an either-or choice between univocal meaning and limitless interpretability, which Aristotle showed to be in general a needless supposition at any given time, must nonetheless hold over time.[12]

This, then, is the rather quotidian remnant of the initially, perhaps, somewhat provocative-seeming claim that "the Constitution is what the Supreme Court thinks it is" (as we have seen, not even this much remains of its companion claim that "the ball is foul if the umpire thinks it is"). It is in the nature of the case that a text such as the Constitution—that is, one semantically rich enough to play a significant role in human affairs—is neither wholly unambiguous nor contains an algorithm permitting a mechanical application of all its provisions to every one of the myriad possible situations to which it can be seen in some way to pertain. It is, however, often necessary, especially in the sorts of cases with which political constitutions tend to deal, that ambiguity be resolved and some definite application be made. Therefore we in the United States have provided a particular institutional framework by which this can be accomplished. The Supreme Court, however, no more creates the Constitution ex nihilo than a literary critic creates the text of Goethe's *Faust*. The overwhelming majority of the Constitution's provisions are no more ambiguous or in need of interpretation—and hence no more open to variant readings—than are, for example, the names of the characters in *Faust* or the order of the scenes and acts. And even in those instances—relatively few in the case of the Constitution, rather more in that of *Faust*—where professional intervention is needed to establish what the interpretation and application of a given passage shall be, the range of possible readings, in the sense of logically, conceptually, and, for the Constitution, legally, permissible ones, remains in principle always circumscribed by the language of the text itself.[13]

II

One hallmark of Rorty's neopragmatism is a persistent conflation of the realms of the factual and the evaluative. "Pragmatists," he declares, "doubt that there is much to be said about th[e] common feature [which all true statements share]. They doubt this *for the same reason* they doubt that there is much to be said about the common feature shared by . . . morally praiseworthy actions" (*CP*, p. xiii; emphasis added). Epistemological and ethical inquiries thus turn out to be at bottom merely two versions of a single chimerical pursuit. It follows from this position, however, that it is, among other

things, impossible for any of us ever to determine in advance of any
given set of circumstances how we ought to act in those circumstances.
For if all we can say is that "certain acts [are] good ones to perform, under the circumstances" (p. xiii), but never what *about* those circumstances, in conjunction with the nature of the acts themselves, *makes*
those acts good ones, then what we have all along thought of as a matter
of basically rational moral decision making reduces merely to radical im-
provisation from one situation to the next. We are, on this view, condemned always merely to *re*act to whatever fate happens to throw our
way. But that is tantamount to saying that there is no such thing as ethics
at all. And from that, in turn, it follows that there is not even any such
thing as right or wrong.

The concept of right, as Kant noted, is logically dependent on the
possibility of *principled* action: I have to have some way of determining
before the situation actually arises in which I am called on to choose between, say, telling the truth and not doing so which of these is the right
thing to do. Whether that way turns out to be the one on which Kant
himself insisted, with its well-known consequence that lying is impermissible under any circumstances, absolutely without exception, is another matter altogether. The point is simply that, absent *some* way of
making this determination, specifically *moral* choice is impossible, and
talk of "morally praiseworthy" actions accordingly becomes vacuous.
Both moral choice and moral evaluation require that the one performing
the action and the one evaluating it have a basis independent of any
given set of circumstances in particular for distinguishing between what
is commendable and what is blameworthy; but even the possibility of
such a basis is just what Rorty appears to deny. In fact, of course, as is
surely plain to almost everyone, both moral choice and moral evaluation
are not merely possibilities, they are full-fledged realities. Of primary
interest at the moment, however, is the way in which this consideration
points in turn to a recognition of one of the signally important respects
in which the pursuit of good *differs* from the pursuit of truth (i.e., science). For scientific research is distinguished precisely by the fact that,
unlike ethics, one does *not* know in advance of particular circumstances
what the outcome of inquiry is likely to be.

In the realm of ethics, that is, we know, at least in general terms,
what we want to achieve. As suggested above, our most basic intuitions
of right and wrong, the ones correlative with human civilization itself,
do not differ significantly from one time or place to another (when they
do so at all). The real difficulties arise at the level of trying to determine
what constitutes in any given case the best application, or "fit," of these
general principles to the shifting exigencies of concrete experience. That
problem tends to present itself with particular acuteness today in the

form of situations in which technological advance (especially, though by no means exclusively, in medicine and the biological sciences) confronts us with both radically unprecedented and yet also radically objective alternatives. These are situations, in other words, in which a decision cannot *not* be made one way or the other, but in which little or nothing in our experience (moral or otherwise) seems able to serve as a guide for the actual determination of which course is the right one to follow. It is, I think, a fundamental mistake, however, to say in such cases (as is nonetheless commonly done) that our morality has not yet developed to the point of being able to orient us in making these difficult choices—that our technical know-how has, as it were, for the moment outrun our know-what-to-do-with-it. Morality does not "develop" at all, any more than logic does. Were either of these actually to do so, per impossibile, that would be equivalent to our having somehow become an entirely different species of being from what we are now. (What not uncommonly does stand in need of development in these situations is rather the willingness, or sometimes the sheer ability, to, as it were, believe in what one already knows: to confront squarely, for example, the realization that not only does technological feasibility not of itself confer moral permissibility, but—and this is, admittedly, a recognition sometimes fraught with considerable pain—that resort to what the former makes possible may nonetheless on moral grounds be permanently impermissible. What is ultimately at issue in such cases, in other words, is at bottom almost always a matter of individual character, not the principles of morality themselves.) In ethics, to sum up, we know *what*, but not always *how*.[14] In science, however, the situation is precisely the reverse. Here we know in general *how* to go about pursuing our objectives. That is simply what it means to have a—or rather, the—scientific method, the reality of which not even Kuhn, if one examines closely what he actually says about scientific practice, denies. It requires a commentator of the eccentricity of, for example, a Feyerabend to assert that science ever does, or ever could, proceed in the absence of fixed procedures for formulating and evaluating hypotheses—and not even he is able to maintain that position consistently. What we neither know nor should expect to know in advance in the realm of science is to *what* particular results the search thus conducted will lead us.

In the final paragraph of *SSR*, Kuhn raises in explicit fashion the question that has been hovering in the background of his exposition throughout:

> Anyone who has followed the argument this far will nevertheless feel the need to ask why the evolutionary process [of "the development of scientific knowledge"] should work. What must nature,

including man, be like in order that science be possible at all?
Why should scientific communities be able to reach a firm consensus unattainable in other fields? Why should consensus endure
across one paradigm change after another? And why should paradigm change invariably produce an instrument more perfect in
any sense than those known before?

Kuhn's response to this question, however, is at best somewhat disappointing: "That problem—What must the world be like in order that
man may know it," he says, "is as old as science itself, and it remains
unanswered" (SSR, p. 173). This response is disappointing because, as
we shall see in the next chapter, it is simply not correct to say without
significant qualification that the problem "remains unanswered." It has,
indeed, not been correct to say this since the latter half of the eighteenth century. To anticipate a bit: as Herder and Kant first recognized,
and as Wittgenstein showed us again in this century, the key to the puzzle lies in reversing the terms of the question. Since knowledge of the
world—or, more generally, human engagement with it in a host of different forms, the cognitive being only one among these—plainly *is* a reality (the contrary hypothesis being, as we shall see, incoherent),
analysis of the structures of that engagement, in particular linguistic
structures, must perforce eventually enable us to answer all the questions that it could ever make sense for us even to ask about "[w]hat . . .
the world [must] be like." There have, indeed, already been quite substantial achievements registered in this regard. But it is no less clear
that much remains to be done, and in that restricted sense, to be sure,
we can agree with Kuhn that the "problem . . . remains unanswered."
More important in the present connection, however, is Kuhn's tacit acknowledgment that there is a legitimate and worthwhile question to be
pursued here at all.

For that is precisely what Rorty neither acknowledges nor, consistently with his overall project, can acknowledge. The conspicuous success of science since the Renaissance in illuminating the nature of reality
is the great thorn in the side of the skeptically inclined philosopher in
the present day. He cannot very well deny the success itself, of course,
certainly not if that were to involve, for example, communicating the
denial via any sort of electromagnetic medium; this would be a bit like
concluding on the basis of published reports that only oral communication can be relied on. Thus he must seek instead to deny, as it were, that
that success entails actually having accomplished anything. And this is in
fact the tack Rorty takes. In *PMN*, citing a passage from Kuhn's *The Essential Tension* in which the latter again leaves on the table the same

open question just noted from the conclusion of *SSR*,[15] Rorty chides him for "suggest[ing] that there is a serious and unresolved problem about why the scientific enterprise has been doing so nicely lately" (*PMN*, p. 339). And he continues:

> In the view I am advocating, the question "Why, if science is merely . . . , does it produce powerful new techniques for prediction and control?" is like the question "Why, if the change in moral consciousness in the West since 1750 is merely . . . , has it been able to accomplish so much for human freedom?" We can fill the first blank with "adherence to the following binding algorithm . . ." or with "a succession of Kuhnian institutionalized disciplinary matrices." We can fill the second with "the application of secular thought to moral issues" or "the guilty conscience of the bourgeoisie" or "changes in the emotional constitution of those who control the levers of power," or with a lot of other phrases. In no case does anyone know what might count as a good answer. (*PMN*, pp. 340–41)

The move here, by which Rorty attempts to represent the first question as somehow fundamentally like the second, and in that way then to dismiss them both, is merely one instance of the general conflation of fact and value that, as noted above, informs the neopragmatist argument throughout. We recall his denial, on the opening page of *CP*, that there is much of anything to be said about the truth of facts "for the same [unnamed] reason" that, in his view, we ought to adopt a corresponding skepticism with regard to the goodness of good actions. This sort of lateral shift in the exposition—with, not incidentally, the supposed link between the two allegedly parallel spheres of discourse remaining itself always wholly unspecified—is a technique particularly favored by Rorty in arguing for his views, one to which he frequently has resort in a variety of contexts. The passage at hand enables us to see particularly clearly why this move nevertheless invariably fails. For it is surely as plain as anything could be that the two supposedly analogous questions have in fact nothing whatever of importance in common with one another.

The problem posed by the first question is this: if science is not ultimately constrained by the real world, but is rather, for example, purely a matter of imaginative constructs, themselves in principle always subject to change whenever one's "values" might call for making that "choice," how then does it repeatedly manage, not merely to get things right, but to get them righter and righter all the time, as evidenced precisely by the ever more "powerful new techniques for prediction and control" that it produces? The second question, however, raises no issue at all, or none that would enable us to see in it an analogue of the first. It simply asks, in effect: why, when people come to think differently about matters pertaining to morality, do they then also act differently, in particular in their dealings with other people? But that is as perfect an example of a nonquestion as one could wish. To think differently from the way one formerly did about matters of morality just *is* to act differently. It is a commonplace that any change that one might profess in one's understanding of the requirements of morality that is not also reflected in concrete form at the level of one's actions is merely verbal (not to say hypocritical). We may, of course, be interested in learning what sorts of things have from time to time occasioned such changes in people's convictions (with the concomitant transformations in their behavior). That is a question for the intellectual historian, however, and has nothing to do with the (non-)issue of how a change in conviction can itself produce a change in behavior. The only way in which the first of these questions could be read as an analogue of the second would be on the (obviously absurd) assumption that to think differently about the world *is* of itself literally to change the world. But virtually no one, it is surely safe to say, seriously believes that the fabric of reality itself is infinitely malleable to our descriptions of it. With this, however, we come back again to the problem posed by Kuhn: how can science be both a human construct and yet also sufficiently constrained by reality that it finds itself obliged to undergo continual change and, as a result of that change, also gets continually better at what it is about (namely, predicting and controlling reality)? At this point, however, Rorty simply forecloses further discussion by asserting peremptorily that such questions as these "survive only as names for a certain inarticulate dissatisfaction" (*PMN*, p. 341).

This "for the same reason as"-maneuver, the tactic of claiming that "to ask *x* is like asking *y*," is, as indicated, one of Rorty's favorites—as well it might be, inasmuch as it employs as an instrument of argumentation one of the very theses that he is most intent on establishing as a conclusion, namely that there is ultimately no very great or important difference between what a scientist does and what, for instance, a poet or a politician does. In *PMN*, he characterizes as "[t]he only real question which separates Kuhn from his critics" the one that asks "whether the sort of 'deliberative process' which occurs during paradigm shifts in the sciences . . . is different in kind from the deliberative process which occurs concerning, for example, the shift from the *ancien régime* to bourgeois democracy, or from the Augustans to the Romantics" (*PMN*, p. 327). Again, his contention is that it is not fundamentally different.

Yet the very examples that he cites surely make plain that these three cases—the scientific, the political, and the literary-cultural—are in fact differentiated from one another by factors far more numerous and substantial than any that might be thought to point to significant similarities between them. We can bring this out by distinguishing somewhat more sharply than Rorty does between the two moments of "deliberative process" and "shift," and by noting in each case the nature of the relationship in which these moments stand to one another.

What should strike us most immediately, I think, is that in the case of the scientific "paradigm shift," and in that case alone, the "deliberative process" and the "shift" itself coincide. The shift from one "paradigm" to another occurs precisely as, and only to the extent that, the members of the relevant scientific community deliberate the respective merits of the various candidates for paradigm-status. The procedure is governed throughout by the overarching aim of achieving the best and most effective description of the world, and hence any candidate for acceptance must be regarded as always open to refutation by reality.[16] Much too much, as Kuhn himself seems to have recognized, has been made of the supposedly nonrational character of this process—of the extent to which it is supposed to depend ultimately on a change in "gestalt" perception or indeed a "conversion" on the part of the one undergoing the "shift."[17] Little or nothing of this sort of relationship between "deliberative process" and actual "shift," however, was involved in either of the other two "shifts" to which Rorty refers. In the case of the political transition "from the *ancien régime* to bourgeois democracy," it is surely obvious that the two moments of "deliberation" and "shift" were in fact more or less radically distinct. Rorty does not make entirely clear which revolution (or revolutions) in particular he has in mind here. If it is the French Revolution of 1789, however, the whole example is, to be sure, somewhat infelicitously framed.[18] For "bourgeois democracy" represented in this case merely a relatively brief interlude between feudal absolutism and nationalist totalitarianism; the invention of the latter in its modern form has actually proved the principal legacy of the French Revolution to the contemporary world.[19] And here as well, not coincidentally, the gap between "deliberation" and "shift" is especially pronounced. Though a considerable amount of talk preceded, accompanied, and even followed the events of the Revolution, the actual transformation of the political order stemmed ultimately from the imposition of the will of one group (in the end, indeed, one man) on the society at large. That "deliberation" played no essential role in this process can be seen from the fact that precisely the same series of events could have transpired had no one bothered to try to construct a rational (or in any sense discursive) justification for it at all, just as, in the other direction, one could have gone on "deliberating" endlessly (as people had in fact been doing in France for over a generation prior to the summoning of the Estates General), without this making the slightest difference to the actual structure of the polity. But this is precisely what can never happen in the case of a scientific "paradigm shift." For, again, it is uniquely characteristic of the latter that in it "deliberation" and "shift" coincide. Perhaps the ultimate reason this is so is simply that the elucidation of reality, unlike the construction of political systems, cannot be compelled. One has but to recall the disasters of Lysenkoism in the Soviet Union and both the Great Leap Forward and the Cultural Revolution in China to be reminded of the folly inherent in attempting to determine the outcome of scientific inquiry on the basis of political considerations. And, conversely, political systems, unlike scientific theories, are not in general open to refutation by reality—at least not in the minds of their adherents. If this really were a genuine possibility, a host of misconceived theories and programs (beginning, perhaps, with Marxism, but by no means ending there) would long since have drawn the obvious conclusion and retired of their own accord from the world stage.

The other of the two major political revolutions of the eighteenth century, the American, actually did culminate in the invention of modern pluralist democracy, of course, and thereby established against totalitarianism the other of the two poles that since about 1800 have defined the political landscape of modernity. Even had Rorty made explicit reference in his political example to this revolution, however, the analogy to the scientific "paradigm shift" would still have failed, although use of the American Revolution as the illustration would have made it possible to develop at least a more plausible argument for the analogy. Here as well the actual "shift," no matter how well motivated "deliberatively," could not have taken place if the citizens of the colonies had not willed it so. And here also, again unlike the situation in the realm of science, it was sufficient for that transformation to occur that the citizenry will that it do so. One crucial step in this whole process that brings out particularly well the decisive role of volition in the entire transformation was the frank decision on the part of the Framers of the Constitution to go beyond the mandate given them by the Congress, which was merely to see what they could do to improve the working of the system under the already established Articles of Confederation, and, on no one's authority save their own, in effect to remake the entire polity from scratch. It is difficult to imagine anything analogous to this step even being open to a team of research scientists. The latter's task is to explain the world, or some portion of it, not to reinvent it. In the terms we used earlier to distinguish cognitive enterprises from value-related ones, the Framers knew the relevant "what" of the matter and believed they could find a better "how." Their success in doing so was to a large extent the result of *reanalyzing* that "what" precisely *in terms of* a specific "how." And this in turn lends to the American experiment in democracy its appearance of partial similarity, alluded to a moment ago and about which there will be more to say presently, to a scientific undertaking.

The link between the "shift . . . from the Augustans to the Romantics" and anything that might be called a "deliberative process" is, if anything, still more tenuous than in the case of the political revolutions just discussed. The supplanting of Neoclassical by Romantic sensibility throughout Europe (to the specifically British version of which Rorty alludes) was the result of a combination of factors—aesthetic and philosophical, but also political, economic, and sociological—so complex that scholars will doubtless be working on illuminating aspects of it for years to come. Let us, however, assume for the moment that there really was nothing more involved here than merely a shift in taste. One can no more be persuaded to change one's taste, literary or otherwise, than one can be induced to find funny or interesting what does not already strike one in either of those ways—not even if that is precisely what one wants to do. In situations of this sort, choice, and hence reasons, play virtually no role at all. Tastes can, of course, be acquired, as well as (though significantly less often) changed; but in neither case does that occur as the result of anything remotely resembling a "deliberative process." It is worth recalling that the "shift" from Augustan (or, again, more generally Neoclassical) to Romantic sensibility spanned considerably more than a generation. Of course, the same can also be true of scientific "paradigm shifts," as Kuhn notes. But, as he also observes, this need not be the case. Simply waiting for the older generation to die off does not in itself constitute an essential feature of such "shifts."[20] If, in other words, it is the exception rather than the rule that an Augustan becomes a Romantic, or an adherent of the *ancien régime* a proponent of republican democracy, it is the rule rather than the exception that any given scientist in a time of "paradigm shift" can eventually be persuaded on unimpeachably rational grounds to abandon the old in favor of the new "paradigm." In part precisely because it is the objective truth about things that is at stake in science, rather than, for example, matters of ethical conviction or aesthetic taste, scientists are, among other considerations, simply far better situated, both professionally and psychologically, to change their minds than are either politicians or poets.

In *CP* we find another instance of the same rhetorical gambit that we have been discussing from *PMN*, again fraught with the same difficulties.

"Very few thinkers," Rorty maintains, "have suggested that maybe science doesn't *have* a secret for success—that there is *no* metaphysical
or epistemological or transcendental explanation of why [for example]
Galileo's vocabulary has worked so well so far, any more than there is an
explanation of why the vocabulary of liberal democracy has worked so
well so far" (*CP*, p. 192). Once more, however, Rorty's example tells precisely against rather than for his position. First, the sense itself in which
science "works"—namely, that it enables us to predict and control reality on the basis of the descriptions that it produces—has in one obvious respect nothing whatever in common with the sense in which liberal
democracy can be said to "work." Indeed, I would urge that the "secret"
of the latter's success consists above all in its ability, unique among political systems, to combine social coherence (virtually by definition the
fundamental requirement that must be met by any form of political organization) with a principled inability to predict or control the specific
behaviors of its citizens (for purposes of this contrast, the counterparts
of natural phenomena as dealt with by science). And in noting this, in
turn, we also see that we are in fact able to account perfectly well for the
historical success of liberal—or, as it would better be put, to avoid an
obvious ambiguity, pluralist—democracy.

The key lies in recognizing that pluralist democracy is not in the first
instance a system of prescribed *ends* to which a given population is
obliged to conform (something that *is* the hallmark of all forms of totalitarianism, whether of the nominal left or right). Rather, it is above all a
system of *procedures*, which specifies only the—in most cases, fairly
broad—terms in which any ends, whatever they may be, are to be pursued and which, accordingly, excludes as impermissible only those ends
the realization (or, in a few cases, even the pursuit) of which would be
incompatible with the continued functioning of those procedures themselves. The lesson to be drawn from the historical success of systems so
constituted is that the broad latitude thereby afforded individuals to
chart their own destinies, rather than being compelled to reenact a vision of the good life already formed in the mind of someone else (not
infrequently, long dead), is evidently in profound accord with a basic,
deep-seated urge in all people to determine their lives for themselves.
We all wish, to the extent possible, to embody in the reality of our own
experience the concept of autonomy that we intuitively recognize as of
the essence of human dignity. This is also what I was getting at a moment ago in suggesting the existence of at least an approximate parallel
between scientific rationality in general and the political rationality of
the American system in particular (not forgetting the sense, just noted,
in which science and pluralist democracy "work" in exactly opposite

ways). Just as in science we know "how," but, prior to experiment, never "what," so, under the Constitution, we *provide for* "how" in such a way that, within the broad limits thus established, we *don't care* precisely "what," recognizing that it is of the essence of freedom that the individual decisions of free people affecting their own lives not be preempted by those who would presume to know better than they do themselves what is good for them.[21] Freedom, as the overarching value at stake here—as it were, the Big "What" in this regard—turns out to be best secured by saying as little as possible about all the little "whats," in the sense of all the particular, concrete, local ends that for each of us largely determine what our lives are about.

There are thus in fact two distinct sorts of difficulty to which Rorty's picture of the relationship between "deliberative process" and "shift" gives rise. He contends that scientific deliberations are at bottom in no wise different from political or aesthetic ones. And he concludes from this that the former are therefore every bit as ad hoc, unsystematic, subjective—in a word (not his, although it might as well be), irrational—as the latter always are. But, as we have seen, neither side of this characterization withstands scrutiny. The rationality of specifically scientific inquiry is *not* the informing principle of such deliberations as may accompany political or aesthetic change (in those circumstances that involve deliberation at all). Yet there *is* at the same time a form of rationality peculiar to the latter as well, or at any rate to the realm of political affairs; I am not sure that the notion of "rational aesthetics" does not represent something of an oxymoron on any construction of *rational*. It is perfectly possible, in other words, to construct a rational politics, in the sense of one in basic accord with fundamental intuitions of right and wrong by virtue of systematically incorporating in its very structure what we might call the entelechy of human dignity (just as it has historically proved all too possible to create political systems whose essential irrationality is in direct proportion to their systematic flouting of those standards). Politics, like ethics generally, is not condemned to irrationality simply because it is not the same thing as science.

Much of Rorty's anti-realist argument, as suggested above, comes down to an attempt to make vanish the question of why science works, without thereby having to commit to a denial that it does work. The same essay cited a moment ago in connection with our alleged inability to explain "why the vocabulary of liberal democracy has worked so well so far" opens with the (by now familiar) claim that the discoveries of modern science "do not, *pace* Descartes and Kant, point any epistemological moral. They do not tell us anything about the nature of science or rationality. In particular, they did not result from the use of, nor do they

exemplify, something called 'the scientific method' " (*CP*, p. 191). Rorty
indicates why he believes this is so as follows:

> The tradition we call "modern philosophy" asked itself "How is it
> that science has had so much success? What is the secret of this
> success?" The various bad answers to these bad questions have
> been variations on *a single charming but uncashable metaphor:
> viz., the New Science discovered the language which nature itself
> uses* [emphasis added]. When Galileo said that the Book of Nature
> was written in the language of mathematics, he meant that his new
> reductionistic, mathematical vocabulary didn't just *happen* to
> work, but that it worked *because* that was the way things *really
> were*. He meant that the vocabulary worked because it fitted the
> universe as a key fits a lock. Ever since, philosophers have been
> trying, and failing, to give sense to these notions of "working *be-
> cause*," and "things as they *really* are." (*CP*, pp. 191–92)

Metaphors, of course, are "uncashable" only if they actually are *metaphors* to begin with. There is, to be sure, a certain figurativeness involved in speaking of a "language which nature itself uses," for nature
qua nature obviously does not use language at all. Nature in and of itself
is as mute as anything could be; that is what makes science necessary in
the first place. But in addition to being something of a straw man (for the
expression in question is, of course, Rorty's to begin with, and not, so far
as I am aware, the actual idiom of any philosopher or scientist), this is
not even what he really has in mind in speaking of a "metaphor" here at
all. For he proceeds at once to cash the image of nature-as-language-
user himself with his reference to the notion of " 'things as they *really*
are.' " In this, however, we also see just how thoroughly the entire passage remains governed by the assumptions of pre-critical epistemology.

Rorty is entirely explicit in his rejection of any suggestion that the
notion of things as they are—that is, objectivity—might be given a perfectly plausible and defensible analysis in critical terms. Adverting back
to his key-in-the-lock image in the passage just cited, he dismisses what
he calls "Kant's rather desperate suggestion that the key only worked
because we had, behind our own backs, constructed the lock it was to
fit" (*CP*, p. 192). His way of following up on this dismissal, however,
points to one fundamental respect in which his own understanding of
the history of philosophy appears to be seriously flawed:

> In retrospect, we have come to see Kant's suggestion as giving the
> game away. For his transcendental idealism opened the back door
> to all the teleological, animistic, Aristotelian notions which the in-

tellectuals had repressed for fear of being old-fashioned. The speculative idealists who succeeded Kant dropped the notion of finding
nature's secrets. They substituted [for it] the notion of making
worlds by creating vocabularies. (*CP*, p. 192)

It is true, as we shall see at greater length in the next chapter, that
Kant's way of formulating the "critical turn" did leave the door open to
the various misunderstandings and misappropriations of it that were
perpetrated in the next generation by the post-Kantian Idealists. And
we shall also have something to say about how that unfortunate chapter
in the history of thought might have been avoided. What Rorty consistently fails to see, however, is that the development in question
stemmed precisely from a *misunderstanding* of what was in itself a fundamentally correct insight and that it thereby actually fell back behind
the level of philosophical attainment that had been achieved with that
insight. In aligning himself to the extent that he does with the specifically Hegelian version of the Idealist position, moreover, he thus also
fails to see that his own theory simply reenacts that same retrograde
movement.

Let us look back to the passage just cited beginning, "The tradition
we call 'modern philosophy.' " Everything that Rorty wants to say here
turns ultimately on the question of whether it is possible to make sense
of the distinction between a theory's "just *happen[ing]* to work" and its
"work[ing] *because* that [is] the way things *really [are]*." One mark of
the pivotal role that this distinction plays in Rorty's argument is that he
is not content to state it only once, but rather returns to it twice over the
two immediately following pages, each time in a slightly different form.
The first restatement also involves the conflation of specifically cognitive and broadly ethical considerations that we have now seen on numerous other occasions:

> We shall not think there is or could be an epistemologically preg-
> nant answer to the question "What did Galileo do right that Aris-
> totle did wrong?", any more than we should expect such an answer
> to the questions "What did Plato do right that Xenophon did
> wrong?" or "What did Miraheau do right that Louis XVI did
> wrong?" We shall just say that Galileo had a good idea, and Aris-
> totle a less good idea; Galileo was using some terminology which
> helped, and Aristotle wasn't. Galileo's terminology was the *only*
> "secret" he had—he didn't pick that terminology because it was
> "clear" or "natural" or "simple," or in line with the categories of
> pure understanding. He just lucked out. (*CP*, p. 193)

And, on the next page, at the same time varying slightly the image of
"the language which nature itself uses," he speaks once again of "[t]his
fantasy of somehow discovering, and somehow *knowing that* one has discovered, Nature's Own Vocabulary" (*CP*, p. 194).[22]

The question then becomes: can we, after all, imagine a situation in
which someone's theory "just happens to work," but in which it does not
do so "because that is the way things really are"? I think we can, but not
in a way that helps Rorty's argument. To begin with a preliminary observation or two: the first thing to note in this connection is surely that
for a given theory to come up for consideration at all, it must "work"
consistently. A "theory" that claimed the ability to predict the sex of unborn children, for example, but that yielded the right answer only about
half the time, would not be a candidate for "just happening to work"
even in those cases where the prediction was correct. A theory cannot
be said to "work" at all if the predictions that it generates are not *regularly* borne out by the facts. Or consider the case of "Clever Hans."
The "theory" that Hans was able to give the correct answers to arithmetical problems because, although only a horse, he was nonetheless
somehow able actually to perform the necessary calculations is similarly
not a candidate for "just happening to work." For although it did seem
for a time, at least to some people, a perfectly good explanation, it
turned out in fact not to work at all when an important but previously
unnoticed variable was changed (specifically, when Hans was not permitted to see the person posing the problem). But what of this case:
asked to explain why a certain light goes on at certain times and not at
others, someone proposes as his "theory" the following: "When the light
goes on, it is because I flip this switch here, saying as I do so 'abracadabra.' " Clearly this explanation "works" in the requisite sense. For the
light indeed does go on (assuming all components of the electrical system in working order) every time anyone flips the switch and says "abracadabra." But it is just as clear that, insofar as the "theory" insists on
an intrinsic connection between the efficacy of flipping the switch and
pronouncing the magic word, it nevertheless does not work "because of
the way things really are." And to that extent the individual proposing
the theory might perhaps be said to have "just lucked out."

It would appear that for Rorty this is basically the situation in which
scientists always find themselves. Because it is inherently impossible
both to discover and to know that one has discovered "Nature's Own Vocabulary," there can never be any assurance that in proposing one's "theory" (no matter how well that theory may work), one is not simply saying
"abracadabra" at the same time that one flips the light switch. Thus formulated, however, this permanent suspicion has a decidedly familiar

ring to it. We have encountered something like this before in the history of thought. It is, in fact, nothing other than the specter of Descartes's Omnipotent Deceiver returned to haunt us again. There is an obvious irony in Rorty, of all people, turning out to be a kind of closet Cartesian. But that is merely to emphasize again, from a slightly different direction, the extent to which his thinking remains inextricably bound to precisely the pre-critical epistemological model that he believes he is overcoming once and for all. The very denial of the *substance* of the claim to have divined "the thoughts which are Nature's Own" (*CP*, p. 194), and the corresponding desire to replace all such claims with a "pragmatic" contentment with whatever "happens to work," is itself intelligible at all only on the tacit assumption that the notion of "Nature's Own Language" (*CP*, p. 192) is *formally* intelligible in its own right to begin with. As we shall see, however, the assumption in question is equivalent to the belief that man, language, and the world are not (or, at any rate, need not be) co-original with one another. And that belief turns out to be fraught with insuperable logical difficulties. In other words, to anticipate a bit, the supposition that a neopragmatist account of the success of science in describing the world would be either necessary or possible depends from the outset on a basic assumption that is itself strictly unintelligible.

Neopragmatism and the
History of Philosophy

CHAPTER FIVE

I

RORTY SHARES WITH HEIDEGGER THE CONVICTION THAT IN THE
history of Western philosophy a fundamental wrong turn was taken in
antiquity. In consequence of this early but crucial misstep, the philosophical thought of the West has essentially been mired in error and
confusion ever since. For Heidegger, the wrong turn consisted in what
he terms the "oblivion of the question of Being" (*Vergessenheit der Seins-
frage*), with the subsequent emergence of that bête noire of more than
a few others in the twentieth century as well, "Western metaphysics."
For Rorty, on the other hand, the real mistake seems to have been that
people started doing philosophy at all. Where Heidegger still finds good
things to say at least about some of the pre-Socratics (notably Anaxi-
mander, Heraclitus, and Parmenides), it appears that in Rorty's view
things went wrong as soon as specifically philosophical questions began
to be formulated in any fashion. Just as Rousseau lays the blame for all
the ills to which culture and civilization have made us heir ultimately at
the feet of a single historical archvillain (namely, "The first man who,
having enclosed a piece of ground, bethought himself of saying 'This is
mine,' and found people simple enough to believe him"[1]), so Rorty often
seems, implicitly if not in quite so many words, to be pointing to something analogous in the realm of ideas: a kind of philosophical Original
Sin, whereby someone began wondering aloud about such things as the

nature of reality or how we can be certain of the things we believe we know, and who also managed to persuade others (to their cost) that these were questions worth taking seriously. Rorty also sees at least a glimmer of hope, however, that the long night may be nearly over. Thus, for him, the intellectual history of the West falls, at least prospectively, into two principal stages, a philosophical and an (incipient) post-philosophical age.

It is a notable feature of Rorty's discussions of his philosophical fore-bears that he has almost nothing to say about the tradition of skepticism in Western thought. In his version of the story, the leading actors in the drama (prior to Hegel, in whose work he sees the first breakthrough to-ward the eventual overcoming of philosophy) are virtually all propound-ers of positive doctrine. Again and again in his writings one encounters the same names: Plato, Aristotle, Descartes, Locke, Kant, perhaps one or two others. For Rorty, these thinkers constitute a single, essentially continuous tradition that is for all intents and purposes identical with Western philosophy itself. The reader not already aware of another, dis-tinct body of thought developed over the centuries in opposition to this one and represented in varying degrees by, among others, Pyrrho, Sex-tus Empiricus, William of Ockham, Montaigne, Bayle, and Hume will not be appreciably the wiser in this regard for having read Rorty. Pre-cisely that omission, however, is of pivotal importance for the overall de-velopment of his argument. For on it largely depends the possibility of making plausible to the reader either of the two claims just noted: first, that until very recently Western philosophy has been, with a few ex-ceptions, at bottom all pretty much of a piece; and, second, that the turn to "post-philosophical" thinking advocated by Rorty represents a radically new departure in thought, unprecedented (again, with the same few exceptions) by anything attempted, or even conceived of, prior to it. Had the skeptical strain in the Western tradition received some-what more attention in Rorty's exposition, however, it is hard to see how there would have been any avoiding precisely the opposite twofold con-clusion: first, that that tradition (prior to the latter half of the eighteenth century) has not one, but rather two—and two at least nominally quite different—sides to it; and, second, that the neopragmatist position as Rorty develops it represents merely an attempt to rehabilitate one of these sides in up-to-date, "post-analytical" garb. What Rorty offers, in other words, is in the end simply skepticism with a new and (it is hoped) finally respectable face.

Rorty himself, of course, rejects this characterization of his views. And yet it seems to me that what he actually advocates is indeed skep-ticism, on any plausible understanding of that notion. For skepticism, again, as noted at the outset, is simply the view that certain knowledge of objective reality is either impossible in principle—what might be called the "atheistic" version of the doctrine—or at any rate beyond the capacity of anyone to guarantee—its slightly milder, "agnostic" form. The reasons for holding this view may, in any given case, have more to do with the aspect of certainty or more with that of reality. Perhaps one feels that we can never really be *sure* about anything; perhaps one feels that there is not even anything for us to be sure *about*. The history of skepticism presents us with as richly variegated and finely nuanced an array of combinations of these basic directions of thought as one could wish. And it is a tradition to which Rorty, his reluctance to accept the designation notwithstanding, quite unmistakably belongs.[2] How else, after all, is one to view the fact that he expressly counsels "denying [that there is such a thing as] 'objective physical reality' " (*PMN*, p. 374), or his reference to the (allegedly) "hopeless 'epistemological' quest for a way of refuting the skeptic and underwriting our claim to be talking about nonfictions" (*PMN*, p. 293)? In a passage germane to the discussion in chapter 4 he is even prepared to maintain that "skepticism [regarding "whether other people have, for example, pains"] is no more refutable . . . than skepticism about whether the table exists when there is no one about to perceive it. It is, after all, quite possible that tables vanish when nobody is around. It is quite possible that our companions always simulate pain-behavior without having any pains" (*PMN*, p. 112). There is a very basic confusion reflected in this passage, one that Wittgenstein in particular helps us clear up. Much of the work in the last year or so of his life in particular was devoted to precisely the point at issue here.[3] What he enables us to see is that it is in fact *not* the case that "certainty cannot be had" regarding such things as pains or tables, and thus that it *is* "impossible"—not merely, in Rorty's words, "just pointless" (*PMN*, p. 112)—to formulate a coherent expression of doubt with regard to them.

One of Rorty's principal arguments for the thesis that "nothing can refute the skeptic—nothing can do what epistemology hoped to do" is that "we discover how language works only within the present theory of the rest of the world, and one cannot use a part of one's present theory to underwrite the rest of it" (*PMN*, p. 294). But this is to get things precisely backwards. The burden of proof is on the skeptic to make his case plausible in the face of our commonsense intuitions of objective reality. And yet the very inability of any of us ever to get outside the linguistic-cultural context in which we operate, to which the skeptic believes he can appeal for support of his view, in fact deprives his argument, whether for radical error or for radical indeterminacy, of even the possibility of a starting point. As Donald Davidson notes, "In sharing a language, in whatever sense this is required for communication, we share a picture of the world that must, in its large features, be true"; hence, to approach the same point from the opposite direction, "massive error about the world is simply unintelligible."[4] The fact that "our present views about nature are our only guide in talking about the relation between nature and our words" (*PMN*, p. 276) thus points to precisely the opposite conclusion from the one Rorty wants to draw from it. For those same "views about nature" are *themselves* obviously inseparable from "our words" and how we use them.[5] The very ineluctability of our dependence on particular forms of expression (and thus of conceptualization) for *whatever* we say about *anything* is what also ensures that no attempt to doubt *everything* or to call *everything* radically into question—and, as noted earlier, a skepticism that did not do this would not even be skepticism, but rather, at most, a desire to avoid being overly credulous—can coherently be undertaken.

More important than the mere fact of Rorty's basic skepticism, however, is the reason he felt compelled to adopt that position in the first place. It is the same reason shared by the adherents of all the myriad other attempts to rehabilitate skepticism so much in evidence today. Regardless of the different names by which these attempts have come to be known—in addition to neopragmatism and anti-foundationalism, postmodernism, post-structuralism, and deconstruction are, of course, among the more familiar ones—and notwithstanding the various, more or less minor, differences in detail in formulation, these are all united, as we have seen, by a common conviction that there are two, and only two, possible epistemological standpoints that one can adopt. Either we assume the existence of an *independent* (immutable, neutral, ahistorical) reality, or we acknowledge that what is sometimes called "reality" is in fact never anything other than *interpretation*, merely some way in particular of talking about things. That way, whatever it may be in any given case, is in turn held to be always relative to some particular historical or cultural "context" and the various "conventions" specific to that context. And for this reason it is also held to be permanently subject to (in principle) unlimited change—indeed, to be constantly in process of undergoing such change. I doubt that there is another pair of alternatives more frequently encountered today in one form or another across the entire range of intellectual disciplines than this one. And yet, in addition to the fact that there is evidently no prima facie reason why one ought to accept this bipolarity as exhaustively determinative of logical space, there are some extremely good reasons why one should not do so, reasons, moreover, that have been open to view by anyone for over two centuries.

Beginning in the 1760s and 1770s, a number of thinkers, chiefly in Germany, pursuing a wide variety of individual interests and acting more or less independently of one another (though, at the same time, in most instances at least aware of each other's work, and in some cases actively collaborating), survey the philosophical scene from the vantage point of the particular issues with which they are engaged, and, one after another, they come to the same conclusion: we are not getting any answers to our questions; and the reason we are not is that we are not formulating those questions in the right way. The common problem underlying all these questions is how to give an adequate account of the relationship between man and the world. And the conclusion to which these thinkers come is that once one has posed the problem in these (at first glance, it would seem, wholly unproblematic) terms, all possibility of resolving it has been permanently blocked from the outset. As Wittgenstein would observe almost two centuries later, in connection specifically with the question of how "the philosophical problem about mental processes and states and about behaviourism arise[s]," but with more general application as well:

> The first step is the one that altogether escapes notice. We talk of processes and states and leave their nature undecided. Sometime perhaps we shall know more about them—we think. But that is just what commits us to a particular way of looking at the matter. For we have a definite concept of what it means to learn to know a process better. (The decisive movement in the conjuring trick has been made, and it was the very one that we thought quite innocent.) (*PI*, § 308)

So also with the problem of accounting for the relationship between "man" and "the world." Once the degree of separation of the two that is implicit in that way of framing the issue has been assumed, then, just as with Descartes's "mind" and "body" (and for basically the same reason), it remains ever thereafter impossible to get them back together again.

From Descartes to Leibniz, continental rationalism had labored with (on its own terms) impressive success to develop an at once comprehensive and internally consistent description of reality. The various systems of the rationalists, however, were in every case hampered by an ultimately fatal inability to provide from within themselves the requisite validation of the whole—the guarantee, that is, that the entire edifice of deductively linked propositions actually did in the end also hook up with the world outside the system, of which it claimed to provide a perfectly perspicuous representation. And thus they proved defenseless against the assault of a thoroughgoing phenomenalist such as Hume. Hume had but to ask at every turn for the concrete, empirical counterpart of whatever concepts the rationalists might invoke (notably, of course, those of causality and personal identity) and, receiving no answer, did not hesitate to declare the entire rationalist undertaking a sham. A critique of the Humean sort, however, though (likewise on its own terms) no less impressively successful than its apparently now-vanquished adversary had seemed, also brings with it its own distinctive set of problems. For if, as a result of that critique, we have now been guaranteed all the contact with the world we could ask for, in the form of rock-solidly-based sense perceptions, this has been achieved only at the cost of simultaneously reducing the world, and ourselves with it, to a congeries of radically discrete sensory points. The orderly, law-governed cosmos in which we had supposed ourselves situated—of which, indeed, we had often thought ourselves the quintessential microcosmic embodiment— turns out on examination to rest on nothing more than an unfounded and unfoundable act of faith. But of course, as Hume himself recognized full well, no one can actually live as if the world truly were the scene of utter randomness and fragmentation that his analysis purportedly shows it to be. Our belief in such things as the law of cause and effect and our own identities as persons over time is, as a practical matter, indispensable, regardless of whether or not that belief can be defended on strictly philosophical grounds. In view of this, however, the wholesale critique of rationalism itself in which Hume's analysis issues begins to lose much of its bite. For if we are, so to speak, condemned to faith in any case, we may be moved to ask how our position would be made any worse by accepting a body of doctrine such as Descartes's, Spinoza's, Leibniz's, or any of a number of other possible candidates, with all the extraordinary range of explanatory power such systems seem to offer us. Once embarked on this line of reasoning, however, we then simply find ourselves batted back and forth endlessly between the two poles of rationalist metaphysics and empiricist phenomenalism, alternately succumbing to the blandishments of each, only to reject it in turn on the strength of the critique offered by the other.

What I have just described in outline is, of course, the familiar opposition of dogmatism and skepticism, which dominated the philosophical landscape of the West prior to the major works of, in particular, Kant and Herder. It is also, however, as far as epistemological structure is concerned (and notwithstanding that in two hundred years the names of both the players and their equipment have changed somewhat) *precisely* the same opposition embodied in the contemporary alternatives of reality-as-independent and "reality"-as-interpretation. Thus whatever can be said of either of these pairs—and for ease of exposition I will continue to stick for the most part, as I have been doing, with the terms *dogmatism* and *skepticism*—applies in precisely equal measure to the other as well. And the first thing to note is that the apparent diametric opposition separating the two points of view is in fact at bottom not an opposition at all. For both the dogmatist and the skeptic conceive of knowledge in accordance with the age-old model of the *adaequatio intellectus ad rem.* According to this model, the attainment of knowledge consists in our having brought our minds in some way into correspondence with an object of knowledge, itself understood to exist prior to and independently of both the knower and the act of cognition. Separating the dogmatist and the skeptic is, in the end, nothing more than a difference of opinion on the question of whether or not this ideal relationship is, or ever could be, actually realized. The dogmatist thinks that it can (he is in fact convinced that he has done so himself in exemplary fashion); the skeptic either denies that this could ever happen at all (if he is a skeptical atheist), or he holds that at any rate we could never truly be certain that it had been accomplished (if he leans toward skeptical agnosticism). The dogmatic standpoint leads, in one form or another, to what today has become known more or less generically as "the metaphysics of presence," an expression that, like its companion term *logocentrism,* has by now grown well beyond the specific context in which it was originally introduced to become a virtually all-purpose instrument of denunciation in the hands of contemporary skeptics. Against this, the skeptical view issues in any of a host of versions of perspectivism, relativism, contextualism, conventionalism, and the like. The common theme of these various -isms is a single thesis: because no one ever has access to reality as such—again, either because that is something we simply can't get at or because there just isn't anything by that name to get at at all—the most anyone can do is to express his particular belief, or opinion, or interpretation of things, without it, however, being even remotely possible—or perhaps even intelligible—to claim that what is uttered in this way provides a definitively true representation of the way things objectively are.

It strikes me as implausible to suppose that anyone has ever actually set out to hold a view as thoroughly counterintuitive as the skeptical one plainly is. I have difficulty imagining someone not driven by exceptional intellectual perversity selecting this as his prime hypothesis from among all the possible positions that one might adopt and then searching for arguments to support it. Rather I think that those who do adopt this position (or, as I have been suggesting, who mistakenly believe they have adopted it) do so for the most part only as a last resort, because they cannot see any way not to. Convinced that the only alternative to it is the now thoroughly discredited "metaphysics of presence," they fall back on what seems to them the least objectionable form of skepticism and try to make the best of it. The more articulate among the defenders of the skeptical position—and whatever else one may say about his views, Rorty is certainly that—may even command a kind of grudging admiration for their ability to render at least momentarily plausible a standpoint that a little reflection nevertheless reveals to be wholly untenable, in large part, as we shall see below, because it is in several different respects simply self-contradictory. The great philosophical lesson of the eighteenth century, however, is that the choice between dogmatism and skepticism is itself entirely unnecessary. That is the true and enduring legacy of the critical turn in philosophy. It is also, however, a lesson that has historically proved strangely easy to forget, or at least to overlook, and is thus something of which it seems necessary to remind ourselves from time to time. As Wittgenstein observes, much of the work of philosophy consists, indeed, in nothing other than this, in merely "assembling reminders for a particular purpose" (*PI*, § 127).

Though often regarded as the work primarily, not to say exclusively, of Kant, the critical turn is in fact, as suggested earlier, better viewed as the collective achievement of an entire generation of thinkers. Again, this was not so much a matter of active collaboration on the part of those who contributed to it. Such collaboration did occur, to be sure, although it is also true that in the case of the two principal figures, Kant and Herder, the relationship tended over the years to move in quite the opposite direction. It is rather that for a variety of reasons, some of which we are able to specify fairly unequivocally, while others remain much more speculative, the condition of aporia generated by the antinomy of dogmatism and skepticism came to be felt especially acutely at about the same time across virtually the entire range of intellectual and artistic activity in one nation in particular, Germany. From the standpoint of sheer conceptual power and architectonic brilliance, the Kantian response to the problem in the *Critique of Pure Reason* continues in many ways to stand as the most imposing one—a philosophical tour de force unrivaled, at least in these respects, by anything since antiquity and, with the exceptions perhaps of Hegel's *Phenomenology* and Wittgenstein's *Tractatus*, not seriously approached by anything produced since its time. Kant's way of formulating his response, however, also contains (as is demonstrated all too clearly by the course that philosophy was to take immediately after him) the potential for giving rise to significant misunderstanding of what the critical turn itself actually consists in.

Kant recognized that an acceptance of the model of the *adaequatio intellectus ad rem* united, even as it separated, the dogmatic and skeptical standpoints; this single (pre-critical) epistemology was at the root of the apparently insuperable difficulties to which those standpoints had individually and jointly given rise. He therefore proposed, as is well known, that rather than assume that we must in some way correspond to phenomena to have knowledge of them, we instead try the hypothesis that phenomena to be known must in some way correspond to us.[6] Kant characterized this move as his "Copernican revolution" in philosophy. In describing his project as analogous to Copernicus's overthrowing of Ptolemaic astronomy he had in mind, of course, a correspondingly massive realignment of our view of the relationship between ourselves and the world. The problem with adverting specifically to Copernicus in this connection, however, is that the two realignments, though in both cases enormously far-reaching in their consequences, actually take place in opposite directions. Whereas Copernicus removes mankind from the center of the cosmos by relocating us to a comparatively marginal position in the overall scheme of things, Kant proposes to place us precisely in the center, as the nearly godlike creators of our own reality. To be sure, this difference would hardly be worth noting, if nothing more were at stake than a punctilious concern with details of intellectual history. There is, however, a larger consideration involved here, and it is one that drawing out the implications of the "Copernican revolution"-analogy helps bring into focus. Kant is determined, as he needs to be, to block the opening of a metaphysical gap between "man" and "world," which, as noted earlier, once admitted, remains forever unbridgeable. He is so intent, however, on securing that goal by means of an overthrow specifically of the *adaequatio* model, in which he (not incorrectly) sees the "man"-"world" gap paradigmatically embodied, that at times (such as the juncture in his text under consideration at the moment) he appears simply to invert the terms of that model, rather than, as he ought to do, rejecting the entire model itself outright. That is, however, a move with potentially fateful consequences. It does ensure the desired integral connection of "man" and "world." But in analyzing man as the agent who *constructs* the world of experience in accordance with forms of cognition inherent in the structure of his own mind, Kant also opens the door at least slightly (especially given a certain fundamental misreading of his analysis, about which more in a moment) to all the excesses and absurdities of post-Kantian Idealism, with its extravagant metaphysics of subjectivity.

Kant himself, of course, was among other things simply far too level-headed ever to have gone in for speculative metaphysics at that level of self-intoxication. One cannot well imagine the sage of Königsberg, with his resolutely down-to-earth instincts, embracing such a product of dialectical genius out of control as, say, Fichte's subjective idealism, with its conception of the Absolute Ego that was to be so ruthlessly, but also pointedly, satirized by writers from Jean Paul[7] and the anonymous author of the *Nachtwachen*[8] to Heine[9] and beyond. Nor does the really central argument of the first *Critique* provide any support for a doctrine of this sort. Kant actually demonstrates the reciprocally constitutive nature of the relationship between man and world. Each of these at once presupposes and is presupposed by the other, and thus they are both inseparable from one another and ontologically on precisely the same objective footing.[10] Neither man nor the world of human experience— and, as Kant shows, that is the only world of which we are able to form a coherent notion—is even conceivable, much less possible, in the absence of the other. There neither is nor could be anything outside that linkage of which it would make sense to speak as even a conceptual possibility, much less an actual one. Talk of the "transcendent," as opposed to the "transcendental,"[11] though, as Kant observes, apparently something to which we are by nature all but irresistibly inclined,[12] is nonetheless strictly unintelligible. A characterization of the world of experience as somehow less than objectively real, however, in order to make sense at all, as we noted above in connection with the theory of anti-foundationalism, would have to assume the existence of just such a "transcendent" level of reality on which the world of experience would be supposed somehow to rest. Precisely this, however, is what the argument of the first *Critique* shows to be impossible. And it follows, accordingly, that any suggestion that that world is not objectively known by us is not even mistaken so much as it is incoherent.

Although the point is actually fairly simple, it can in practice prove exceptionally difficult to see clearly. There seems to be little overestimating the hold on the mind capable of being exerted by the idea that if one is to avoid falling into an *un*critical realism (the "metaphysics of presence" again, according to which reality is simply "there," prior to and independently of any of us), it is necessary to posit what might be called the doctrine of the ubiquity of interpretation.[13] To be sure, that doctrine does avoid uncritical realism. But it pays a high price to do so, inasmuch as it is compelled at the same time to reject realism of any sort. It is thus forced into the position of having to deny our commonsense intuition that some things—the facts—are, after all, objectively, definitively, and unalterably the case.[14] That position is, indeed, so counterintuitive that, as suggested earlier, I think it overwhelmingly unlikely that anyone has ever truly held it. This does not mean, of course, that there are not many today who claim to hold it; it merely means that in general we should be extremely reluctant to believe them. It is not that we suppose them to be lying, of course; rather we simply recognize

that they are confused. For much the same reason, to borrow a Wittgensteinian example, we would not be inclined to believe someone who
claimed to know what time it was on the sun either (see *PI*, § 350).

Some things we say, of course, *are* interpretations. It is difficult to
imagine anyone wanting to deny something so obvious. And in many
cases we may believe so firmly in the correctness of these interpretations that virtually nothing could shake our conviction. One person may
see in the sinking of the *Titanic*, for example, a judgment of God, while
another sees simply an unfortunate combination of incompetence, arro-
gance, and bad luck. And there is probably little prospect of either person persuading the other to his point of view, so different are the overall
outlooks in which the respective interpretations are embedded. To argue that everything we say is (merely) an interpretation, however, is
then to be unable to distinguish in kind between this sort of assertion
and the one that says no more than that the *Titanic* sank, period. But
that is surely an impossible position to sustain. It is no help to the doctrine of ubiquitous interpretation to argue that even the bare assertion
that the *Titanic* went down is possible only relative to some context of
belief and some perspective in particular. For if this is meant to point to
anything more than the obvious and uncontroversial fact that at any
given time everybody believes something and is somewhere, while no
one can believe everything or be everywhere at once, then some context
of belief and some perspective must actually be produced—and not
merely postulated as an abstract possibility—from or in terms of which
the *Titanic* in fact did *not* sink.[15] Otherwise the notions of "context of
belief" and "perspective" themselves have no "cash value" whatever
here. We again simply "divide through" (*PI*, § 293) by all such "contexts" and "perspectives" and come out with nothing more than the bare
fact itself of the *Titanic* sinking, in which all the various "contexts" and
"perspectives" converge.[16] And so it is necessary that someone actually
assert, for example, that the *Titanic* is still afloat (having never disap-
peared beneath the waves), or that it met some other end (perhaps, say,
being sold for scrap), or that nothing at all happened to it (because no
such ship ever existed in the first place). It is important to recognize that
making some choice among these or other similar alternatives is not itself an optional move in the game, in the sense of being something that
we could simply elect not to do in any form. When one's king is in
check, to avoid checkmate one must either block or flee or take the at-
tacking piece. What one cannot do—and still be playing chess—is nothing (i.e., leave the king in check). Similarly, one cannot, as it were, take
the *Titanic* off the board, in the sense of declining to say anything whatever about it—even that there never was a ship by that name—and still

be speaking English (or any other language). Of course, if one does not happen to know what the name *Titanic* refers to, then one has not yet gotten into the game at all, or at least not this part of it, just as someone who does not know the ways of escaping check has not yet begun to play chess. The remedy in each case is the same: we either explain the point in question ourselves or we direct the person to the appropriate reference work to look it up for himself.

But what if someone actually were prepared to assert one of these things about the *Titanic*, claiming that, given his particular perspective and context of belief, he was fully justified in doing so? The best answer here, I think, is the simplest one: we'll cross that bridge when we get to it. For, of course, we never will get to it. No one who does not wish to be considered mad or who is not so in reality is going to try to convince people that he seriously believes any of these things.[17] And in this way the burden of proof remains on the person wishing to argue for the doctrine of ubiquitous interpretation. At the same time, however, one may still have the feeling that this is somehow too ad hoc a solution, that the issue has not really been addressed but merely postponed, albeit indefinitely. Such a feeling overlooks the fact that to dispose of a pseudo-problem, it is entirely sufficient to show that it is not a *problem* at all. And that has surely been done when it has once been shown that the supposed difficulty does not represent anything that anyone will ever actually encounter that would require a decision one way or the other on which anything would depend. For the sake of argument, however, let us grant the point anyway and suppose that someone really has come forward to advance one of the claims in question. Now, for any issue at all to be joined between parties in disagreement, clearly there must first be agreement at least to the extent of what it is they are talking about, even if that is no more than acknowledging that they are just trying to establish what it is they are talking about. In the case at hand, both must already know at least what the name *Titanic* refers to. Otherwise a difference of opinion no more arises than it would if one person were to say, "The *Titanic* went down in 1912," and the other to respond, "But the *Andrea Doria* sank in 1956." But what if even the reference of the name *Titanic* is held to be merely an interpretation? Well, we may then inquire, do both of us know what a ship is? Still interpretation, may come the response. How about floating and sinking objects? Same thing. Liquids and solids? No better. Time and space? Sorry. And so it may go, at least for a time.

The most obvious thing to note here, of course, is that by this point in the discussion the proponent of ubiquitous interpretationism has long since ceased to be able to convince anyone other than the most ardent among his fellow partisans that he really means what he is saying (again, not in the sense that he is lying, but in the sense of not having thought through the implications of his words). Rather it is clear that he is merely trying doggedly to hold on to a doctrine to which he has committed himself (perhaps, as suggested earlier, from a belief that this is the only way to avoid the "metaphysics of presence") but on which, as he now recognizes, he cannot give an inch without the whole structure collapsing around him. The more important consideration, however, is precisely that this sort of thing *cannot* go on indefinitely. As we have noted several times now, life (in this respect at least, unlike logic) has no infinite regresses. Sooner or later—in circumstances where one party to the dispute has not merely gotten the bit in his teeth in pursuit of a purely academic obsession, ordinarily much sooner than later—a stage will be reached at which either something in common is found or where it may seem that absolutely everything has been tried with no resonance whatsoever. But—and this is the crucial consideration—how could it ever be *determined* in the first place that the *latter* was in fact the case? Clearly, that determination, like every other, requires that the parties making it have enough in common to recognize and agree upon the fact. But surely it is plain that, in this case in particular, the ostensible recognition and agreement would at once undo itself, just to the extent that it were to occur at all. And that means, in turn, that the stark alternative just envisaged can in reality never arise. At this bedrock level, in other words, it is just logically impossible to agree to totally disagree. If one is *communicating* at all, which is to say, if language is being employed on both sides in any form, there is by that very fact at least some degree of overlap between the "contexts of belief" or "perspectives" represented in the exchange. And what must be true in the case of any two interlocutors can easily be shown to obtain with the same necessity for everyone. For when a third party comes along, we simply treat the first two (or as much as they have in common) as a unit in relation to the third (now actually the new second) and repeat the process we have just gone through, deriving the same result and thereby expanding by one the membership in the common human set. And so it will go until we have run through the entire human race. We can, moreover, obviously begin this process anywhere, with any two interlocutors, between whom the bedrock degrees of overlap that we discover will presumably now and then be different from the one first discovered. And because we can then build back up in the same way to what, however, we now *already* know to be a *single* human race with a *common* context of belief (however initially modest in scope), the extent of that common context can itself clearly only expand. But at this point, again, the notions of "context" or "perspective" are themselves no longer doing any conceptual work. For they are no longer distinguishing between the single, common human standpoint and anything else. And so, as before, we simply "divide through" by them and come out with objective reality pure and simple, as it exists (to add what is really a superfluous qualification) for human beings at large.

Something at least very much like this argument seems to me the one on which Kant was actually intent in the *Critique of Pure Reason,* notwithstanding that his manner of exposition sometimes tends to obscure the fact. The point emerges as well—as it were, in negative reflection— from a consideration of what became of that argument in the hands of a thinker alluded to earlier, Fichte, who had actually begun his career with the aim of defending the Kantian critical philosophy against all comers.[18] In Fichte's view, the otherwise admirable edifice that Kant had erected is marred by the inclusion in it of one element too many, the "thing-in-itself" (*Ding an sich*). And he therefore proposes to set matters right by simply dispensing with that notion altogether. Unfortunately, however, he makes only half a job of it. He drops the idea of a "thing-in-itself" behind the phenomena of the external world, but he fails to take the corresponding step on the side of our internal experience of ourselves. He thereby creates a fundamental imbalance between, on the one hand, a now radically productive Self, or Ego, viewed as the metaphysical ground of all Being, and, on the other hand, the mere projections of that Ego's ceaseless activity of creation and self-creation. What he needed to do—the step that Kant himself should have taken—was to drop the *Ding an sich* on *both* sides of the relationship. The result would have been to leave the empirical self and the world of concrete experience, again, on exactly the same ontological footing with one another, with both of them grounded in unimpeachably objective fashion.

To be sure, a problem of exposition arises here. For if the notion of the *Ding an sich* is as essential as it appears to be in reaching the conclusion of Kant's critical argument at all, how can that argument, without self-destructing, then go back and, as its final stage, knock a key component of its own foundation out from under it? Essentially the same problem, of course, is familiar to readers of Wittgenstein's *Tractatus,* whose famous (not to say notorious) penultimate numbered section seems determined to render retroactively impossible the very argument that has led up to it with apparently seamless logical inevitability. This is not the place to attempt an exhaustive answer to the question of how what has struck some readers as a manifest self-contradiction, ultimately fatal to the entire project of the *Tractatus,* is in fact overcome by Wittgenstein; this answer, if successful, would presumably also suggest how a counterpart of that dilemma could have been handled by Kant as well. It seems to me, however, that the approach to such an answer must in any case be by way of a conception of philosophical heuristic and discursive recursion capable of representing the truth of an argument as literally *emergent* in the course of the text that constitutes it.[19] It is perhaps worth noting in passing that there is after all nothing inherently mysterious in this phenomenon, inasmuch as there exists a counterpart to it of which most people have had actual experience in ordinary life. It has been said of any activity that one might choose to pursue for which more or less extensive training is required that in school you learn all the rules and in life you learn all the exceptions. That is, in learning to apply the rules one has assimilated, the shape of the rules themselves changes, sometimes quite considerably. As a result, they gradually cease over time to be exactly what they were when one first learned them. And yet the very possibility of this adaptation and transformation depends in its own right on one's having initially bought unreservedly into the same rules that are now undergoing that change. No matter what the field of intellectual or artistic endeavor, access to the more advanced levels of proficiency and sophistication is to be had only by first learning to regard as hard-and-fast precepts precisely those principles that one later qualifies or modifies in significant degree, to the extent that one does not abandon them altogether. And in this fairly common experience I think it is possible to see a kind of pragmatic instantiation of Wittgenstein's famous image, in the penultimate section of the *Tractatus*, of "throw[ing] away the ladder after [one] has climbed up it" (*TLP*, 6.54).[20]

It is also possible, however, to avoid this whole problem of exposition in the first place.[21] That is an important realization to which Wittgenstein comes after his return to philosophy in 1929 (and is, accordingly, one of relatively few really significant points of difference between his so-called "earlier" and "later" periods). The same recognition, however, at least in implicit form, is also visible much earlier, in the contribution to the critical turn made by Kant's younger contemporary and one-time student Herder. The key text here is the latter's *Treatise on the Origin of Language*.[22] Responding to the question set by the Berlin Academy for its essay competition for the year 1770—"Assuming man left to his natural faculties alone, is he capable of inventing language? And by what means would he accomplish that invention?"—Herder argues, in effect, that the solution to the problem lies in seeing that the question rests on a faulty assumption and so cannot be answered at all on its own terms. The question envisages a situation in which man and the world stand over against each other, each already completely formed in all respects. Man already possesses all his "natural faculties," the world is already fully stocked with the familiar inventory of objects and events. The only thing not yet in place is the bond of language necessary to bring the two together. And the question is then: could man have bridged that gap on his own, or do we not rather have to assume, as some had argued, that such a feat far exceeds mere human powers and could in fact only have been accomplished by God, who, having himself invented language, then imparted it to the earliest humans? Herder's great insight is to recognize that this line of reflection takes as its starting point a supposition that is itself fatally flawed. For there is no such thing as prelinguistic man to begin with. The reason, as Herder shows, is that there is no such thing as prelinguistic consciousness, and in the absence of consciousness it plainly makes no sense to speak of human beings. Similarly, there can be no such thing as an extra-linguistic reality external to us. The world of human experience (again, the only one we are, or ever could be, talking about at all), precisely by virtue of being *human* experience in the first place, is of necessity already conceptually—and that is at once to say, linguistically—ordered. Thus there is strictly speaking no such thing as the "origin" of language, if by that is meant the sort of invention of it contemplated by the question of the Berlin Academy. For prior to language there are neither human beings to have invented it nor a world that could have motivated them to do so. To express the same point in positive terms, language, man, and the world are, of necessity, entirely *co-original* with one another.

II

Neither the Kantian nor the Herderian version of the critical turn is at all in evidence in Rorty's discussion. His argument is developed throughout on the assumption of an exhaustive bipolarity of dogmatic and (protestations to the contrary notwithstanding) skeptical outlooks. Although the exact formulation of the antithesis varies somewhat from one context to another, everywhere one looks in his writings one finds only the same two possibilities envisaged. "There . . . are," we are told, "two ways of thinking about various things. . . . [I]t is the difference between regarding truth, goodness, and beauty as eternal objects which we try to locate and reveal, and regarding them as artifacts whose fundamental design we often have to alter" (*CP*, p. 92). Again, "there are two senses" of such terms as *good, true,* and *real.* These are, respectively, a "special philosophical sense"— the one in which they refer, in the language of the previous passage, to "eternal objects"—and a "homely and shopworn sense"—Rorty's folksy way of speaking of the ordinary, everyday uses of these terms, which he interprets (again in the language of the previous passage) as referring to endlessly alterable "artifacts" (*PMN*, p. 308). We are urged, accordingly, to "view language as conventional behavior, *rather than* as hooking on to the world at designated spots" (*CP*, p. 116; emphasis added). For "we have only *two* alternatives: a 'pure' language-game approach which dispenses with these notions ["of 'correspondence' and 'reference' "] altogether, or a rigidly physicalist approach which interprets them in terms of physical causality" (*CP*, pp. 126–27). On the latter view, that of "[t]he true realistic believer," "our notion of the world" is one "of a hard, unyielding, rigid *être-en-soi* which stands aloof, sublimely indifferent to the attentions we lavish on it"; Rorty terms this notion "an obsession rather than an intuition." On the former we are content to regard the world as simply a system of "ideally coherent beliefs"; for "the only intuition we have of the world as determining truth," he contends, "is just the intuition that we must make our new beliefs conform to a vast body of platitudes, unquestioned perceptual reports, and the like" (*CP*, pp. 13–14).

There is something extraordinarily seductive about an argument that says: it is *either* this way *or* that. And Rorty is nothing if not adroit in repeatedly framing the issue in these terms. Indeed, I think his skill in doing so goes a long way to explain the obviously considerable success his argument has enjoyed in recent years. Exactly two alternatives seems to be, at some psychological level, the most effective number with which to present the person one wishes to convince. One has not quite said simply: this is *the* way things are, take it (if you are intelligent) or leave it (if you are not). And one has thereby significantly reduced the chances of provoking an immediate adverse reaction to one's position by making the person feel patronized. At the same time, however, once one has persuaded one's interlocutor to accept that initial bipolarity as definitive, one has all but eliminated any chance that he will not adopt the position for which one is arguing; for as a practical matter there will now be no alternative to doing so, save to turn to something that one will in the meantime have done one's best to paint in such colors that it would not be found by anyone an even remotely plausible candidate for acceptance. This is a time-honored rhetorical strategy, and I am obviously in no position to criticize the use of it, inasmuch as I am in the end also urging on the reader a choice between two alternatives—what I am calling the "pre-critical" and the "critical" standpoints, respectively. Complicating matters somewhat, however, is the fact that to do so, I must first represent Rorty's bipolarity as itself consisting merely of two versions of a single, common outlook—the "pre-critical" one. Specifically, as I have indicated above, these versions represent merely two different possible reactions to a single basic conception of the relationship between man and the world, one to which both of them are committed in precisely equal measure. And this means in turn that the focus of my argument is inevitably blurred to some extent by the need to shift back and forth between a bipartite and a tripartite perspective.

That still seems to me a comparatively enviable position, however, when contrasted with the lengths to which Rorty is obliged to go to keep his two-stage, "philosophical/post-philosophical" schema intact. To do so, it is necessary that he represent virtually the entire philosophical tradition of the West, from Plato (or, as on some occasions in his writings, Parmenides) up to nearly the present day, as engaged in essentially the same activity. To be sure, he does not shrink from the challenge; but the task is not made any easier merely by facing it squarely. It depends above all on denying that the eighteenth-century "critical turn" really did constitute a fundamentally new direction in thought; and that denial requires imputing to Kant and company a commitment to the very same epistemological model of the *adaequatio intellectus ad rem* that had dominated the tradition up to their time, but to the overthrow of which their "critical" efforts were explicitly directed. Rorty, however, finds this anything but an insuperable difficulty. He speaks easily, for example, of "the Cartesian–Kantian problematic" (*PMN*, p. 8), and, in the paragraph immediately following the one in which this passage occurs, he expands the group to "the Descartes-Locke-Kant tradition" (*PMN*, pp. 8–9). It should be noted, by the way, that Rorty does not always make entirely clear whom he regards as the true initiators of the long-running error of "philosophy." In some places he expressly traces its roots all the way back to the Greeks, while in others he seems to imply that it is largely a post-Renaissance phenomenon. In fact his view seems to be a combination of both positions: while Socrates, Plato, and Aristotle took the first, fatal steps down the "philosophical" path, it was Descartes, Locke, and their successors—including Kant—who imparted to the project the specific form in which it continues to plague us today.

In what, then, does this allegedly unitary "tradition" consist? Its defining mark, says Rorty, is a conception of knowledge dominated by what he calls the "ocular metaphor" (*PMN*, p. 39, passim). Knowledge of anything, understood in accordance with this "metaphor," is conceived of paradigmatically as a matter of "*looking at*" (*PMN*, p. 39) the thing known. The reason for terming this a "metaphor" (apart from the fact that Rorty doesn't think it is what really happens at all when we know, or claim to know, something) is because the "looking" in question is not primarily a matter of literal vision; rather it is something supposed to take place in some way inside us, as a result of the workings of what he calls "the Eye of the Mind" (*PMN*, p. 38f.). But that is only the beginning of Rorty's optical imagery. As he says elsewhere, adding to what turns out to be a rather large and multifaceted complex of images the single element that is for him finally the decisive one, "The picture which holds traditional philosophy captive is that of the mind as a great *mirror*, containing various representations" (*PMN*, p. 12; emphasis added). And further,

> [P]erhaps it helps to think of the original dominating [ocular] metaphor as being that of having our beliefs determined by being brought face-to-face with the object of belief (the geometrical figure which proves the theorem, for example).[23] The next stage is to think that to understand how to know better is to understand how to improve the activity of a quasi-visual faculty, the Mirror of Nature, and thus to think of knowledge as an assemblage of accurate representations. Then comes the idea that the way to have accurate representations is to find, within the Mirror, a special privileged class of representations so compelling that their accuracy cannot be doubted. These privileged foundations will be the foundations of knowledge, and the discipline which directs us toward them—the theory of knowledge—will be the foundation of culture. *The theory of knowledge will be the search for that which compels the mind to belief as soon as it is unveiled.* Philosophy-as-epistemology will be the search for the immutable structures within which knowledge, life, and culture must be contained—structures set by the privileged representations which it studies. (*PMN*, p. 163; emphasis added)

To the extent that this is supposed to apply to Kant as well as, for example, to Descartes or to Locke—and Rorty makes plain that that is indeed his intention—it shows as clearly as I think anything could the extent to which he has simply failed to grasp what is involved in the critical turn.

For a literary critic, especially one (such as myself) whose work has tended to focus on the eighteenth and early nineteenth centuries, the first thing that talk of a "Mirror of Nature" is likely to call to mind is M. H. Abrams's classic study of Romanticism, *The Mirror and the Lamp*. What Abrams describes, in a series of brilliantly executed chapters, are the manifold ways in which at precisely this time the "Mirror" *was replaced by* the "Lamp" as the paradigmatic image of the relationship between man and world. As he explains in his Preface,

> The title of the book identifies two common and antithetic metaphors of mind, one comparing the mind to a reflector of external objects, the other to a radiant projector which makes a contribution to the objects it perceives. The first of these was characteristic of much of the thinking from Plato to the eighteenth century; the second typifies the prevailing romantic conception of the poetic mind.[24]

The qualification "*poetic* mind" reminds us that for the Romantics the "man" whose relationship to the world is at issue is in the first instance the poetic genius. The poet at this time appears as the archetypal embodiment of humanity at large; this is, indeed, a key idea, gradually taking shape over the course of the eighteenth century, that ultimately makes the transition from the "Mirror" to the "Lamp" possible at all. And thus the supplanting of the "Mirror" by the "Lamp" brings with it, at the same time that it is brought about by, a radical reconception of human nature and the human condition generally. That reconception, however, is simply another way of referring to the "critical turn," as characterized above. Or rather, it refers to *both* the critical turn *and* the Idealist metaphysics of subjectivity that followed almost immediately in its wake. The point is of some importance for our understanding of why the critical turn (then as now) only temporarily resolved the philosophical problem to which it was addressed, and thus also why it is something that must be repeated from time to time (a consideration to which we shall return below). The conception of man and world as reciprocally constitutive, which I have been arguing is the key insight marking the critical turn, proves in practice to be extremely difficult to sustain. Poised between the two sides of the pre-critical outlook, it tends to be squeezed by them, so long as they persist as habits of thought, into a vanishingly small logical space. And thus no sooner had the critical turn been introduced in the latter decades of the eighteenth century than it began to slide almost irresistibly into a form of metaphysical dogmatism more or less closely resembling it. As we saw earlier, this was initially the Fichtean system of subjective idealism, followed then in relatively short order by all the other versions of post-Kantian Idealism. The transformation from the critical (back) to the dogmatic drew additional support, moreover, from another development of the time. This was the tendency, which had been growing in strength and influence for

decades largely independently of the particular set of issues at stake
here, to view things as much as possible in aesthetic terms in any case.
And out of this there then emerged, at the turn of the eighteenth century, a mammoth, if relatively short-lived, celebration of the supposedly
limitless capacity of "productive imagination" literally to recreate reality
in its own image.[25]

Now, on one possible reading of the passages from Rorty cited a moment ago, with their implicit insistence that even Kant's thinking about
fundamental questions of epistemology continues to be informed by the
model of the "Mirror," one might conclude that he was simply (if unac-
countably) unaware of the transformation in thought to which Abrams
refers. That supposition, however, strikes me as too implausible to be
entertained seriously. The possibility of a lacuna on this scale in the historical knowledge of someone of Rorty's background and experience
strains credulity to the breaking point. And if we look again at the passages in question, in conjunction with one or two others from elsewhere
in *PMN*, we see that things are in fact not quite so simple as they may
appear at first glance. I believe that Rorty can still be shown to be
wrong, both about Kant in particular and about the critical turn generally. But the error cannot be attributed to mere lack of awareness of the
history of thought.

There is no mistaking, of course, that the passage in which Rorty offers his relatively extended explanation of the "ocular metaphor" is governed throughout by the pre-critical model of the *adaequatio intellectus
ad rem*. He speaks of the conception of knowledge implicit in that "metaphor" as, for instance, one according to which "our beliefs [are] determined by being brought face-to-face with the object of belief" or with
"that which compels the mind to belief as soon as it is unveiled" (*PMN*,
p. 163). The enabling picture for this account is clearly the familiar one
of man and the world in their original state as not yet in contact, but
rather as standing apart from one another in pristine isolation, each already whole and complete in itself. And within the context established
by that picture, to be sure, it makes perfect sense for Rorty then to say,
as he does elsewhere, that "[a]ny theory which views knowledge as accuracy of representation, and which holds that certainty can only be rationally had about representations, will make skepticism inevitable"
(*PMN*, p. 113). Of course, it is also true, as we have seen, that within this
same context skepticism makes dogmatism no less inevitable, and thus
that the two remain permanently deadlocked, with neither able to gain
a decisive advantage over the other. It does not follow, however, although Rorty seems simply to take for granted throughout that it does,
that an understanding of "knowledge as accuracy of representation" can

be had only on the model of the *adaequatio*. This single non sequitur, I think, is ultimately the source of all the problems to which the neopragmatist position gives rise.

To return for the moment to the passage in which Rorty develops the implications of the "ocular metaphor," the question remains: how is Kant to be assimilated to that model without doing obvious violence to the language of the *Critique of Pure Reason*, with its clear rejection of the notion that either man or the world exists, or could exist, prior to or independently of the other? Without that notion, as Kant recognizes, there is nothing to give rise to the *adaequatio*-hypothesis in the first place, and the very idea that an explanation would be needed of how the (assumed) gap between man and world is bridged, with all the paradoxes and confusions to which that idea inevitably leads, is accordingly seen to be otiose. Rorty seems instinctively aware of the problem, and in response to it he introduces an interestingly subtle shift in his characterization of the objects of knowledge to which the "ocular metaphor" would have us trying to make our "representations" somehow correspond:

> The next stage is to think that to understand how to know better is to understand how to improve the activity of . . . [our internal] Mirror of Nature, and thus to think of knowledge as an assemblage of accurate representations. Then comes the idea that the way to have accurate representations is to find, *within the Mirror,* a special privileged class of representations so compelling that their accuracy cannot be doubted. (*PMN*, p. 163; emphasis added)

The fact that this sounds like nothing so much as a gloss of Cartesian rather than Kantian epistemology should not obscure for us the real significance of the move Rorty has made here. He has, as it were, brought everything *inside;* but in so doing he has continued to assume that talk of that internal realm can *only* be in terms of precisely the same *adaequatio*-model that governs the pre-critical conception of our knowledge of the external world. That this move is intended, in particular, to block any attempt to distinguish the Kantian project from the Cartesian or Lockean ones as something not merely different, but indeed radically different in kind, from them is made all but unmistakably clear by the way in which Rorty continues the passage:

> These privileged foundations will be the foundations of knowledge, and the discipline which directs us toward them—the theory of knowledge—will be the foundation of culture. . . . Philosophy-as-epistemology will be the search for the immutable

structures within which knowledge, life, and culture must be contained—structures set by the *privileged representations* which it
studies. (*PMN*, p. 163; emphasis added)

Thus, notwithstanding Kant's analysis of experience as something we
construct rather than something given to us whole and entire in advance, when it comes to identifying the *apparatus* itself by which that
act of construction occurs, he is, in Rorty's view, at bottom every bit as
pre-critical as any of his predecessors. The "pure concepts of the understanding" and the various types of synthesis in which they are engaged are, on this reading, themselves unavoidably posited by Kant as
independently existing objects of knowledge, of which we then seek to
form "accurate representations." And so the very effort to escape the
pre-critical morass only mires him all the more deeply in it. From this
point of view, it is possible to see how a number of otherwise puzzling
things that Rorty says elsewhere about Kant are, at least on their own
terms, plausible, for example, that "the [Kantian] notion of 'transcendental constitution' is entirely parasitical on the Descartes-Locke notion
of the mechanics of inner space" (*PMN*, p. 151, n. 31), or that "Kant was
never troubled by the question of how we could have apodictic knowledge of these 'constituting activities,' for Cartesian privileged access was
supposed to take care of that" (*PMN*, pp. 137–38).[26] In this way, even
the gulf between Kant and Plato may seem to shrink to insignificance:
"[N]othing deep turns on the choice . . . between the imagery of making and of finding" (*PMN*, p. 344).

Let us pause for a moment to consider the implications of all this. At
bottom, Rorty is urging us to view the man who possessed perhaps the
most powerful purely philosophical mind since Aristotle as having been
nevertheless so oblivious to the structure of probably his single most important argument that he incorporated into its very foundations precisely the epistemological model it was designed to overcome.[27]
Fortunately, there is no need to make that assumption. The tip-off that
something is fundamentally amiss in Rorty's account comes (at the latest) when he includes among the implications of the "ocular metaphor"
an implicit desire "to understand how to know *better*," a desire that is to
be realized, as he goes on to say, by "understand[ing] how to *improve*
the activity of . . . the Mirror of Nature" (*PMN*, p. 163; emphasis
added). For while talk of this sort perhaps makes sense against the backdrop of the *adaequatio*-model, it makes none in the context of the effort
in which Kant is engaged. At issue for him is not how to acquire a "better" knowledge of the world (or, for that matter, of ourselves); doing that
is the job of science. The goal of the "critical" philosophy is at once to

ground[28] our knowledge of anything whatever, in whatever degree of scope or precision we may possess it, and, precisely in so doing, to provide a perspicuous account of the *structure* of that knowledge. To do so, it proves necessary to develop, not merely a new set of arguments, but an entirely new type of argument, the transcendental deduction.[29]

The primary concern of this type of argument is not with objects of knowledge under any description. Rather it is with modes of activity, specifically, as Wolff says, "with the methods, limits, sources, and nature of all branches of human inquiry. . . . Transcendental Philosophy is a self-reflective, second-level investigation whose purpose is to test and pass judgment upon the claims of reason in all its manifestations. Hence it presumably should not issue in substantive propositions" (*KMA*, p. 35) at all.[30] Nor should the fact that "[i]n keeping with the practice of his time, Kant employs a faculty psychology" mislead us

> into supposing that a rejection of eighteenth-century psychology necessarily carries with it the repudiation of the Critical Philosophy, for in the *Critique of Pure Reason*, and to varying degrees in the other works as well, the language of mental faculties can be replaced by a more modern vocabulary of mental functions. When Kant discovers a clear distinction between two activities of the mind, he embodies it in a corresponding distinction of faculties. . . . The argument always runs from function to faculty, however, and Kant rarely attempts to infer any substantive fact about mental operations from some unverifiable premise concerning faculties. (*KMA*, pp. 35–36)[31]

Even recognizing all this, however, we do not yet have quite enough to meet Rorty's objection. The key consideration is the way in which, in Kant's view, we actually get at these various "activities of mind" and how what we are able to say about them is derived.

As Wolff notes, for Kant the "cognitive activities" through which the world of experience first comes into being "are performed according to innate rules of the mind." The locus of that activity is above all the *judgments* we make—in more nearly contemporary parlance, the propositions we assert—and "[j]udgment can be understood only if we first analyze judging" (*KMA*, p. 323). That is, however, precisely *not* something to be accomplished through a process of introspection, at least not of the Cartesian sort. Although "Descartes's method of doubt is . . . the first step in the recognition of the priority of the epistemological,"

> Descartes did not carry through the consequences of his method. He continued to employ the categories of substance and cause to

> describe the self which he had discovered. . . . [H]e still viewed
> his problem as that of reestablishing contact between the con-
> scious subject, whose substantial nature he never doubted, and an
> independent objective world order. (*KMA*, p. 321)

Kant, however, aware of the insoluble difficulties to which that assumption inevitably leads, proceeds differently:

> Descartes had asserted, as the premise of his philosophy, that he
> was conscious of himself as a thinking being. But Kant does not
> believe that this is the proper way to phrase the primary evidence
> of an introspective analysis of consciousness. Rather, as he says in
> the Deduction in B [i.e., the revised second edition of the *Cri-
> tique of Pure Reason*], the premise is: "It must be possible for the
> 'I think' to accompany all my representations" [B 131]. The *formal
> unity of all consciousness*, and *not the immediate awareness of a
> thinking being*, serves as the starting point for philosophical argu-
> ment. Mere consciousness without intuition can never yield
> knowledge of any entity, even of myself. (*KMA*, p. 300; emphasis
> added; see also p. 192, *passim*)

The *only* thing necessary to enable Kant to set his argument in motion,
in other words, is the acknowledgment that one is conscious at all (*KMA*,
pp. 56, 60, 111–12, *passim*). He at no point requires an assumption that
we have some special, "privileged" insight into a kind of inner sanctum
of the self, replete with cognitive equipment of all sorts. And it is surely
plain, if anything is, that one cannot without absurdity deny that one is
conscious[32] (any more than, for the opposite reason, one could truthfully
say that one was asleep[33]).

The transcendental deduction in its entirety is an argument of fear-
some complexity, and I do not propose to attempt a comprehensive reconstruction of it here. My concern is rather simply to indicate enough
about the *kind* of argument it represents to show that Rorty's effort to
reduce it to little more than a variant of Cartesianism reflects a fundamental misapprehension of what it is actually about. For almost the first
time in the history of Western thought, Kant bases an argument from
the outset on the recognition that we can never get outside ourselves or
our situatedness. He is intent, in other words, on taking seriously, and
so drawing the full consequences of, precisely the insight that skeptics
and relativists typically believe is their own, but to which in fact they
merely pay a kind of lip service.[34] For in order even to assert the various
claims of conventionalism and contextualism that are the distinguishing
marks of the skeptical or relativist position[35]—the position that I earlier

termed the doctrine of the ubiquity of interpretation—it is necessary that one have adopted oneself vis-à-vis all (and one cannot underscore *all* too strongly here) discourses, all perspectives, all points of view, a standpoint that is not merely by the terms of one's own argument self-contradictory, but one that, if that argument is thought through to the end, literally cannot exist at all.[36]

This last observation, to be sure, may seem to be merely two ways of saying the same thing; and in fact the two points are at bottom not far apart. Nevertheless, I think there is also a useful distinction to be drawn between them. The first is more a matter of straight logic, namely the familiar charge that skepticism-cum-relativism is self-referentially inconsistent. The argument goes like this: if relativism really were universally true (and if it did not claim to be that, it would pack approximately the same philosophical punch as the cliché that it takes all kinds of people to make a world), because it denies the possibility of any such thing as universal truth (that denial being simply what relativism *is*), then it could not after all be true in the first place. For to assert that it is a universal truth that there is no universal truth is plainly absurd. Q. E. D. Some professed relativists today believe they can escape this dilemma. Because the price of doing so, however, is at the same time to reject the principle, fundamental to rationality itself, that one cannot coherently assert a contradiction, while there is not much that can be said to them in response, there is obviously not much that needs to be either. We will have occasion later to look more closely at the ways in which Rorty's argument in particular issues ultimately in a kind of programmatic irrationalism. The second of the two points just noted—the literal impossibility of a standpoint from which skepticism and relativism could together be enunciated—cuts, however, if anything even more deeply against that ostensible position. Logic by itself, after all, may seem to be not merely a fairly abstract business (as, of course, in one sense it is), but also a fairly remote one, something that, while it may impinge on one's most fundamental and deeply held convictions, need not do so. But let us consider what radical conventionalism or radical contextualism (again, ultimately two ways of referring to the same thing), on the assumption that it were possible at all, would actually entail, this time not so much in the sense of the inferential relationships among propositions that would result, but at what we might call the existential-pragmatic level.

To speak of something as (merely) a context of belief entails, first, the existence of a plurality of such contexts. Otherwise, as we saw earlier in a slightly different connection, the expression itself would simply be devoid of content. Talk of a single "context of belief" would be as uninformative (and thus as useless) as would be, for example, the concept of "life," if everything were held to be, in some sense, alive. Schopenhauer makes a similar point in the realm of theology when he characterizes pantheism as merely a polite form of atheism. Just as the attempt to propound a theory of radical animism, so to speak, would ineluctably deprive itself of its own starting point, so also would radical contextualism, if it did not posit the existence of multiple contexts. But, second, there must also be some way of comparing and contrasting different contexts. Otherwise, again, the concept of "context" would itself be emptied of meaning, this time from the other side. If acceptance of that concept commits the one who believes in it to the existence of a set or class that it defines, precisely this acceptance also commits the believer to at least some degree of commonality among the members of the set. For just as the notion of "life" means nothing if absolutely everything is held to be "alive," so the class of living things is not a class at all (or at any rate not that class) if it numbers among its members things that are not alive. This much, of course, is so uncontroversial as to be virtually trivial. What else after all, it may be asked, have the proponents of radical contextualism been maintaining all along? Indeed, this *is* what they have been maintaining, at least in part. It is important, however, to recognize that all this is in fact strictly entailed if the radical contextualist position is even to be coherent, which is obviously the minimal condition of its being either true or false. But let us see where this line of reflection has now brought us.

There is, first of all, on this view, no single (or, as it is sometimes put today, "master") context of belief. Second, however, all the contexts that there are must have at least enough in common with one another for them to be identifiable as such. That point in common is precisely their contextuality, which is to say, their partiality, their determination in accordance with some perspective in particular. And that in turn entails their necessary *inability* to provide a definitive account of how things objectively are. Finally, there is nothing but an (indefinitely large) plurality of such contexts; this last claim is, of course, just the first one again, expressed in slightly different form. Left out of account in all this, however, is any consideration either of the nature of that context itself in which these three claims must, of necessity, be situated in their own right (for there is, by hypothesis, simply nowhere extra-contextual for them to be) or of the status of this context in the very system that those claims purport to describe. Once this question is raised, however, it at once becomes clear that the system is so structured that there can be no place in it for such a context at all. For this (non-)context has the unique property of seeking to locate itself between positions that, on its own terms, together already exhaust logical space. The upshot of the argument for radical contextualism is thus to leave that argument itself with literally nowhere to go and thus nowhere to be.

On the one hand, it cannot be a (or the) "master" context (however much it may appear to resemble a candidate for that role), for, again, by hypothesis, there just is no such thing. But neither is this "contextualist context" simply one context among all the many others. Again, it cannot be. For unlike any of them, it is the one from which it is purportedly possible to speak precisely of contexts themselves, and, moreover, to speak comprehensively of them. (Here, of course, the proximity of the present line of argument to the one from self-referential inconsistency seen a moment ago becomes especially apparent.) It is, in other words, at least in implicit intent, the *meta*-context embracing all first-level contexts. But at the same time, inasmuch as its very arrogation to itself of that status depends on the assertion that there are *only* first-level contexts—its assumption of that position is, indeed, identical with this assertion—it must itself, if it is to be (literally) anything at all, strive to represent itself as every bit as much a first-level context as any other. It must, that is, simultaneously define and so constitute the set of all contexts and be itself a member of that very set. It has long been recognized, however, that that sort of bilocation is impossible. (Russell's Paradox, as is well known, neatly illustrates the incoherence that results from supposing that sets can be members of themselves.) In perhaps somewhat more down-to-earth terms, the reason that the "contextualist context" reserves for itself as the only possible position it can occupy a position that it has at the same time firmly closed off from being occupied by anything (and which is thus literally no position at all) is that it must on its own terms be in two mutually exclusive places at once. And the reason for that, in turn, as I have suggested, is simply that there neither is nor can be any such thing as a thoroughgoing skepticism at all. Skepticism, in the end, is merely the form that dogmatism assumes when it develops a bad conscience about itself.

If all this still seems merely so much logic-chopping, let me see if I cannot make use of a familiar (and, it is sometimes supposed, unanswerable) question to render things more concrete. If a tree falls in the forest, and no one is around to hear it, does it make a sound? A Berkeleyan idealist, committed to the doctrine of *esse est percipi* (and leaving out of account for the moment the hypothesis of an all-perceiving God, which is itself not merely thoroughly ad hoc but, on Berkeley's own terms, actually incoherent), has to say that it does not. The pre-critical realist objects that this entails the counterintuitive conclusion that the laws of physics can be, as it were, suspended for lack of a quorum. But he founders in turn on the idealist's retort that he must then present an account of what (for example) sound *is*, absent anyone's (or anything's) perception of it. For he discovers that he is unable even to conceive of the situation that gives rise to the problem—let us say, the majestic pine, weakened by age or disease or infestation or some other cause, toppling to earth amidst the surrounding trees, slowly at first, but with ever-increasing speed, until it finally comes to rest in a shower of dust and debris—without in the same moment implicitly placing an observer (himself) on the scene. That scene need not, of course, be envisaged in anything like this much detail. But it cannot not be envisaged at all, however abstractly. And once that has happened, there is inescapably already someone present, perceiving for all he is worth. Precisely the point at issue here was made once, interestingly enough, in the course of an episode of the television comedy *Cheers*, with both wonderful conciseness and the sort of slightly off kilter brilliance sometimes exhibited by the character who provides the key observation. The would-be know-it-all mailman Cliff Clavin has just introduced the tree-falling-in-the-forest case as an example of what he wants to say is an unanswerable question. To this, Coach (the character in question) responds, "If no one was there, how do you know it fell?" It is easy, I think, to miss just how apt a response this is. Cliff certainly does. Undaunted, he tries to save the example by expanding it: "I saw the tree standing in the forest yesterday," he says, "and I came back today and saw it lying on the ground." Coach's philosophical instincts, however, are far too sound for him to be fazed by this (even if his grip on reality at large is occasionally a bit tenuous): "What if," he asks, "a group of beavers came along and chewed through the tree and then lowered it gently to the ground?" Cliff at least knows when he is licked: "You got me there, Coach," he concedes; to which Coach responds, obviously a bit disappointed in his interlocutor, "I don't know, Cliffy, you're just not prepared at all tonight."

The point, of course, is not that the tree-falling-in-the-forest question cannot be answered. It is that the question cannot even be *asked*. Cliff, however, is far from alone in thinking that it can. One reason this confusion occurs as readily as it does appears to have something to do with the ostensible question's being framed specifically in terms of sound. I have no idea what it is about auditory phenomena in particular that is so conducive to this sort of confusion. Whatever the reason for it, however, what happens in such cases seems to be basically this. We find ourselves confronted with two possibilities, both of which, at least initially, we feel able to formulate as prima facie coherent hypotheses, but neither of which, on reflection, seems at all plausible as a description of an actual state of affairs. On the one hand, we have, as it were, the silent-movie version of the story. We imagine the tree falling, with bark cracking, wood splintering, branches being torn off, and the trunk finally slamming into the ground with tremendous force, but all of this occurring (because, by hypothesis, no one is there to hear it) in the complete absence of sound, as if the whole forest had been placed in a vacuum. And, we think to ourselves (rightly, of course), surely that is absurd. So we try what seems the only other possibility. We turn up the volume, while at the same time consciously removing from our imagined scene all trace of an audience. Then we are left with what might be called free-floating sound, however, and that does not prove appreciably easier to deal with than the picture we just rejected. For we now have to imagine that precisely the same thing that *we* would have experienced, had we actually been present, as a result of the vibrations in the air generated by a falling tree striking our ears is somehow still "there," even though we are not. But that does not seem to be a position that anyone could very well take either. And so in the end, unwilling to opt for either of these views, we fall back on the conclusion that we simply have one of those "unanswerable questions" on our hands and let it go at that.

In all this we have failed to notice, however, that the problem with which we are having so much difficulty is by no means peculiar to the realm of auditory phenomena. Precisely analogous questions can be formulated about the tree in connection with any mode of perception, including the one we have been taking for granted all along, the visual. Here we see the brilliance of Coach's initial response to Cliff. What he in effect points out is that if you can ask whether a tree falling in the forest with no one around to hear it makes a sound, you can with equal right ask whether a tree falling in the forest with no one around to *see* it falls at all. But nobody, it is surely safe to say, has ever thought that the latter constituted an "unanswerable question," fraught with deep, yet at the same time never quite accessible, philosophical significance.[37] Events relatable primarily to our visual sense seem perfectly unambiguous with regard to their status as phenomena. One would have to be a determined idealist indeed to maintain that a necessary condition of the bare occurrence of such an event was the presence on the scene of somebody to watch it taking place.[38]

I think it unlikely, however, that everyone is going to be satisfied with this. All well and good, I can imagine someone interjecting at this point, but nothing that has been said thus far amounts in the end to anything more than evading the issue. Do trees fall silently in certain circumstances, or don't they? The law of excluded middle tells us that it's got to be one or the other: x or $\sim x$, *tertium non datur.* This apparently entirely natural question, together with the difficulty that I think more than a few people experience in not asking it (I certainly know this to be true in my own case), or, conversely, the degree of effort that is required both to recognize why it is in fact a non-question and also to sustain that recognition, testifies as forcefully as I think anything could to just how deeply ingrained the pre-critical outlook is in us. And because frontal assaults are almost invariably ineffective in cases such as this, I want to try another flanking attack on it, this time from the opposite direction.

One of the most distinctive of all scents is that of a pine forest. Does a pine forest have a scent, however, if there is no one around capable of smelling it? And what about the feel of pine needles or pine cones or pine bark? Do they feel like anything at all if there does not happen to be someone at the moment touching them? And, having gone this far, we may as well proceed all the way to the end. To my knowledge, I have never eaten any part of a pine tree, but presumably if I were to, it would taste like something—that is, it would have *some* flavor, whether or not I would be able to characterize that flavor in terms of anything more generally familiar. But what does, for example, a pine needle taste like when no one is around to sample it? By this point, to be sure, the reader could not very well be blamed for feeling that we had left the realm of (more or less) down-to-earth philosophy for the conceptual twilight zone of such things as Zen koans. The point, however, is to recognize that these questions of smell, touch, and taste are precisely analogous to our earlier ones regarding what (if anything) a falling tree sounds like when no one is listening or, indeed, what that same tree does at all if no one happens to be looking. Nonetheless, despite that recognition of the formal indistinguishability of these phenomena, our virtually automatic inclination is to arrange them on a scale as follows. What we think of as primarily visual events are unambiguous in one direction; they happen whether there are witnesses to them or not. Olfactory, tactile, and gustatory events are correspondingly unambiguous in the other direction; they require for their very existence the participation and thus, obviously, the presence of the one whose sensations they are. And auditory events, finally, occupy a kind of mysterious middle ground, not quite assignable to either end of the scale; thus they give rise to ultimately "unanswerable" questions. That inclination itself, however, is possible only on the basis of a thoroughly pre-critical epistemology. And in this way, again, we are able to see that it is precisely the pre-critical outlook that is ultimately at the root of all the confusions and aporias from which we are endeavoring to extricate ourselves here.

The pre-critical outlook, we recall, is essentially the belief that man and the world can each be thought of apart from the other. On this view, it makes sense to say that we can, as it were, "think away" the world— everything, that is, that is not man, whatever we take that to consist in in its own right—and be left simply with man alone, absolutely un-changed from what he is now. And so also in the opposite direction: we can imagine man removed from the cosmos (an all-too-real possibility, of course, in the latter half of the twentieth century)—we can, indeed, imagine that the human race had never evolved at all (a by no means implausible scenario, as even a modest acquaintance with the physical-chemical conditions of human life makes clear)—and not thereby change the world one iota (apart, obviously, from those respects in which human actions of one sort or another had, or would have, affected it). From quarks to galaxies, everything would be exactly as it is now and would function exactly as it does now, with the sole exception that we would no longer be part of the scene. I think it is safe to say that most people have always found this picture, or some variant of it, entirely plausible, especially the latter half of it. For while it may require some-thing of a leap of abstractive faith to give any actual content to the notion of man-as-he-is in a completely worldless state, it seems at first glance no more than common sense to acknowledge that the world-as-it-is is not (or not in any way that has any important philosophical implications) dependent on our being part of it. For, after all, we have *not* always been part of it. The cosmos is vastly older than the human race. Are we to suppose, for example, that the solar system would not have formed, that the continents would not have taken shape as they did, or that dino-saurs would not have roamed the earth, if evolution had taken a slightly different turn and *homo sapiens* had never arisen? Such a retroactive cancellation of history—for that is what, at least initially, it would ap-pear to amount to—is surely as absurd a hypothesis as any could be.

On the other hand, however, once the apparently so commonsensical pre-critical view has been adopted, we have seen that insuperable dif-ficulties at once present themselves in explaining how the two, by hy-pothesis, mutually independent sides of the man-world relationship can get together even in principle, much less how they ever in fact do so. And in that circumstance, again, two, and only two, paths appear to be available to us. We can become dogmatists, taking an even greater leap of faith than before, and say, in effect, that although we don't actually know how it gets done, plainly it does, somehow, and that is enough. Or we can become skeptics and deny that it ever gets done at all. But hav-ing made that denial, we cannot very well stop there. For the world is clearly full of people saying all sorts of things about all sorts of things, and because, as skeptics, we have ruled out as philosophically unsup-portable the supposition that any of them is actually establishing contact with the world as it really is, we have to find some other way of char-acterizing the activity in which they are engaged. At this point talk of

ubiquitous interpretation, of the inescapability of "contexts of belief,"
and all the rest begins. What remains unnoticed throughout this process, however, is that precisely in opting for the skeptical path one has
not only not overcome the pre-critical gulf between man and world, one
has actually institutionalized it. To put the matter in slightly different
terms: one has concluded that the idea of a completely extra-contextual,
non-perspectival, wholly disinterested standpoint from which one could
survey the totality of objects of knowledge while at the same time not
being oneself part of that totality—an epistemological "Archimedean
point" outside of and distinct from *everything*—expresses an impossible
aspiration. So far, so good. But, as we have seen, the skeptical approach
leaves one no way of doing away with that view except by adopting oneself—only provisionally, of course, and not for an instant longer than absolutely necessary—the position of precisely such an Archimedean
point. One occupies the discredited throne but believes that one is
thereby doing something different from the dogmatists who held it previously because, unlike them, one is using the authority it confers only
to dismantle it. That, of course, never happens, however, and not (or not
primarily) because of any conscious disingenuousness on the part of
those whose professed goal it is. It never happens because the goal itself
and the way in which one is trying to reach the goal are hopelessly in
contradiction with one another.

The only way in which any sense can be given to the doctrine of ubiquitous interpretation or radical contextualism—that is, again, the notion
that we can never talk of things as literally being such and such a way,
but only of their seeming so, or of their being interpreted in that way—
is on the assumption of a radical separability of man and world. That
assumption, however, is itself not merely false; it is incoherent. Reduced
to its bare essentials, this is the burden of my argument here. So far as
I am aware, it is an insight that was first achieved by Kant, Herder, and
a few others in the eighteenth century. It represents the essence of what
I am here calling the "critical turn." Another way to express the same
insight is to say (borrowing a phrase used several times by Rorty, though
obviously not with the same end in view) that situatedness "goes all the
way down." Precisely because we *cannot* get outside of ourselves—ourselves as reflected specifically in our language, but more generally in
our form of life at large—there neither is nor could be a perspective
available to us from which *everything* that we think, say, and do could
appear as (much less actually be shown to be) merely one context of belief, one interpretation, one set of interests among others.

But what of the objection that the critical turn is after all just subjective idealism all over again? How, in other words, starting from this

alleged insight, are we to account, for example, for the reality of the dinosaurs, as well as for everything else that happened long before there
were human beings around to be "situated" in any fashion, not to speak
of everything that has gone on in the universe since the time that humans first appeared but of which we are only now gradually becoming
aware? The answer is the same in both cases: it is that there is no other
way of providing a coherent version of the desired account except in the
terms of the "critical" insight. Let us recall what we saw to be the implications of the tree-falling-in-the-forest example. The notion of *factuality* itself—or, as Kant might put it, *phenomenality*—includes, as part
of its very concept, that we are (in one of the most overworked, as well
as most frequently misused, phrases in recent memory, but to which,
alas, I am unable to find an alternative) *always already* there. Not necessarily any one of us in particular, of course, and not necessarily literally on the spot. One principal confusion giving rise to Berkeleyan
idealism is traceable to just this sort of excessive literalism in our thinking. Like most deep confusions, however, it also arises through what
seems initially a perfectly unproblematic application of common sense:
sometimes, we say, forests have people in them; sometimes they don't.
In general, sometimes there is somebody around; sometimes there
isn't. In the terms of a passage from the *Philosophical Investigations*
cited earlier, however, it is precisely here that we have taken the fatal
"first step" into conceptual quicksand, and it was "the one that altogether escape[d] notice," indeed "the very one that we thought quite
innocent" (*PI*, § 308). The way out of this impasse, as we also saw earlier,
is, in Charles Altieri's words (speaking fluent Wittgensteinian), "to deny
the way in."[39] And that means to deny that *facts* ever occur in the radical
absence of human beings.[40] Alternatively, to express the same point in
positive fashion, it is to assert the thesis, introduced earlier, of the reciprocal constitutiveness of man and world. We cannot even conceive of
a fact without implicitly locating ourselves in what we might call *conceptual presence* to that fact. We recall, for example, the impossible situation that arises when we try both to imagine the tree falling with no
one around to hear (or see or smell or touch or taste) it and, at the same
time, to clear the scene completely of all observers, including ourselves.
Nor, on the other hand, can we so much as conceive of ourselves absent
all experience of anything whatever. Even a sensory deprivation tank involves an experience of something. To invert another shibboleth of contemporary skepticism, absences are also presences.

This "conceptual presence"[41] is not simply a kind of metaphor for literal presence. It is logically prior to notions of both literalness and met-
aphoricity, inasmuch as both those notions express possibilities that

occur within the world. Here we are speaking, however, of the shape of
the world in toto. And we have found ourselves ineluctably led to the
conclusion that that world is in no sense even so much as conceivable,
except as indissolubly linked to the human beings whose world it is. And
just as "conceptual presence" is not dependent on any one spatial location in particular (for example, the literal spot at which the fact in question occurs), neither is it bound to any given moment in time (for
example, the present). The reason in each case, as we might put it in
Kantian terms, is that among its defining elements are the forms of spa-
tiality and temporality themselves. Thus there is no difficulty in acknowledging that we can be (indeed, are) "conceptually present" to, say,
the dinosaurs in a way that is epistemologically in no wise inferior to,
and hence no more problematic than, the way in which we are present
to what is going on in front of us this minute. The fact that I could right
now give for all intents and purposes an exhaustive inventory of the contents of the desk at which I am writing this, while we obviously still have
quite a bit to learn about the dinosaurs, is a purely contingent matter
and hence one with no bearing on the underlying epistemological issue.
The questions of what in particular we happen to know, when we happen to know it, how we happen to have learned it, and even how we go
about revising our views in light of subsequent developments, are all
logically subsequent to, and insofar distinct from, the question of the
nature and conditions of factuality itself.

III

Heidegger expresses essentially the
point at which I am getting here with his notion of "Being-in-the-world".
(*In-der-Welt-sein*), understood as a basic—more basic than which literally *nothing*—constitutive category of the mode of being that he calls
Dasein. As usual, however, Wittgenstein both grasps the point fully and
is also able to formulate it without resorting, as Heidegger all too often
finds necessary, to the almost limitless capacity for neologism that German grammar makes available to the dedicated metaphysician. In passage after passage, Wittgenstein refers to what he calls the ultimate
"ungroundedness" of our most fundamental ways of thinking, speaking,
and acting. Such passages are found perhaps most frequently in *On Certainty*, but the same insight is clearly visible in his thought from the
beginning.[42] This is, indeed, one important respect in which his work in

philosophy is essentially continuous from beginning to end. His use specifically of the term "ungroundedness," however, along with a number of other similar expressions, has provided fertile ground for misapprehension of the point that he is actually intent on making. That we are "ungrounded," in Wittgenstein's sense, does not mean that there is somehow a kind of space beneath us in which a "ground" could go, but which unfortunately just happens to be empty, and that we are therefore left, as it were, epistemologically floating in mid-air. His point is that there is no such space at all. We are, again, always already as "far down," so to speak, as it is possible to be, or even to conceive of being. There is nothing beneath us, not in the sense that there is nothing beneath someone who has just stepped off a cliff. Rather it is in the sense that if there is *nothing* between two objects, then those objects are entirely contiguous with one another. To vary the image, the sense in question is that of there being, for example, nothing beneath a fish in water that is not at the same time on every other side of it as well. In that case, however, the notion itself of there being "nothing beneath one" drops out. We are from the outset thoroughly immersed in our linguistic-epistemological-existential element, and any further question of "support" or "ground" simply does not (because it cannot) arise, any more than we could intelligibly ask what is under the center of the earth or what holds up the earth itself. It would be as if one were to try to go further north from the North Pole (or in any direction *but* south from there). To put the same point in slightly different terms, to suppose that there is something either marvelous or problematic about the bedrock indissolubility of the link between man and world—which supposition, as we have seen, is what first sets one on the path of skepticism—is analogous to regarding it as a matter of our great good fortune that the earth's atmosphere is composed of precisely those gases, and in precisely those proportions, that are necessary to sustain human life, for otherwise we would certainly find ourselves in a pickle.[43]

All this, as I have indicated, was recognized more than two centuries ago by Kant, Herder, and others. Thus Kant's argument in particular, to remain with it a moment longer, nowhere depends—Rorty's assertion to the contrary notwithstanding—on a claim of "privileged" access to an inner realm of, as it were, super-representations. In Wolff's words, "The unity of consciousness is [for Kant] a fact of logic, not a datum of introspective psychology" (*KMA*, p. 105, n. 19). As Kant himself expresses it in the *Critique of Pure Reason:* "It must be possible for the 'I think' to accompany all my representations; for otherwise something would be represented in me which could not be thought at all, and that is equivalent to saying that the representation would be impossible, or

at least would be nothing to me" (B 131–32). The phenomenon to which
Kant refers here is usually termed the "transcendental unity of apperception." It is of pivotal importance for an understanding of the "critical"
philosophy to recognize that this "transcendental unity of apperception"
is itself *identical with* the Kantian "transcendental ego." The latter expression, which, as Wolff notes, also identifies "the locus of the activity
of synthesis" (*AR*, p. 10) by which the world of experience is constituted,
is simply another name for the former. The term *transcendental ego*
thus refers *not* to some separate entity in its own right, although this
appears to be how Rorty understands it, on analogy with the Cartesian
"soul." Rather it points to a merely *logical* feature of human experience,
namely, again, the necessary possibility of "I think" being attached to all
my mental representations, if they are to be *my* representations at all.[44]
For Kant, at bottom, as later for Wittgenstein, "everything lies open to
view" (*PI*, § 126), and it is simply a matter of displaying in as perspicuous
a fashion as possible the logic of what we are already doing: "The problems are solved, not by giving new information, but by arranging what
we have always known" (*PI*, § 109).[45]

If Kant's argument is not in any sense dependent on Cartesian introspection itself, however, it is nonetheless also true that the argument
gives needless hostages to fortune in the extent to which it relies on the
thoroughly introspective vocabulary of rationalist metaphysics, even as
it attempts to adapt that vocabulary to the expression of the "critical"
insight. The influence of the inventor of the German version of that vocabulary, the (in his own time) much-celebrated *praeceptor Germaniae*
Christian Wolff, would be difficult to overestimate in this regard.
Wolff's work represents, indeed, a far more important chapter in the
history of the German language than it does in the history of philosophy,
German or otherwise. Modern German philosophy begins, of course,
with Leibniz. But Leibniz, as is well known, and despite an occasional
nod in the direction of his native language as a legitimate vehicle for
serious philosophy, himself wrote almost nothing in German, preferring
to work in the two then-dominant languages of philosophy, Latin and
French. It thus fell primarily, if not quite exclusively, to Wolff, whose
own work consists largely in a kind of eclectic systematization of Leib-
nizian themes in conjunction with ideas derived from a number of other
thinkers, for all intents and purposes to invent a German philosophical
idiom. And this, then, was the vocabulary that Kant inherited a generation later. Not until the appearance on the scene of a group of extremely gifted semi-outsiders from the standpoint of professional
academic philosophy, among them Herder, were the first serious efforts
made to shake off this vocabulary, with all the difficulties it inevitably

created for the formulation of a body of thought intent on moving beyond the very sort of philosophizing for which it had originally been developed.

Interestingly, both the essence of the problem itself and the indication of how it could nevertheless be resolved appear together at the same juncture in the overall architectonic of the first *Critique*. The first step in the exposition of the Transcendental Analytic (the section containing the heart of the entire "critical" argument) is what Kant terms "The (Transcendental) Clue to the Discovery of All Pure Concepts of the Understanding" (A 67–83, B 92–109). Also known as the "Metaphysical Deduction," this is the point at which he produces what he calls the "Table of Judgments" (A 70, B 95). From that, in turn, he derives the "Table of Categories" (= "Pure Concepts of the Understanding") (A 80, B 106), the argument for the objective validity of which is then the primary concern of the remainder of the Analytic. That argument, the *transcendental* deduction of the categories, consists in showing that these categories are objectively valid for our experience, precisely because they constitute that experience in the first place. The argument develops this conclusion by demonstrating that the constitutive function of the categories is inherent in the logic of consciousness itself, as reflected above all in the "transcendental unity of apperception."[46] Thus, as indicated earlier, it requires no assumption beyond one that cannot coherently be denied—namely, that one is conscious at all—in order to be undertaken. If we have learned anything from Wittgenstein, however, it is, again, surely that we need to be especially alert to what is going on when apparently innocent first steps are taken in putting together a line of argumentation. Certainly the importance of such alertness becomes especially clear in the case at hand.

What perhaps strikes us most immediately is that, despite Kant's express concern to have provided with the Table of Judgments a comprehensive schematic representation of "the function of thought in judgment" (A 70, B 95) and his evident belief that he has succeeded in doing so, the Table of Judgments with which he in fact presents us is, to put it mildly, a less than exhaustive survey of the territory it purports to cover. Moreover, as Wolff notes,

> Kant's own papers, in which he can be seen working up the doctrines of the Critical Philosophy, reveal that he tinkered endlessly with the lists of Judgments and Categories before hitting on the principle of four sets of three.[47] Furthermore, in contradistinction to the order of argument of the Metaphysical Deduction, Kant quite evidently adjusted the Table of Judgments so that it would yield the desired Table of Categories. (*KMA*, p. 62)

More serious than this, however, as Wolff also notes, is the consideration that the basic *connection* Kant claims to have discovered between the Table of Judgments and the Table of Categories, a connection clearly necessary to justify regarding the former as the decisive "clue" to the latter, is itself nowhere demonstrated:

> [T]he argument is arbitrary in the extreme. No proof is given for the key statement that "The same function which gives unity to the various representations *in a judgment* also gives unity to the mere synthesis of various representations *in an intuition . . .*" [B 104-5]. . . . This is probably the weakest link in the entire argument of the Analytic. The appearance from nowhere of the Table of Judgments and the rather flimsy argument to the Table of Categories are entirely unconvincing. (*KMA*, p. 77)

Wolff adds at once, however, that "[t]he failings of the Metaphysical Deduction are not fatal, . . . for in the Analytic of Principles Kant returns to the individual categories and deduces them from the characteristics of time-consciousness" (*KMA*, p. 77).

There is no doubt, of course, that this is Kant's intention; whether the argument intended to achieve that end is in all respects successful is as may be. As noted earlier, the particulars of the transcendental deduction itself lie outside the scope of the present discussion. With their reconstructions of that argument scholars such as Wolff, Allison, and others have in any case, it seems to me, probably presented about as strong a case for its validity as anyone is likely to be able to offer. But, as I have indicated, it is primarily the *type* of argument that Kant develops here that is of interest, not each of its components considered in its own right, nor even whether the entire argument in precisely the form in which Kant presents it can in the end withstand every sort of objection that might be brought against it. Wolff himself notes that in fact there seems little prospect of presenting even the specifically epistemological portion of the "critical" philosophy as both a complete and a wholly consistent structure of thought; and this is not yet to speak of the still greater difficulties, alluded to above, that one encounters in trying to fit every section of the overall Kantian edifice—epistemological, ethical, aesthetic, as well as historical, theological, scientific, and the rest—together with all the others. Again, however, for purposes of the argument I am putting forward here, none of this constitutes a serious objection. To profess oneself a Platonist, for example, it is by no means necessary that one find compelling every argument without exception that Plato presents on the entire range of topics—virtually co-extensive with philosophy itself—that are addressed at one point or another in his works. The notion of a "Platonist" standpoint on this or that question has a well-understood sense, sanctioned by long usage in philosophical discourse. And so also with the notion of a (broadly) Kantian outlook, in particular as it pertains to the nature and status of knowledge or knowledge claims.

In his Introduction to the collection *Critical Theory Since 1965*, Hazard Adams speaks of "the thought of Kant" as "seem[ing] to us today to cry out for transference of the notion of the constitutive from the mind to language."[48] In light of what we have now seen, however, it might be better to speak, not so much of a "transference" of Kant's central notion to a realm by implication more or less foreign to the one in terms of which he himself originally conceived it, but rather of a *return* of that notion to precisely the ground on which the first steps toward its formulation were actually taken. Kant, that is, begins his argument as basically a *linguistic* one; the Table of Judgments is, in essence, simply an attempt to express what Wittgenstein would later call "the general form of a proposition" (*TLP,* 4.5, *passim*).[49] Committed as he is, however, to the very vocabulary of rationalist faculty psychology that he is in process of rendering obsolete, Kant almost immediately turns the argument in the direction of a conceptual apparatus fundamentally incompatible with it. In doing so, he to a certain extent betrays his own best insight (in addition to creating the problem for the logic of the exposition at large that we have just seen noted by Wolff) by in effect introducing a fundamental separation of *language* and *mind.* The gap separating the Table of Judgments and the Table of Categories cannot be bridged, any more than a gap between *man* and *world* can be bridged once *it* has been admitted. The point, of course, is that the gap between the two Tables was never necessary in the first place, just as the acknowledgment of a fundamental split between man and world never was or ever could be necessary either, and for ultimately the same reason.

The central insight of the Kantian "epistemological turn" is perfectly—with the benefit of hindsight, one might even say obviously—correct. In Wolff's words:

> The epistemological turn is the progressive substitution of epistemological for ontological or metaphysical considerations. It is the recognition that the knowing subject can never be ignored, or bracketed out. Since all knowledge is the knowledge by a subject, even the most general investigation of the modes and categories of being will have to begin with an analysis of the limits and preconditions of knowing. We may abstract from the perceptual peculiarities of the individual, from the particular state of scientific

advance of his age, and even from the most pervasive social and
cultural biases, but we can never abstract from the subject *qua*
knowing human being. If there are forms of perception and cognition which are inherent in the fact of consciousness itself, then
these will constitute the limits of Being, so far as it can be discussed at all. To extend our investigation beyond those limits will
involve us in an empty play of words for which no content can ever
be provided. . . . [I]t is self-contradictory to inquire what objects
are like independently of being perceived and conceived . . . [that
is] what they are like *in themselves.* (*KMA*, pp. 320–21)

Or as Allison puts it:

The objective validity of the categories is to be explained in terms
of their role in judgment. Thus to say that the categories are objectively valid is to claim that they make possible, "ground," or "legitimate" an objectively valid synthesis of representations, that is,
a judgment. But since it is only in and through judgments that we
represent objects, the objective validity of the categories can also
be said to consist in the fact that they are necessary conditions for
the representation of objects. (*KTI*, p. 135)[50]

To the objection that our " 'ordinary sense' [of reality] includes and
must include the idea of an ontologically independent object" and thus
that "the result [of Kant's argument] is scepticism, no matter what one
calls it," Wolff continues,

there can be no answer beyond a careful reiteration of all the reasons why such a demand is self-contradictory. Universality and necessity are all you can get, Kant says in effect. Therefore, they are
all it has ever been legitimate to demand. Anyone who persists in
asking what the world is *really* like—in other words, who wishes
to know what an object is like independently of the conditions of
his knowing what it is like—must then simply be dismissed as un-
serious. In the terminology of a later philosophical school, he
needs to be cured, not answered. (*KMA*, pp. 322–23)

The allusion at the end of this passage is, of course, to Wittgenstein,
specifically to the latter's conception of philosophy as a kind of "therapy"
(*PI*, § 133). To recognize this, however, is at the same time to be reminded all the more forcefully of the one pivotal respect in which Kant
and Wittgenstein do differ from one another, the respect in which, as we
might say, Kant stops just short of drawing the decisive consequence of
his own breakthrough. If the quintessential activity of mind by which we

come to know the world, understood to include not merely phenomena external to us but even ourselves as well, is that of *judgment;* if, indeed, the only satisfactory account we can give of how the world, again including ourselves, comes into being at all is in terms of that activity of mind; and if, as Wolff notes, "[j]udgment can be understood only if we we first analyze judging" (*KMA*, p. 323); then it would appear to follow that our primary concern must be with what is necessarily the locus of all judging, namely language. And that is to say that the critical turn has not yet truly been completed so long as it remains (merely) "epistemological." It realizes itself fully only when it has constituted itself as "linguistic."

As suggested earlier, this was precisely Herder's move. It was, moreover, one that he had made even *before* Kant's more nearly exclusively "epistemological" version of the "turn" appeared in 1781.[51] The primary texts here are the *Treatise on the Origin of Language* of 1770, mentioned above, and the somewhat later *On Knowing and Feeling in the Human Soul*, the final version of which was published in 1778, but on which Herder had been working for some time prior to that date, as reflected in preliminary drafts from the years 1774 and 1775. The foundations of the Herderian "linguistic turn," however, had already been laid in his first published work, the essay *On Diligence in Several Learned Languages* of 1764, as well as in another short piece composed at about the same time but not prepared for publication entitled *Essay on Being.* The latter was in fact written under the direct influence of Kant, to whom it is addressed, and whose lectures Herder had attended as a student in Königsberg from 1762 to 1764. The relationship between Herder and Kant is a fascinatingly·complex one, in which a deep-seated philosophical kinship is mixed with an at least equally deep-seated difference in intellectual temperament, as well as, in later years, on the side of the notoriously thin-skinned and irascible Herder, an abiding personal antipathy occasioned by Kant's critical reviews of the first two volumes of his projected magnum opus, the *Ideas on the Philosophy of the History of Mankind.*[52] The unfortunate result of this mixture of competing elements, however, has been that the first, and by far most important, aspect of the relationship—the extent to which, beneath all the obvious differences in formulation, the two are saying almost exactly the same thing about the essential linkage of man and world—has regularly been obscured (not to say rendered invisible) by either or both of the latter two considerations. The first to fall prey to this confusion were, indeed, Kant and Herder themselves. That state of affairs is especially apparent—strikingly so—in the case of Herder. In one of his last works, the *Metacritique of the 'Critique of Pure Reason'* of 1799, while setting out expressly to demolish what he takes to be Kantian epistemology, what he in fact does is to (re-)accomplish precisely the critical turn as both he and Kant, in their different ways, had done for the first time years earlier. The differences between what I am calling these "different ways," while by no means insignificant in their own right, are nonetheless in the long run of far less importance than the single, fundamental insight that the two thinkers shared in common.[53]

With Herder, however, that insight is also located firmly "out there," in the world of concretely lived experience.[54] And thus his argument does not afford even the opening for misinterpretation that Kant's does in virtue of what we have seen to be the largely outmoded philosophical vocabulary employed by the latter. Before Nietzsche at any rate, there is probably no more consistently or more vigorously outspoken opponent of faculty psychology or of the presuppositions underlying pre-critical Continental rationalism generally than Herder.[55] With his version of the critical turn, the sort of misreading of Kant that we have seen to be central—indeed, indispensable—to Rorty's neopragmatism is thus deprived from the outset of any point of departure. Although it may require a considerable effort to see Kant, as Rorty does, "inside" the mind, endlessly measuring and polishing our "mirror of nature," there is nevertheless at least something in Kant's own words—suitably decontextualized, to be sure—that might be taken as conferring a kind of prima facie legitimacy on that approach to his texts. Even that minimal condition, however, is absent in the case of Herder. One would have to reinvent him out of whole cloth to achieve a comparable misunderstanding of his thought. For his central argument, as indicated earlier, takes the form essentially of a demonstration that any supposition that man, language, and the world are *not* what Heidegger would later call *gleichursprünglich* (i.e., again, co-original) is of necessity incoherent. Thus we do not begin "within" ourselves (as, for example, Descartes had done) and from that starting point then try to get "outside" and establish contact with what we suppose is already "there" in advance of us. We start from where and what and how we are—always already in a condition of reciprocal constitution of man and world, a condition primarily brought about by, at the same time that it is paradigmatically embodied in, language—and simply seek to render explicit, in philosophically articulated form, what we have always already known.

So far as I am aware, Herder is mentioned nowhere in Rorty's work. Certainly he does not appear in any of the three books that together constitute what might be called the neopragmatist canon. And here, unlike the state of affairs seen earlier in connection with the shift from the paradigm of the "Mirror" to that of the "Lamp," I believe it may actually be for once a case of a genuine gap in Rorty's otherwise impressive erudition. In this, however, he is scarcely alone. Even among Germanists, whose business it presumably is to know these things, Herder has long been the poor relation of Western intellectual history. That situation, indeed, had already been recognized fifty years ago by Gadamer, when he noted that, among the leading figures in the German literary tradition, Herder was the only one who was no longer read.[56] So nearly complete is the oblivion into which he has lapsed for most of those working on questions of contemporary interest in philosophy and critical theory, that it in fact registers as something of a shock to find Charles Taylor referring, in a recent essay, to the epochal significance of "[t]he new theory of language that arises at the end of the 18th century, most notably in the work of Herder and Humboldt, [which] not only gives a new account of how language is essential to human thought, but [thereby] also. . . . totally upsets the outlook of the mainstream epistemological tradition."[57] The consequences of having overlooked Herder are, however, everywhere visible in Rorty and everywhere fatal to his argument. In failing to note Herder's position at (or nearly at—it is important not to neglect the key contribution of Vico in this regard either) the head of the line of thinkers who point to the integral relationship of language and thought as the fundamental determinant of the human condition at large, Rorty also fails to see the specifically "critical" dimension central to that insight from the beginning. For him, given the pre-critical framework in which he operates throughout, the line of thought in question represents simply one aspect of a general "anti-Platonist insistence on the ubiquity of language" (CP, p. xix).

To be sure, this last formulation may strike us, at least at first glance, as after all not too far off the mark. The giveaway, however, comes with the qualifier "anti-Platonist." For Rorty, as we have now seen repeatedly, there is no alternative to Platonism (i.e., in the terminology we have been employing, dogmatism) other than skeptical relativism. And thus what he calls "the ubiquity of language" is in his argot equivalent to the doctrine of ubiquitous interpretation, which in turn, as we have also seen, forms the centerpiece of the contemporary version of the skeptical outlook. Again, however, as we saw in the previous chapter, Rorty undermines his own argument by means of the very examples he adduces in support of it. Immediately following the passage last cited, he groups together as putative illustrations of the point in question selections from the works of both explicitly "critical" thinkers (Peirce and Wittgenstein) and programmatic skeptics (Derrida and Foucault), in the belief nevertheless that they are all saying basically the same thing:

> Peirce . . . and Wittgenstein are saying that the regress of interpretation cannot be cut off by the sort of "intuition" which Cartesian epistemology took for granted. . . . Derrida [is] saying that

our culture has been dominated by the notion of a "transcendental signified" which, by cutting off this regress, would bring us out from contingency and convention and into the Truth. Foucault is saying that we are gradually losing our grip on the "metaphysical comfort" which that Philosophical tradition provided—its picture of Man as having a "double" (the soul, the Noumenal Self) who uses Reality's own language rather than merely the vocabulary of a time and a place. (*CP*, pp. xx–xxi)

His text by Derrida (taken from *Of Grammatology*) runs as follows: "Peirce goes very far in the direction that I have called the deconstruction of the transcendental signified, which, at one time or another, would place a reassuring end to the reference from sign to sign." From Wittgenstein he offers the well-known thesis (from the *Investigations*): "It is only in language that one can mean something by something" (*CP*, p. xx).

Now Derrida, in the passage just cited, is referring in turn to the following selection from Peirce (as given in *Of Grammatology*):

The science of semiotics has three branches. The first is called by Duns Scotus *grammatica speculativa*. We may term it *pure grammar*. It has for its task to ascertain what must be true of the representamen used by every scientific intelligence in order that they may embody any *meaning*. The second is logic proper. It is the science of what is quasi-necessarily true of the representamina of any scientific intelligence in order that they may hold good of any *object*, that is, may be true. Or say, logic proper is the formal science of the conditions of the truth of representations. The third, in imitation of Kant's fashion of preserving old associations of words in finding nomenclatures for new conceptions, I call *pure rhetoric*. Its task is to ascertain the laws by which in every scientific intelligence one sign gives birth to another, and especially one thought brings forth another.[58]

What has obviously caught Derrida's eye in all this, the point on which he has fastened with characteristic avidity, is the third of Peirce's "three branches" of "semiotics." And, simply ignoring the first and second of these branches, he then proceeds to read into it an early version of his own doctrine of the endless deferral of meaning, as expressed in probably his most famous neologism, the (anti-)notion of *différance*.[59] In fact, of course, what Peirce quite clearly has in view here with his references to "what must be true of the representamen used by every scientific intelligence in order [first] that they may embody any *meaning*" and, second, "that they may hold good of any *object,* that is, may be true," is a transcendental (i.e., "critical") analysis of what might be called the conditions of possibility of making sense—something that recalls both Kant and Herder and points ahead directly to Wittgenstein. (That precisely the same is true as well of the passage from Peirce's writings that Rorty himself cites at this point in his text perhaps goes without saying.[60]) And it is clearly only in light of this overall project that the part of it that Peirce calls *"pure rhetoric"* can even begin to be understood.[61] For Derrida, however, for whom there is no such thing as determinate meaning, much less truth, such a project can obviously have no place in his system, and thus Peirce's manifest commitment to it is simply passed over in his gloss of the passage.[62]

What Derrida and his disciples are in the end doing when they speak of such things as an "endless deferral of meaning" or an "infinite play of semiosis" is simply to refer, both somewhat melodramatically and ultimately misleadingly, to the singularly undramatic fact that every term in a language must be defined by means of other terms in the language.[63] This is the same state of affairs to which Wittgenstein points when, for example, he observes that we never get individual elements of a language by themselves, as discrete entities, but rather that any such element, precisely by virtue of being recognized as an element in a language at all, of necessity already implies the whole system to which it belongs. Language is, in this sense, holistic, a characterization that Rorty also frequently employs (see, e.g., *CP,* p. xxi), though always drawing from it, in the ways we have seen, the opposite conclusion from the one it actually entails. When we acquire a language, we do so, as it were, by stages all at once. As Wittgenstein puts it in a characteristically effective image, the process is analogous to the sun coming up over an entire landscape, all the parts of which pass by degrees from darkness to light in step with one another.[64] The Derridean (or Rortyan) formulation of the truism of linguistic holism goes wrong, however, when it adopts the mistaken belief that the system itself is somehow infinite, which it plainly is not.[65] That misconception then leads to the further erroneous conclusion that (Wittgenstein notwithstanding) explanation does not "come to an end somewhere" (*PI,* § 1), for the reason that, in the nature of the case, it cannot do so. But, of course, here (as, by and large, elsewhere) Wittgenstein has it right. It is not merely that, as a practical matter, we do not continue beyond a certain point to ask questions about linguistic meaning. It is that, beyond a certain point, we *cannot* continue intelligibly to do so. For either we will come round in our chain of definitions sooner or later to something that has already been defined earlier in the chain, which simply points us back to the basic fact of linguistic holism, or we will reach a point at which we have run out of possible explanations and nothing more can be said beyond, " 'This is simply what [we] do' " (*PI*, § 217). In the latter case, we advert to what Wittgenstein calls the "ungrounded way of acting" (*OC*, § 110; see also, e.g., § 204) that ultimately underlies all uses of language. (Recall in this connection our earlier discussion of the notion of "ungroundedness" as it functions in Wittgenstein's thought generally.)

The fact that "[i]t is only in a language that I can mean something by something" (*PI*, p. 18) is thus not even so much opposed to Derrida's imaginary project of a "de-construction of the transcendental signified," or to Rorty's correspondingly imaginary notion of an in principle infinite "regress of interpretation" (*CP*, p. xx), as much as it shows the literal senselessness of both those (pseudo-)notions.[66] It is not, in other words, as if Wittgenstein were somehow intent on defending either the idea of a single, master repository of meaning "which, at one time or another, would place a reassuring end to the reference from sign to sign" (Derrida), or "the sort of [ultimate] 'intuition' which Cartesian epistemology took for granted" (Rorty). It is rather precisely because "[i]t is only in a language that I [or anyone] can mean something by something" that it can never make sense to assume the position of radical skepticism vis-à-vis language at large, and, in particular, its capacity to function as a conveyor of determinate meaning, that both Derrida and Rorty attempt. For if it is true, as it surely is, that to "mean" anything, one must do so "in a language," it follows that there neither is nor can be any quasi-extra-linguistic point from which one could coherently call in question that very linkage of language and (determinate) meaning. Derrida's and Rorty's respective bêtes noires of the "transcendental signified" and "Cartesian intuition" are, again, merely the remnants of a now thoroughly obsolete and superseded pre-critical epistemology. Having made the critical turn, we have no more need to concern ourselves with them in any fashion, whether it be to assert or deny their existence, than it is necessary (for most people at any rate) to answer either "yes" or "no" to the question, "Do you still beat your wife?"

The need is rather—assuming a willingness to carry on with the philosophical project of the West at all—to continue working out the implications of the critical turn in its specifically linguistic form. That is, of course, an effort in which a number of contemporary thinkers are actively engaged, among them Donald Davidson, Hilary Putnam, Karl-Otto Apel, and Jürgen Habermas. For Rorty, however, as we have seen, this very tradition of philosophical inquiry, which constitutes not merely the distinctive, but indeed virtually the defining, mark of Western culture at large, is itself precisely what is to be swept aside. (In reading

Rorty, one is sometimes put in mind of a phrase with which Russell once characterized another body of thought—albeit with far less justice— namely that it represented "the metaphysics of the new Stone Age."[67]) In particular, he has no use for the view—central to the "linguistic turn"—that to the extent that we learn more about the workings of language, we eo ipso learn more about the nature of reality itself. He speaks rather of "the *so-called* linguistic turn" (*PMN*, p. 162; emphasis added), contending flatly that "there is no way to . . . say something about the scheme of representations we are employing which will make clear its tie to the content we wish to represent" (*PMN*, p. 295). " 'Our language,' " he maintains, "is . . . hopeless [as] an explanation of truth or necessity" (*CP*, p. 33). And he adds:

> The point about the so-called "linguistic turn" in recent philosophy is supposed to be that whereas once we thought, with Aristotle, that necessity came from things, and later thought with Kant that it came from the structure of our minds, we now know that it comes from language. . . . [The] only problem is whether language (as one more social practice) is strong enough to stand the strain. If language is not constrained by things, or the transcendental ego, or *something*, then when one finds its limits is one really finding anything that counts as *necessary?* And if one isn't, is one doing *philosophy?* (*CP*, p. 27)

Rorty's answers to these questions are, in effect, "no" and (by virtue of that first negative response) "who cares?" He proposes that we simply "drop. . . . the concept of necessity" (*CP*, p. 27) altogether, where "necessity" is equivalent to something like "the limits of the intelligibly sayable." The prospect of the collapse of discourse into mere noise—or, what amounts to the same thing, the inability any longer to distinguish between the two—that would obviously follow from the wholesale abandonment of that criterion is one that he is evidently prepared to contemplate with equanimity.

As the longer passage just cited makes clear (and similar indications are not difficult to find elsewhere in his writings), Rorty's difficulty is not, or not exactly, that he does not understand what the "linguistic turn" itself is about.[68] He characterizes twentieth-century " '[a]nalytic' philosophy," for example, as "one more variant of Kantian philosophy, a variant marked principally by thinking of representation as linguistic rather than mental, and of philosophy of language rather than 'transcendental critique,' or psychology, as the discipline which exhibits the 'foundations of knowledge' " (*PMN*, p. 8). And in the same vein: "[T]he contemporary notion of philosophy of language as 'first philosophy' is not so much a change from the older claim that epistemology was 'first' as a minor variant upon it" (*PMN*, p. 134, n. 4). Though, as we have seen, this characterization of the development in question is basically correct—the linguistic turn *is* a continuation of the critical turn by other than purely "epistemological" means—the use in the first of these passages of the expression "one more variant" provides at least some grounds for suspicion that Rorty's understanding of it is nevertheless still not quite complete. That suspicion becomes more acute in the second passage, where he in effect dismisses the linguistic version of the critical turn as merely a "*minor* variant" on its earlier, epistemological embodiment. And we find ourselves confirmed in our suspicion by what follows that second passage: "The central claim of philosophy since Kant has been that the 'possibility of representing reality' was what needed explanation, and for this project the difference between mental and linguistic representations is relatively unimportant" (*PMN*, p. 134, n. 4).

Perhaps it would indeed be the case (though I am inclined to doubt it) that the distinction between the linguistic and the mental really did not make much of a difference, if what Rorty represents as "the central claim of philosophy since Kant" really were so in its own right. But, notwithstanding what many among Kant's successors have thought, down to the present day, it is not, and never has been. The issue that Kant (and Herder) engaged, and which in so doing they bequeathed to their philosophical descendants as the central concern of the discipline (regardless of whether that fact has been recognized by any given thinker at any given time), is not the "possibility of *representing* reality"; it is the possibility of there *being* reality at all and how that reality is to be accounted for. With the issue thus understood, however, it clearly also makes literally all the difference in the world, as we have seen, whether one grounds one's explanation in the comparatively abstract terms of forms of mental activity or in the concrete, lived world of everyday linguistic experience. Kant himself, it should be noted, shares at least part of the blame for this confusion. He frequently writes as if the real question he is addressing were, "How are synthetic judgments a priori possible?" (i.e., in Rorty's terms, "How is it possible that we are able accurately to represent reality?"). And the number of readers who have simply taken him at his word when he speaks in this way is distressingly (if also, given the complexity of his exposition, more or less understandably) large. But, of course, merely to assume that synthetic judgments a priori *are* possible, that we do *in fact* represent reality accurately to ourselves, which is what this way of putting the question does, is to make of the argument from the outset no more than an extended exercise in question begging.[69]

To counter a skepticism as sweeping as that of Hume, it clearly does not suffice to start from the assumption that we do possess objectively valid knowledge of a law-governed natural order and then simply proceed to an analysis of the sources and composition of that knowledge. For the initial assumption is precisely what a Humean skeptic denies. Rather it is necessary to begin from some still more fundamental premise—for Kant, as we have seen, the (unavoidable) acknowledgment that one is conscious at all—and on that basis to show, as the *conclusion* of the argument, that we do in fact possess such knowledge. At issue is thus not a need to account for how synthetic judgments a priori are possible; the need is rather to demonstrate *that* they are possible in the first place, and indeed not merely possible but necessarily valid. That demonstration, however, brings with it in turn a fundamental reanalysis of our very notion of objectivity, and thereby also of our conception of reality itself. In other words, we make the "critical turn."[70] As we have also noted, however, that turn is not complete, even in conception, much less in execution, until it has been understood and carried out primarily in terms of language.

Thus, Rorty to the contrary notwithstanding, not only *is* there a "way to . . . say something about the scheme of representations we are employing which will make clear its tie to the content we wish to represent" (*PMN*, p. 295). Inasmuch as that "content" is itself dependent on the specific qualities of that "scheme of representations" for its very existence as such—that is, in precisely the form that it has for us, which is, however, again, by hypothesis, the only form we could ever so much as conceive of its having at all—it is impossible that there should not be some such "way." We see here, again, Rorty's tacit commitment to the pre-critical model of the *adaequatio intellectus ad rem*. For him, "we" stand on one side of an imaginary divide, already completely formed in our hermetic self-enclosure, while the "content" that we seek to "represent" occupies a corresponding position on the other side of that divide. And the object of the game is (or would be, if it were a game that, in his view, we ought to be playing at all) to employ a "scheme of representations" in such a way as to both bridge that gap and, at the same time, provide an ironclad guarantee that the bridging effort had in fact been successful. (How "we" are supposed to have developed an interest in "representing" this "content" in the first place prior to our even being aware of it—"it" being, by hypothesis, not yet "represented" to us in any fashion—remains, of course, something of a mystery in all this.) Thus conceived, however, the project is obviously open to a slightly modified version of Gorgias's skeptical triple whammy: first, absolute truth is in principle unknowable (i.e., the gap dividing "us" from any "content" we might wish to "represent" is inherently unbridgeable); second, even supposing the truth to be somehow knowable, the knowledge in question could never be given a definitively adequate expression; and, finally, even if per impossibile such an expression were to be achieved, nonetheless no assured method of communicating this knowledge could ever be found, for there could never be any way of guaranteeing that the communication had been successfully carried out—that is, that the message as received was actually the same as the one transmitted. And in fact these are, as we have seen, essentially the consequences that Rorty embraces.

CHOICE AND INCOMMENSURABILITY

CHAPTER SIX

I

FOR RORTY, AS SEEN, LANGUAGE IS MERELY "ONE MORE SOCIAL practice" (*CP*, p. 27) among others. And thus, in addition to committing himself to the thesis that both man and world must be (somehow) logically prior to language, he is, if anything, even more strongly committed to what we might call the doctrine of radical linguistic voluntarism. I noted earlier that there is probably no general theoretical claim more frequently encountered today than the one that says that in formulating a theory of knowledge, we have in the end two and only two choices: we can go the way of the "metaphysics of presence"; or we can become perspectivists and relativists by adopting the view that I have been calling the doctrine of ubiquitous interpretation. The correlative doctrine of linguistic voluntarism, which one hears enunciated with scarcely less frequency than its companion, constitutes, I think, one important reason why so many people apparently find themselves drawn so irresistibly to ubiquitous interpretationism. It is, in brief, as Rorty puts it in a characteristic passage, the claim that "man is always free to choose new descriptions" (*PMN*, p. 362, n. 7) of anything whatever, unconstrained by anything inherent in either the objects of description or language itself.[1] Now, to be sure, there is a trivial sense (or rather, several related trivial senses) in which this doctrine, or something more or less resembling it, might be said to be true. Being trivial, however, these senses also offer no support for Rorty's position, nor, indeed, do they capture what he really has in mind in asserting it. In the first place, there obviously exists a considerable number of different "natural" languages, in any one of which we might in principle elect to express ourselves. There is, however, also a crucial distinction—one to which we shall return below—between the sense in which "It's raining" and "Es regnet" might be said to constitute different descriptions of a state of affairs, and the one in which either "It's raining" and "It's not raining," or "Es regnet" and "Es regnet nicht," do so. In addition, there is no limit in principle to the number of "artificial" languages that we can construct for any of the probably innumerable purposes for which language is employed, including, but by no means limited to, giving descriptions of states of affairs. And in many instances there may well be good reasons for preferring such newly invented linguistic systems to any of those previously available. Even within a given natural language, moreover, and limiting ourselves for the moment to the area of factual description (or rather to one particular aspect of that area), it is always possible in principle to produce an indefinitely large number of different accounts, all of them nonetheless fully compatible with observed phenomena (however implausible any of them may prove on other grounds).

Minus the concluding parenthetical qualification, I think this last sense of "different descriptions" probably comes closest to what Rorty is actually getting at with his doctrine of linguistic voluntarism. In itself, however, it expresses nothing more than the familiar notion of the underdetermination of theory by fact.[2] And it is a very long way indeed from here to the conclusion that the entire extent of what can either plausibly or intelligibly be said about the world stands under no limits or constraints whatsoever. It does not follow, in other words, from the fact—itself surely obvious—"that all problems, topics, and distinctions are language-relative" that they are therefore "the results of *our having chosen* to use a certain vocabulary, to play a certain language-game" (*CP*, p. 140; emphasis added). This is among Rorty's most glaring non sequiturs, one that appears repeatedly in one form or another throughout the entire neopragmatist argument. And despite his recourse to the Wittgensteinian vocabulary of "language-games" to formulate the point, it is once again Wittgenstein himself who provides the decisive counter to Rorty's position. "Can I say 'bububu' and mean 'If it doesn't rain I shall go for a walk'?" Wittgenstein asks (*PI*, p. 18). And the answer, interestingly enough, is the very statement that in the previous chapter we saw Rorty cite in conjunction with a passage from Derrida that he mistakenly interpreted as making essentially the same point as the one on which Wittgenstein is intent: "It is only in a language that I can mean something by something." As we have already seen to some extent, the implications of this deceptively simple observation are manifold, and they all tell against Rorty's theory.

One of the more bizarre assertions nowadays associated with, in particular, the deconstructionist or post-structuralist strain of contemporary skepticism is that whereas it used to be supposed that people speak this or that language, we now recognize that precisely the opposite is the case—that in reality "language speaks man."[3] Even if this were grammatically a sufficiently well-formed utterance to be capable of being either true or false, that would still elevate it no further than from unintelligibility to absurdity. The prima facie nonsense of the locution "language speaks man" notwithstanding, however, there is nonetheless also discernible in that (pseudo-)claim at least a glimmer of insight into the actual nature of the relationship between man and language, and that glimmer is of interest here. For Rorty's doctrine of linguistic voluntarism would be reconcilable with Wittgenstein's observation that "[i]t is only in a language that [anyone] can mean something by something," only if it were possible for anyone to invent his particular language entirely from scratch whenever he chose to do so. Only if that were a genuine option could any nontrivial content be given to the claim, not merely that "man is always free to choose new descriptions," but that the descriptions we in fact employ are "the results of our having chosen to use a certain vocabulary, to play a certain language-game." But this is precisely what the usable kernel of insight underlying the assertion "language speaks man" reminds us is impossible. That impossibility, to be sure, already follows directly from the co–originality of man, language, and world, discussed at some length above. Rather than simply advert to that fundamental fact and be done with it, however, I want to develop this kernel of insight a bit further by means of two additional considerations: one, the Wittgensteinian recognition, alluded to several times now, that *all* meaning, precisely in order to *be* meaning, must be located in a broader linguistic *context;* the other, a Herderian argument demonstrating the fallacy inherent in any attempt to account for the origin of language that requires us to postulate a state of *human* existence *prior* to our becoming creatures of language-use.

At the time that Herder wrote his *Treatise on the Origin of Language*, there were two primary theories in competition with one another purporting to explain the phenomenon in question. In more or less contemporary parlance, we might call these, respectively, linguistic creationism and linguistic conventionalism. Though, to my knowledge, only the latter continues to find serious adherents, to the extent it has any at all that is, as Herder showed, still too many. For although

unencumbered by any specifically theological presuppositions, it nonetheless suffers from the same flaw as does its more overtly devout counterpart. Briefly, as noted earlier, linguistic creationism is the view that
human language was actually produced by God, who in an act of divine
beneficence then imparted it to mankind; the argument is that the manifold perfections of language—its complexity, subtlety, limitless capacity
for expression, and so forth—far exceed anything that could have been
achieved through the exercise of mere human faculties and so compel us
to postulate an original supernatural source. Linguistic conventionalism, on the other hand, sees the human race as more than a match for
the task of creating language, operating as a kind of committee of the
whole. The idea is that, just as we today settle questions of definition
by getting together and agreeing on how we will refer to things (as in
the case, for example, of the redefinition of the basic unit of length
in the metric system, first, from one ten-millionth of the distance between the North Pole and the equator to the length of the "standard
meter," and subsequently from the standard meter to a certain number
of wave lengths of a particular range of light given off by a particular
gas), so we may suppose our earliest ancestors to have done essentially
the same thing with designations of all sorts. This would presumably
have occurred initially within individual families, but from that starting
point there would gradually have been created a common vocabulary for
the larger units of clans, tribes, and eventually whole nations.

As Kant notes on several occasions in the *Critique of Pure Reason*, a
prime source of the confusions that philosophers regularly create for
themselves is the attempt to extend the range of application of descriptions that hold good for parts of the whole to the whole itself. And that
is in effect, as Herder recognized, precisely the error that makes possible both the conventionalist and the creationist views of how human
language came about. In his *Treatise*, Herder asks with respect to linguistic conventionalism how the original meeting of the language committee is supposed to have been conducted. Obviously no one could
have communicated with anyone else, for, by hypothesis, there existed
as yet *no* language of any sort in which communication could have taken
place (such things as grunts or gestures, for example, insofar as they
could function as bearers of meaning, would, of course, by that very fact
already constitute a language, merely a somewhat less articulated one).
But this is precisely what the linguistic conventionalist has overlooked.
The situation that his theory tacitly envisages as primary in the case of
language formation is essentially the same one that Wittgenstein sees
implied by Augustine's account in the *Confessions* (cited in *PI*, § 1) of
how as a child he (as he believes) initially acquired the ability to use lan-

guage: "Augustine describes the learning of human language as if the child came into a strange country and did not understand the language of the country; that is, as if it already had a language, only not this one. Or again: as if the child could already *think*, only not yet speak. And 'think' would here mean something like 'talk to itself' " (*PI*, § 32). For the linguistic conventionalist argument even to get off the ground, the ability to communicate with one another on the part of those who are supposedly establishing the original "conventions" must already be presupposed. But, as Herder also shows, the state of affairs implicitly taken for granted by the linguistic creationist does not differ materially from this one. For here as well the existence of language prior to its presumed point of origin has already in effect been posited, this time in the form of our ability to comprehend the divine instruction through which language is supposedly imparted to us in the first place.

But—and this is finally the point of this brief excursus via Herder and Wittgenstein—Rorty's doctrine of linguistic voluntarism faces precisely the same difficulty encountered by the doctrines of linguistic creationism and conventionalism. Here as well language must already be in place if what the doctrine envisages as primary is to occur at all—in this case, that we ourselves "choose" all the "descriptions" or "vocabularies" with which we propose to engage reality.[4] For unless Rorty has in mind some special exemption from his principle "that *all* problems, topics, and distinctions are language-relative" (emphasis added), which, apart from involving him in more or less flagrant self-contradiction, would also, in my view, simply be to assert something manifestly false, no such supposed "choice" is going to be able to get back behind the language in which it is itself articulated and—the point of crucial importance here— that it did *not* itself create. Once again, as we have several times had occasion to note, language is always already there. The point becomes clearer still, I think, if we look more closely at yet another key Wittgensteinian notion that, as just seen, Rorty believes he can invoke in support of his argument, that of a "language-game." Of all the various concepts and expressions to have been given widespread currency by Wittgenstein's work in philosophy, it may be that none has been so persistently misunderstood and misapplied as has this one.

So far as I know, the first instances of "language-games" that Wittgenstein expressly identifies as such are those in the opening sections of the *Philosophical Investigations*, in particular § 2, where we find the now famous example of the builder and his assistant:

A [the builder] is building with building-stones: there are blocks, pillars, slabs and beams. B [the assistant] has to pass the stones,

and that in the order in which A needs them. For this purpose
they use a language consisting of the words "block", "pillar",
"slab", "beam". A calls them out;—B brings the stone which he
has learnt to bring at such-and-such a call.—Conceive this as a
complete primitive language. (*PI*, § 2)

The term *language-game* itself is introduced a few sections later:

We can . . . think of the whole process of using words in (2) as one
of those games by means of which children learn their native language. I will call these games "language-games" and will sometimes speak of a primitive language as a language-game. . . . I
shall [however] also call the whole, *consisting of language and the
actions into which it is woven*, the "language-game". (*PI*, § 7; emphasis added)

It is above all the key linkage of "language" and "actions" in the notion
of a "language-game" that tends to be left out of account when allusion
is made to that notion today. And that tendency is especially pronounced
when such allusion is by those intent on defending an essentially skeptical point of view.

In the section of the *Investigations* immediately preceding the one
last cited, developing some of the implications of § 2, Wittgenstein introduces the theme of contextual determination, both of meaning itself
and also of type of meaning:

We could imagine that the language of § 2 was the *whole* language
of A and B; even the whole language of a tribe. The children are
brought up to perform *these* actions, to use *these* words as they do
so, and to react in *this* way to the words of others.

An important part of the training will consist in the teacher's
pointing to the objects, directing the child's attention to them, and
at the same time uttering a word; for instance, the word "slab" as
he points to that shape. . . . This ostensive teaching of words can
be said to establish an association between the word and the thing.
But what does this mean? Well, it may mean various things; but
one very likely thinks first of all that a picture of the object comes
before the child's mind when it hears the word. But now, if this
does happen—is it the purpose of the word?—Yes, it *may* be the
purpose. . . . But in the language of § 2 it is *not* the purpose of the
words to evoke images. (It may, of course, be discovered that that
helps to attain the actual purpose.)

But if the ostensive teaching has this effect,—am I to say that it
effects an understanding of the word? Don't you understand the

call "Slab!" if you act upon it in such-and-such a way?—Doubtless the ostensive teaching helped to bring this about; *but only together with a particular training. With different training the same ostensive teaching of these words would have effected a quite different understanding* [emphasis added].

"I set the brake up by connecting up rod and lever."—Yes, *given the whole of the rest of the mechanism. Only in conjunction with that is it a brake-lever, and separated from its support it is not even a lever; it may be anything, or nothing* [emphasis added]. (*PI*, § 6)

What Wittgenstein leaves implicit here (though it is a point that becomes more explicit in the subsequent course of the *Investigations*) is in each case the converse of the two passages I have emphasized. That is, if the particular context of activity in which a given instance of "ostensive teaching" takes place is a necessary condition of the words that are taught in that way acquiring for the student the specific meanings they do, it is also the case that, *within that context of activity,* these words could acquire by means of this "ostensive teaching" *no other meanings* than the ones they in fact acquire; just as, for the same reason, if it is true (as it clearly is) that a piece of metal is a "brake-lever" only when hooked up in a certain way to a particular type of "mechanism," it is no less true that, once hooked up in this way, that piece of metal cannot *not* be, precisely, a brake-lever.

The implications of this for Rorty's doctrine of linguistic voluntarism would seem to be the following. Though any given language-game, taken by itself, is not in general something that anyone *has* to play, neither is it—and this holds true for all language-games without exception—something that one is free to play or not to play either *whenever* or *however* one chooses. To take the case of describing the weather, alluded to briefly in passing above, weather reporting is itself, of course, by and large something that one can engage in or not engage in, as one wishes. One is not reporting the weather at all, however, if, for example, one simply utters the words "It's raining" to an audience that understands no English, or "Es regnet" to one that does not know German. It is possible, of course, that one is teaching one's audience the meaning of the expression in question, by pronouncing (say) "It's raining," while at the same time directing the audience's attention to the rain coming down. This is, however, not yet weather reporting. It is rather precisely the sort of "ostensive teaching" to which Wittgenstein refers in the passage from the *Investigations* last cited and which is a necessary condition of the audience's subsequently being able to do anything whatever with the expression "It's raining," including, though by no means limited to, describing the weather or understanding descriptions of it. But it would be at best misleading, and I would prefer to say simply false, to characterize "It's raining" and "Es regnet" as themselves "different descriptions" of a phenomenon. Rather they are precisely the same description of that phenomenon, merely rendered in two different languages.

The pairs "It's raining" and "It's not raining," or "Es regnet" and "Es regnet nicht," are, however, at least in ordinary usage, genuinely different descriptions. But here as well, although for different reasons, one is not "free" to choose whichever member of the pair one happens to feel like choosing, at least not without, depending on the choice, having to make some fairly substantial compensatory adjustments in all other areas of one's language use at the same time. Suppose it is in fact raining and someone nonetheless says to us, "It's not raining." (I am leaving out of account here borderline cases such as drizzle or "heavy mist," from which skeptics sometimes believe they can derive support for their position, but which in fact present no difficulties whatsoever. That belief is simply a version of the "difficult calls fallacy" discussed in chapter 4 in connection with Rorty's baseball example.) If, after having been shown that water really is coming down from the sky, perhaps even having been taken outside so as to get wet, the person nonetheless persists in asserting that it is not raining, there are several courses open to us. Probably the most natural of these is to inquire what he then calls it in *his* language when the state of affairs in question obtains. But what if he denies that there is any difference at all between our vocabularies in this regard, maintaining that we both mean precisely the same thing by the expression *it's raining?* We will then presumably conclude that he is using *not* in a rather eccentric way, and that in his idiolect "It's not raining" means what "It's raining" means in standard English. We will, of course, then expect to encounter the same inversion of affirmation and negation in all other cases, whenever this person delivers himself of statements regarding matters of fact. Thus understood, the person is not really speaking English at all, but rather some other language more or less similar to it, in which "It's not raining" translates the English "It's raining," just as the German "Es regnet" does. But what if the person denies this as well and insists that he means by "It's not raining" what all other speakers of standard English mean by it and that it is in fact not raining? Here we may feel inclined to say, with Wittgenstein, that we "have reached bedrock, and [our] spade is turned" (*PI*, § 217).

Now, at one level, the choice between Rorty's skeptical view and the commonsense realism of most people may appear to turn on how one evaluates this state of affairs. For Rorty, it is simply a standoff, with nothing further to be said on either side that might ultimately decide the issue between the two parties one way or the other—no way, in other words, to establish definitively what is *really* the case (that notion itself, as we have seen, having no meaning in Rorty's theory). For the vast majority of people, however, the person who denies that it is raining when it in fact is, whether from ignorance or insanity or some other cause, is simply wrong. Those people are, of course, correct in that view, obviously so; at the same time, however, an important consideration is in at least some danger of being obscured here. For if one permits the point at issue between Rorty and virtually everyone else to be framed in the terms just suggested, one has in a certain sense already conceded the victory to him or at any rate as much of a victory as he is interested in obtaining. For "evaluation" is itself, as it were, Rorty's home turf, and once one has accepted *that* as an adequate characterization of how things are to be determined in this regard, one is already for all intents and purposes playing his game, which is all he really needs. The doctrine of linguistic voluntarism is itself a game without ultimate rights or wrongs, truths or falsehoods, corrects or incorrects; that is, indeed, the whole point of this game. The only counters in it are the "choices" we (supposedly) make to talk in one way or another and so to "describe" things in this way or that. And thus, precisely in casting the difference in views that is at stake here as itself a question of how to "evaluate" a particular state of affairs—that is, as a *choice* between one way of speaking of that state of affairs and some other way of speaking of it—one has already, in effect, consented to play "linguistic voluntarism" with Rorty.

Fortunately for the tenability of common sense, we might say, it is in fact by no means necessary to commit oneself, however tacitly, to "linguistic voluntarism" in order even to be able to come to grips with Rorty's argument. Here in particular we see the importance of Wittgenstein's characterization of a "language-game" as "the whole, consisting of language and the *actions* into which it is woven" (emphasis added). Just as "a brake-lever . . . separated from its support [i.e., "the rest of the mechanism"] is not even a lever," so words uttered in the absence of the actions they entail are not even words, but merely sounds. Specifically, to stay with our meteorological example, someone who (ostensibly) asserts, "It's not raining," but who does not also *act* as one does when it is not raining, has not in fact asserted anything. Rather he has merely produced a series of noises that happen to be homophonic with a well-formed proposition in the English language. In making this observation, moreover, we once again, as earlier in connection with the doctrine of ubiquitous interpretation, place the burden of proof back on

Rorty and those who believe themselves persuaded by his argument.[5] Either (the most likely outcome) no one is going to claim that it is not raining when it actually is, in which case the issue is decided by default in favor of common sense; for if everyone always "chooses" precisely the same vocabulary, the notion of "choice" itself drops out, as contributing nothing in its own right to our understanding of the cognitive-linguistic process that is taking place. All that remains is, again, the Wittgenstein-ian recognition, " 'This is simply what [we] do' " (PI, § 217). Or (against all expectation) someone really does make the claim in question, in which case we all become good Missourians and say, "Show me." When it's not raining, people go outside without umbrellas or foul weather gear; they plan baseball games and picnics; they don't (other things be-ing equal) bother about rolling up the windows of their cars; if the lack of rain persists long enough, they begin to observe plants withering and water levels dropping in lakes and reservoirs, and they typically begin to express some concern about these things; and so on virtually ad infini-tum. At this point, the "choice" (so to speak) rests squarely with the neopragmatist. In asserting that it's not raining when it actually is, he can either act in all the ways indicated (and in many more besides), in which case, among other things, he will simply get soaked for his trou-ble; or he can act as people generally do when it's raining, in which case, however—and this is the crucial point—*he will not in fact have asserted at all* that it is *not* raining, no matter how much he may insist that that is what he has done.[6]

II

The notion of a "language-game," at least as that notion is understood by Wittgenstein, is thus not only of no help to Rorty's argument; it actually enables us to see all the more clearly why that argument inevitably fails. In seeing this, moreover, we have also come round by another route to a conclusion in some respects very similar to one reached earlier in connection with the example of the sinking of the *Titanic*. This is that it is in the end impossible even to give sense to the currently widespread belief in the existence of what might be called a multitude of discrete centers of meaning—semiotic "windowless monads" between which at bottom no real contact ever does, or ever could, occur. In his Introduction to the English translation of Habermas's *Der philosophische Diskurs der Moderne*, Thomas Mc-

Carthy indicates some of the ways in which this belief manifests itself in contemporary critical discourse:

> To the necessity that characterizes reason in the Cartesian-Kantian [sic] view, the radical critics [of enlightenment] oppose *the contingency and conventionality of the rules, criteria, and products of what counts as rational speech and action at any given time and place;* to its universality, they oppose *an irreducible plurality of incommensurable lifeworlds and forms of life, the irremediably "local" character of all truth, argument, and validity;* to the apriori, the empirical; to certainty, fallibility; to unity, heterogeneity; to homogeneity, the fragmentary; to self-evident givenness ("presence"), universal mediation by differential systems of signs (Saussure); to the unconditioned, a rejection of ultimate foundations in any form. (emphasis added)[7]

Nearly all the familiar apparatus of the pre-critical, dogmatic-skeptical antinomy is, of course, on display here. Nonetheless, even after everything we have seen thus far of the untenability of that dichotomy, it may perhaps still be wondered whether we have really dealt adequately with the challenge posed by its skeptical side, as embodied in the latter member of each of the pairs listed by McCarthy. For is it not after all the case, first, that people, both at any given time and perhaps even more strikingly over time, believe and have believed, not merely different things, but *incommensurably* different things; second, that those incommensurably different beliefs often go to the very foundations of these people's respective belief-systems; and, third, that there is therefore no possibility of deciding between these belief-systems, inasmuch as the possibility of such an ultimate decision in favor of one or the other would presuppose precisely the sort of transcendent perspective (or nonperspective) that, by hypothesis, is never available to anyone?

The answer to this question, in all three of its parts, is no. "Incommensurability" is the third of the great pillars of contemporary skepticism, and, like the related doctrines of ubiquitous interpretation and linguistic voluntarism, it, too, is a fiction. Indeed, in Rorty's hands, it becomes something of a multiple fiction. For, in his view, the first thinker to whom it is supposed to have occurred to render thematic the notion of "incommensurability" was Hegel. He speaks in this connection of "the sense of liberation from science which was Hegel's chief legacy to the nineteenth century. Hegel left Kant's ideal of philosophy-as-science a shambles, but he did . . . create a new literary genre, a genre which exhibited the relativity of significance to choice of vocabulary, the bewildering variety of vocabularies from which we can choose, and the intrinsic instability of each" (*CP*, p. 148). How Hegel is supposed to have "exhibited" this, in light of the way in which Rorty, a page earlier, characterizes his overall style of philosophizing, is, to be sure, somewhat bewildering in its own right:

> Hegel decided that philosophy should be speculative rather than merely reflective. . . . If Kant had survived to read the *Phenomenology* he would have realized that philosophy had only managed to stay on the secure path of a science for about twenty-five years. Hegel kept the name of "science" without the distinctive mark of science—willingness to accept a neutral vocabulary in which to state problems, and thereby make argumentation possible. Under cover of Kant's invention, a new super-science called "philosophy," Hegel invented a literary genre *which lacked any trace of argumentation* [emphasis added], but which obsessively captioned itself *System der Wissenschaft* or *Wissenschaft der Logik, or Encyklopädie der philosophischen Wissenschaften*. (*CP*, p. 147)

For Hegel or anyone else to have "exhibited" something without "any trace of argumentation" would be an undeniably impressive achievement. As a matter of fact, there is a bit more (though, so far as I can tell, not much more) of genuine "argumentation" in Hegel than Rorty acknowledges. But it follows in turn, precisely from that general lack of reliance on argumentation to which Rorty himself points, that there is also a good deal less that is actually "exhibited" by Hegel—if by that is meant something like "conclusively (or even plausibly) demonstrated"—than either of them seems to believe.

This is, however, only the beginning of the difficulties encountered by Rorty's effort to enlist Hegel as not merely a powerful supporter, but indeed virtually the inventor, of the doctrine of radical meaning-incommensurability. For in fact, of course, Hegel did not believe in anything remotely resembling this doctrine, in either of its aspects to which Rorty refers. That is, he neither denied the possibility of a "neutral vocabulary," nor did he claim that, whatever the vocabulary we happen to be employing, our use of it is a result of our having "chosen" to do so. And even if he had believed either of these things, he would in any case not have been the first to see in the question of (possibly) incommensurable modes of conceptualization and expression an issue of philosophical importance. All these points, moreover, can be made simultaneously by reference to a single figure, one already mentioned earlier in several related connections, namely Herder. It is, in the first

place, Herder, not Hegel, who (at least among German thinkers[8]) first
explicitly challenges the Enlightenment assumption of a fundamental
uniformity of human nature (intellectual and otherwise) at all times and
places. Before Hegel had even been born, much less begun his philosophical career, Herder had already formulated the key notion of a distinctive "mode of thought" (in his writings, variously *Denkart* or
Denkungsart) peculiar to each people (*Volk* or *Nation*) and reflected
above all in the characteristic features of its language.[9] But neither
Herder nor Hegel supposed that a language (equivalent to a particular
conceptual matrix) ever is, or even in principle could be, created ex nihilo by anyone who might "choose" to do so. This is not the place to
undertake a detailed consideration of Herder's conception of the dialectic of context and originality that, in his view, necessarily informs all
uses of language.[10] Briefly, however, neither of these elements is for him
separable from the other or even conceivable apart from it. And thus
while language is always already there—there could never be so much
as a single instance of language use were that not the case—it is nonetheless also true that every linguistic event in particular is in its own
right strictly speaking unprecedented; for each such event instantiates
hitherto unactualized possibilities latent in that already extant context.
In this way, however, the enabling context itself, in and by virtue of
which alone the *next* such event will take place, is altered in turn. And
so the process continues, always combining in a kind of permanently incomplete totality the moments of continuity and disjunction, wholeness
and partiality, with each of these at once the necessary condition and
inevitable consequence of the other.

The Hegelian counterpart of this dialectic is far more widely known
than its Herderian predecessor and so for present purposes can be dealt
with still more summarily. One need, for example, merely advert to so
generally familiar a notion as that of the reciprocal interrelationship of
individual (or, in any sense, local) intention, on the one hand, and the
famous (or, as the case may be, notorious) "cunning of reason," on the
other. In recalling the inextricability of this linkage for Hegel, we are
also reminded that he would surely have responded to the suggestion
that we even could be, much less ever actually are, entirely on our own
in "choosing" our particular basic vocabularies with the same incredulity with which Herder would have greeted it. So far, indeed, is Hegel
from *denying* the possibility of a "neutral," or "master," vocabulary, in
which everything without exception would find, not merely an adequate, but in fact its quintessentially correct, expression, that his insistence precisely on the reality of such a vocabulary permits him to
avoid altogether a problem with which Herder struggles throughout his

career, never wholly convinced that he had found a satisfactory resolution of it. In an earlier study of Herder, I described the difference between him and Hegel in this respect as follows:

> The linguistic-cultural terms in which Herder primarily conceives his version of the problem of the One and the Many create for him, in his effort to realize the synthesis that would mark the completion of human development, requirements of a sort that Hegel's system does not oblige him to meet. When Hegel describes the essential character of a given culture and thereby locates it within the overall historical development of the *Weltgeist, he does so in his own language, from his own perspective. Since that is, however, by hypothesis also the perspective of the whole, the fact that that description has captured everything necessary about its object is guaranteed.* Hegel does not feel constrained to evoke a flesh-and-blood sense for what it felt like to be, for example, a Greek in the age of Pericles or a Roman in the era of the Republic, much less for the way of life of the Eskimo or the Tibetan or the American Indian. Herder, however, feels precisely that obligation. (emphasis added)[11]

In light of this, it is not surprising to learn that the idea of a sympathetic identification with other peoples and their cultures as the only way of ever achieving a true understanding of them—an idea that reappears, for example, in Coleridge's concept of "empathy" (the word itself being derived from the German *Einfühlung*), as well as in Dilthey's notion of *Verstehen*, conceived as the epistemological mode appropriate to the sciences of man (as opposed to the *Erkennen* proper to the natural sciences)—originates with Herder.

The frustration that Herder experiences in his attempt to achieve a combination of the absolutely global and the absolutely particular in his depictions of the nature and development of humankind—something attested to implicitly by the fact that all his larger projects, from the early *Fragments on Recent German Literature* to the late *Ideas on the Philosophy of the History of Mankind*, remained unfinished—is, in part, simply a consequence of the way in which he tends to frame the starting points for his expositions. In still greater measure, however, that frustration reflects an at least occasional failure to appreciate the full implications of his own insight into the thoroughly *historical* character of human existence. With respect to the former consideration, Herder (like Schiller) has a marked predilection for formulating oppositions in such a way that a synthesis of the opposed poles appears effectively precluded from the outset, by virtue of each of those poles having been defined precisely as the negation of the other.[12] This has often been held to be the case, for example, with regard to his categories of nationality and humanity (*Humanität*), or those of individual cultural autonomy and universal human progress.[13] The way out of the dilemma, however, as Herder also recognizes, at least in his better moments—and this is something that is in any case implicit in his thought throughout—is always to historicize the *problem* itself. This means viewing the opposition in question, whatever its specific terms or the shape it happens to assume in any given context, not as a static antinomy, but rather dynamically, as one structural moment in a continuing process of change and development. And thus the very perception (or presumed perception) of irreducible relativism among a host of ostensibly "incommensurable" historical-cultural centers of activity, when viewed as consistency demands in historical perspective in its own right, contains the implicit assurance that it cannot be the last word on what it purports to describe. For the putative apprehension of universal relativism is itself inseparable from the very moment of universality that, in part, constitutes it. One cannot, in other words, be talking of the *entirety* of the human race as describable only in relativist terms, without invoking at the same time the notion precisely of the entirety of the *human race* and thereby tacitly acknowledging that relativism cannot by itself represent the exhaustive account it claims to be. But that is at once to say that it cannot be even a partially adequate account. For, as we noted earlier, a relativism that does not claim to be *totally* descriptive of the field with which it is concerned is no longer even relativism. Relativism, in other words, taken by itself, is merely the hypostatization of one aspect of a particular level of cultural development, one that is still in process of moving from a view of humanity as an undifferentiated whole to a conception of it as a differentiated, articulated, and, above all, continuously developing, totality. In postulating what McCarthy, glossing the contemporary skeptical position, terms "an irreducible plurality of incommensurable lifeworlds and forms of life" as *the* once-and-for-all definitive reality of the human condition, it betrays precisely the *historical* insight that made it possible in the first place. And thus its practical effect is (or would be, in the surely unlikely event that it were ever actually to gain general acceptance) to ensure the stagnation of the human race, by substituting a negative ideal of infinite entropy for a vision of humanity as analogous to an organism, that is, an ultimately ordered whole, though also one that is still (as always) in process of unfolding itself.[14]

But—to return to Rorty and the support he believes he can derive from Hegel for his own position—what if we prescind from the somewhat baroque teleology of the Hegelian self-realizing *Weltgeist* and concentrate our attention exclusively on "the relativity of significance to . . . vocabulary" (whether, in some sense, "chosen" or not) that Hegel is supposed to have "exhibited" (*CP*, p. 148)? What if, in other words, we "naturalize" Hegel by ignoring the transcendent, totalizing aspect of Absolute Idealism and treat the various moments prior to the final stage of the dialectic as if they were themselves, each in its own right, all there were to the story (instead of, as Hegel himself views them, merely so many stages in the single, all-embracing development of reality, of which his system is intended to be at once the description and the culmination)? Surely then, it may be supposed, we will be able to derive the requisite support for the "incommensurability"-thesis. Once again, however, the attempt fails. It is not, of course, as if people had not over time invented a multitude of different ways in which to express things. Plainly, no one would think of wanting to deny anything so obvious. Davidson refers to "the pedestrian and familiar fact that the truth of a sentence is relative to (among other things) the language to which it belongs."[15] But, as he also notes, "The dominant metaphor of conceptual relativism, that of differing points of view, seems to betray an underlying paradox. Different points of view make sense, but only if there is a common coordinate system on which to plot them; yet the existence of a common system belies the claim of dramatic incomparability."[16] Specifically, "speakers of different languages may share a conceptual scheme provided there is a way of translating one language into the other."[17] The case for radical incommensurability of meaning thus ultimately stands or falls with the possibility of finding (at least) two languages that, while on the one hand clearly recognizable as such—that is, about whose status *as languages* there is no doubt—are nonetheless, either wholly or at least in significant part, not translatable one into the other. Yet, apart from the fact that, as an empirical matter, no such language-pair has ever been found,[18] it is by no means clear that such a discovery is even logically possible.

One way of seeing the difficulty involved here is to recall again Wittgenstein's argument in the *Philosophical Investigations* against the possibility of a "private language" and to recognize that that argument can be applied to whole linguistic communities in essentially the same way as to individuals and their use of language.[19] The incommensurability-thesis commits the one asserting it to a view of linguistic communities and the modes of conceptualization peculiar to them precisely analogous to the view of the individual's perceptions and sensations against which Wittgenstein directs what has come to be known as the "private language"-argument. And just as Wittgenstein is able to show that the supposition that *only I* know, or ever can know, for example, what the color green looks like *to me*, or what the pain of a headache feels like *to me*, is actually incoherent (notwithstanding that it has often been regarded as not merely true but, indeed, virtually tautological), similar considerations can be brought to bear against the claim that only a member of a given language community is in a position to say how the world appears *to him*, by virtue of the (it is assumed) absolutely distinctive shape that the conceptual scheme peculiar to his language imparts to reality.

To be sure, the idea of a distinctive "reality" uniquely the domain of the speakers of a given language may seem, at least initially, to lend the incommensurability-thesis a certain prima facie plausibility (again, precisely the superficial plausibility of the belief in individual "private languages"). But the thesis does not stop here. It cannot do so, without ceasing to make the very claim on which it is intent. For the claim is not merely that people who have grown up speaking as their native language, say, Hopi or Navaho (to recall examples made famous by Whorf) as a matter of fact tend to see things differently from native speakers of, say, English or German, and so in a kind of quasi-metaphorical sense inhabit different "worlds" from theirs. It is that those speakers of Hopi or Navaho *cannot* communicate to their English or German counterparts what their "worlds" are like, even if that is precisely what they wish to do. "Incommensurability" can make no compromise with communicability and still *be* incommensurability. In the moment that a bridge of communication is established, we have, not incommensurable languages, but (obviously) intertranslatable ones. And that in turn entails the existence of "a common coordinate system" of the sort to which Davidson refers. As Putnam notes, responding specifically to writers such as Kuhn and Feyerabend who seek to demonstrate the incommensurability-thesis by means of arguments purportedly establishing the radically paradigm-specific character of all cognition, but making a point of more general application as well:

> [I]f Feyerabend (and Kuhn at his most incommensurable) were right, then members of other cultures, including seventeenth-century scientists, would be conceptualizable by us only as animals producing responses to stimuli (including noises that curiously resemble English or Italian). To tell us that Galileo had 'incommensurable' notions *and then to go on to describe them at length* is totally incoherent.[20]

But surely, it may be objected, translation from one language to another is never absolutely exact or complete—never without at least some remainder, some residuum of significance that ultimately eludes a wholly adequate rendering in the terms of the new linguistic framework. Again, however, who would think of denying anything so obvious?[21] But what of it? As Herder observes, in *On Diligence in Several Learned Languages* and elsewhere, that is merely an argument for learning more languages, not a demonstration that any meaning is ever in principle inaccessible to anyone. Whatever human beings can create is eo ipso always available to other human beings. That does not necessarily mean, of course, immediately available or available without any difficulty of access. But to suppose that some quantum of meaning were somehow absolutely inaccessible would be tantamount to removing it entirely from what Rorty himself likes to call, borrowing from Michael Oakeshott, "the conversation of mankind." It would, in effect, be to invoke on a kind of macroscale the notion that Wittgenstein characterizes by means of probably the best known element of the "private language"-argument, the famous image of the "beetle-in-the-box" seen earlier (*PI*, § 293).

The "incommensurability"-thesis, at least in the form that we have considered thus far, simply reflects an insufficiently thought through attempt to place oneself simultaneously in two mutually exclusive positions—at once *within* a *given* language and, at the same time, surveying *all* languages from a standpoint *outside* any one of them in particular. For it is, on the one hand, only from the perspective of the former that what we might call the entirety of that language's uniqueness is available. Only the native speaker of a language (or someone who has managed to acquire something very close to native fluency) has a full sense for every aspect of the range and texture of its distinctive idiom. Yet, on the other hand, it is only from the latter perspective that that distinctive quality, qua distinctive, can become an object of awareness. What Whorf, for example, found to be the specific, distinguishing qualities of the *Weltanschauung* implicit in the language of the Hopi have that status only for someone, such as himself, who has some other *Weltanschauung* with which to compare them. For the individual who knows no other language, they are neither distinctive nor nondistinctive, but simply the way things are; they provide (or are capable of providing) no more occasion for special note than the color of the air or the difference between up and down or whatever else goes literally without saying. But the very fact that Whorf was able to identify the (as he believed, at any rate) distinctive features of the physical universe of the Hopi reflected in their language, and, furthermore, that he was able to describe these features to his non-Hopi-speaking audience, testifies precisely to the ultimate commensurability of that language with others, or at least of as much of it as he was in this way able to capture. And whatever (if anything) he was unable to capture—because, one might be inclined to suppose, radically "incommensurable" with his own "conceptual scheme"—becomes in the perspective of the whole simply a "beetle-in-the-box," about which, from *that* perspective, nothing whatever can be said—not even that it is "there" (or, for that matter, not "there"). It is only "there," if at all, for the speaker of Hopi. But in that case as well, as just seen, it also vanishes—this time, as it were, in the opposite direction—simply blending into the overall background of the Hopi world.

An analogous set of considerations holds, moreover, in the case of any two languages that one might take to be *wholly* "incommensurable," on the ground that no key has (yet) been found for translating the one into the other. Let us recall the case of Egyptian hieroglyphic, alluded to earlier, which prior to the discovery of the Rosetta Stone in 1799 had successfully resisted all efforts to decipher it. For those who could not read hieroglyphic—and, between the time when the ability to do so was lost (whenever that was) and 1821 (when the solution to the puzzle was found on the basis of the Rosetta Stone texts), that was everybody—hieroglyphic was not strictly speaking a language at all, notwithstanding its obvious resemblance to language in both form and (at least apparent) function. It plainly had once been the language of a people, or at least one particular subgroup of that people, which had ceased to exist in its earlier form. With the passing of that people, however, and with, as far as anyone knew, no key having been left for those who came after that would display the correspondences between it and other languages, the entirety of hieroglyphic became, in effect, a "beetle-in-the-box" in precisely the same way as those (presumably comparatively few) individual aspects of Hopi just alluded to that one might for the sake of argument suppose to be untranslatable. And thus not merely this or that element of hieroglyphic, but rather hieroglyphic itself was not properly regardable as one species of the genus "language." What tends to make this difficult to see from the vantage point of the present is simply that, since the work of Champollion and others, we have grown so accustomed to seeing in hieroglyphic not merely, as it were, a language-schema, but rather an actual language, that is, a system of expression and communication that can in fact be understood as such, that to think of it in any other terms seems not simply mistaken (as, of course, it now would be) but somehow vaguely irrational. But let us consider a parallel case.

Imagine that we see before us two individuals seated facing each other, with between them a flat surface marked off in alternately light and dark colored squares. On the surface are a number of small figures of different shapes and sizes, each of them of one or the other of two colors. Next to the surface is what appears to be a timepiece of some sort (actually two timepieces in one instrument). From time to time one of the individuals changes the position of one (or sometimes, though this occurs much less often, two) of the figures on the surface. It may also happen that he removes another figure from the surface as he does so. In every case, he also presses the nearer of two buttons atop the time-keeping instrument, which has the effect of stopping the timepiece nearer to him and starting the one nearer the other individual; both individuals also make written notations on tablets kept next to them for that purpose. Occasionally, one or the other of the individuals may leave his seat for a time, but he will on no account speak to anyone else. After a certain period, both individuals rise and depart the area, leaving the figures on the surface as they are. They return the next day and recommence the ritual as just described, continuing it until one or both of them determine, expressly or tacitly, that it has been completed. What are we to make of all this?

For anyone familiar with the format of officially sanctioned chess matches, the answer is, of course, obvious. But if for the moment we "bracket out" our prior knowledge of this and ask ourselves the same question, little or nothing is obvious—not even that the individuals in question are playing a game, or, for that matter, that they are engaged in any sort of competitive enterprise. For all we can tell, they might be performing a religious ceremony, or conducting a scientific experiment, or carrying out a financial transaction, or exchanging messages of some sort, or any of countless other possibilities. To be recognized even as a game, much less as the specific game that it is, the activity in question must first be locatable in some way in an overall context of "game-hood." It is not sufficient that it have, or appear to have, about it certain features in common with other games—in this case, for example, the moving of pieces on a playing surface. For prior to the activity's being identified as a game at all, its various elements are not recognizable as "pieces" or "moves" to begin with, however much they may resemble what in other contexts we know to be gamepieces and the moves made with them. And so also with the "signs" that constitute Egyptian hieroglyphic. It is not, of course, as if, as a practical matter, anyone ever actually supposed that hieroglyphic might not be a language (but rather, say, marks produced by some not yet fully understood process of nature); that purely contingent fact, however, has no bearing on the conceptual point at issue here. It became possible to regard hieroglyphic as a language properly so called only at such time as it became possible to locate it in fact, and not merely in prospect, in the context of "language-hood" in general. And that required, in turn, actually deciphering it and so demonstrating its intertranslatabilty with all other languages.

Expressions such as "game-hood" and "language-hood" are liable to be misunderstood, of course, as if the intention were to endorse some version of Platonic (or, for that matter, Aristotelian) essentialism. The pre-critical assumption implicit in this view—that it is either essentialism or relativism, with no third possibility (again, dogmatism or skepticism, *tertium non datur*)—is, to be sure, as we have seen repeatedly, one to which Rorty is in fact wholly committed. Again, however, Wittgenstein in particular helps us see, from yet another direction, why there is no need to adopt that assumption—indeed, why it is a fundamental mistake to do so:

> Consider for example the proceedings that we call "games". I mean board-games, card-games, ball-games, Olympic games, and so on. What is common to them all?—Don't say: "There *must* be something common, or they would not be called 'games' "—but *look and see* whether there is anything common to all.—For if you look at them you will not see something that is common to *all*, but similarities, relationships, and a whole series of them at that. . . . a complicated network of similarities overlapping and criss-crossing: sometimes overall similarities, sometimes similarities of detail.
>
> I can think of no better expression to characterize these similarities than "family resemblances"; for the various resemblances between members of a family: build, features, colour of eyes, gait, temperament, etc. etc. overlap and criss-cross in the same way.— And I shall say: 'games' form a family. (*PI*, § 66–67)

As a skeptic, however, Rorty remains merely an inverted essentialist, which means that neither the notion of "family resemblance" itself nor any of its implications can find a place in his theory. This has consequences for his conception of human nature at large, in particular as it relates to the human capacity for language. From the fact that it is not possible to specify necessary and sufficient conditions that would determine the set containing all and only languages—impossible, that is, to find a single, Platonic form of language in which all "*particular* language[s]" (*CIS*, p. 177) could be shown in some sense to participate—he concludes that it is therefore impossible to find in language in *any* general sense the distinguishing mark of human nature. He thereby rules out in advance, however, the possibility that such a distinguishing mark might be found precisely in those features of the "family" of languages that, for example, enable us in virtually any given, concrete case to say with complete confidence what is a language and what is not, in just the same way that those who have the concept "game" are in general always able to tell what is a game from what is not, even though they are

similarly unable to provide, in Platonic fashion, an exhaustive definition of the term *game* (in this regard, see also *PI*, § 68–69, 71, *passim*).
For Rorty,

> there is nothing deep inside each of us, no common human na-
> ture, no built-in human solidarity, to use as a moral reference
> point. There is nothing to people except what has been socialized
> into them—their ability to use [some] language [in particular],
> and thereby to exchange beliefs and desires with [some] other peo-
> ple. . . . To be a person is to speak a *particular* language, one
> which enables us to discuss particular beliefs and desires with par-
> ticular sorts of people. It is a historical contingency whether we
> are socialized by Neanderthals, ancient Chinese, Eton, Summer-
> hill, or the Ministry of Truth. Simply by being human we do not
> have a common bond. For all we share with all other humans is the
> same thing we share with all other animals—the ability to feel
> pain. (*CIS*, p. 177)

So far as I can tell, the book from which the passage just cited is
taken, *Contingency, Irony, and Solidarity,* adds only two new features to
the theory of neopragmatism developed in *PMN* and *CP.* Neither of
them, however, does anything to strengthen the argument already presented in those earlier works—if anything, quite the contrary. The notions in question were evidently intended to shore up the theory at two
of its most conspicuously weak points: first, its helplessness in the face
of issues of morality, and second (not unrelated to the first), its inability
to provide any account of the human *individual* as in part a *social* being.
The fact that they are nevertheless wholly inadequate to the task simply
testifies that much more strongly, it seems to me, to the basic untenability of neopragmatism in its very conception. One of these notions we
see in the passage at hand (though this is by no means its only appearance in *CIS*), in the form of the attempt to define human beings by reference exclusively to our capacity to feel pain. As just indicated, this
seems clearly to be an effort to find some way of avoiding the genuinely
disturbing implications of neopragmatism as presented in both *PMN* and
CP for questions of morality. At issue here is the evident difficulty of
reconciling neopragmatism with even the possibility (much less the reality) of principled ethical behavior. In the Introduction to *CP,* for example, Rorty allows that

> seeing all criteria as no more than temporary resting places, con-
> structed by a community to facilitate its inquiries, seems morally
> humiliating. . . . [For it] means that when the secret police come,

when the torturers violate the innocent, there is nothing to be said
to them of the form 'There is something within you which you are
betraying. Though you embody the practices of a totalitarian society which will endure forever, there is something beyond those
practices which condemns you.' This thought is hard to live with.
(*CP*, p. xlii; see also pp. 158, 172–74)

In the end, Rorty appears to have found it too hard to live with. The
resort to our capacity to feel pain as the defining mark of our being,
however, notwithstanding the accompanying effort "to try to isolate
something that distinguishes human from animal pain" (*CIS*, p. 177),
not only does not do the job for which it was designed. It actually creates
fresh difficulties for Rorty's theory. The idea is to try to derive something like basic ethical categories from the recognition of what a really
terrible thing it is to inflict pain on someone. Now, in at least a great
many cases, of course, this is clearly true: it *is* a really terrible thing to
do.[22] But that fact alone is scarcely sufficient to provide the foundation
of either a general conception of human nature or an ethics capable of
taking due account of the distinctive character of what it is to be human.
Rorty's definition, for example (to mention but one of a number of objections to it that come to mind immediately), would still deprive us of
any way of explaining why it is all right to kill an animal to prevent a
human being from starving to death, even if that requires inflicting extreme pain on the animal, but not all right—indeed, absolutely impermissible—to take the life of a human being against his will to save a
starving animal, even if that human being is terminally ill, with virtually
no time left to live, and death can be induced completely painlessly.[23]
  The specifically ethical difficulties that follow from Rorty's "pain"-
criterion of humanness are, however, by no means the only ones to
which it gives rise. Let us suppose that the time has finally come, at
some distant point in the future, when, after centuries of trying, scientists have at last realized the age-old dream of the universal anesthetic.
Pain has been abolished, psychic and emotional no less than physical,
and, of course, in such a way that we are now equipped with other
means of getting ourselves out of harm's way when necessary. For example, when I inadvertently place my hand on a hot surface, the message that I am in imminent danger of sustaining severe tissue damage is
flashed virtually instantaneously—as, of course, it is now—to the appropriate center in my brain, which in turn automatically initiates the
withdrawal of my hand from the surface, without, however, my ever becoming conscious of a sensation of discomfort. In this circumstance, it
would appear to follow for Rorty that people who happen to have been

"socialized" in sufficiently different ways must be regarded as having (apart from certain, presumably incidental, physiological similarities) no more in common with one another—or, for that matter, no less—than any one of them has with, say, a (correspondingly anesthetized) salamander, or a tomato plant, or a piece of gravel. The temptation is very great, of course, simply to dismiss as not worthy of serious consideration any position that entails consequences such as these. In this case, however, I think that would be a mistake. There are specific, identifiable reasons why views of the sort that Rorty is propounding tend to appear at certain junctures in the history of culture, as well as why, at such times, they are able to command a certain, not inconsiderable, following, at least in some sectors of society.[24] And in order to get at the root of that problem it is necessary to examine the claims in question closely, in step by step fashion, and in that way to identify precisely what has gone wrong with the thinking that has produced them.

Perhaps the first question to be raised here is: what will count as *sufficiently* different modes of "socialization" for Rorty? For, after all, no two people are ever "socialized" in exactly the same way. The experiences that have contributed to my becoming the person I now am could never be duplicated in every detail by any other person (perhaps, as some recent studies with identical twins suggest, not even in principle, and certainly not as a practical matter). But, if that is so, how different do two contexts of socialization then have to be before "incommensurability" between their respective vocabularies sets in? Rorty evidently has no answer to this question. His ostensible boundaries of incommensurability between different "criteria" and different "vocabularies" are in the end merely more or less arbitrary reifications of various group-concepts—national, cultural, religious, anthropological, or what have you—combined with the claim, which years of being repeated countless times by innumerable commentators have not succeeded in rendering any less false than it always was, that there is no such thing as a "value-free vocabulary" (*PMN*, p. 364). This latter claim, of course, is merely another way of formulating the doctrine of linguistic voluntarism, discussed above. In reality, however—and this is something that was at least implicit in that earlier discussion—there is hardly anything easier than to list as many propositions as one likes to which, under one description or another, individuals holding the most disparate "values" imaginable would nonetheless all assent without hesitation. They would do this for the very good reason that the propositions in question are true. If it is objected that this shows no more than that in some cases different value-sets converge or overlap with one another, the response is that in such cases—which, not incidentally, constitute the vast majority of things that anybody at all would ever want to say about anything whatsoever—it is possible, again, to "divide through" by "value-ladenness" and be left with nothing more than plain, uncontroversial factuality, relative (though the term is at least potentially misleading in contexts such as this) to nothing more than what Wittgenstein calls "[t]he common behavior of mankind" (*PI*, § 206; see also, e.g., § 54, 201, 244, 288). In all but a minuscule percentage of cases (if that), the notion of the "value-relativity" of different "vocabularies" thus turns out to be itself wholly lacking in pragmatic "cash value."

Rorty, however, maintains that a "view of intellectual life [according to which "intellectual justice would be made possible by finding theses which everyone would, given sufficient time and dialectical ability, accept"] presupposes either that, contrary to the prophets of the ubiquity of language . . . , language does *not* go all the way down, or that, contrary to the appearances, all vocabularies are commensurable" (*CP*, p. xxx). But, he continues,

> The first alternative amounts to saying that some intuitions, at least, are *not* a function of the way one has been brought up to talk, of the texts and people one has encountered. The second amounts to saying that the intuitions built into the vocabularies of Homeric warriors, Buddhist sages, Enlightenment scientists, and contemporary French literary critics, are not really as different as they seem—that there are common elements in each which Philosophy can isolate and use to formulate theses which it would be rational for all these people to accept, and problems which they all face. (*CP*, p. xxx)

It is, however, precisely the fact that language *does* "go all the way down," or, in other words, that "there is *no* way to think about [*any* part of] either the world or our purposes *except* by using language" (*CP*, p. xix; emphasis added), that, as we have seen, guarantees the very opposite of the conclusion that Rorty believes he can derive from it. Precisely the co-originality of man, language, and world, discussed at some length earlier, ensures that "the attempt to say 'how language relates to the world' by saying what *makes* certain sentences true," though by no means automatically assured of success in any given case in particular, nevertheless *cannot* be "impossible" (*CP*, p. xix) in principle. Only if it were possible for us to go *radically* wrong in our language, only if it were possible that *everything* might turn out to be after all merely an enormous illusion, only if it were possible to give sense to precisely what Rorty quite correctly denies makes any sense whatsoever—that is, the notion of something extra-linguistic against which the totality of what we conceive linguistically could be weighed and found wanting— only on this assumption would it be possible to rule out as unachievable in principle a demonstration of the relationship between language and reality. This does not mean, of course, the relationship between what on any given occasion we happen to say and what on that occasion happens to be the case; that is always a contingent matter, dependent on our getting the facts right in that particular instance. The relationship in question is rather between the structure of what we say and the structure of what is the case. The latter is a question, not of fact, but rather of logic, of the nature of factuality itself. And precisely *because* apart from language there is neither an "us" in the first place about which it could be said (for example) that we had gone radically wrong about anything, nor a world about which it would be possible for anyone to have gone radically wrong at all, the "impossibility" that Rorty means to assert can be seen—in part, on the strength of his own argument—to vanish.

This tendency to mistake the implications of his own best insights is everywhere visible in Rorty's work. Elsewhere, for example, he glosses the recognition that language "go[es] all the way down" as the claim *both* "that there is [no] kind of awareness of facts which is not expressible in language" *and* that there is accordingly none "which no argument could render dubious" (*CP*, p. xxxv). If the latter half of the claim means anything, however, it is surely that there is no fact whatsoever that I could not be presented with some good reason to doubt. But if that were really true, then, among other things, the former half of the claim, which Rorty nevertheless appears to regard as equivalent to it, might not be; for precisely the assertion "that there is [no] kind of awareness of facts which is not expressible in language" could itself in principle be called in question. We see here once again the confusion inherent in Rorty's attempt to go *completely* linguistic and yet at the same time still to find, precisely in that recognition of the exhaustive linguistic constitution of reality, a plausible basis for skeptical relativism. Doubt, however, like every other part of our experience, exists only *within* the triad of man, language, and world, not, as Rorty's alleged permanent possibility of dubiousness would need to have it, as a sort of free-floating phenomenon hovering just beyond that threefold structure, always poised and ready to strike at any element of it in particular. There *is* no "beyond" that structure. This does not mean, of course, that we can never be induced (and properly so) to revise our beliefs; in certain circumstances, we may even revise those that had been to one degree or another central to our understandings of ourselves and the world. "Revision," as Quine notes, "can strike anywhere."[25] There are, however, two crucially important observations that need to be made in conjunction with this one.

The first is that revision is never, as it were, radically individuated. The body of what we take to be the case changes (when it does) only as a whole. Indeed, it seems not unreasonable to speculate that precisely this recognition, or at least something similar to it, was among the considerations that eventually led Wittgenstein to abandon what was by far the single weakest element in the argument of the *Tractatus*, namely the doctrine of "elementary propositions." In the first section of that work he asserts: "Each item can be the case or not the case while everything else remains the same" (*TLP*, 1.21). Now, of course, there is at least one way to read this thesis such that, although still not strictly speaking quite correct, it is also not to such an extent incorrect that much damage is done. For example, at this moment it is not raining where I live; it is, in fact, a beautiful early autumn day, with just a touch of the summer lingering before the air turns cool and the leaves change color. It might, however, equally well be raining, as in fact it was only a few days ago. If that were so, however, the rest of the universe—the unimaginably large number of other things that are the case, including the manifold relations between and among "things" in the narrower sense (i.e., persons, objects, events, and the like)—would, on the whole, not be dramatically different from the way it is right now, with the sun shining outside, here in southern Durham county, North Carolina, USA. Similarly, I am at this moment composing this paragraph in longhand, in pencil, and writing with my right hand. Were I instead using a typewriter, or writing with a pen, or if I were left-handed, the world at large would be changed from the way it is now, if anything, still less than in the case of my weather example. What is *not* possible, however, is that good reasons could be given that would *both* persuade me (or anyone else who happened to be here, including, of course, Rorty himself) that it actually was raining outside right now (when it in fact is not) or that I was writing this with my left hand (when I am in fact using my right hand) *and* that would nonetheless at the same time leave the rest of the world unaltered. I cannot myself, as a practical matter, begin to imagine all the changes in my (or anyone else's) sense of what is and is not the case that would be necessitated by actually adopting the views in question; such changes would, in any case, clearly be considerable. At least since Wittgenstein, however, and probably earlier still, it has been widely recognized as an elementary fact of philosophical logic that a cognitive transmogrification of this sort is at any rate conceivable, however vanishingly small its real probability. But for this very reason—that is, that it is precisely an *elementary* fact of logic—it is hard to see why, if there were nothing more than this involved in Rorty's "universal dubiousness"-thesis, he thought it necessary to make a point of emphasizing it at all. On the other hand, if there is supposed to be something more to that thesis—and it seems to me clear that Rorty does want somehow to say that there is—it is difficult to see what that "something more" could be that would still be consonant with the recognition of linguistic constitutivism, which he apparently also wants to preserve.

The second of the two observations alluded to above makes essentially the same point from a slightly different direction. Rorty wants to deny "that there is a kind of awareness of facts . . . which no *argument* could render dubious" (*CP*, p. xxxv; emphasis added). This way of putting the matter, however, seems at least tacitly to acknowledge that doubt, in order genuinely to *be* doubt, always requires a *reason*. The Cartesian project of methodological doubt—doubt on demand, as it were, of anything whatever—is, as Wittgenstein observes, a merely verbal exercise, devoid of any existentially substantive content. One can no more doubt whatever one wishes, whenever one chooses to do so, than one can, for example, bring about an experience of surpassing joy by repeating to oneself, "Don't worry, be happy." But what, then, is the status of the "argument" itself that in any given case provides the reason(s) impelling us to doubt? In the first place, such an argument must obviously refer in some way to other things that we already know and that are themselves, at least for the moment, *not* in doubt. But, more than this, it must do so in ways that our *overall* structure of linguistic conceptualization can recognize as even admissible. The impetus to a revision of some part of our system of beliefs must come, in other words, from *within* the system itself—there is, as we have emphasized repeatedly, literally nowhere else from which it could come—and it must, moreover, be expressed precisely *in the terms of* that system. It must, that is, be grounded not only in other, non-controversial facts but also, no less indispensably, in the structure of factuality at large. From this there follows in turn not merely the quasi-negative conclusion that it is impossible for the whole of our system of beliefs to be called in question simultaneously; it also follows—and this positive recognition is perhaps the single most important aspect of the interrelationship of man, language, and world that Rorty's skepticism overlooks—that the very constitution of reality embodied in that triadic relationship contains in itself the possibility of its own modification. Inasmuch as both the fact of legitimate doubt and the fact of doubt being resolved through determination of what actually is the case are plainly realities—things of which everyone has had actual concrete experience—it clearly could not very well be otherwise. For Rorty, however, the fact that beliefs are altered can be accounted for only by invoking a notion of radical "ungroundedness" of belief, in the privative sense of that term discussed earlier: beliefs are mutable because there is not really a sense in which they hook up with anything "real" to begin with.[26] The "critical realist" view, on the other hand, incorporates into *its* notion of "ungroundedness"— the notion that we are always already as far "down" as it is possible even to conceive of being—an essentially *historicist* dimension. In this way it enables us to see in our interaction with the world a process characterized at once by fundamental continuity and yet also a kind of persistent discontinuity in the form of constant self-examination and self-correction.[27]

Put in slightly different terms, this in the end really says no more than that our form of life, which is, however, at the same time, of necessity, also the form of reality itself, includes a capacity for reflection on itself. And to find anything either mysterious or suspiciously metaphysical in *that* statement would be rather like finding grounds for suspicion that something philosophically illicit was going on in the fact that the periodic table of the elements is arranged as it is. To wonder why the relationship of man, language, and world, including the dimension of reflexivity inherent in that relationship, is as it is, would be at bottom analogous to wondering why, for example, hydrogen is lighter than uranium. In neither case is there available, even in principle, the basis for comparison with some other state of affairs that would be required to render the question meaningful. Perhaps the best-known instance in the twentieth century of a question to which precisely this difficulty attaches is Heidegger's famous query, "Why is there anything at all, rather than nothing?"[28] One may, to be sure, from time to time and in a certain state of mind, experience a kind of inarticulate sense of wonder at, as it were, the sheer being-of-it-all. That is a long way, however, from being able to formulate coherently a question as to the *why*-of-it-all, that is, something to which an answer could be given in the form of a *reason*. At the level of totality, *why* no longer has any meaning; *everything* that there is, just *is*.[29] In this circumstance, the genuinely interesting, as well as possible, question is the one that, to my knowledge, Herder first posed in sharply delineated fashion: how can one develop an account of (in Rorty's words) "language-as-a-whole" (*CP*, p. xix) from *within* language itself—that being, by hypothesis, the only position available to us?[30] It is not clear why accomplishing this should be in principle any more difficult, much less impossible, than, say, the physicist's project of developing a description of the universe from a position inside—where else would he be?—the object of his efforts.

Nor does this effort to gain a more adequate understanding than we currently possess of the linguistic constitution of reality amount to what Rorty terms an "attempt to step outside our skins . . . and compare

ourselves with something absolute" (*CP*, p. xix). The reference to the
shadow of an unattainable but constantly pursued "absolute," separate
from and ontologically prior to human beings, is, again, merely Rorty's
pre-critical straw man. The physicist in the age of quantum-mechanical
indeterminacy, Einsteinian relativity, Heisenbergian uncertainty,
Gödelian incompleteness, and the newly emergent field of "chaos theory" does not for any of these reasons regard the project of describing
the universe correctly as a chimera. Quite the contrary, such notions as
these are what the correct description of the universe consists in thus
far. They reflect part of what the notion of "correctness" itself means as
applied to such things as elementary particles, the macro-behavior of
galaxies, or axiomatized formal systems.[31] The physicist recognizes, at
least tacitly, precisely what Rorty all too often seems to overlook,
namely the fundamental rootedness of the meanings of words (and so
the content of concepts) in the contexts of actual use in which alone they
exist at all. So long as one continues to frame the issue in the obsolete
terms of successful or unsuccessful "correspondence" to something understood as itself "given" in advance, it will not be difficult to produce
an argument for skeptical relativism; the long history of pre-critical
thought contains few, if any, lessons more unambiguous than this one.
If, however, as we have seen, one simply rejects that intitial formulation
of the issue altogether and instead interprets such notions as "correctness" or "objectivity" in critical (i.e., Kantian-Herderian) terms, then
the skeptical temptation dissolves of itself, as nothing more than a legacy
of confusions past.

One additional note before returning to the main line of the discussion: I assume that few readers of a skeptical bent will have allowed the
qualifier "thus far" in the preceding paragraph to pass without a mighty
"Aha!," or words to that effect (and any who nonetheless did so might
well be thought to have allowed their cognitive atheist or agnostic instincts to grow deplorably slack). It is not as if the skeptic were actually
on to anything here, of course; it is merely that this is one point at which
skeptics are particularly inclined to think that there is something for
them to be on to. The confusion in this case is between an *incomplete*
description of something and a *universally corrigible* one. From the fact
that our understanding of the universe is properly characterized in the
former terms, however, it does not follow that it is even in principle
characterizable in the latter, much less that it must actually be so characterized. It, of course, belabors the obvious to say that we still have
more to learn about things. Indeed, as Quine's likening of the body of
knowledge to an ever-expanding circle neatly suggests—the image, that
is, that represents the extent of what we know at any time as the area

bounded by the circle and the number of new questions to which what we know gives rise as that circle's circumference—we will always have more to learn about things. The skeptic, however, if he wishes to remain a skeptic, has to deny that we ever really learn anything at all. One currently popular way of expressing this claim among skeptics—it is, in particular, a hallmark of Rorty's neopragmatism—is to deny the "convergence" of what we we say about the world with the way the world is in itself. Apart from the fact that this denial clearly presupposes the precritical model of the *adaequatio intellectus ad rem*, however, the rejection of "convergence," thus formulated, has the additional unwelcome consequence of making science itself impossible in any form: first, because nothing could ever be ruled out as an explanation of any natural phenomenon; and second, because, by virtue of that first impossibility, there could also be no rational or principled selection of a scientific heuristic. Any "discovery," whatever that term itself might now be taken to mean, would have to be regarded both as purely a matter of chance and, in any case, as always radically revocable in favor of *any* other explanation whatever. In place of, for example, Galileo's declaration that "mathematics is the language in which God has written the universe" (or, for a post-Nietzschean age, a secular counterpart of the same, according to which mathematics reflects part of what Wittgenstein calls "the logical form of reality" [*TLP*, 2.18]), we would have to limit ourselves to saying, as, indeed, Rorty unabashedly does, that Galileo "just lucked out" (*CP*, p. 193) in making the discoveries that he did. And instead of acknowledging that we still, and presumably always will, have more to learn about, say, the etiology of disease, we would in fact have to deny that, for example, Pasteur's germ theory took us in any real sense a step closer to the solution to that problem than we had been previously. For there is on this view no such thing as a "solution" to be approached at all, not even asymptotically. In so doing, however, we would also at least tacitly leave open the possibility that, instead of being obliged to *incorporate* the explanatory power of Pasteur's breakthrough in any subsequent advance in our understanding of disease (however otherwise different the science of a later age might turn out to be from its nineteenth-century counterpart), we might after all someday want to drop the germ theory entirely, in any version of it, and go back to accounting for disease by reference to such things as imbalances of bodily humors or demonic possession. Such are the consequences of a resolute refusal to acknowledge that science does in fact discover *truths* about the world, and that it does so, in particular, through a process of continual *synthesis*, in which earlier achievements are at once assimilated and transformed in the context of those that come after.[32]

Indeed, if precisely this Herderian dialectic of context and innovation were not a reality, however imperfectly it may yet be understood in all respects (and, so far as I can tell, that is extremely imperfectly at best), it is plain that Rorty's development of his own theory would, by the very terms of that theory, never have been possible in the first place. If it were not the case, that is, that, contrary to his own assertion seen earlier, "some intuitions, at least," are *not*, or not solely, "a function of the way one has been brought up to talk, of the texts and people one has encountered" (*CP*, p. xxx); if, in other words, it were not possible to develop "intuitions" other than those that our respective upbringings have drummed into us; it would remain utterly mysterious how Rorty was able to achieve the cognitive vantage point from which it became clear to him that precisely these most basic intuitions were what needed to be, as he says, "deliberately repressed" (*CP*, p. xxxv). The self-contradiction inherent in Rorty's call for massive cognitive "extirpat[ion]" (*CP*, p. xxxi)—extirpation, not merely of those individual items of belief that we are most inclined to accept, but of the framework itself in which our beliefs in anything whatever are cast—is inescapably of the essence of his neopragmatism. For without this demand, neopragmatism clearly cannot hope to bring about the total overhaul of the epistemic practices of contemporary civilization that is its avowed goal. But the demand itself is thoroughly self-undermining. For the epistemology that is supposed to provide the conceptual foundation capable of supporting it— the reduction, again, not merely of our actual knowledge-claims, but even of what we are able to conceive of as knowledge at all, to nothing more than expressions of what we happen to have been "socialized" into believing—precisely in carrying out its appointed task, cannot help rendering impossible in advance the emergence of the very program that generated both the need for and the possibility of that epistemology itself. Rorty has thus locked himself into a circle of genuinely classic viciousness[33]:

> *Of course* we have such intuitions [e.g., "to the effect that 'truth is more than assertibility' or 'there is more to pains than brain-states' or 'there is a clash between modern physics and our sense of moral responsibility' "]. How could we escape having them? We have been educated within an intellectual tradition built around such claims. . . . But it begs the question between pragmatist and realist to say that we must find a philosophical view which "captures" such intuitions. The pragmatist is urging that we do our best to *stop having* such intuitions, that we develop a *new* intellectual tradition. (*CP*, pp. xxix–xxx)

Nor does Rorty always take quite this kid-gloved an approach to the issue. He continues on the same page: "[T]he pragmatist's quarrel with the intuitive realist should be about the *status* of intuitions—about their *right* to be respected" (*CP*, p. xxx). It is, however, not the somewhat ominous tone of voice in the argument at junctures such as this that is of primary concern here. The point is rather simply to observe that no question at all can be begged against Rorty's position until such time as he actually has a position, which is to say, something that can be asserted without more or less flagrant self-contradiction. But, as we have now seen, that is precisely what he does not have.[34]

III

The last string to Rorty's bow thus becomes the claim, seen earlier,

that the intuitions built into the vocabularies of [for example] Homeric warriors, Buddhist sages, Enlightenment scientists, and contemporary French literary critics, are . . . really as different as they seem—that there are [not] common elements in each which Philosophy can isolate and use to formulate theses which it would be rational for all these people to accept, and problems which they all face. (*CP*, p. xxx)

Let us suppose for the sake of argument that it would still be possible to preserve something of the thesis that Rorty wants to defend here minus the straw man of essentialism on which, as formulated, it clearly depends, but which, as noted earlier, the Wittgensteinian concept of "family resemblance" enables us to recognize as in fact an entirely dispensable notion. It remains nevertheless striking—all the more so given the central importance of this thesis for neopragmatist doctrine generally—that, so far as I can tell, Rorty nowhere in any of the three books that constitute what I have termed the neopragmatist canon actually undertakes to develop an argument for it. Instead, he simply adverts to what he calls "the appearances" (*CP*, p. xxx), in light of which we are apparently just supposed to see that there is no sense in which the basic "intuitions" of "Achilles and the Buddha, Lavoisier and Derrida" (*CP*, p. xxx) have anything at all in common with one another.

In fact, as we saw earlier in connection with the alleged "value-relativity" of different discourses, there is not the slightest difficulty in assembling innumerable instances of "theses which it would be rational for all these people to accept, and problems which they all face." Perhaps the most obvious of these involve the conditions that must be met to sustain life at all. Plainly, these conditions are by and large the same for all the individuals in question, as well as for all other people, simply by virtue of their being human, which, by hypothesis, they are (notwithstanding that one differs from the others in being a fictional character rather than a real person). There is, accordingly, at least to this extent—and the actual extent is vastly greater still—a set of "problems which they all face" and which it would be "[ir]rational," if anything would be, for them not "to accept" as such. All the different "vocabularies" of mankind, from pre-Homeric (even) to post-structuralist, are in basic agreement with regard to literally countless things. And conversely, if utter incommensurability ever were to be encountered, there would, again by hypothesis, not be enough common ground even to formulate the *fact* of disagreement in the first place, as opposed to merely registering mutual incomprehension. Indeed, Rorty's own views militate precisely against the possibility of radical incommensurability among human vocabularies. For, as he maintains in *PMN*, one decisive mark by which we distinguish between the human and the nonhuman in any given case is just the possibility or impossibility of entering into a conversation with the being in question, with the obvious presupposition of mutual intelligibility that the possibility of such conversation includes (*PMN*, pp. 188–90).[35] As Wittgenstein notes in a passage cited earlier, referring implicitly to his key notion of "form of life," "If a lion could talk, we could not understand him" (*PI*, II, 223). In light of all this we are perhaps better able to see that in fact there cannot *not* be—in a sense that, of course, still remains to be explicated in full—precisely what Rorty wants to deny, namely "a core language . . . common to all traditions" (*CP*, p. xxxv). That explication is, indeed, as I have in effect been arguing throughout here, the principal outstanding task for the "linguistic turn" in philosophy.[36]

But what of the surely no less obvious differences between what, for example, Achilles, the Buddha, Lavoisier, and Derrida believe to be true? Let us stay for the moment with the bare-minimum, brute-factual conditions of inherently finite human existence. Some years ago I began an essay on the German Renaissance classic, *The Plowman from Bohemia*, by noting: "Great works of literature from the epic of Gilgamesh and the *Iliad* to the novels of Camus speak to man's perennial question: why do we die? and to its tragic intensification: why do the young, the good, the innocent, members of our families, our closest friends seem so often to die first?"[37] One can scarcely fail, I think, to be struck by the astonishing contemporaneity of not merely the thematics but also the sensibility of so ancient a work as the Gilgamesh-epic, a text already centuries old when the *Iliad* and the *Odyssey* were composed.[38] People, precisely qua people, have always known about death; such differences as arise are in what people *think* about death: how, in the broadest sense of the term, they account for it, and how, in a correspondingly broad sense, they assess it. Achilles—at least in the *Iliad*—believes that a short but glorious life is to be preferred to a long but undistinguished one (in the *Odyssey*, having had some time actually to experience non-life, he has, of course, come to a somewhat different opinion). The Buddha teaches that prior to the attainment of nirvana death is merely one part of a continuing process of transformation and, it is hoped, development through the cycle of death and rebirth. Life is in a certain sense inextinguishable, but personality is not; and in this teaching, the extinction of the individual self is the consummation devoutly to be, as it were, unwished for. I have no idea what conception, if any, Lavoisier may have taken with him as he went to the guillotine of what his state of being was shortly to be; but let us suppose him to have been, like many of his contemporaries in the French Enlightenment, essentially an Epicurean materialist. For him, then, the end of life would have meant simply the dissolution of the "soul" into the atoms of which it had been composed. And Derrida, finally, notwithstanding that his (anti-)theory commits him to a denial of the existence of any determinate concept of "death"—just as Hume's radical phenomenalism obliged him to deny the continued existence of the self over time—is, when he ceases from his abstract reflections and rejoins the world of common experience, surely no more in doubt about the fact that people do eventually *die* than was Hume (by his own admission) about the fact that in life *people*, and not merely clusters of discrete impressions and ideas, genuinely exist.

The phenomenon of death, about which people have always known, but about which, as these examples suggest, they have thought the most disparate things imaginable, is in every case the same phenomenon. And the same holds true mutatis mutandis for all facts. Hayden White's analysis of the writing of history as a process of what he calls *emplotment* of *events* reflects basically the distinction I am getting at here. White tends, at least on occasion, it seems to me, to underemphasize somewhat the moment of "event" in favor of that of "emplotment," a disequilibrium abetted by his occasional failure to distinguish sufficiently sharply between figurative and literal discourse. And in this way he perhaps encourages contemporary skeptical outlooks more than he actually

wants, or, in any case, certainly should want. Nevertheless at bottom he
seems entirely clear on the difference between, for example, the fact of
the storming of the Bastille, on the one hand, and either the degree or
the type of significance that a given observer may or may not see as attaching to that event, on the other. To complete the picture, it is necessary only that factuality itself be understood in "critical" rather than
"pre-critical" terms—that is, as inseparable from the human beings who
constitute it, rather than as existing in some sense prior to us. But this
is also precisely the point at which it is most important to be clear on
exactly what it is that we are saying. The caveat, I think, can hardly be
stressed too strongly. For it is above all the failure to exercise sufficient
caution at just this juncture that initially gives contemporary skeptical
outlooks the deceptive appearance of plausibility, not to say inevitability,
that for many they continue to possess. If the world of fact turns out on
reflection to be itself ultimately a human construct, and if, in addition,
our assessments of the significance of facts are also human constructs,
then the all-too-natural question becomes: what, then, after all is the
difference here? Or is there even a difference? Might it not rather be
that the former collapses into the latter, taking with it as it goes all our
old, naive notions of factuality and objectivity? Might it not be that these
can be unmasked as nothing more than particular instances, which as a
rule we merely fail to recognize as such, of a single, all-encompassing
process of radically perspectival world-construction, in the course of
which each of us creates for himself or herself an individually tailored
image of reality?

The view thus expressed is, of course, once again just the doctrine of
ubiquitous interpretation, discussed above. And if we were able to see
then why that doctrine cannot be valid—indeed, why it is incoherent—
we are now able to see why it has nevertheless come to be adopted as
widely as it has, in belief if not actually in fact. For more than two centuries now, we have been living in what we can call at the risk of some
oversimplification a post-Kantian world. But notwithstanding that the
"critical" philosophy of Kant, Herder, and a few others has since the late
eighteenth century continued virtually uninterruptedly to define the
philosophical context of modernity, it is also a body of thought that with
relatively few exceptions has been at best half-digested by those who
would appropriate it. At no time since the post-Kantian Idealists themselves, from Fichte to Hegel, has that been more the case than it is today. Almost everyone, that is, has by now picked up on the idea of
constitutivism; for nearly a generation, it has increasingly become a
commonplace (verging lately on a cliché) of theoretical discourse in one
discipline after another that objects of knowledge are "made" rather

than "found," "constructed" rather than "discovered," in short that, in Herder's words, "We live always in a world that we create for ourselves" (*SWS*, VIII, 252). What has by and large not been picked up on, however, is the accompanying notion—without which, however, as Kant himself recognized perhaps better than anyone else, the very idea of constitutivism dissolves into mere solipsism—of *reanalysis*. Kant, that is, did not *replace* what people had formerly taken to be hard-and-fast, rock-solid "objects" with (mere) "appearances," although it is still possible, as it has always been, to find in the literature more or less direct expressions of that basic misunderstanding of his central argument.[39] Instead he *reanalyzed* the concept of "objectivity" *in terms of* "phenomenality" (and, in that sense, "appearances"). The effect of that reanalysis, however, was to make possible for the first time a philosophically defensible account of precisely the hard-and-fast, rock-solid character that people at large had always known was of the essence of "objects," simply as a matter of common sense. Kant was entirely candid in acknowledging that although most people would in all likelihood never read a work like the *Critique of Pure Reason* (and would for the most part not understand it even if they did), neither was there any need for them to do so, inasmuch as the basic conclusions that it established were already perfectly and unassailably clear to them from their own experience. Only for his colleagues in academic philosophy was such a work necessary; for, as Wittgenstein would observe a century and a half later, only philosophers regularly manage to confuse themselves to the extent of being unable to recognize what they already know.

Or rather, it used to be only philosophers who did so. What was once almost exclusively the hallmark of that particular guild has lately emerged as a prominent characteristic of the philosophically inclined in other disciplines as well. As Rorty rightly observes, the center of gravity of philosophical discourse, especially in American universities, has in recent years tended markedly to shift from departments of philosophy themselves to areas such as comparative literature and literary theory.[40] The latter have indeed become the principal sources of new energy in this regard, but, in something like sorcerer's apprentice fashion, they have in many cases been conspicuously less successful in controlling and so avoiding being swept away by the forces into which they have tapped. Nowhere is that gap between insight and comprehension more strikingly apparent than in the currently widespread inability to see how *not* to take the step of reducing (Kantian-Herderian) constitutivism to (ubiquitous) interpretationism. Even though that reduction comes only at the price of making it impossible to distinguish between, for example, the *fact* of the Bastille being stormed on 14 July 1789 and the *assessment* of that event (in White's term, its "emplotment") in conjunction with various other events as part of what Brinton would call an historical "anatomy" of the French Revolution—for both the ostensible fact and the overtly acknowledged assessment are, from this point of view, equally matters of purely subjective evaluation (in some extreme versions of the doctrine, indeed, mere "taste"[41])—nonetheless, as anyone even moderately familiar with the contemporary academic scene, particularly in the United States, is well aware, precisely this reduction has come to seem to many inescapable.

In this circumstance, it appears, some have simply swallowed hard and tried to make the best of what common sense tells them is an obviously impossible situation. Others, however, whether instinctively or with a conscious eye for tactical advantage as the case may be, have found in this conflation of fact and assessment a singular opportunity. For it offers a way to avoid having to acknowledge that there is, after all, a fundamental difference in kind between, on the one hand, the linguistic-epistemological construction of reality (as reflected in the triad of man, language, and world) and, on the other hand, the manifold interpretations of reality that can always be developed on the basis of what Rorty calls "alternative conceptual schemes" (*CP*, p. 123). And the benefits to be reaped, at least for a certain sort of philosophical or theoretical standpoint, from being able to avoid that distinction are by no means inconsiderable. Instead of being obliged to recognize that reality is simultaneously "relative" to human beings and yet, as we have seen, precisely for that reason, also rock-solidly objective, it now becomes open to one to claim that myriad "alternative conceptual schemes" are in the end all there is. To be sure, this is, in addition to ubiquitous interpretationism, also merely the doctrine of radical meaning-incommensurability all over again—the two doctrines tending, as we have seen, to appear in tandem with one another—and in asserting it, one thus inevitably encounters once more all the insuperable difficulties to which we earlier saw that doctrine giving rise. But if one is intent, for whatever reason, on putting together an at least minimally plausible case for a position that cannot, however, be defended on rational grounds, the possibility of appealing to "alternative conceptual schemes" as ostensibly the basic units of all discourse may nevertheless represent a virtual godsend. For if one is shown that one's argument for the position in question is, for example, inconsistent or self-contradictory, or that it fails to avoid fatal ambiguities in the use of key terms, or that it commits any of a number of other fallacies, and is insofar rationally defective, one may now respond that "rationality" is itself nothing more than a reflection of some "conceptual scheme" in particular: you've got yours (as the song goes), but I've got mine, too; and yours has nothing whatever to say about mine. In particular, yours has and can have not the slightest warrant for asserting that mine is in any respect less rational than yours. In this way, of course, whatever one happens to feel like saying becomes radically self-confirming; moreover, that self-confirmation has at least an initial appearance of avoiding circularity (not that even that logical difficulty would represent, on the terms of this theory, an at all fatal, or even especially serious, problem). As Popper, however, was perhaps the first to observe, at least in this century, an assertion that is not disconfirmable even in principle is vacuous. It says nothing whatever, regardless of what the individual uttering it may believe to the contrary. On the other hand, however, when the only alternative to this is the obligation to abandon one's previously held position altogether, on the grounds that for any of the reasons just mentioned, as well as others that could be cited, it is rationally indefensible, vacuousness may seem a comparatively small price to pay. But even that price can, as a practical matter, be avoided. It is entirely possible for the discursive community with which one primarily identifies to be so constituted that its members are insulated from ever having to confront directly the fact that this is indeed the price they are paying to begin with.

This move typically involves an interestingly double-pronged strategy. As suggested above, one first denies that there is any such thing as disinterested rationality at all and contends instead that any position taken by anyone is merely an expression of some (necessarily local) interest in particular. On this view, the only real differences that arise between competing positions have nothing to do with cognitive legitimacy as such—on this view, there *is* no such thing as cognitive legitimacy as such—but rather reflect at most the extent to which the inherently partial and self-serving character of whatever anyone says or does is either rendered overt or (more or less disingenuously) concealed. On the other hand, however, *rationality* (i.e., the term itself) is simply too great a prize to be allowed to slip away completely. Not to be rational is, in our tradition, inescapably to be accounted *ir*rational, and no one is going to accept that without a struggle. This urgency, then, motivates the effort, regularly encountered today, to reintroduce "rationality" into the very intellectual landscape from which one has just finished removing any trace of it, having substituted, in the way just seen, for even the possibility, much less the reality, of reasoned deliberation a new sort of Hobbesian *bellum omnium contra omnes*. It will now be alleged that each party to the struggle (in particular one's own, of course) embodies its own distinctive *sort* of "rationality."[42] The consequence of having been rescued in this way for the term *rationality* itself, however, is that it has effectively been transformed into a kind of cognitive counterpart of the emperor's new clothes. Though one may continue to employ it, in the hope of retaining for oneself the aura of seriousness and respectability that originally attached to it by virtue of designating the actual discipline of the intellect, that hope cannot but be in vain. For one has now simply dispersed what used to be the concept denoted by that term among all the myriad "alternative conceptual schemes" in existence. Each of these, however, answers only to its own at once radically individuated and entirely self-warranting standards of justification.

Whether or not Rorty actually intends to serve as a spokesman for this sort of world, his neopragmatism has at any rate certainly done nothing to discourage its emergence. Another way of seeing this is to note that he in effect inverts what Davidson takes as the "criterion of a conceptual scheme different from our own." For Davidson, such a scheme would be one that produced statements that, while "largely true," are nonetheless "not translatable" into our own scheme.[43] In Rorty's view, what we have instead is a state of affairs in which the statements produced by each of the various "alternative conceptual schemes" are, while largely translatable into all the other schemes, nonetheless (by the lights of those other schemes) not all true because each scheme is in varying degrees "incommensurable" with all the others.[44] For him, in other words, it is possible that two different "vocabularies" might be entirely intertranslatable with one another but that each might still be capable of producing substantive utterances that could not be evaluated from the standpoint of the other. The reason for this is that the standards of truth and falsity, or even of coherence and incoherence, according to which the utterances in question were produced within the one vocabulary might nonetheless be radically incommensurable with the corresponding standards in the other vocabulary. Rorty, that is, evidently believes it is possible for one person to understand perfectly well what another person is saying, and for that first person nevertheless to have, even in principle, no way of determining whether what the other person has said is true or false, or even whether or not it makes sense. This, however, is surely as incoherent as any view could be. As Davidson notes, the very possibility of "meaningful *disagreement*" itself already "depends on a foundation . . . in agreement" (emphasis added).[45] The terms in which something is understood just *are* the criteria of what does or does not make sense. And making sense is in turn a necessary condition of something's being *either* true *or* false. The actual determination of truth or falsity depends, moreover, while not exclusively, nonetheless in significant degree, on the specific ways in which that issue of coherence or incoherence is settled as well.

One respect in which Rorty's overall philosophical view strikes me as most clearly mistaken is his conviction that (along with perhaps a few others on the contemporary scene) he is actually presenting a new *kind* of argument, rather than merely offering one more contribution of essentially the same sort to a centuries-old discussion of fundamentally the same issues, one that has always been conducted in basically the same terms. Precisely this conviction, however, makes all the more apparent the thoroughly traditional character of both his views themselves and his way of arguing for them. Throughout the history of philosophy, skeptics have regularly regarded themselves as the heralds of a new age, and in this, as in so much else, it seems to me, Rorty is at one with his forebears. As he sees it, what is taking place today is not that "a new way is [being] found to deal with an old problem," but rather that "a new set of problems [is] emerg[ing] and the old ones begin[ning] to fade away" (*PMN*, p. 264). What he terms the "naturalistic, behavioristic attitude toward language" has, he believes, made it possible for him and others in the "Nietzsche-Heidegger-Derrida tradition" "to transcend [the] Kantian motive" in thought and in that way to give rise to the present moment, in which we are "living between a repudiated past [i.e., the bad old days of Philosophy, writ large] and a dimly seen post-Philosophical future" (*CP*, p. xxi). From this point of view, of course, it then makes perfect sense to suggest, as he does, that we might well be "at the end of an era" (*PMN*, p. 393) in the development of the human race, with a new age about to dawn, and that from the vantage point of future generations most of "twentieth-century philosophy [may come] to seem a stage of awkward transitional backing and filling (as sixteenth-century philosophy now seems to us)" (*PMN*, p. 394).

In fact, I think there is little doubt that Rorty is correct in this estimate, though not in the way he intends. Skeptics have always flourished in times of confusion and uncertainty. They are themselves preeminently figures of transition; having by definition no substantive views of their own to impart, this could hardly be otherwise. Prior to the eighteenth century, the skeptical transition was always merely from one form of dogmatism to another. Since the late 1700s, however, it has twice been from dogmatism to critical realism: first, from Continental rationalism to Kant and Herder; second, somewhat more than a century later, from nineteenth-century metaphysics to Wittgenstein. And so it may well be again in the case of contemporary skepticism. Among other considerations tending in this direction is the fact that talk of radical uncertainty, indeterminacy, relativism, perspectivism, ungroundedness, and the like eventually becomes simply tiresome when repeated long enough in the face of objective reality. A general shift in temperament begins to set in, as people in greater and greater numbers grow weary of what Wittgenstein called "just gassing" and return, as they always have, to productive engagement with the real world. From the vantage point of *this* future, the bulk of twentieth-century philosophy is still, I think, unlikely to cut a particularly impressive figure. It is, however, precisely the fact that such writers of the present and recent past as Derrida or the later Heidegger—the very figures whom Rorty regards as in the vanguard of the coming age—were for a time taken seriously by anyone that will surely strike our descendants as little short of incredible.

Several years ago someone likened the state of contemporary criticism to a kind of neoscholasticism. The comparison strikes me as entirely apt. For much of what today is taken for creative energy and innovation in the work of critics and theoreticians in fact calls to mind nothing so much as the ever more subtle production of variations on a basic, unquestioned set of themes that characterized the work of thinkers in the late Middle Ages. In the pursuit of ever more manifold and finely nuanced ways of representing (or rather, "re-presenting") texts as the enactments of their own undoing, "persons" as the constantly self-renewing scenes of rupture and dispersal, and interpretations as the variously self-validating and self-deluding voices of mere interest, partiality, and "will-to-power," it is difficult after a while not to hear echoes of efforts to determine how many angels can dance on the head of a pin. From the vantage point of some future student of intellectual history looking back on the late twentieth century, it seems to me likely that the currently widely shared assessment of contemporary critical theory and practice as showing all the signs of a flourishing age of intellectual vigor and creativity and as holding promise of more and better yet to come will appear as in fact profoundly out of touch with reality. This sort of confidence, I think, will strike our descendants as misplaced in much the same way that the confidence of late-medieval thinkers in the future of their sort of philosophizing was misplaced at a time when Bacon and, shortly thereafter, Descartes were about to arrive and announce that the game was up. It is tempting to invoke Kuhn's notions of "normal science" and "crisis" in this connection. The idea would be to draw a parallel between the contemporary state of criticism and the ways in which, as Kuhn maintains, science comes to be done in the historically late phase of a given paradigm.[46] It seems to me, however, that the analogy ultimately fails. In the late period of Kuhnian "normal science," the "crisis" that leads eventually to the next scientific revolution is occasioned by the emergence within the framework of the old paradigm of what he calls "anomalies." These are problems with which scientists are either unable to deal at all or which they can handle only at the cost of increasingly cumbersome, and in proportion less plausible, adjustments to the old scheme. Scientific paradigm-shifts, in other words, come about precisely through the generation of *new* questions and problems. The mark of the basic exhaustion of the contemporary "paradigm" of critical theory, on the other hand, is just its inability any longer to generate interestingly new questions at all.

Rorty's own example of the philosophy of the sixteenth century is instructive in this regard. Although it did not itself issue directly in the "critical" revolution in thought, it made possible (by making necessary) the great efforts in dogmatic philosophy of the century following it; and these in turn, as we have seen, did ultimately lead by way of the skeptical reaction that they inevitably provoked to that revolution. The sixteenth century itself, however—undeniably outstanding achievements such as the art of the High Renaissance notwithstanding—was for the most part really a rather appalling time. The combination of institutional chaos, intellectual mannerism, and ethical disorientation that had for several centuries increasingly been the dominant characteristics of Western culture was coming to a head at a level of unsustainable intensity. The invention of something dramatically new—the age of modernity—was being made, as it were, existentially obligatory. These same three characteristics, however, have been (as Nietzsche foresaw they would be) all too conspicuously the marks of much of the twentieth century as well, and in ever greater degree the nearer one comes to the present day. Neopragmatism—like anti-foundationalism, post-structuralism, and all the other forms of contemporary skepticism—is merely among the more recent manifestations of this overall spirit of the age. To see in it instead something capable of leading us *out* of the dilemmas in which we are today still caught would be to fall prey to a confusion analogous to the one that Karl Kraus recognized in psychoanalysis when he characterized it, in a memorable phrase, as "itself the disease of the mind for which it purports to be the cure."

PART THREE

NEODOGMATISM

[I]t is lack of confidence, more than anything else, that kills a civilisation. We can destroy ourselves by cynicism and disillusion, just as effectively as by bombs. . . . The trouble [today] is that there is still no centre. The moral and intellectual failure of Marxism has left us with no alternative to heroic materialism, and that isn't enough. One may be optimistic, but one can't exactly be joyful at the prospect before us.

Kenneth Clark, *Civilisation: A Personal View*

"Genuine History"

CHAPTER SEVEN

I

Until a bit more than two centuries ago in the history of Western thought, the options open to anyone interested in developing a theory of knowledge were basically limited to two: dogmatism or skepticism. Prior to that time thinkers intent on coming to grips with fundamental issues of the nature or even the possibility of knowledge had for centuries been going back and forth between these two poles, alternating between primarily dogmatic and primarily skeptical outlooks, with each of these paradigms being exchanged for the other at more or less predictable intervals.[1] There seems, indeed, to be something virtually archetypal about the dogmatic-skeptical antinomy in the efforts of human beings to make sense of their worlds. Certainly it is not difficult to find counterparts of the pendular movement just noted in the history of one discipline after another throughout the humanities, social sciences, and, although to a significantly lesser extent, occasionally even the natural sciences. In the field of literary and cultural studies, this pattern has tended to appear in the guise of what some have described as a periodic movement back and forth between primarily *historicist* and primarily *formalist* modes of analysis. For a good part of this century, and especially in the years immediately following World War II, formalisms of one sort or another had the field largely to themselves. Whenever a situation such as this develops, however, it is usually

241

possible to count on two things happening: first, versions of the dominant paradigm find themselves pushed into assuming ever more extreme, and in proportion ever less plausible, shapes, until the paradigm itself finally reaches what might be thought of as its practical limit of excess; and second, having been thus overstated to the point that its own foundations come to appear in an increasingly dubious light, that paradigm then provokes a reaction in the form of a counterposition that seeks to emphasize as much as possible the differences (or, at any rate, putative differences) between itself and the previously dominant mode of thought.[2]

It is not, of course, as if "formalism" and "skepticism" were simply two ways of referring to the same thing; patently, they are not. Rather it is a matter here of characteristic tendencies or potentials of thought. An example may help clarify the point. Just as the theoretical position widely known today as poststructuralism can be derived, among other ways, by taking structuralist theory and pursuing it in accordance with its own internal logic to the point at which it appears to turn against itself,[3] so something similar can be observed in the case of formalism and skepticism. The cultivated indifference of New Critical formalism to anything outside the text, regarded as itself an autonomous, perfectly enclosed, organic whole—in particular, the willingness to ignore for purposes of analysis considerations of the person of the author, the status, function, or composition of the audience, and the concrete historical circumstances of the text's production—makes it comparatively easy for so-called "textualist" formalism (as it has become more or less widely known), animated by poststructuralist semiotics and the latter's extension of the limits of the "text" to coincide with those of reality at large, then to transform indifference to the outside world into a skeptical denial of determinate factuality or significance altogether.[4] It was at first thought by many in the field, of course, as the latter paradigm began to be put forward some twenty-five years ago, that it held promise of a renewal of critical energy and imagination in the wake of the more or less generally acknowledged collapse into final torpor of the sort of formalism that had dominated the preceding generation or two. This was, indeed, a principal reason that it was able to take hold as quickly and effectively as it did. More recently, however, commentators have increasingly begun to note the extent to which this paradigm, rather than constituting a move in fundamental opposition to the earlier formalist enterprise, in fact merely represents its continuation by other means. Armed with a new vocabulary, it nonetheless continues to rely on the same basic analytic assumptions and procedures as had its predecessor. In this light, it becomes possible to view contemporary skepticism in critical studies as, so to speak, the mannerism of the New Criticism.[5]

Precisely the sort of transition within the overall dogmatic-skeptical framework referred to a moment ago has, of course, been underway for several years now within the field of criticism in particular. With formalism having reached its latent *terminus ad quem* in the form of "textualism," it predictably began to find itself under attack from one "content"-oriented approach after another. There has, however, as yet been little or no effort to give any of the current crop of challengers a theoretical foundation in anything resembling "critical realist" terms (obviously because there has been as yet little recognition of the need to do so).[6] And so we are witnessing instead merely one more repetition of an old and familiar pattern: once again, as so many times before in the history of thought, a predominantly skeptical mode is being challenged by a number of predominantly dogmatic ones. Prominent among the recent contenders for top honors are, in this country, the so-called "new historicism" and, on the other side of the Atlantic, its chiefly British counterpart, "cultural materialism." So far as I can tell, however, neither the politically valorized anecdotalism of the new historicists, nor the cultural materialists' efforts to revive what used to be called simply literary sociology with a more overtly radical-leftist spin, nor any of the other attempts currently in vogue to achieve what has been called "a genuinely historicized critical practice"[7] has any hope of breaking out of the traditional dogmatic-skeptical antinomy. It is, moreover, precisely the failure of contemporary historicizers to recognize this fact that I think all but assures for the immediate future of criticism at least one more aporetic round of claim and counterclaim between these perennial antagonists. The occurrence of the term *genuinely* in the passage just cited tips us off to what is actually going on here. My reason for calling attention to it is by way of reminder that the notion of "history" characteristically invoked in contexts such as this is far from being an ordinary or obvious or uncontroversial one. We rightly become suspicious when we encounter, say, a Rousseau or a Hegel or anyone else with a master plan for organizing all aspects of society talking about *true* freedom, as opposed to the ordinary kind. For we recognize how easily this sort of locution can function as a rhetorical lever creating an opening for what are on their face the most astonishingly counterintuitive claims: for example, in a passage seen earlier, that it is both possible and, on occasion, even necessary for a person to be "forced to be free," or that freedom, properly understood, consists in obedience to a law (such as that of the Prussian state) in the actual formulation of which one has had no voice whatsoever. So also, for the same reason, we have good grounds for caution when we find appeals being made to *genuine* history. For it seems prima facie unlikely that there will turn out to be nothing more involved here than the simple, unproblematic sense in which history, like life itself in Kin Hubbard's laconic observation, "is just one thing after another."

Someone, I am sure, will want to object that what this phrase describes is not "history" at all, but rather simply the past. "One thing after another," it will be said, is the stuff of *chronicles*, and these provide merely the raw material of history. History, properly so called, is always a product of selection and interpretation—what Hayden White, for example, as noted above, terms "emplotment" of "events."[8] The point, of course, is perfectly well taken, as far as it goes. The troublesome aspect of "*genuine* history," however, as we shall see, is precisely its tendency to conflate these two components, and so to treat what is actually a form of "emplotment" (i.e., one interpretation among a great many others possible) as if it had itself the indubitable status of an "event" (i.e., an objective fact). Indeed, the tacit acknowledgment of that very conflation is what motivates the inclusion of the qualifier "genuinely" in Porter's call for a "genuinely historicized critical practice" in the first place.[9]

"Genuine history," in the sense in which that notion is characteristically invoked by its proponents[10]—like "textualism" but, as it were, in mirror image—is exemplary of the tendency of much contemporary criticism to blend together dogmatic and skeptical modes of thought to create what are on their face decidedly strange-looking hybrids.[11] Where "textualism" derives its characteristically skeptical cast of mind by first positing as the only alternative to it a dogmatically conceived ideal of epistemic objectivity and semantic wholeness and then demolishing that straw man, so "genuine history" bases an epistemologically dogmatic politics of analysis and interpretation largely on skeptical premises regarding the possibility of discovering universally valid modes of thought and action among human beings. To adopt a properly "historicized" perspective in the sense at issue here is, in other words, to posit *discontinuity* as the primary reality of human affairs. And it is then to take the additional step of viewing that discontinuity against the backdrop of a specific *political* matrix of belief. "History" thus becomes, in effect, a metaphor for a radical metaphysics of metonymy. Porter speaks several times of what she calls "the social text" as constituting the "ground" of history (*HL*, p. 256, *passim*). The tacit assumption here, of course, is that one simply knows the underlying, a priori principles according to which this "text" is constructed. Chief among these is that history is above all "the scene of heterogeneity, difference, [and] contradiction" (*HL*, p. 253). This "scene" is governed furthermore by the "constraints of social reality," and these "constraints" are in turn to be construed with primary reference to the "material conditions of production, consumption, and exchange" (*HL*, p. 263). The spaces in the grid-work thus laid out are then filled in by "those oppositional, alternative, and sometimes strongly antagonistic forms [of critical practice] which have emerged since the 1960s, first from Marxist, then from Afro-Americanist and feminist, and finally from Third World Studies" (*HL*, p. 256). The object of such "critical practice" is to recognize "the colonized other . . . as having a separate existence," and in that way to guard against simply "reenact[ing] the discursive practice of effacement and appropriation" (*HL*, p. 259) of that "other." We are called on to "construct the discursive field so as to avoid a relapse into formalism, which remarginalizes both the social [i.e., again, "the social text," the principles of which are known a priori] and the 'others' whose voice it should make audible" (*HL*, p. 265).

Some indication of just how involved things can get in fairly short order here is given by the fact that many partisans of the view in question evidently feel the need to distinguish between, as it were, good Otherness and bad Otherness. The latter, in Porter's words, is "always already a cultural product of a dominant discourse" (*HL*, p. 259) and thus "always already subordinated, dominated, othered [in the bad sense]" (*HL*, p. 260). This is, in essence, her objection to the "new historicism"—that in this way it "continue[s] to exhibit the force of a formalist legacy whose subtle denials of history persist" (*HL*, p. 253). The good sort of Otherness, on the other hand, the kind to which on this view we ought to be attending, is the "heterogeneity, difference, [and] contradiction" (*HL*, p. 253) that the particular political, cultural, ethnic, and gendered entities privileged in this framework are supposed to manifest in some sense in and of themselves, prior to being appropriated by the "dominant discourse." It may also happen, however, that the entities in question do not yet actually have the desired status in and of themselves, or not quite. Rather that status may itself be the object of a continuing quest. "To be Latin American," for example, writes one critic, "means to be first recognized and named by the Other. . . . Thus our literary history becomes a search for a true identity, the need to find an authentic self hidden under Columbus's misnomer [i.e., his "call(ing) the Caribbean islanders 'Indians']."[12] Similarly, for another critic, "[i]t is through th[e] knowledge . . . of being born into a condition of being disesteemed, rejected, alienated, and deprived that African Americans have arrived at their identity"; or rather they "endeavor to forge an identity out of this paradoxical status" of having "to live in an atmosphere . . . saturated with notions concerning equality, freedom, and the rights of man."[13] In this situation, so the same critic, "the creation of an autonomous self demands a slow rejection of social elements

extraneous to that self" (ibid., p. 735). For "black imitation of white society was damaging. It led to the loss of a vital folk-culture or tradition,
with its concomitant folk-wisdom, and it stifled black people's sense of
self" (ibid., p. 743). Here is envisaged no possibility of a middle ground,
no continuum running from one pole to another, no prospect of mutual
influence and reciprocal growth—only a stark choice between assimilation and self-abnegation, on the one hand, and radical uniqueness, on
the other. The choice is (obviously) not long in doubt: in circumstances
such as those just described, it is necessary to insist on "the unadapt-
ability of a black folk culture to the Western values [even] of individu-
alism and rationalism" (ibid., p. 744).

It is not difficult to see how the quest for the grail of the "politically
correct" may itself become a kind of self-consuming obsession. Not
enough that one is in perpetual quest of oneself; one may find oneself at
the same time, as it were, constantly looking over one's own shoulder as
one goes, attempting to measure the success or failure of that endeavor
against a standard that is at once given a priori and yet never quite proof
against lingering doubts and uncertainties. Rena Fraden, for example,
quoting in part Raymond Williams, writes that "although it is necessary
to theorize about the alternatives to culture, it is not always easy to recognize the real thing.

> 'It is exceptionally difficult to distinguish between those which are
> really elements of some new phase of the dominant culture . . .
> and those which are substantially alternative or oppositional to it;
> emergent in the strict sense, rather than merely novel.'[14] This is
> not to say that [Williams] denies that alternatives exist, only that
> one can easily be fooled. The pivotal question, of course, is how
> can we judge what is truly oppositional?[15]

The uneasy coexistence of dogmatism and skepticism in contemporary
theory, especially that of the political left, could, I think, hardly be
borne witness to more eloquently than it is here.

In sum, the direction of thought basic to what I am here calling "genuine history" depends above all on two key moves, one conceptual, the
other political. The former, and logically prior one, consists in the postulation of what we can call radical "Otherness" among the peoples of
the earth. It is assumed that certain groups of individuals are in important respects not merely different from one another—for clearly little
could be more commonplace than that observation—but rather that, for
reasons of history, culture, psychology, biology, or other factors, they
are in fact incommensurably different from one another. Certain se-

lected properties of persons are thereby invested with a kind of meta-physically absolute status. Prominent among the properties that are today singled out in this way are, of course, race, ethnicity, gender, and socioeconomic class.[16] The idea is that each entity hypostatized in this way possesses or reflects capacities for experience or ways of conceptu-alizing reality uniquely its own, not merely unshared, but in principle unshareable, by members of any other group. Essentially the same move, moreover, can equally well be made along the diachronic as along the synchronic axis. It is common today to be told, for example, that the characteristic outlooks and beliefs of people in the Renaissance (the home base of the "new historicism") or the Middle Ages were, in much the same way, radically "Other" than the corresponding outlooks and beliefs of those of us living in the late twentieth century.[17] From here it is then a comparatively short step to postulating for any such group one may happen to choose a correspondingly unique set of interests. And finally—for purposes of criticism, obviously a consideration of particular importance—it can readily be maintained that each such group is en-dowed with a unique "voice," in which alone adequate expression of its distinctive experiences and interests is possible. This is, to be sure, al-ready to have assumed quite a lot. But at least in those versions of "gen-uine history" with which I am acquainted, there is one more crucial step yet to come. If the first key move is to posit radical "Otherness" in gen-eral, then the second is to adopt a scheme that privileges certain of these hypostatized entities in particular (and so also, of course, their "voices") as historically "marginalized," "colonized," or "excluded" ones. In this way, it is effectively possible to create for purposes of analysis virtually whatever selected groups of perennial historical "victims" one likes, all of them presumably with a legitimate claim to having that vic-timization redressed.[18] This latter step is, of course, made all the easier to take if one has first adopted the assumption that any analytic frame-work one might employ is of necessity already implicated more or less directly in support of some political agenda or other. If political neutral-ity is a phantom, in other words, and belief in such neutrality, accord-ingly, a delusion, then it may indeed appear that there remains to any of us only the decision as to which side we are going to be on, that of the "victims" or of their "oppressors." And in this circumstance, who, after all, is knowingly going to choose the latter?

Now, while it may be thought churlish to ask why, exactly, anyone should regard any of this as true—what, precisely, the epistemic status of the claims involved is supposed to be and how it is warranted—when we look again at just how many assumptions have to be made in order to find this perspective-*cum*-program plausible, none of them either inconsiderable or obviously valid, the entire project of "genuine history" begins to appear in a significantly different light. Surely the first question that we ought to ask here is whether we can even make sense of the notion of radical Otherness to begin with.[19] I do not think that we can. The thought that qua female, or black, or Latin American, or proletarian, or whatever it may be, one eo ipso experiences or conceptualizes reality in a manner systematically and qualitatively different from the members of other groups doubtless has its psychologically gratifying aspect. And that is something that it is far from my intention to belittle. The prospect of an assured sense of group solidarity, anchored in the very nature of one's being, is nothing to be dismissed lightly in an often inhospitable world. Unfortunately, however, the notion appears to be not even mistaken so much as it is incoherent. Let us recall that the reality of difference itself is not in question here. Even if the fact were not already obvious, we would still know by Leibniz's Law that everybody is different from everybody else in some way; for if any two people were in no wise different from one another, we would not have two people at all, but only one. As a kind of existential complement to this principle of the identiy of indiscernibles, moreover, there is also the principle that *individuum ineffabile est*. If we cannot form any notion of two beings impossible in all respects to tell apart from one another, neither can we form any notion of an absolutely unique single entity, whether that "entity" be thought of as an individual human being or, as in the case at hand, a particular group of human beings defined in terms of some key, essential resemblance that all the members of the group are assumed to bear to one another, and on the basis of which they are assumed to differ fundamentally from all other human beings. Apprehension of anything requires that that thing be located in some context, some class of things like it in whatever may be the relevant respects. That is just another way of saying—as we learn in particular from Kant and Herder—that our most basic and fundamental experience of reality occurs always in the form of judgment and that judgment consists quintessentially in subsumption under a concept. Neither wholly passive intellection nor radical particularity of the objects of intellection forms any part of the world of human experience.

Most of this at least is, of course, entirely familiar to everyone. And its application to the question at hand, it seems to me, is fairly clear. Those inclined to talk of radical incommensurability among various groups of people assume too readily that all we need be concerned with is the "figure" of radical difference; the "ground" against which that figure would have to emerge in order to be perceived at all tends not to appear in their reckoning. But as we know from gestalt psychology and elsewhere, "figures" without "grounds" have no existence whatsoever. In reminding ourselves of this truism, however, we also see how the incommensurability-thesis, when thought all the way through, in the end undoes itself. For it appears that incommensurability among different groups of people could not even be observed without thereby at once ceasing to be precisely incommensurability. What is it, after all, that in such a case would (or could) tell us that we were dealing with people to begin with, as opposed, say, to unusually articulate animals, extremely sophisticated automata, or cleverly disguised extraterrestrials? While, for all I know, we may (or may not) be in some sense "incommensurable" with any or all of the latter, that is in any case clearly not the sort of absolute gulf between groups of *human beings* to which "genuine history" needs to be able to appeal if it is even to get off the ground. My own belief, though one that I am not yet able to articulate (much less actually demonstrate) in wholly adequate fashion, is that an essential dimension of the human condition, both at any given time and also over time, is at some deep level a relationship of mutual presupposition and entailment between sameness and difference, identity and alterity, commonality and otherness. And it must be possible, accordingly, to understand all these phenomena as in some way matters of degree, rather than as considerations compelling a hopeless choice between conceptions of humanity as either completely and fundamentally homogeneous or as divided into a multiplicity of metaphysically distinct units. In particular, as just suggested, I do not see how we could even recognize the Other *as* "other" unless we had at the same time already recognized him as in a certain sense one with ourselves as well; just as, by the same token, I do not see how the recognition of a common nature shared by *different* beings could occur at all (i.e., as a perception distinguishable, say, from viewing a clone of oneself) if that oneness did not also at the same time incorporate a basic element of plurality.

I believe, moreover, that something analogous to this state of affairs must hold true as well even in the case of each of us individually, in our relations to ourselves. As Herder puts it in the *Treatise on the Origin of Language:*

> It is of the essence of the human soul that we learn nothing in isolation, for itself alone, but rather either join it to what we already know or consider what in the future we will join to it. . . . That chain continues in this way until our death; one is, so to speak, never a *whole* person—always developing, in process, moving toward completion. . . . We are always emerging from childhood, however old we may be, are always underway, restless, unsatisfied;

the essence of our lives is never enjoyment, but rather always progression, and we have never become fully human beings until—
our lives are over. (*SWS*, V, 98)

I think it is fair to say that with little or no alteration this could equally
well have been written a hundred years later by Nietzsche. Alexander
Nehamas refers to "Nietzsche's view that the subject of an activity is not
given antecedently of the activity in question."[20] Indeed, he adds, for
Nietzsche each of us is "a conglomeration of 'under-souls,' which may or
may not be in harmony with one another" (ibid.). But a certain difficulty
with this view begins to make itself felt when we try to think it through
consistently, as can be seen by following Nehamas's argument a step or
two further. For purposes of interpretation of any text by Nietzsche (in
this particular case, *Beyond Good and Evil*), he says, "it becomes crucial
to understand the character who engages or who is manifested, in the
monologue which the text constitutes" (ibid.). "To do any of this," however, "we must *first determine*, in an elementary way, who the narrator
of *Beyond Good and Evil* is" (ibid., p. 52; emphasis added).

I am not sure that Nehamas always shows himself quite as sensible as
he might of the existential-hermeneutical paradox involved here. Nor,
for that matter, does it seem to me that Nietzsche always does so either.
Nehamas's justly admired *Nietzsche: Life as Literature* is essentially a
defense of the following propositions. First,

> The self, according to Nietzsche, is not a constant, stable entity.
> On the contrary, it is something that one becomes, something, he
> would even say, one constructs. A person consists of absolutely ev-
> erything one thinks, wants, and does. But a person worthy of ad-
> miration, a person who has (or is) a self, is one whose thoughts,
> desires, and actions are not haphazard but are instead connected
> to one another in the intimate way that indicates in all cases the
> presence of style. A self is just a set of coherently connected epi-
> sodes, and an admirable self, as Nietzsche insists again and again,
> consists of a large number of powerful and conflicting tendencies
> that are controlled and harmonized. . . . [S]tyle, which is what
> Nietzsche requires and admires, involves controlled multiplicity
> and resolved conflict.[21]

Second, the key to understanding Nietzsche is to see him as having
sought literally to realize the truth of this principle himself, in his own
activity as poet-philosopher: "Nietzsche exemplifies through his own
writings one way in which one individual may have succeeded in fash-
ioning itself. . . . This individual is none other than Nietzsche himself,

who is a creature of his own texts," the product of his "effort to create an artwork out of himself" (ibid., p. 8). This "effort" surely presupposes, however, that someone (or, less plausibly, some thing) is in charge of the activity of self-creation to begin with—even (or precisely) as that same "self" is thereby brought into being in its own right, The paramount Nietzschean exhortation "to give style to one's character" loses its point—indeed, I would venture to say, loses its coherence—if the development in question is not in some way so directed but is rather, for example, merely something more or less analogous to a process of nature. I do not myself have the key to untying this particular Gordian knot (if that is the right metaphor); certainly no mere wave of the magic wand of a need to think in some sense "dialectically" is likely to suffice. Perhaps it comes down in the end to a permanent, never wholly resolvable riddle of the human condition, the one to which Nietzsche (like Herder before him, merely in slightly different words) repeatedly gestured with his notion of "becoming what one is." In any case, however, it seems clear that, for reasons of the sort I have suggested, currently fashionable celebrations of the destruction or otherwise dispensability of the "self" are, at the very least, premature. In particular, attempts to find a warrant for that destruction in Nietzsche can appeal at best to only one aspect of his writings. It is an aspect, however, that in being removed in this way from the overall context of his oeuvre at large, is also unavoidably drained of the meaning that he actually intended it should have.[22]

To return to the main line of the exposition, however: Referring to Peter Winch's assertion, in his influential essay "Understanding a Primitive Society,"[23] that " 'the onus is on us to extend our understanding' rather than 'insist on seeing (things) in terms of our own ready made distinction(s),' " Thomas McCarthy notes that "as an account of the logic of the interpretive situation," this "version of the charity principle. . . . is one-sided." He elaborates:

> If there is initial disagreement in beliefs and practices, concepts and criteria, and if there is no extramundane standpoint from which we might neutrally adjudicate the differences, and if neither side is justified in assuming without further ado the superiority of their own way of looking at things, then a discussion of the differences is the only nonarbitrary path open for weighing the pros and cons of the divergent outlooks. If this discussion is to be symmetrical, then 'their' views will have to be given equal consideration with 'our' views. We shall have to try to appreciate how things look from *their* point of view. And this will require expanding the horizon of our own, as Winch points out. What he fails to consider is that symmetry requires the same from them. That is,

they would, correspondingly, have to learn to see things from *our* point of view as well, if discussion of the differences in belief and practice is to proceed without unduly privileging the one or the other side.[24]

In the remainder of the essay from which this passage is taken, McCarthy argues persuasively that "this description of the logical—or, in this case, dialogical—situation has far-reaching consequences for the whole discussion of relativism" (ibid., pp. 84–85). Specifically, "[t]o grant that every point of view is historically situated is not *ipso facto* to surrender all claim to validity, to drop any claim that one view is better than another. . . . [W]hile the open-ended 'conversation of mankind' rules out the assumption that our point of view is absolute, it does not require us simply to drop notions of cognitive advance or learning from experience" (ibid., pp. 85–86).

Peter Haidu contends, rightly I believe, that "the problematic of alterity is one of the key problems of the epoch. To recognize the nonidentical, the different, the other whose limits of differentiation are not predeterminable or predictable is . . . the heart of the problematic located in the domains, not only of textuality, but also of interpersonal relations, political relations at the national scale, and, most obviously, at the international scale of diplomacy."[25] This has, indeed, *been* "one of the key problems of the epoch" since, at the latest, the time that Herder began calling attention to it in 1764. Ultimately, of course, it is a version of the classic problem of the One and the Many, from which in many ways philosophy itself, at least in its Western form, takes its start.[26] Haidu also recognizes the basic incoherence of "the postulate of an 'Entirely Other' " (ibid., p. 683), at least with respect to human beings. *God*, for example, is " 'Entirely Other' " than man, "so different that man cannot formulate a positive discourse regarding that other substance. Hence [as medieval theologians well understood] the necessity for a negative theology, basing itself on the inability of man to say that which he is not" (ibid.). Haidu's notion of "relative alterity," however, strikes me nonetheless as in the end merely a slightly awkward attempt to still have things both ways: to hold on to the old, *radical* alterity, with all the philosophical punch that notion was felt to pack prior to the recognition of its unintelligibility, while at the same time preserving his exposition from the slide into incoherence that actually adopting that notion in full-blown form would entail. As his example of "the experience to which Lévi-Strauss's narrative alludes in the *Tristes tropiques*" (ibid., p. 684) makes clear, "relative alterity" is finally little more than a way of referring to whatever it is with which one does not yet happen to be familiar. Notions such as sameness, commonality, fundamental unity, and the like as applied to human beings have taken such a beating in recent years, however, that even a critic such as Haidu, who appears to have at least a tacit sense for the need to incorporate these notions in our overall understanding of human nature, nevertheless evidently has difficulty in actually coming out and saying so.

Even assuming for the sake of argument that a satisfactory interpretation of the notion of radical Otherness could somehow be found, apologists for "genuine history" would still face the problem of explaining why just these properties in particular are the ones along which the fault lines of incommensurability are held to run. Why specifically gender, race, class, and ethnicity, for example? From what privileged perspective was *that* determination made? And, especially in light of the overall tenor of the theory itself, how is such privileging to be defended? Is it because the categories in question are "natural kinds"? But there are innumerable "natural kinds" comprised in the human race. And in any case, as we saw earlier, there is considerable ambivalence on the part of the proponents of the theory themselves regarding the whole issue of "natural kinds" (or "essentialism") versus social and historical "constructs." Is it then because all the members of the respective categories share a common history of subjugation and exploitation? But plainly not all of them do, or ever have. And even if they did, the members of these groups would not be the only individuals so characterizable. I dare say that there is no form of persecution or repression without exception that has not at one time or another been visited upon virtually every sort of person there is. The claim of a unique common history, in any case, begs the question. For this common history is precisely what must first be demonstrated in some way, not itself used as a prior basis of classification. In sum, although there are doubtless other questions as well that could be raised here, perhaps the foregoing is enough to suggest something of the extent to which anyone who is urged to adopt the perspective of "genuine history" is owed a rather substantial explanation *why.* I am at no point denying that such an explanation might (someday) be found. As I have indicated, however, the only ones that have in fact been offered thus far have all found it necessary to ground themselves exclusively in metaphysically dogmatic terms. And my best guess is that this is in all likelihood unavoidable. I see no way around the answers to the various questions that are at stake here being in the end simply posited in a grand leap of faith, with no assurance either provided in fact or, so far as I can tell, even available in principle that those answers truly do correspond in some way to reality.

To the extent that the neodogmatist tendency in contemporary criticism continues to take its bearings largely from Marxist categories of political, economic, and social analysis, moreover, it is difficult to see any significant change occurring in the almost completely marginalized position that criticism currently occupies in relation to the world outside the academy and the concerns of those (obviously the vast majority of people) who live their lives there.[27] Commentators have been noting for years, of course, that among the very few places in the world where Marxism is truly taken seriously by anyone any longer are universities, in particular in North America and Western Europe. Speculative metaphysics enjoyed a period of growth and expansion in the nineteenth century unlike anything since the great systems of the Continental rationalists in the seventeenth century and, prior to that, the High Middle Ages. Without exception, however, all these products of nineteenth-century imagination have been decisively refuted by twentieth-century reality; and with the sole exception of Marxism, the obvious conclusion has been drawn in each case by virtually everyone. Despite its manifest and repeated failures as an instrument of analysis in the present, a predictor of future developments, or a basis for social organization, Marxism nevertheless continues to demonstrate an almost uncanny ability to attract adherents within the university environment.[28] Those whose lives, professional and otherwise, bring them into contact with objective reality both more often and more directly than tends to be the case with most academics—including, not least, those in nominally "socialist" countries who until recently were obliged to pay lip service to Marxism as, for all intents and purposes, the state religion (and who in the vast majority of cases, unfortunately, still do[29])—have long recognized what the late Kenneth Clark termed its "moral and intellectual failure." What was once perhaps only a more or less mild irony, however, has more recently become a major source of embarrassment for many intellectuals, as people around the world in growing numbers capitalize on any shred of opportunity to liberate themselves from Marxist-inspired rule, even when the attempt to do so entails considerable personal risk. Here in particular, perhaps more than in any other single respect, the gulf between contemporary criticism and objective reality appears to grow wider all the time. Consider, for example, Richard Rorty's contention that "bourgeois capitalist society . . . is irrelevant to most of the problems of most of the population of the planet,"[30] weighed against the eagerness with which which virtually every portion of that population, given half a chance, adopts capitalism as its preferred mode of political, economic, and social organization.

Frederick Turner presents a striking example of what often seems an almost instinctive gravitation on the part of many academics to the radical left: "If sensible economic strategy worked," he maintains, "capitalism would fail. Instead it is the wonderfully rational socialist systems that collapse, undone by inflation or its reflex, the black market, whose fundamental roots are as mysterious as desire itself."[31] Or, we might say, as transparent. Turner is evidently still puzzled as to why collectivization, nationalization, and central-planning schemes invariably fail when tested under real-world conditions. To suggest that one might properly characterize as "rational" a belief in the possibility of such schemes actually duplicating, much less improving upon, the ability of market economies with their countless local decisions and negotiations, driven by the myriad personal incentives of vast numbers of participants, to produce and distribute wealth, must surely strike the reader in the last decade of the twentieth century as a rather remarkable point of view. That view, however, is at least matched in implausibility by Turner's still more sweeping contention that "there can be no such thing as economic justice in a world . . . [in which] it is possible to give a gift . . . and to show mercy"; for gift-giving "is inherently unfair to those who did not get a gift," and showing mercy "is inherently unjust and unequal" (ibid., p. 750). Now, a gift is, by definition, something that one is not owed. But justice consists precisely in the determination of deserts—that is, what people *are* owed. It can therefore never be the case that one is done an injustice by not being made the recipient of a gift. Mercy, on the other hand, is compassion unconstrained by principles of justice *as formally codified;* it is the tacit acknowledgment that, in a world of imperfect beings such as ourselves, the ideal of justice and the reality of legal systems can never be made perfectly congruent with one another. From the fact that it is not within our power to develop a legal code capable of anticipating all possible cases and to which, accordingly, reasonable exceptions would never be either possible or necessary, it scarcely follows, however, that "a merciful act . . . cannot be fully accounted for by the merits of the recipient of it" and still less that "mercy is necessarily undeserved and necessarily unequal" (ibid., p. 759). What else, after all, could account for "a merciful act," if not precisely "the merits of the recipient of it"? The predicates "undeserved" and "unequal" would be properly applied to judgments that would, say, free Jean Valjean today but condemn him (or someone just like him in exactly similar circumstances) tomorrow. They are not applicable to judgments that would free Jean Valjean and condemn Raskolnikov on the basis of the respective presence and absence of extenuating circumstances in the two cases (leaving out of account for the moment the enormous difference in the gravity of the crimes themselves). The concept of mercy is demeaned if applied to the sort of case in which Jean Valjean goes free or not depending merely, as it were, on the luck of the draw. Mercy is not whim or caprice. From the fact that one is never, strictly speaking, owed mercy, in other words, it does not follow that one cannot *merit* mercy. The commonsensical distinction between how we would act in formulating a legal code, given perfect knowledge of the future, and the ad hoc ways in which in reality we sometimes have to apply our moral intuitions to particular cases, prevents the conflation of the concepts of justice and mercy that Turner fears (ibid., p. 759). But it does not do so at the price, which he is forced to pay, of positing a stark opposition between the two.

Events of the last few years notwithstanding, however, it would surely be an unimaginative Marxist dialectician at best who could find no way of turning the lemon of socialist collapse into some sort of lemonade. And in fact a number of expedients to that end are lately more and more in evidence among the faithful. Prominent among these are efforts to put as much distance as possible between one's own Marxism and the now hopelessly discredited former regimes of Eastern Europe and the Soviet Union (as well as the equally discredited, but, alas, still surviving, ones of Cuba, North Korea, and China).[32] Those regimes, it is now alleged, not only did not reflect what *we* believe; they were never *really* Marxist to begin with, or not in the good sense. Rather they represented, for example, merely "Stalinist aberrations." This, however, seems a little like calling the beliefs of the Flat Earth Society a "planar aberration" of geocentrism—as if geocentrism also came in tenable forms.[33] When a given system of belief has, as Marxism has, produced throughout the entire history of its existence, whenever and wherever it has actually been tried, nothing but results that one finds oneself constrained to term "aberrations," the notion of "aberration" itself loses content. Nonetheless, this strategy has an undeniable attraction for those who are determined to hold on to "Marxism" in some form. Michael Ryan, for example (and he is, of course, only one among many who could be cited here), distinguishes between what he calls "scientific marxism . . . grounded in . . . 'dialectical materialism' [and] closed to new advances in philosophy and critical analysis" and "critical marxism," distinguished precisely by its "rejection of the model of authoritarian central state communism" and support for "models of socialism which are dehierarchized, egalitarian, and democratic."[34]

An interesting feature of this move is the effort, as it were, to go generic, dropping the proper noun format altogether and styling oneself simply a "marxist," writ small.[35] In this same general vein we can locate references to such notions as "post-Marxism" or even "postmodern Marxism."[36] And still other variations on the theme would not be difficult to cite. Once steps of this sort begin to be taken, however, the question more or less inevitably arises: What is supposed to be the point of keeping the designation "Marxist" (whether upper or lower case) at all? This whole effort has about it something more than a little reminiscent of the insistence on the part of many Roman Catholics today, especially in the United States and including not a few members of the clergy, that, notwithstanding their rejection of significant portions of the doctrine of their Church as reflected both in Scripture and in the teachings of the Vatican, they nonetheless remain in some sense "Catholics." The difficulty, of course, is in how to give any cash value to that claim, once the possibility has been removed of grounding it in an appeal to a distinctive body of doctrine accepted by all members of the particular community of belief. And, in similar fashion, one may be moved to wonder: What is particularly "Marxist" about (for example) "critical marxism"? In addition, however, there is the further question of whether this purportedly rehabilitated version of Marxism can avoid the epistemological pitfall, fatal to its predecessor, of having to ground itself solely in metaphysically dogmatic terms. The answers to these two questions, I think, are not much and almost certainly not, respectively.

With respect to the former question, one does not exactly set one's outlook apart from others by characterizing it as a "rejection of . . . authoritarian central state communism." Virtually everyone today rejects that "model." And, similarly, it would be a not inconsiderable feat to find someone who did *not* claim to be in some sense in favor of "dehierarchized, egalitarian, and democratic" policies. To talk in vague terms, as is common today, of a need to be "oppositional," or "subversive," or "transgressive," or to support "alternative discourses," is so far to have said very little. Things get both more interesting and more controversial when, for instance, the notion of "socialism" invoked by Ryan in his characterization of "critical marxism" actually begins to be unpacked. For now the question becomes one of what precisely either the techniques of analysis or the principles of policy formulation that this notion implies really have to do with the realization of such generally agreed-upon values as, say, freedom, justice, and peace. Indeed, it is necessary to look more closely into just how those values themselves are construed in the first place in accordance with the model in question; for, again, the mere words *freedom, justice*, and *peace*, taken by themselves, refer to goals that are supported in *some* sense by virtually everyone. This is not a task I want to pursue at any length here. In general, however, what support of "socialism" in the sense at issue seems to amount to, when one finally gets down to cases, is simply the familiar political and economic agenda of those of a broadly left-liberal to radical persuasion. Such classic Marxist concepts as the theory of surplus value are now, for the most part, folded into a kind of all-purpose notion of "exploitation." Gone, similarly, are such once key policy objectives as the "dictatorship of the proletariat" and the concentration of ownership of the means of production in the hands of the state. Replacing them on the agenda are such items as steeply "progressive" taxation for purposes of income redistribution, a tendency to reject private enterprise in favor of a leading role for government in determining the direction of the economy, and, perhaps most characteristically of all, the establishment of a system of privileges and entitlements in the apportionment of society's goods for the benefit of certain selected interest groups (defined, in particular, by race, gender, ethnicity, and, more recently, sexual orientation).

This last-mentioned policy objective points, in turn, to the second of the questions raised above, that of the epistemological status of the "new" Marxism. We saw earlier, in connection with the discussion of "genuine history," something of the extent to which the appeal to concepts of race, gender, and the like in contexts such as this actually involves little more than an old-fashioned positing of metaphysical essences; and to that extent, of course, it also entails an actual denial of history, at least insofar as history is understood to be a matter of real change. Robert Markley, immediately preceding his reference to Ryan's distinction between "scientific" and "critical marxism" cited above, asserts as "the basic premise of Marxist thought" what he terms "the materialist grounding of all structures or systems of thought" ("What Isn't History," p. 654). We may presumably take it then that this "premise" at least is central to all the "variety of complex 'Marxisms' " (ibid.), all the "sophisticated 'critical' Marxisms that," Markley contends, "have emerged in the wake of Mikhail Bakhtin, Louis Althusser, Jean Baudrillard, Antonio Gramsci, Fredric Jameson, and others" (ibid., p. 655). Again, however, this notion needs to be unpacked, if we are to be clear on what is actually being asserted. Once that is done, however, this "basic premise" either proves to be something largely unexceptionable, but, in proportion, also not particularly informative; or it makes some very specific and sweeping claims indeed, but, in proportion, also does so in a way every bit as metaphysically dogmatic as anything that was ever postulated by the "old-fashioned dialectical materialism" (ibid.) now ostensibly being put out to pasture.

If the only thing meant by a "materialist grounding of all structures or systems of thought" is that our explanations of mental phenomena must in principle always be referable ultimately to concepts of physical science (even if we have at the moment no very adequate notion of how actually to go about doing that)—if, in other words, we are to make no appeal in such accounts to Cartesian dualisms or "ghost-in-the-machine" models—then I think there is surely not much basis for disagreement. But if anything is clear in all this, it is certainly that "the basic premise of Marxist thought" in question is by no means limited to any such modest conception of a "materialist grounding" of thought as this one. Rather there is a large and intricate set of concepts pertaining to structures of society and forms of human activity—in particular, though by no means exclusively, poltical and economic activity—that is posited in this "premise" as the *explanans* of such things as consciousness, belief, characteristic attitudes of people, and so forth. Or rather, a number of such sets of concepts have been proposed (e.g., by Bakhtin, Althusser, Baudrillard, and others), each of them differing to some extent from the others, but among which there is also a considerable degree of overlap. And among the most important of the common features linking these various sets is precisely that the relationship of explanatory theory to the reality that that theory purports to explain is in every case simply *asserted* (or, as in some instances, merely assumed), but always without anything remotely resembling a supporting argument. With respect to epistemological structure, in other words, these various systems are all more or less unabashedly dogmatic in character.[37] It was always a non sequitur to conclude from the supposed fact that a variety of allegedly more "sophisticated" forms of "ideological criticism" had succeeded the older " 'vulgar' Marxist maxims" and "Stalinist caricature[s]" ("What Isn't History," p. 655) that the underlying epistemological modality of the former had itself undergone any fundamental change from the one that characterized the latter in their heyday. Markley's and others' protestations to the contrary notwithstanding, it remains the case that " 'ideological criticism' . . . assumes for itself a metaphysical objectivity, a privileged analytical authority, that it denies to those '-ologies' and '-isms' that it attacks" (ibid., p. 654).[38]

As Oscar Kenshur observes, this is "a difficulty that has long bedeviled the theory of ideology, namely the difficulty of privileging the standpoint from which ideological analysis is to be carried out. . . . [T]he [ostensible] historical self-consciousness that underlies the analysis of ideologies cannot in itself ensure that the perspective of the person carrying out the analysis represents science rather than ideology" in its own right.[39] In particular, as Kenshur points out in his critical rejoinder to Markley's attack on his analysis of "ideological essentialism," "the claim that all language is an ideological construct cannot be justified by an implicit appeal to a historical consensus or to one's own advanced place on a historical continuum"; for the very attempt to do so inescapably commits one to "arguing that there is a *transhistorical* perspective yielded by a progressive philosophical project, namely, the perspective

that sees all language as an ideological construct and that sees itself as
the happy culmination of theoretical advances" (emphasis added).[40] The
assumption of such a perspective is obviously fatal to the program of universal ideological "historicization" that Markley and others would
clearly like to be able to undertake in neo-Marxist fashion. And yet that
same assumption is evidently unavoidable on the terms of the program
itself. There appears to be, in other words, no way of reconciling with
one another the *historical*-materialist and the *dialectical*-materialist
components of the system in question, neither of which it can afford to
abandon, but each of which also excludes the other. To effect such a reconciliation it would be necessary to show how the system can be at once
the comprehensive, global description of human affairs that it purports
to be, necessarily valid for all people in all times and places, and yet at
the same time remain faithful in its own right precisely to the relativist
and particularist principles that are of the essence of that very description, with its denial that any such all-embracing "grand narrative" can
ever legitimately claim to be *the* once-and-for-all true story.

Discussing the fallacy he terms "ideological essentialism," Kenshur
develops an argument showing that "the claim that views about knowledge have some intrinsic connection with political views does not rest—
to use a metaphor popular among early-modern philosophers—on very
solid foundations" ("Demystifying," p. 343). "[N]o epistemological position can be *intrinsically* reactionary or *intrinsically* progressive"
(ibid., p. 347), for the fairly obvious reason that there is no epistemological position that cannot be (and historically has not been) used in the
service of "political views" not only different from, but wholly incompatible with, one another.[41] And he adds, significantly:

> Nor is philosophical skepticism or relativism an exception to this
> rule. For while many contemporary theorists seem to assume that
> skepticism is intrinsically subversive of established authority, a
> glance at Sextus Empiricus, or at the long history of skepticism,
> will reveal a tradition of skeptical arguments to justify obedience to
> religious and civil authority: since our own investigations cannot
> yield certainty, the argument goes, we have no basis for question-
> ing established authority. ("Demystifying," p. 347)[42]

And, on the other hand, although "contemporary polemicists . . . refer
to connections" between "the objectivist notion that there can be a standard of correctness in the interpretation of texts" and what they regard
as "unsavory . . . political implications" in the form of "right-wing tendencies" in thought and action, they "generally omit to demonstrate the

existence of such a relationship" (ibid., p. 335). I think "generally" is putting it rather kindly here. I have myself never seen anything remotely resembling such a "demonstration." And the reason I have not, I believe, is the very good one that no such demonstration is possible, neither of the alleged "implications" themselves nor of their, also allegedly, "unsavory" character.

Where I would like to have seen Kenshur press his argument further, however, is with regard to the whole matter of the supposed permanent possibility (or even relevance) of "ideological analysis." While recognizing that "an epistemological stance is not intrinsically linked to one political stance or another" ("Demystifying," p. 351), he is nonetheless unwilling to go all the way and acknowledge the possibility of an epistemological stance not linked to any political stance at all. And yet that very conclusion appears to be entailed precisely by his own anti-essentialist argument. For if "[t]hose who, on the basis of perceived homologies, claim that a given theory or belief logically entails a given [ideologically] legitimating function are . . . guilty of ideological essentialism . . . inasmuch as they treat historical questions as if they were theoretical ones" (ibid., p. 353); if, in other words, the standpoint in question "treats a historically contingent relationship as if it were a relationship of logical implication" (ibid., p. 347); then we can ask how the situation is any different from this if one automatically assumes that there is of necessity always some "legitimating function" discernible in the case of every "theory or belief" without exception. For surely the same considerations as those just invoked must apply here as well. This assumption, too, appears intent on transforming the merely "historically contingent"—that is, the presence or absence of a (so-called) "legitimating function" in any given case in particular—into a matter of "logical implication." And thus a new sort of epistemological-ideological essentialism is posited, differing from the first sort only in its location one level higher up in the order of abstraction.

If "to engage in ideological analysis is . . . to examine a theory or structure of thought . . . in the context . . . of its role in legitimating sectional interests" ("Demystifying," p. 351), there is still the logically prior question to be addressed of why such analysis should simply be assumed to be required, or even appropriate, in the case of absolutely every "theory or structure of thought" to begin with. And yet Kenshur appears entirely committed to that assumption. While allowing that "the status of an epistemological stance as ideological is not its essence, but merely one of the ways in which it may be considered," he nonetheless adds at once: "I am not, I hasten to say, supposing that philosophical or scientific theories are the products of purely disinterested contemplation, and that theories are put to ideological uses only after the fact" (ibid.). But if we substitute, say, something like "mental activity" for the straw man of "contemplation" here—I am not sure that it makes sense to speak of contemplation producing anything (apart, perhaps, from certain aesthetic or quasi-aesthetic states of consciousness), and I am sure that it makes no sense at all to speak of theories being so produced, whether philosophical, scientific, or any other kind—I see no reason why we should not say precisely this about the vast majority of our beliefs and knowledge claims. An actual demonstration of, or even a plausible argument for, the thesis that disinterestedness, and specifically disinterested rationality, do not exist is as lacking as one showing the alleged "connections between objectivist theory and right-wing tendencies." There is, of course, again, as noted a moment ago, no lack of dogmatic assertions to this effect today, but that is obviously not the same thing. And in reflecting on the difference between the two, we can also begin to see why there could never be such a demonstration either. No one has to believe a mere assertion. Assertions, in the sense in which I am using the term here, are statements made in the absence of (sufficient) reasons. In itself, of course, that does not mean that they are not true; it merely means that we have as yet no reason to regard them as true. What both compels and constrains belief are precisely reasons. Linked together in sufficient numbers and force, reasons yield demonstrations. One can take or leave mere assertions without, so to speak, epistemological penalty. One cannot, however, deny the conclusion of a demonstration without either self-contradiction or absurdity. A demonstration that would purport to show either the nonexistence or the nonbinding character of rationality is thus, on its own terms, a logical impossibility. And because that is so, it follows in turn that we have more than adequate reason to reject any and all assertions to the effect that there is no such thing as rationality, or that there are not criteria of rational deliberation universally binding on all discursive agents.

The commonsense view of most people, based on extensive, concrete experience of the real world, is that while "a single epistemological stance can be used to support divergent sectional interests" and, contrariwise, "the same sectional interests can be served by surprisingly divergent epistemological claims" ("Demystifying," p. 350), by far the most usual case is the one in which a given epistemological "stance" or set of "claims" is altogether indifferent to any particular body of "sectional interests." The overwhelmingly largest portion of our beliefs tends neither to "legitimate" nor to undermine such "interests" but rather does not intersect with them at any point at all. And we have now seen one way—there are doubtless others—in which that commonsense view can be defended on logical grounds as well. Foucault and others to the contrary notwithstanding, life just is not the all-consuming struggle for power between competing truth-regimes that they would have us believe it is. No one not suffering from acute paranoia actually experiences life that way. And the effort to develop an argument showing that it is nevertheless the case (i.e., regardless of whether or not one happens to be aware of it) founders, as just seen, on the fact that no such argument could establish its validity without committing itself in the same moment to precisely the opposite thesis from the one it wants to demonstrate. As Habermas points out, Foucault and his followers assume much too readily that the very situation of universal, constant power struggle, which they want to contend represents the basic stratum of the human condition at large, does not call for an explanation in its own right as to its own possibility. And yet, as Habermas shows, it requires only a little reflection to see that, on its own terms, such a situation could scarcely have arisen in the first place:

> When, like Foucault, one admits only the model of processes of subjugation, of confrontations mediated by the body, of contexts of more or less consciously strategic action; when one excludes any stabilizing of domains of action in terms of values, norms, and processes of mutual understanding and offers for these mechanisms of social integration none of the familiar equivalents from systems or exchange theories; then one is hardly able to explain just how persistent local struggles could get consolidated into institutionalized power. . . . Foucault presupposes in his descriptions institutionally sedimented disciplines, power practices, technologies of truth and of domination, but he cannot explain "how there can be derived from a social condition of uninterrupted struggle the aggregate state of a network of power, however momentary one conceives it as being."[43] . . . Foucault, the theorist of power, encounters . . . the same problems as the institutionalist Arnold Gehlen;[44] both theories lack a mechanism for social integration such as language, with its interlacing of the performative attitudes of speakers and hearers.[45]

But, it may be countered, what if rationality itself is at bottom not really a disinterested matter at all? As Martin Matusik frames the issue, "[M]ust postmodernity be allowed to sidestep the *tu quoque* charge of self-referentiality by offering its own *tu quoque* retort to a critical modernist: 'you are merely *deciding* to be rational, hence your choice of modernity is irrational'?"[46] That is, what if electing rationality is itself a wholly arbitrary choice, neither grounded nor groundable in reason in its own right, but rather dictated solely by some "sectional interest" in particular that the person making that choice hopes in this way to be able to promote more effectively? The key premise of the postmodernist *tu quoque* is clearly that one can apply a "decisionist" model to rationality itself. But Wittgenstein had already noted in the *Tractatus* that the premise is false: "What makes logic a priori," he remarks in a passage seen earlier, "is the *impossibility* of illogical thought" (*TLP*, 5.4731). The point is misunderstood, moreover, if Wittgenstein is taken to be asserting a merely psychological impossibility here. In this context a "thought" is for him a "logical picture of facts" (*TLP*, 3), and that is in turn to say "a proposition with a sense" (*TLP*, 4). The "impossibility" in question is thus *logical* in nature. As he puts it elsewhere in the *Tractatus:* "It used to be said that God could create anything except what would be contrary to the laws of logic.—The truth is that we could not *say* what an 'illogical' world would look like" (*TLP*, 3.031). For only propositions are sayable in the first place, and propositions, again, are precisely logical pictures of facts.

As Matusik's essay helps remind us, Habermas's position in response to the postmodernist *tu quoque* coincides in its essentials with the Wittgensteinian one just seen. For Habermas, too, it is a question finally of what is logically possible or not. And in this way he is able to show that the attempt to reduce or relativize rationality to mere local (or "sectional") interest, as reflected in an ultimately arbitrary choice on the part of the one advocating it, is blocked before it can get underway. As Matusik puts it: "Habermas establishes the universal and objective validity of a discursive paradigm of reason without . . . leaning on decision or allowing for a silent retreat from communication. Communication is not a matter of decidability. . . . One cannot decide to use or not to use language because, in Gadamer's words, 'being that can be understood is [already] language' " (ibid., pp. 162–63).[47] "[T]o be human," in other words, is eo ipso "[t]o be a potential participant in discourse. . . . The decision not to communicate, not to have any authority in discourse," thus itself "depends . . . on this prior [communicative] competence. Participation and nonparticipation are moves within the same language game that already structured [among other things] the [very] modernist-postmodernist debate" (ibid., p. 164) that is at issue here. Rationality, accordingly, *cannot* be radically interest-relative—one cannot "*decid[e]* to be rational" (or not)—because interests themselves, and a fortiori the decisions prompted by them, already presuppose rationality for their very existence. For Habermas, as we saw at some length earlier, "the claims [of "communicative rationality"] to truth, normative rightness, and authenticity" can therefore legitimately be regarded as "universal crosscultural and transhistorical invariants of communication" (ibid., p. 158). Such "universal validity claims constitute all linguistically mediated communicative interaction and are always implicitly amenable to redemption in an argumentative discourse" (ibid., p. 159). In Habermas's own words: "No matter how the intersubjectivity of mutual understanding may be deformed, the *design* of an ideal speech situation [i.e., the structural principles of communicative rationality] is necessarily implied in the structure of the potential speech act, since all speech, even of intentional deception, is oriented toward the idea of truth."[48]

II

In the preceding section I have tried to sketch at least some principal features of the direction in contemporary criticism that I am calling neodogmatism. Regardless of what forms in particular "content"-oriented approaches to criticism such as these may happen to assume, however, the more important point to note for purposes of the overall argument here is that they are no more assured of a permanent spot atop the marquee than is—or, as the case may be, depending on one's assessment of the current state of the struggle, was—the "textualism" they are bidding fair to replace. As noted earlier, dogmatic systems of thought, which, despite what we have seen to be a significant admixture of skeptical strains, the ones in question here basically are, have always both called forth and eventually been undermined by unabashedly skeptical assaults on their epistemic foundations. It would be historically naive in the extreme, I think, to suppose that the same thing will not in time happen in this case as well. The only way off this Ixion's wheel of dogmatism and skepticism, foundationalism and anti-foundationalism, is to break firmly with the single, fundamental assumption on which both these positions depend in precisely equal measure. Showing how that can be done—or rather, offering some reminders of how in their different ways Kant, Herder, and Wittgenstein showed us it could be done—has been the principal negative concern of this study. What the positive consequences might be, whether for literary criticism in particular or for critical theory generally, should a recognition of this "negative" insight actually take hold on a large scale, I am unable to say. Kant saw his "critical" analysis of the limits of knowledge as securing at the same time a space for the possibility of morality. Similarly, Herder regarded his "negative philosophy" as above all a way of removing a series of obstacles to productive pursuit of the ideal of *Humanität*. For Wittgenstein, to be sure, a corresponding answer to this question—what happens to the "fly," once it has been shown the way out of the "fly-bottle"—is perhaps not quite so easy to specify. We recall, however, his famous characterization of the *Tractatus* as composed of two parts, one of them consisting of everything actually said in the work, the other of everything left unsaid in it; and it was the latter—the part concerned, above all, with ethics—that was in his view by far the more important one.[49] Like Kant, whom he greatly admired in this regard, Wittgenstein, too, is intent on achieving a delimitation of the realm of the factual for the sake of that of the ethical. As his friend Paul Engelmann put it in a well-known and frequently cited remark, while both Wittgenstein and the logical positivists believed that one could only be silent on matters of ethics, unlike Wittgenstein the logical positivists had "nothing to be silent about."[50] And although the idea of such a delimitation seems to me plainly not the sole object of his later philosophizing, in which a more generalized notion of "therapy" tends to assume primary importance, I doubt that it was ever very far from his thoughts either. But to the question what would a criticism freed of both dogmatic and skeptical urges look like, again, I have at the moment no, or no very extensive, answer.

The search for a way out of the otherwise endless cycle of dogmatism-skepticism-new dogmatism-new skepticism is, in any case, by no means tantamount to an effort to "bring history to an end" in the realm of criticism.[51] If anything, quite the contrary. The prospect of breaking the dogmatic-skeptical deadlock brings with it a renewed possibility of something that we rightly regard as of the essence of history, but which, as suggested earlier, has for some time now largely been absent from the scene of our endeavors, namely *change*, the emergence of the new, the unexpected, even (or especially) the unprecedented and unpredictable. Charles Altieri has sought to lay the theoretical foundation for a rehumanized practice of literary criticism, one that would be capable of orienting itself in productive fashion to the lives and interests of people at large. And he has himself also offered several concrete examples of how such a program might be translated into reality.[52] Reed Dasenbrock, too, has provided a number of stimulating suggestions in the same direction.[53] Mention should also be made of John Ellis and Paisley Livingston in this connection.[54] And there are certainly others who could be included here as well—although, by the same token, not yet a great many of them. The dogmatic-skeptical paradigm—what I have been calling the "pre-critical" standpoint—remains for the most part (as, with few exceptions, it always has) the dominant outlook of professionals and laymen alike, with, at the moment, as we have seen, in the field of criticism in particular predominantly skeptical modes largely holding the upper hand, though also facing a stiff challenge from a reinvigorated, politically charged dogmatism. Even the theoretical case capable of overthrowing this paradigm still has some way to go before it can be said to have been made in wholly adequate fashion. And working out all the practical implications of that case for the actual work of critical analysis will doubtless be a much longer task still. If anything is already clear in all this, however, it is surely that there is in any case no going back to the sort of formalism that until comparatively recently dominated the field. Though most of those active in the profession today were trained more or less in the mold of the New Criticism—we were taught, that is, to be first and foremost "close readers" of texts—and although the various techniques that we acquired in the course of that training will in all likelihood continue to be an important part of our approach to our work, there seems nevertheless no serious prospect of any of us ever being content again merely to produce the sorts of readings that once came out of that school and which, in their time, did set the tone for criticism generally. But exactly how we move forward from the point at which we now find ourselves can be determined, I think, only in the process of actually trying to do so.[55]

Two important questions still requiring attention from the theory of critical realism are what might be called the problem of *error* and the (very big) problem of *history*. With respect to the former, Donald Davidson writes in a slightly different, though related, connection:

> It should not be assumed that if we cease to be bullied or beguiled by the scheme-content and subjective-objective dichotomies, all the problems of epistemology will evaporate. But the problems that seem salient will change. Answering the global skeptic will no longer be a challenge, the search for epistemological foundations in experience will be seen as pointless, and conceptual relativism will lose its appeal. But plenty of questions of equal or greater interest will remain, or be generated by the new stance. The demise of the subjective as previously conceived leaves us without foundations for knowledge and relieves us of the the need for them. New problems then arise, however, that cluster around the nature of error; for error is hard to identify and explain if the holism that goes with a nonfoundational approach is not somehow constrained.[56]

In other words, while adopting a position such as Davidson's (or my own) means that there is no longer any difficulty in accounting for our ability to be *right* about things, it becomes in proportion somewhat more difficult to explain how we ever go *wrong* about them.[57]

Though the problem of error is certainly a philosophically challenging one, there is at any rate for each of us a thoroughly concrete and unambiguous point of orientation toward its eventual resolution in our own experience, specifically in all the incontrovertible reminders of our all-too-fallible natures with which the world sometimes seems only too glad to provide us. A correspondingly unequivocal point of reference in the case of the problem of history seems, however, to be lacking. The problem is essentially this: it seems equally necessary to say each of two different things about history, and yet it is not at all easy to see how those two things can be made compatible with one another. On the one hand, we are evidently always *inside* history, the objects of its continual movement, formed in accordance with the characteristics of our own particular historical situations. Our being is insofar radically contextual, determined in accordance with the myriad specific details uniquely constitutive of our present location and the tradition in which it is embedded. And yet if we really were in all respects as utterly time- and place-bound as this picture represents us as being, it is not clear how history itself would even be possible. The very assertion of the "inside-history" principle as a universal condition of human existence appears, in other words, to presuppose the possibility of precisely what the principle itself would deny, namely a global perspective, not bound to any individual moment in particular, and insofar actually *outside* of history. To put it another way, history is nothing if not a human artifact; it is made by people, not merely in the sense that it is the activities of human beings with which history is primarily concerned, but in the sense that one of those activities is precisely the creation of the very stories in which history itself consists. It thus appears that we are of necessity the subjects as well as the objects of history, ourselves the creators of what, by hypothesis, creates us.[58]

Both Herder and Hegel were acutely aware of this apparent paradox, and both of them made impressive efforts to resolve it. That these efforts may nonetheless not have been in all respects entirely successful is attested to, as much as anything else perhaps, simply by the fact that the problem is evidently still with us. It reappears, for example, in only slightly modified form, as the central issue in the famous Habermas-Gadamer debate, the key points of which are lucidly summarized by Thomas McCarthy in his critical exposition of the former's thought.[59] To begin with, as McCarthy notes:

Gadamer explicitly takes into account . . . the essentially historical dimension of *Sinn* and *Sinnverstehen*. By drawing out the dependence of interpretive understanding on the sociocultural
"initial situation" of the interpreter and disclosing the essentially
historical nature of the latter, hermeneutics forces us to reflect on
the relations of theory to history and, more particularly, to the
philosophy of history. (*CTH*, p. 177)

And further, emphasizing the element of commonality in the two thinkers' views:

For Habermas, as for Gadamer, the ideas of a society freed from
history and for a technical mastery of its future, of a history that
has been disempowered as *Wirkungsgeschichte*, and of a post-
historical social science freed from context-bound interpretation
of its historical situation are equally illusory. They themselves
have to be hermeneutically comprehended in their relation to the
sociocultural development of modern society. In reality, the allegedly universal theories of social action remain rooted in, and reflect, this very development. . . . If the social scientist is not to
proceed with his head in the sand, he must reflectively take into
account the dependence of his conceptual apparatus on a prior
understanding that is rooted in his own sociocultural situation.
He must become hermeneutically and historically self-conscious.
(*CTH*, pp. 178–79)

Differences begin to arise, however, as attention turns to the question of
substantive claims to truth and how to assess them. "In Gadamer's view
the dismissal of beliefs and values as mistakes pure and simple is an admission of a failure to understand" (*CTH*, p. 181). Against this standpoint, while "Habermas accepts, at least in its general outlines, the
argument that the interpreter necessarily relates what is to be understood to his own concrete hermeneutic situation,. . . . he has serious
reservations about Gadamer's account of that relation and the conservative implications he draws from it" (*CTH*, p. 181). As Habermas writes
in *Zur Logik der Sozialwissenschaften:*

In Gadamer's view, on-going tradition and hermeneutic inquiry
merge to a single point. Opposed to this is the insight that the reflected appropriation of tradition breaks down the nature-like
(*naturwüchsige*) substance of tradition and alters the position of
the subject in it. . . . The hermeneutic insight is certainly correct,
viz. the insight that understanding—no matter how controlled it
may be—cannot simply leap over the interpreter's relationship to

tradition. But from the fact that understanding is structurally a part of the traditions that it further develops through appropriation, it does not follow that the medium of tradition is not profoundly altered by scientific reflection. . . . Gadamer fails to appreciate the power of reflection that is developed in understanding. This type of reflection is no longer blinded by the appearance of an absolute that can only be self-grounded; it does not detach itself from the soil of contingency on which it finds itself. But in grasping the genesis of the tradition from which it proceeds and on which it turns back, reflection shakes the dogmatism of life practice. (*CTH*, p. 181)

In other words, as McCarthy puts it, summing up Habermas's position here, "The fact that 'the moment of historical influence is and remains effective in all understanding of tradition' is itself no justification of the legitimacy and authority of tradition" (*CTH*, pp. 181–82).[60]

Thus the issue is joined between "hermeneutics," on the one hand, and "critique," on the other. Habermas writes: "Gadamer's prejudice for the rights of prejudices certified by tradition denies the power of reflection. The latter proves itself however in being able to reject the claim of tradition" (*CTH*, p. 182). And, accordingly, notes McCarthy, "Although he accepts Gadamer's point about the finitude and context-boundedness of human understanding, Habermas rejects his relativistic and idealistic conclusions regarding the logic of *Verstehen*" (*CTH*, p. 182). For "the critique of ideology," which Habermas sees as not merely indispensable to an understanding of any discourse in the present but as something that must be extended to the "tradition" as well, plainly "requires a system of reference that goes beyond tradition, one that deabsolutizes tradition by systematically taking into account the empirical conditions under which it develops and changes. . . . A reduction of social inquiry to *Sinnverstehen* could be justified only on the idealist assumption that linguisticaly articulated consciousness determined the material conditions of life" (*CTH*, pp. 183–84). Citing Habermas again: " 'Social action can only be comprehended in an objective framework that is constituted conjointly by language, labor and power [or domination—*Herrschaft*]' " (*CTH*, p. 184). Against "Gadamer's point about the situation-dependency of historical understanding—thought is always rooted in actual history; there is no point outside of history from which to view the whole, as if it were given to consciousness as a completed totality" (*CTH*, p. 184), Habermas thus insists on the reality of what we might think of as a number of historical "existentials." Though, like Heidegger's "existentials," nowhere fully realized save as actually instantiated in some way in particular historical contexts—as Heidegger puts it, "Being is always the

Being of beings"[61]—in Habermas's view they are evidently also always instantiated in some form or other everywhere.

McCarthy rightly notes that "the contemporary debate between hermeneutics and critical theory [the latter term referring, again, specifically to Habermas's program in philosophy and social thought] . . . has been carried out at a 'transcendental' . . . level" (*CTH*, p. 187). I am puzzled, however, at his apparent suggestion that this somehow distinguishes "the contemporary debate" from "the Enlightenment versus Romanticism controversy of the late eighteenth and early nineteenth centuries" (*CTH*, p. 187). For it was precisely at this time, of course, as we have seen, that the notion of a "transcendental" analysis was first developed at all. At least if McCarthy is thinking of figures such as Kant, Fichte, and Hegel as among the parties to the "controversy" in question, I do not see how what is involved there can well be understand without reference to the level of the "transcendental." However this may be, though, McCarthy clearly makes an important point in emphasizing that "Gadamer does not simply plead the advantage of tradition; he argues that participation in a cultural heritage is a condition of the possibility of all thought, including critical reflection" (*CTH*, p. 187). In this way Gadamer seeks, in effect, to outflank Habermas, by showing that the latter's points against him cannot even be formulated without implicitly confirming what they profess to deny. Because "critique is necessarily partial and from a particular point of view. . . . Gadamer concludes, Habermas's concept of critique is 'dogmatic': he ascribes to reflection a power that it could have only on idealistic premises. . . . Reflection is no less historically situated, context-dependent, than other modes of thought. In challenging a cultural heritage one presupposes and continues it" (*CTH*, pp. 187–88).

In particular, "[w]hat Habermas designates as 'real determinants of social processes' (such as economic and political factors) and sets against language and culture are themselves linguistically mediated and accessible to interpretive understanding" (*CTH*, p. 188). Moreover, "[h]ermeneutics does not imply a blind subjugation to tradition; we also understand when we *see through prejudices* that distort reality. 'In fact [says Gadamer] this is when we *understand most of all* ' " (*CTH*, p. 189; emphasis added). This is, I think, a crucial juncture in the debate. For it seems that Gadamer may finally have overreached himself here by trying to have things both ways at once; it is a move, however, that his theory may also in the end leave him no alternative to at least attempting. Were we not told a moment ago that "[i]n Gadamer's view the dismissal of beliefs and values as mistakes pure and simple is an admission of a failure to understand" (*CTH*, p. 181)? And further:

In the strong (hermeneutic) sense, to understand is to explicate to
a point at which the belief or value in question appears worthy of
consideration from a common point of view of humanity. It is only
when we fail in this attempt that we have to appeal to error, self-
delusion, and so forth to explain something that we are not able to
understand. . . . Since we have no monopoly on truth and goodness, we must maintain an openness to the beliefs and values of
others; we must be prepared to learn from them. (*CTH*, p. 181)

But how are we simultaneously to maintain this attitude, which seems to
come very close to the standpoint of *tout comprendre c'est tout pardon-
ner,* and yet also be able to "see through prejudices that distort reality"?
How will we even be able to recognize such "prejudices" *as* prejudices
(in the pejorative sense of the term clearly intended in this context—
Gadamer, of course, also has a more positive notion of *Vor-urteil*), if a
necessary condition of our having understood them at all—that is, *before* we have passed one way or the other on their possibly "prejudicial"
character—is to have established a kind of sympathetic identification
with them? It is all well and good to say, as McCarthy quotes Peter
Winch as saying—the latter perhaps unaware that he is in effect quoting
Herder in turn—that " '[s]eriously to study another way of life is necessarily to seek to extend our own' " (*CTH*, p. 181). That is surely true.
But it does not yet answer, or even address, the criticism, which
Friedrich Schlegel brought against Herder as Habermas now does
against Gadamer, that a historical hermeneutics of this sort, with its fu-
sion of understanding and identification, amounts ultimately to a mas-
sively holistic justification of everything, leaving us no alternative to
saying simply, as Schlegel implied Herder was committed to saying,
"daß alles sein müßte, was es ist und war."[62]

As I have tried to show on other occasions, this is a problem to which
Herder was in fact thoroughly attuned well before the time of Schlegel's
criticism and one with which he continued to wrestle throughout his
life.[63] In general, the extent to which Herder anticipates both the
shape of contemporary critical debate and the positions taken by parties on *both* sides of the various controversies current in it, though not
yet widely recognized, is nonetheless remarkable. Nowhere is that
more clearly the case than in the field of cultural anthropology, as Mc-
Carthy implicitly demonstrates in a long footnote dealing with Habermas's analysis of a fundamental problem confronting contemporary
ethnomethodologists:

Stressing the "indexicality" or context-dependence of communication, ethnomethodologists have argued forcefully that the social

scientist as interpreter must enter, at least as a virtual participant, into the context in which the action to be interpreted is embedded.[64] . . . The methodological implications of this thesis are far-reaching: "If a context of action can be opened up only from within, that is through (at least virtual) participation in a communication that is set within, and at the same time further develops, this context, the sociologist must in principle assume the same position as the lay member. He has no privileged access to the object domain."[65] . . . This, of course, raises the question of what ethnomethodologists conceive themselves to be doing. Some . . . have accepted the radically relativistic implications of applying this insight to their own work: "Interpretive sciences must give up the claim to produce theoretical knowledge . . . If the insight into the unavoidably self-referential character of research practice cannot open a way to context-independent knowledge, then social research can exist only as one particular form of life alongside others. . . . It cannot dissolve its situational ties." . . . Others. . . . have attempted to analyze formally the invariant properties of the "practices" through which "members" produce the objective appearance of a stable order. . . . But this immediately raises the question: "How can this type of research into universals be carried through if social-scientific interpretations are context-dependent in the same way as everyday interpretations?" According to Habermas, the ethnomethodologist is here confronted with a dilemma from which he cannot escape without altering his basic self-understanding. Either he claims a privileged access to his object domain—an analogue of Husserl's epoche—and thus betrays his original methodological insight or he remains true to that insight and surrenders the claim to theory (to reconstruct the general presuppositions of communication). The only way out of this dilemma of either a "Husserlian absolutism" or a "confessed relativism" is, Habermas argues, to show "how social-scientific analysis must unavoidably fasten onto the everyday interpretations it examines, and how it can nevertheless reflectively penetrate them and transcend the given context." . . . To do this, he goes on, requires that one acknowledge the "binding force of general structures of rationality" rather than regarding them as mere phenomena: "Garfinkel [for example] treats standards of rationality, like all other conventions, as the result of a contingent interpretive practice that can be described, but not systematically reconstructed and evaluated. . . . He regards unconditional and universal validity claims merely as something that the participants take to be unconditional and universal. . . . Garfinkel thus once again reserves for the ethnomethodologist the position of neutral observer. . . . But then the ethnomethodologist has to claim for his own statements standards of validity which *a fortiori* lie outside the domain

of those claimed by the participants; to the extent that he does not
credit himself with such an extramundane position, he cannot
claim a theoretical status for his statements." (CTH, pp. 411–12)[66]

Gadamer's earlier point against Habermas—that because, in McCarthy's words, "there is no alternative to dialogue as a medium for clari-
fying and evaluating opposing validity claims[, t]he critic of ideology
[i.e., Habermas] assumes a superiority for his point of view that he cannot in reality justify[,] . . . pretend[ing] to anticipate the outcome of rational dialogue before it has taken place" (CTH, p. 189)—would thus
appear to be turned back against Gadamer himself. But that does not
necessarily mean that the latter is ready to sue for terms. For it is still
open to him to insist that, again in McCarthy's words, "the point at issue
is not whether we accept or reject a given validity claim."

> The question is rather how we become conscious of and evaluate
> preconceptions and prejudgments. This is not, he argues, some-
> thing that can be done all at once in a supreme act of reflection. It
> is rather precisely in trying to understand other points of view, in
> trying to come to an understanding with others, that my own, as
> well as their, "structure of prejudices" becomes perceptible. Re-
> flection is not something opposed to understanding; it is an inte-
> gral moment of the attempt to understand. To separate them as
> Habermas does is a "dogmatic confusion." (CTH, p. 189)

And so the controversy continues. As McCarthy sums up:

> Gadamer's universalization of hermeneutics rests on a logical ar-
> gument against the possibility of methodologically transcending
> the hermeneutic point of view: any attempt to do so is inconsistent
> with the very conditions of possibility of understanding: the lin-
> guisticality and historicity of human existence. Habermas's coun-
> terposition is an attempt to mitigate the radically situational
> character of understanding through the introduction of theoretical
> elements; the theories of communication and social evolution are
> meant to reduce the context-dependency of the basic categories
> and assumptions of critical theory. (CTH, p. 193)

As I have indicated, I do not yet have a solution to this problem, or
not a complete one at any rate. But I do not believe that anyone else
today does either. A comprehensive solution to the problem of history
ultimately entails, I think, showing how reason itself can be, in Hilary
Putnam's words, "both immanent (not to be found outside of concrete

language games and institutions) and transcendent (a regulative idea that we use to criticize the conduct of all activities and institutions)." In other words, Putnam maintains:

> There are two points that must be balanced . . . : (1) talk of what is 'right' and 'wrong' in any area only makes sense against the background of an inherited tradition; but (2) traditions themselves can be criticized. . . . What I am saying is that the 'standards' accepted by a culture or a subculture, either explicitly or implicitly, cannot *define* what reason is, even in context, because they *presuppose* reason (reasonableness) for their interpretation. On the one hand, there is no notion of reasonableness at all without cultures, practices, procedures; on the other hand, the cultures, practices, procedures we inherit are not an algorithm to be slavishly followed. As Mill said, commenting on his own inductive logic, there is no rule book which will not lead to terrible results "if supposed to be conjoined with universal idiocy."[67]

McCarthy as well has recourse to the vocabulary of "immanence" and "transcendence" in this regard. He writes:

> What is important is the common idea that any adequate account of truth as rational acceptability will have to capture not only its immanence—i.e., its socially situated character—but its transcendence as well. While we may have no idea of standards of rationality wholly independent of historically concrete languages and practices, it remains that reason serves as an ideal with reference to which we can criticize the standards we inherit. Though never divorced from social practices of justification, the idea of reason can never be reduced to any particular set of such practices.[68]

In his Introduction to the English translation of Habermas's *Der philosophische Diskurs der Moderne*, McCarthy observes similarly:

> Habermas . . . readily agrees with Foucault that reason is a "thing of this world." But for him this does not obviate the distinctions between truth and falsity, right and wrong; nor does it make them simply equivalent to what is de facto acceptable at a given time and place. The undeniable "immanence" of the standards we use to draw these distinctions—their embeddedness in concrete languages, cultures, practices—should not blind us to the equally undeniable "transcendence" of the claims they represent—their openness to critique and revision and their internal relation to intersubjective recognition brought about by the "force" of

reasons. . . . *The challenge, then, is to rethink the idea of reason in line with our essential finitude*—that is, with the historical, social, embodied, practical, desirous, assertive nature of the knowing and acting subject—and to recast accordingly our received humanistic ideals. (emphasis added)[69]

Regardless of the particulars of how this challenge is eventually met, however, it is in any case clear, I believe, that that solution will have to reflect in some way the epistemology of what I have here been calling critical realism. For if I am right, the only alternative—I believe, the only even logically possible alternative—to critical realism is a surely unacceptable choice between the blind faith of dogmatism on the one hand and the incoherence of skepticism on the other. As I have also indicated, I regard the implications of critical realism for both literary studies in particular and critical theory generally as, in the first instance, negative ones. I have no idea what a criticism of the future, no longer dominated by skepticism, dogmatism, or any combination of the two, might look like; and I certainly have no wish to try to prescribe what it ought to look like. I shall regard the work of developing the argument for critical realism as more than amply repaid, if it can contribute in even a small way to the emergence of a climate for criticism somewhat more hospitable than the current one often appears to be to reasoned deliberation and a balanced weighing of arguments, and in direct proportion to that to one more conducive to the ideal of what Woodrow Wilson called "the passionate search for dispassionate truth."

NOTES

INTRODUCTION

1. For overviews of the history of skepticism in Western thought as well as extensive bibliography on the subject, see the articles "Skepticism," in *The Encyclopedia of Philosophy*, ed. Paul Edwards (New York: Macmillan Co., 1967), VII, 449–61; and "Skepticism in Antiquity" and "Skepticism in Modern Thought," in the *Dictionary of the History of Ideas*, ed. Philip P. Wiener (New York: Scribner, 1973), IV, 234–51.

2. For a lively and insightful examination of (among other things) this sort of epistemic double vision in the work of Marxist, feminist, and Freudian critics, see Richard Levin, "The Poetics and Politics of Bardicide," *PMLA* 105 (1990): 491–504. Mark Kelman offers a generally quite lucid analysis of the same confusion on the part of many in the legal community, particularly those of a more leftist political persuasion, in "Reasonable Evidence of Reasonableness," *Critical Inquiry* 17 (1991): 798–817 (esp. 806–8).

3. Donald Davidson, "The Structure and Content of Truth," *The Journal of Philosophy* 87 (1990): 298–99.

4. Immanuel Kant, *Critique of Pure Reason*, trans. Norman Kemp Smith (New York: St. Martin's Press, 1965), p. 26 (B xxiv–xxv).

5. Johann Gottfried Herder, *Sämtliche Werke*, ed. Bernhard Suphan (Berlin: Weidmannsche Buchhandlung, 1877–1913), II, 17. For an English translation of the passage in question, see Michael Morton, *Herder and the Poetics of Thought: Unity and Diversity in On Diligence in Several Learned Languages* (University Park: Pennsylvania State University Press, 1989), pp. 127–28.

6. *TLP*, 4.112; *PI*, § 124, 126, 128.

7. *TLP*, 6.53; *PI*, § 464.

8. *TLP*, 6.52; *PI*, § 109, 133, 255, 309.

9. The predilection for defining oneself in terms of what one is not is apparent as well in the proliferation of "posts" in contemporary theory: *post*-modernism, *post*-structuralism, *post*-analytic philosophy, *post*-Marxism, and so on. This, of course, more or less inevitably invites speculation as to what is supposed to come next. For it is not easy

to see how one can continue indefinitely to think of oneself as merely subsequent to something else, especially as that thing, whatever it may have been, continues in its own right to withdraw ever further from one into an ever more distant past.

10. The passage is misunderstood, however, if taken as evidence of a fundamentally perspectivist bent in Wittgenstein's thought—though, of course, not merely the *Investigations* but the so-called "later" Wittgenstein generally are today often read in just that way. This is a point to which we shall return at greater length later in the discussion.

11. Frithjof Bergmann speaks rather scathingly of "the modish postmodernist talk about the relativistic and perspectivalistic Nietzsche, whom a host of writers now want to make into the pope of their nihilism," noting that in fact Nietzsche "often wields the most cutting and 'objective' standard." In particular, Bergmann reminds the reader, "The bifurcation which runs like a spine through the body of Nietzsche's writings is the division between what debilitates and maims *life*, versus everything that strengthens and invigorates it. He reiterates this again and again and with as few circumlocutions and qualifications as one could wish." See "Nietzsche's Critique of Morality," in Robert C. Solomon and Kathleen M. Higgins, ed., *Reading Nietzsche* (New York: Oxford University Press, 1988), pp. 44–45.

12. As one example, culled more or less at random from recent critical literature, a discussion of Julia Kristeva's *Revolution in Poetic Language* notes that "according to Kristeva's theory, poetry is essentially antiformal—in fact, so profoundly antiaesthetic that the proper words for describing it are not *beauty, inspiration, form, instinctive rightness, inevitability,* or *delicacy* (to leave aside unaesthetic terms such as *perception* and *truth*, which the theory also renders inappropriate). Instead, it attracts terms drawn from politics and war: *corruption, infiltration, disruption, shatterings, negation, supplantation,* and *murder*. Poetry is the *chora's* guerrilla war against culture." See Calvin Bedient, "Kristeva and Poetry as Shattered Signification," *Critical Inquiry* 16 (1990): 809. And further, citing Kristeva herself: "[I]n poetry 'the repeated death drive (negativity, destruction) withdraws from the unconscious and *takes up a position as already positivized and erotized in a language* that, through drive investment, is organized into prosody and rhythmic timbres'. . . . What the text manifests 'through language' is 'the jouissance of destruction (or, if you will, of the 'death drive'), which . . . passes through an unburying of repressed, sublimated anality.' " See ibid., p. 811; passages cited according to *Revolution in Poetic Language,* trans. Margaret Waller (New York: Columbia University Press, 1984), pp. 163, 150. In sum, Bedient maintains, citing again Kristeva, as "[a]nti-'art,' the modern text is art only to the degree that it knows and shows itself angry at God as meaning, meaning as God. Knowledge of textual practice as 'that most intense struggle toward death, which runs alongside and is inseparable from the differentiated binding of its charge in a symbolic texture'; knowledge of the subversion of 'the symbolic function' by an 'anal drive that agitates the subject's body'; knowledge of 'matter in the process of splitting' (*RPL*, pp. 180, 149, 180)—such is the burden of the modern or 'twentieth-century text' " (ibid., p. 814).

13. Francis Golffing, trans., *The Birth of Tragedy and The Genealogy of Morals,* by Friedrich Nietzsche (Garden City: Doubleday Anchor, 1956), p. 299. Nietzsche's text reads: "[L]ieber will noch der Mensch *das Nichts* wollen, als *nicht* wollen." See *Nietzsche Werke: Kritische Gesamtausgabe,* ed. Giorgio Colli and Mazzino Montinari (Berlin: de Gruyter, 1967ff.), 6. Abt., 2. Bd., 430.

14. Arthur Danto, "Some Remarks on *The Genealogy of Morals*," in Solomon and Higgins, ed., *Reading Nietzsche*, p. 25.

15. Ibid., pp. 26–27.

16. The allusion, of course, is to the legendary Cratylus, a disciple of Heraclitus and firm believer in the latter's doctrine of permanent flux. Heraclitus, as is well known,

asserted that "it is not possible to step twice into the same river." See *Ancilla to the Pre-Socratic Philosophers*, trans. Kathleen Freeman from Diels, *Fragmente der Vorsokratiker* (Cambridge: Harvard University Press, 1957), p. 31, Fr. 91. As Richard Popkin relates, however, "The purported development of this theory by Cratylus [led] to the view that since everything is changing, one can't step [even] once into the same river, because both that river and oneself are changing. . . . Cratylus apparently became convinced that communication was impossible because, since the speaker, the auditor, and the words were changing, whatever meaning might have been intended by the words would be altered by the time they were heard. Therefore, Cratylus is supposed to have refused to discuss anything and only to have wiggled his finger when somebody said something, to indicate that he had heard something but that it would be pointless to reply, since everything was changing." See Richard H. Popkin, "Skepticism," *The Encyclopedia of Philosophy*, VII, 449.

17. Robert Scholes, "Deconstruction and Communication," *Critical Inquiry* 14 (1988): 291–93.

18. Jean-François Lyotard, "Answering the Question: What Is Postmodernism?" Appendix to *The Postmodern Condition: A Report on Knowledge*, trans. Geoff Bennington and Brian Massumi (Minneapolis: University of Minnesota Press, 1984), pp. 79–81.

19. Ibid., p. 81.

20. Bernd Magnus, "The Deification of the Commonplace: *Twilight of the Idols*," in Solomon and Higgins, ed., *Reading Nietzsche*, p. 167.

21. In at least partial extenuation of Nietzsche, this point needs to be qualified to some extent. As Ivan Soll rightly notes, and as other commentators have recognized as well, the "significance that Nietzsche attributed to this idea had . . . nothing to do with the question of its truth"; rather, for him, the "[c]onfrontation with the idea of eternal recurrence . . . serves as a crucial test of human strength and one's attitude toward life." Nevertheless, as Soll also points out, Nietzsche was in fact convinced of its literal truth, continuing to regard the eternal recurrence as, in his words, "the most scientific of all hypotheses." See Soll, "Pessimism and the Tragic View of Life: Reconsiderations of Nietzsche's *Birth of Tragedy*," in Solomon and Higgins, ed., *Reading Nietzsche*, p. 119. For a fuller discussion, Soll refers the reader to his essay "Reflections on Recurrence," in Robert Solomon, ed., *Nietzsche*, Modern Studies in Philosophy (Garden City: Doubleday, 1973).

22. See, in *Twilight of the Idols*, the section " 'Reason' in Philosophy," § 5.

23. Cf. Wittgenstein: "Self-evidence . . . can become dispensable in logic, only because language itself prevents every logical mistake.—What makes logic a priori is the *impossibility* of illogical thought" (*TLP*, 5.4731; see also 3.03–3.032).

24. As Richard Rorty shows (perhaps in part against his own intention), this is basically the insuperable dilemma confronting Derrida in his attempt to give a coherent formulation to his theory of language and meaning. See "Deconstruction and Circumvention," *Critical Inquiry* 11 (1984): 1–23 (esp. 8–10). I discuss this point at greater length in "Strict Constructionism: Davidsonian Realism and the World of Belief," forthcoming in Reed Way Dasenbrock, ed., *Literary Theory After Davidson* (University Park: Pennsylvania State University Press).

25. Not least, interestingly enough, by Derrida himself. See his essay "Différance," in *Margins of Philosophy*, trans. Alan Bass (Chicago: University of Chicago Press, 1982); cited in Hazard Adams and Leroy Searle, ed., *Critical Theory Since 1965* (Tallahassee: University Presses of Florida, 1986), p. 122. Scholes (semi-facetiously?) finds in the notion of *différance* and its obviously central place in Derridean theory a version of the doctrine of "original sin"; see "Deconstruction and Communication," p. 281.

26. This is, as it were, the nihilism of secularization. The notion of secularization, by the way, remains, in my view (Blumenberg to the contrary notwithstanding), indispensable to our understanding of the formation of modern sensibility generally—as, indeed, much of the evidence cited by Blumenberg himself tends to confirm. See Hans Blumenberg, *The Legitimacy of the Modern Age*, trans. Robert M. Wallace (Cambridge: MIT Press, 1983). Still one of the best statements of the "secularization-thesis" is Carl L. Becker's classic *The Heavenly City of the Eighteenth-Century Philosophers* (New Haven: Yale University Press, 1932).

CHAPTER ONE

1. Richard Rorty, "Philosophy as a Kind of Writing: An Essay on Derrida," in *Consequences of Pragmatism (Essays: 1972–1980)* (Minneapolis: University of Minnesota Press, 1982), p. 92. This duality, basic to Rorty's neopragmatism, is asserted on numerous occasions throughout his writings. For example, "Pragmatists are supposed to treat everything as a matter of a choice of context and nothing as a matter of intrinsic properties" ("Philosophy without Principles," in W. J. T. Mitchell, ed., *Against Theory: Literary Studies and the New Pragmatism* [Chicago: University of Chicago Press, 1985], p. 134). Or, "as long as we view language as conventional behavior, rather than as hooking on to the world at designated spots, ability to identify should be enough to keep conversation going" ("Is There a Problem about Fictional Discourse?" in *CP*, p. 116). For "we have only *two* alternatives: a 'pure' language-game approach which dispenses with these notions ["of 'correspondence' and 'reference'"] altogether, or a rigidly physicalist approach which interprets them in terms of physical causality" (*CP*, pp. 126–27). It would be an easy matter to continue multiplying examples in this way. This epistemological opposition, moreover, is regularly accompanied by a metaphilosophical one of great importance. Without the latter, indeed, I think the former would have little prospect of being sustained for very long at all. It is the opposition between "think[ing] of philosophy as entirely a matter of deductive argument" and viewing it "as a matter of telling stories" ("Philosophy without Principles," pp. 134–35). Once again, it would by no means be difficult to cite one statement after another of this duality in Rorty's writings. Cf., e.g., "There are two principal ways in which reflective human beings try, by placing their lives in a larger context, to give sense to those lives. The first is by telling the story of their contribution to a community. . . . The second way is to describe themselves as standing in immediate relation to a nonhuman reality" ("Solidarity or Objectivity?," in J. Rajchman and C. West, ed., *Post-Analytic Philosophy* [New York: Columbia University Press, 1985], p. 3). One way of regarding the argument I am trying to develop here is as an effort to show that the "storytelling" option (which, as hardly needs to be said, is Rorty's preferred one) cannot even be formulated as an option without at the same time ceasing to be the position it purports to be, and insofar rendering itself, practically speaking, unintelligible.

2. Haskell Fain, "Some Comments on Stern's 'Narrative versus Description in Historiography,' " *New Literary History* 21 (1990): 573–74. Both the article by Laurent Stern to which Fain responds here and Stern's "Reply to Professor Fain" also appear in this number of *NLH*.

3. Thomas S. Kuhn, *The Structure of Scientific Revolutions*, 2d ed. (Chicago: University of Chicago Press, 1970), p. 4.

4. Ibid., p. 110. Cf. T. Kuhn, "Postscript—1969," included as an appendix to the second edition of *SSR*: "If two people stand at the same place and gaze in the same di-

rection, we must, under pain of solipsism, conclude that they receive closely similar stimuli. . . . But people do not see stimuli; our knowledge of them is highly theoretical and abstract. Instead they have sensations, and we are under no compulsion to suppose that the sensations of our two viewers are the same. . . . Individuals raised in different societies behave on some occasions as though they saw different things. If we were not tempted to identify stimuli one-to-one with sensations, we might recognize that they actually do so" (pp. 192–93). And further: "A scientific theory is usually felt to be better than its predecessors not only in solving puzzles but also because it is somehow a better representation of what nature is really like. . . . [Yet] there is, I think, no theory-independent way to reconstruct phrases like 'really there'; the notion of a match between the ontology of a theory and its 'real' counterpart in nature now seems to me illusive in principle" (p. 206).

5. Paul Feyerabend, *Against Method*, rev. ed. (London: Verso, 1988), p. 260. Cf. in the same work: "Who is right. . . . depends on what kind of information has privileged status and this in turn depends on the culture, or the 'cultural leaders' who use the information. . . . [E]ven the apparently hardest scientific 'fact' can be dissolved by decisions undermining the values that make it a fact. . . . The (cultural) measuring instruments that separate 'reality' from 'appearance' change and must change when we move from one culture to another and from one historical stage to the next" (pp. 254–55). Peter Galison cites Feyerabend to the same effect: "[My] thesis can be read as a philosophical thesis about the influence of theories on our observations. It then asserts that observations (observation terms) are not merely theory-*laden* (the position of Hanson, Hesse and others) but *fully theoretical* (observation statements have no 'observational core'). But the thesis can also be read as a historical thesis concerning the use of theoretical terms by scientists. In this case it asserts that scientists often use theories to restructure abstract matters *as well as* phenomena, and that no part of the phenomena is exempt from the possibility of being restructured in this way" (Feyerabend, *Realism, Rationalism, and Scientific Method* [Cambridge: Cambridge University Press, 1981], p. x; cited in Galison, "History, Philosophy, and the Central Metaphor," *Science in Context* 2 [1988]: 204). Against this view, Galison rightly notes that "[t]he critical model we need [for the history and philosophy of science] must . . . avoid the unwarranted assumption—shared by both positivist and antipositivist [in the idiom I will be using here, both dogmatist and skeptic]—that there is a universally fixed, hierarchical relation between experiment and theory. There certainly is no a priori reason to assume (with the positivists) that experiment 'comes first' epistemically or historically. Nor should one assume (with the antipositivists) that theory is privileged over experience. In individual instances, it is frequently the case that one may impose structure on the other. But this is exactly the task at hand: to discover and articulate the mediative processes by which experiments and theories each constrain the other's activity" (ibid., p. 208).

6. The evident affinities between Feyerabend's view and Rorty's are, I think, by no means fortuitous. Notwithstanding Rorty's frequent references to Dewey, Heidegger, and Wittgenstein, joined more recently by Derrida, as the principal twentieth-century influences on his thinking, it appears that his views on the history of modern science in particular, including his denial of the existence of any such thing as "scientific method," owe at least as much to Feyerabend as to any of the others named. Both the degree of similarity between his and Feyerabend's discussions of Galileo, for example, as well as the considerable extent to which both of them base their arguments regarding the nature and validity of science at large on that one case in particular are striking, to say the least.

7. Fredric Jameson, Foreword to Jean-François Lyotard, *The Postmodern Condition*, pp. viii–ix. Jameson goes on to speak of what he calls the "many family resemblances

elsewhere in contemporary thought" (ibid., p. ix) to the point of view that generates the opposition in question. He refers the reader in particular to "Louis Althusser's essays in epistemology" and to Rorty's *Philosophy and the Mirror of Nature* and *Consequences of Pragmatism* (ibid., p. xx).

8. *PMC*, pp. xxiii–xxiv; subsequent references are given in the text.

9. Barbara Herrnstein Smith, *Contingencies of Value: Alternative Perspectives for Critical Theory* (Cambridge: Harvard University Press, 1988), p. 15; subsequent references are given in the text.

10. Several pages earlier, to be sure, Smith makes at least a nod in the direction of most people's intuition that literary works, once completed by their authors, do *not* change, any more, for example, than do the identities of those authors themselves. If Shakespeare wrote the works generally attributed to him, then he *always* did so. If—as seems rather unlikely—it were someday to be shown that the author was actually someone else, then we will have learned that *that* person always did so. What makes the past the past is, above all, precisely that it is unalterable. Smith acknowledges that the "texts" read by different critics of Shakespeare's sonnets "were the same." This admission turns out not to count for much, however, for it is followed at once by the claim that nevertheless "the *poems* [that these critics read and to which they responded] weren't" (*CV*, p. 4). The distinction between "text" and "poem" would not, I think, be an entirely easy one to sustain (or perhaps even to explain). In any case, no attempt is made to do so, and by the time we reach the passage cited a moment ago regarding "the properties of literary works," it seems to have been altogether forgotten.

11. Note that the *work* itself, and not merely its *meaning*, is at issue. It is, in other words, not merely a restatement of *Rezeptionsgeschichte* with which we are dealing here, but rather a view with significantly more far-reaching implications.

12. Felicity Nussbaum refers without comment or elaboration to what she calls "the vexed problem of objectivity" in "The Politics of Difference," *Eighteenth-Century Studies* 23 (1990): 378. I am suggesting that in fact there is nothing that could even make sense for us to be vexed at in this regard. Objectivity is both inescapably and indispensably simply part of what it is to be human. The need is rather to develop an *understanding* of objectivity that does not at the same time commit us to an untenable (because merely dogmatic) metaphysics of a priori "givenness" of the objects of our knowledge.

13. Stanley Fish, *Is There a Text in This Class? The Authority of Interpretive Communities* (Cambridge: Harvard University Press, 1980), p. vii; subsequent references are given in the text.

14. *Doing What Comes Naturally: Change, Rhetoric, and the Practice of Theory in Literary and Legal Studies* (Durham: Duke University Press, 1989), p. ix; subsequent references are given in the text.

15. "Rhetoric," in *DWN*, p. 474. Fish concludes this essay, by the way, with the same passage from Rorty's *Consequences of Pragmatism* cited at the beginning of the present chapter. He explicitly associates Rorty's contrast between "two ways of thinking about . . . things" with his own "oppositions," and insofar, I think, lends that much more credence to the general thesis regarding contemporary critical outlooks that I am trying to develop here.

16. The contrast between "serious man" and "rhetorical man" is taken from Richard Lanham, *The Motives of Eloquence* (New Haven: Yale University Press, 1976); see "Rhetoric," *DWN*, pp. 482–83.

17. "Rhetoric," *DWN*, pp. 484–85.

18. In a footnote Smith speaks of the need for a "postaxiological study of public art or art in public places, with attention to the disputes between experts deploring philistine

taste and citizens outraged by expenditures of communal funds on what they see as non-uplifting, depressing, insulting, and/or ridiculous objects" (CV, p. 196). Smith leaves little doubt (here or elsewhere) as to her sympathy with the "experts" in such disputes. She has been among the most vocal of those criticizing attempts in the wake of the controversy surrounding exhibitions of works by Robert Mapplethorpe, Andres Cerrano, and others to "censor" artists by placing certain restrictions on funding of artists' projects by the National Endowment for the Arts. The distinction between censoring an activity and not subsidizing it with public funds has not for the most part, I think, received the attention it might have from those objecting to the shift in NEA policy in question. That particular issue aside, however, it is hard not to be struck by the sometimes remarkably patronizing, even contemptuous, tone of many of Smith's remarks. She speaks, for example, of "the revulsion of academics and intellectuals at the actual literary preferences, forms of aesthetic enjoyment, and general modes of cultural consumption of nonacademics and non-intellectuals—including those whose *political* emancipation they may otherwise seek to promote" (CV, p. 26).

19. "Introduction: Going Down the Anti-Formalist Road," *DWN*, pp. 29–30. The passage is interesting for another reason as well, inasmuch as it occurs in the context of an effort by Fish to acquit his position of the charge of self-referential inconsistency. Smith, too, recognizes the need to address this charge. Her way of doing so differs in some particulars from Fish's but is in the end no more successful than his. The entire issue of self-refutation will occupy us at much greater length later in the discussion.

20. The citations here are from Habermas's "What Is Universal Pragmatics?" in *Communication and the Evolution of Society*, trans. Thomas McCarthy (Boston: Beacon Press, 1979), p. 3.

21. See Edwin A. Abbott, *Flatland: A Romance of Many Dimensions*, 6th ed. (New York: Dover, 1952).

22. It may happen, of course, that textual criticism has not yet established the definitive version of a given work. In this case, the locus of unambiguousness simply shifts to the level of the variants of the text, each of which will itself be viewed in precisely the same unchanging way by anyone and everyone who cares to examine it. And analogous considerations apply to the portions or fragments of those works (such as Büchner's *Woyzeck*, for example) for which it seems unlikely that a single, definitive version can ever be established.

23. Jean Jacques Rousseau, *The Social Contract and Discourses*, trans. G. D. H. Cole (New York: Dutton, 1950), p. 18.

24. Discussing Foucault, Anthony Close notes that "[k]nowledge of the outlooks and ideas of individuals, *qua* individual systems of thought, is not his concern . . . because 'rules of formation have their place, not in the mentality of individuals, but in discourse itself; thus they impose themselves by a sort of uniform anonymity on all the individuals who undertake to speak within a discursive field.' " See "Centering the De-Centerers: Foucault and *Las Meninas*," *Philosophy and Literature* 11 (1987): 28. The passage by Foucault is from *The Archaeology of Knowledge* (Paris: Gallimard, 1969), pp. 83–84.

25. See I. Kant, *Critique of Pure Reason*, A viii–x.

26. In a footnote at this point, Smith attempts to get around the clearly somewhat awkward implications for her theory of the use of the term *information* here. She asserts that that notion is actually merely one way in which "traditional discourse . . . hypostasizes [sic] the complex processes through which our behavior is modified by our interactions with our environments" and adds that "[i]n an account more rigorous than that offered here, the entire problematic terminology of 'information' would be replaced by a

description of the specific dynamics of such interactions" (*CV*, p. 204). In adding this remark, however, it would seem that Smith has actually accomplished precisely the opposite of what she intended. For it now appears that, in her view, there is an even greater body of objective fact than the one posited thus far that we are presumed to be capable of identifying with absolute certainty.

27. Anthony Kenny, *Wittgenstein* (Cambridge: Harvard University Press, 1973), p. 192; subsequent references are given in the text.

28. Cf., again from the "private-language argument": "In what sense are my sensations *private?*—Well, only I can know whether I am really in pain; another person can only surmise it.—In one way this is wrong, and in another nonsense. If we are using the word 'to know' as it is normally used (and how else are we to use it?), then other people very often know when I am in pain.—Yes, but all the same not with the certainty with which I know it myself!—It can't be said of me at all (except perhaps as a joke) that I *know* I am in pain. What is it supposed to mean—except perhaps that I *am* in pain?" (*PI*, § 246).

29. Lewis Carroll, *Alice's Adventures in Wonderland and Through the Looking Glass* (New York: Collier, 1962), p. 247.

CHAPTER TWO

1. "Critical Self-Consciousness, Or Can We Know What We're Doing?" in *DWN*, p. 436; subsequent references are given in the text.

2. There is, of course, also what might be thought of as a kind of "hermeneutics of suspicion" (to borrow Ricoeur's well-known phrase) with a political twist to it that effectively decouples the notion of the "political" from anything having to do in any important way with intentionality and the like at all. On this view, one is always and necessarily politically implicated, *regardless of anything one may believe and no matter how one may choose to act.* Althusser, for example, with his notion of the all-pervasiveness of "ideological state apparatuses," would seem to take this position. As we shall see to some extent below, however, maintaining this view is possible only on the condition that one also commit oneself to a particularly unabashed version of dogmatic metaphysics.

3. Ludwig Wittgenstein, *Über Gewißheit/On Certainty*, ed. G.E.M. Anscombe and G. H. von Wright, trans. Denis Paul and G.E.M. Anscombe (New York: Harper & Row, 1972).

4. There is, of course, at least one other important respect in which the *Tractatus* differs from *On Certainty*. The former was composed over a period of many years and so had the benefit of repeated revisions and emendations in the formulation of the argument; the remarks collected in the latter represent, in the words of the editors, "all first-draft material, which [Wittgenstein] did not live to excerpt and polish" (Anscombe and von Wright, Preface, *On Certainty*, p. vi). Thus it is not surprising to find that the latter does not present us with the sort of well-rounded and, in virtually all respects, internally consistent line of exposition characteristic of the former. In particular, some passages here and there in *On Certainty* (not many, but a few), *taken by themselves*, do appear to support a reading of Wittgenstein as endorsing a basically perspectivist and decisionist standpoint with regard to linguistic meaning and the determination of what will count as "reality." Such passages are frequently cited by those who would like to enlist Wittgenstein as an (obviously influential) advocate for their own acceptance of that position. To do so, however, as we shall see in more detail below, entails overlooking or ignoring at least two important considerations: first, the overall context established by the vast majority of the remarks in *On Certainty* (not to speak of the characteristic direction

of Wittgenstein's thought at large) is precisely contrary to a perspectivist or decisionist outlook; and second, and even more telling, virtually every passage in *On Certainty* in particular that might appear to support the view in question is sooner or later answered in a way designed to show why that view can nevertheless not be sustained. In the jottings and notes that constitute *On Certainty*, as elsewhere in his unpublished writings, Wittgenstein is *trying out* different positions and the various arguments that can be adduced in support of them. These include perspectivism and decisionism, and it seems clear that Wittgenstein is far from insensible to the attractions those standpoints might hold for someone, at least initially. They are, accordingly, given a full and fair opportunity to prove their worth. The result, however, is always to find that they cannot in the end be coherently or intelligibly adhered to. To cite *only* those passages in which Wittgenstein is trying to present them in the most favorable and compelling light (or, indeed, in which he may have felt himself, for the moment at any rate, inclined to accept them) is thus to give (at best) a seriously distorted impression of his considered views. Although the two situations are in obvious respects not entirely parallel, this way of representing Wittgenstein is nonetheless at least slightly reminiscent of those commentators on Nietzsche who claim to be able to find in the discarded and posthumous fragments of *The Will to Power* the real keys to his thought, seizing on these in preference to those expressions of his views that he himself saw fit to give to the world in published form.

5. Donald Davidson, "The Structure and Content of Truth," p. 279.

6. Gary Shapiro, "*The Antichrist* and the Semiotics of History," in Solomon and Higgins, ed., *Reading Nietzsche*, p. 206.

7. Ibid., p. 205. Habermas notes, in a similar vein, that "the [Peircean] 'final consensus' that we anticipate for a particular statement or a special set of statements does not signify that we have to represent to ourselves the limit value of a cumulative progress of knowledge in the form of an 'actual sequence of future theories'. 'Final consensus' expresses only an idea that is implicitly posited with the concept of truth, an idea that determines the assertoric meaning of assertions, each *in its place and at its time*. . . . Peirce's language-theoretic concept of reality is connected with the idea of a convergence point towards which the lines of all theoretical descriptions run in the end. But this idea . . . is always here and now, and indeed is in force only at the moment in which we *raise* a validity-claim with the conviction that it can be discursively redeemed." And he adds, drawing out an implication of the foregoing that is of importance for a later stage of the discussion here: "This may explain why it would be senseless for us to reckon with future theories as we do with the appearance of events. The truth of tomorrow is an empty concept. . . . Anyone who seriously puts forward a theoretical proposition unavoidably finds oneself in the role of the 'last' theoretician" ("A Reply to my Critics," p. 277). There will be more to say later on the pivotal difference in outlook between Peirce and Derrida. This is a point on which it seems all the more important to be clear, in view of Derrida's own belief that Peirce's philosophy can actually be viewed as at least a partial forerunner of deconstruction.

8. As we shall see at greater length below, Herder's way of dealing with the problem of "origins" (e.g., the origin of language) is effectively to *dissolve* the problem, such that it becomes no longer possible even to raise the question in any interesting (or, for that matter, coherent) form. See in this connection Michael Morton, "*Verum est factum*: Critical Realism and the Discourse of Autonomy," *German Quarterly* 64 (1991): 149–65.

9. Ludwig Wittgenstein, *The Blue and Brown Books* (New York: Harper & Row, 1965), pp. 14–15.

10. Ludwig Wittgenstein, *Zettel*, ed. G.E.M. Anscombe and G. H. von Wright, trans. G.E.M. Anscombe (Oxford: Blackwell, 1967), § 693. In the same collection of notes and remarks, Wittgenstein asserts flatly that "there is no such thing as an infinite list"

(Z, § 705). And similarly, with reference specifically to the ability to perform arithmetical operations, he maintains that the person who has once acquired this ability must be able to "go on [i.e., continue applying what he has learned in new situations] *without a reason.* Not, however, because he cannot yet grasp the reason but because—in *this* system—there is no reason. ('The chain of reasons comes to an end.')" (Z, § 301).

11. Thomas McCarthy, *The Critical Theory of Jürgen Habermas* (Cambridge: MIT Press, 1978), p. 319; subsequent references are given in the text.

12. Confusion on this point seems to be rife among contemporary "historicizers." For an especially clear instance of it, see Thomas McLaughlin's discussion of the notion of artistic "unity" in his Introduction to Frank Lentricchia and Thomas McLaughlin, ed., *Critical Terms for Literary Study* (Chicago: University of Chicago Press, 1990), p. 4.

13. Stephen Toulmin, "The Construal of Reality: Criticism in Modern and Postmodern Science," *Critical Inquiry* 9 (1982): 93–111.

14. The reference is to Stephen Toulmin, *Human Understanding* (Princeton: Princeton University Press, 1972), p. 95.

15. The passages cited by Fish are from "The Construal of Reality," p. 109, and *Human Understanding*, p. 500, respectively.

16. "Either Toulmin means what he has just said and the warranting rationality is itself intepretive, in which case it cannot be used to discriminate between interpretations, or the warranting position exists independently of interpretation, in which case Toulmin's acknowledgment of the inevitability of interpretation is no more than an empty gesture. Either Toulmin is committed to the coherence of his argument and the notion of rationally warranted choice is problematized, or he affirms the rationality of choice and his argument falls apart in the space between these two sentences. He simply cannot have it both ways" (*DWN*, p. 438). I should perhaps make clear that it is no part of my intention here to try to rescue Toulmin's view from Fish's assault on it. For it seems to me that Fish is obviously correct: Toulmin really can't have it both ways. But neither should he *want* to have it both ways. Toulmin is but one in a long and distinguished line of critics and theoreticians who have made themselves easy targets for Fish's dialectical artillery. Once he has taken the position that "the doctrines of the natural sciences are critical interpretations of their subject matter no less than those of the humanities" ("Construal of Reality," p. 95; cited by Fish, *DWN*, p. 436), there will indeed be no way for him then to introduce as a check on interpretive practice a notion of impartial rationality, without being at once caught on the horns of the dilemma just described by Fish. His mistake, however, does not lie in the direction of a belief in rationality—as I am trying to show, that belief is not an optional matter for anyone, Fish included (and hence is not, properly speaking, even a "belief")—but rather in his commitment in the first place to the doctrine of the ubiquity of interpretation. Toulmin, however, like Fish at least to this extent, continues to operate in a pre-critical context of thought, still bound to the dogmatic-skeptical duality of "what there (independently) *is*-what gets (interpretively) *said.*" He, too, seeks to reject the former alternative in favor of the latter, but, as Fish is able to show without much difficulty, he is simply not very consistent in doing so. By this I do not mean to suggest that there actually is some way in which that might have been done consistently. Fish as well, though certainly more dogged in his pursuit of undiluted interpretivism than Toulmin, cannot in the end avoid lapsing into his own version of (dogmatic) foundationalism, as we have already seen to some extent and will see still more clearly as we proceed. A reminder of what we might call the ineluctability of the rational is given with Fish's very formulation of the dilemma in which he traps Toulmin. The argument that culminates in the assertion that the latter "cannot have it both ways" is an exemplary bit of reasoning, showing how, on his own terms, Toulmin cannot avoid self-contradiction. But in order

that this demonstration have any force, basic *logic* must itself be valid—universally and invariably so. Of course, it *is* universally and invariably valid. But that is clearly not something that Fish is going to have an easy time reconciling with his insistence on radical historicity, partiality, interest-governedness of assertions, and all the rest of the "anti-foundationalist thesis."

CHAPTER THREE

1. Fish's page references, unless otherwise noted, are to Jürgen Habermas, "What Is Universal Pragmatics?," in *Communication and the Evolution of Society,* trans. Thomas McCarthy (Boston: Beacon Press, 1979).

2. Neither of the two phrases for which Fish refers the reader to page 12 of "What Is Universal Pragmatics?" is actually to be found there, by the way. The second of them, with which we are at the moment concerned, in fact comes on page 8 (following by a bit the first of the passages from that text cited here). If the other—that is, the reference to the "prevailing realm of purposes"—occurs at all in "What Is Universal Pragmatics?," I have not been able to locate it. Certainly it appears neither on page 12 nor on page 8. Nor is it mere philological pedantry to make a point of noting this; for as I have suggested, the lapse points to a larger pattern in Fish's overall argument against Habermas, one that contributes in significant measure to its ultimate failure. Although there is surely no question of willful misrepresentation here, neither is there any denying that Fish is at least somewhat casual in his practice of citation at this point. And that in turn, as we shall see, does contribute to some extent to the *objective* misrepresentations of Habermas that do occur in the course of his critique.

3. A terminological clarification is in order here. Habermas, too, speaks of his project in philosophy as in certain respects a "critical" one. His sense of that term, however, insofar as it reflects merely a holdover from the political-sociological program of the Frankfurt School, has nothing to do with (indeed, is in many ways diametrically opposed to) the transcendental, Kantian-Herderian-Wittgensteinian sense in which I am using it. Unlike Wittgenstein, in Habermas's case it really is possible to distinguish between two almost completely separate philosophical personae, something already reflected in the distinction noted earlier between the transcendental and the programmatic aspects of his thought. It is only with one of these, however, that we are at all concerned here.

4. In general this remains Habermas's preferred terminology. But cf., for example, still later in the essay, where he completes the identification of his idiom with the traditional one, asserting that "all speech actions . . . contain a locutionary component (in the form of a sentence with propositional content) and an illocutionary component (in the form of a performative sentence)" (*UP,* p. 50).

5. "Still Wrong After All These Years," in *DWN,* p. 358; subsequent references are given in the text.

6. By "presupposed norms" (*UP,* p. 38) Habermas means in this context the defining marks or conditions of "institutionally bound speech acts" such as (to give the examples he lists) "betting, christening, appointing, marrying, and so on." As promised earlier, we will shortly be considering Habermas's distinction, which Fish thinks fatal to his theory, between "institutionally bound" and "unbound" speech acts.

7. Reed Way Dasenbrock notes: "One does not have to be, as Fish claims, an essentialist or a positivist to want to ask why we see certain things at certain times. And to ask that question is to ask what permits us to see them, which is to move from the level of

the individual perception to the level of what makes perception possible. This move is a move Fish never makes, at least in a sustained way." See "Accounting for the Changing Certainties of Interpretive Communities," *MLN* 101 (1986): 1039.

8. John R. Searle, "What Is A Speech Act?," in Adams and Searle, ed., *Critical Theory Since 1965*, pp. 60–69.

9. If Habermas's reference, in the passage from *UP* last cited by Fish, to "the claims to validity that [participants in an idealized case of communicative action] reciprocally raise" does not outright invite the misunderstanding of "universal validity claims" as substantive assertions, it certainly does nothing to discourage such a misunderstanding either. Even if we suppose, moreover, that Habermas is still thinking, consistently with the overall bent of his theory, of these claims as formal entities here, the much more serious problem just alluded to would remain. For if it were to turn out that the theory of "universal pragmatics" did require for its development the incorporation of a fundamental element of decisionism, there would, indeed, so far as I can tell, no longer be any way to avoid Fish's perspectivist critique of that theory.

10. Jürgen Habermas, "A Reply to my Critics," in Thompson and Held, ed., *Habermas: Critical Debates*, pp. 226–27; subsequent references are given in the text.

11. Habermas's works are, of course, replete with tables. Perhaps not the least of the respects in which he can be seen as working in an essentially Kantian tradition is simply this love of architectonic that he shares with the master.

12. Following the passage from *RC* last cited, Habermas notes parenthetically that "[f]or the egocentric calculation of success"—that is, in order to undertake "strategic action"—"it suffices if each *privately attributes or denies* truth-value to his or her views or to those of others" (*RC*, p. 267; emphasis added). Again, I think this is surely correct as far as it goes. It seems to be simply another way of saying that the "suspension" of validity-claims in "strategic action" must be covert if it is to have any chance of being effective. But, again, as Wittgenstein repeatedly points out, private states are in need of public criteria. To speak of a state or condition of the self of which in principle *only* the person who is actually in that state could *ever* have knowledge is so far to have said nothing (or nothing intelligible) at all.

13. For more on this point, see *CTH*, pp. 287–88 (and 428, n. 38) and 323.

14. See Adams and Searle, ed., *Critical Theory Since 1965*, p. 525.

15. For Habermas's understanding of both the distinction and the relationship between the two senses of "self-reflection" in his writings—the transcendental-analytic and the socially critical, respectively—see also *RC*, p. 229, with the passage from his "A Postscript to *Knowledge and Human Interests*" cited there.

16. The fact that in practice—that is, in describing the actual behavior of real gases—scientists employ, instead of the classical, universal gas laws themselves, equations based on these laws but also relativized to the specific characteristics of each gas in particular seems also to bear a certain analogy to Habermas's principle that, in order to develop an adequate analysis of concrete speech-acts in the actual contexts in which they occur, it is necessary to supplement the principles of "universal pragmatics," valid for all speech-acts, with "empirical pragmatic" considerations specific to a given "milieu" (see again *UP*, p. 32).

17. Jürgen Habermas, "Wahrheitstheorien," in H. Fahrenbach, ed., *Wirklichkeit und Reflexion*, pp. 258–59; cited in *CTH*, p. 310.

18. As we have also seen in connection with the notion of ideality in particular, there is a certain extent to which, given the ultimate convergence of the theoretical and the practical in Habermas's analysis, this ambiguity—or, perhaps better, simply dual signification—is not merely unavoidable, but, indeed, positively essential to the completion

of that analysis. It is, however, not a logically vicious ambiguity, of a sort that would vitiate the argument on formal grounds. For, so far as I am aware, Habermas nowhere depends for the demonstration of a given conclusion on a shift in the meaning of a key term *within* the context of that demonstration itself.

19. The specific criticism that Fish brings against Habermas here reflects, in turn, his more fundamental contention that critical reflection on our most basic convictions, in the sense of either analysis or evaluation of them, is inherently impossible. The fact of our being always exhaustively situated in some interpretive-motivational context in particular entails, in his view, that the very conceptual matrix in terms of which such reflection would have to be undertaken would itself be "intelligible only within the conditions it would [seek to] escape. . . . [R]eflection can never get off the ground because it is always tethered to the ground from which it claims to set us free" (*DWN*, pp. 454–55). This argument, however, depends for its force on the tacit assumption that situatedness is itself radically *plural*—in other words, that there is no such thing as what I earlier termed the Big Situation. The critical realist overcoming of skeptical positions such as Fish's consists largely in showing, against this view, that the assumption of radical situational plurality is itself finally unsustainable.

20. Habermas's usual way of identifying his four universal validity claims is, of course, to speak of claims to "comprehensibility," "truth," "truthfulness" (or "sincerity"), and "rightness" (or "appropriateness"). In light of this, it is interesting to see how the enumeration in the passage at hand matches up with the terms in the more frequently encountered list. "Grammaticality" obviously corresponds to "comprehensibility," "truth" to "truth," and "rightness" to "rightness," which leaves—and this is the point I find particularly noteworthy—"consistency" as the counterpart of "truthfulness" or "sincerity." That is, a notion that we would ordinarily be inclined to regard as primarily an *ethical* one is, for Habermas, evidently analyzable in terms of a corresponding *logical-epistemic* one (and vice versa). In this we catch perhaps an additional glimpse of the overriding tendency of his thinking to move always in the direction of an ultimate convergence of the theoretical and the practical, toward the ultimate end of constructing what might be thought of as a transcendental deduction of civilization itself.

21. This is, of course, precisely the confusion from which Derrida's development of the deconstructionist assault on meaning takes its start. For a particularly thorough statement of this confusion, see Samuel Wheeler, III, "The Extension of Deconstruction," *The Monist* 69 (1986): 3–21.

22. As Habermas also notes: "To be sure, 'institutional bond' is a criterion that does not always permit an unambiguous classification. Commands can exist wherever relations of authority are institutionalized; appointments presuppose special, bureaucratically developed organizations; and marriages require a single institution (which is, however, found universally). But this does not destroy the usefulness of the analytic point of view. Institutionally unbound speech actions, insofar as they have any regulative meaning at all, are related to various aspects of action norms in general; they are not *essentially* fixed by particular institutions" (*UP*, p. 39; emphasis added). The fact that we cannot specify an algorithm that would enable us to separate institutionally bound from unbound speech-acts a priori and in wholly unambiguous fashion is in its own right, of course, in keeping with Wittgenstein's recognition that for the most part language functions not by means of essentialist definitions at all, but rather precisely in terms of "family resemblances."

23. "How to Do Things with Austin and Searle," in *ITC*, p. 241. Although I realize that there is some danger of becoming tiresome in continually pointing this out, I will risk trying the reader's patience one more time by observing that here again, as elsewhere, Fish cannot even begin to develop his theory purporting to undermine our confidence in

the reality of objective factuality without appealing to "the fact of" *something's* being un-ambiguously and apodictically the case. This may be the most obvious respect in which skeptical theories, insofar as they are enunciated at all (presumably the minimal condition of qualifying as a "theory" in the first place), are without exception incoherent. Again, as noted earlier, determinate factuality and determinate meaning are not existentially op-tional notions for human beings. The *only* choice we have in this regard is in how these notions will be construed—whether in pre-critical (i.e., metaphysically dogmatic) or in critical terms.

24. See also, for example, among many other instances that could be cited, "Don't Know Much About the Middle Ages: Posner on Law and Literature," in *DWN*, pp. 300 and 302; and "Anti-Foundationalism, Theory Hope, and the Teaching of Composition," ibid., pp. 342–43. The latter essay also appears in Clayton Koelb and Virgil Lokke, ed., *The Current in Criticism: Essays on the Present and Future of Literary Theory* (West La-fayette: Purdue University Press, 1987).

25. "How To Recognize a Poem When You See One," in *ITC*, p. 331.

26. Habermas, too, as McCarthy notes, sees that "correspondence theories of truth are fraught with insuperable difficulties; they 'attempt in vain to break out of the sphere of language' " (the citation is from Habermas's "Wahrheitstheorien," p. 216). Such theo-ries, McCarthy continues, "are not only unable to supply a criterion of truth (which state-ments correspond to reality?) independent of critical discussion; they are incapable of giving a coherent account either of the 'reality-in-itself' to which true statements are said to correspond or of the relation of 'correspondence' that is said to obtain" (*CTH*, p. 302).

27. It would be interesting, of course, to be told precisely why the number of "stan-dard stories" is supposed to be comparatively limited. Certainly there are innumerable particular beliefs on which somebody somewhere can be found to disagree with somebody else. How massive does disagreement have to be before we are talking about whole "sys-tems of belief" distinct from one another, and thus about different "standard stories"? What are the criteria for regarding one difference of opinion rather than another as the cutoff point? In fact, it seems to me, what we see here again (albeit in relatively mild form) is merely one further instance of the sort of apodictically foundationalist assertion with which anti-foundationalism can never entirely dispense.

28. It is perhaps worth noting that neither irony nor metaphor nor any other form of tropological discourse constitutes a counterexample to this thesis. To suppose the con-trary is to confuse the fact that it is entirely possible to mean precisely what one says in many different ways with the self-contradictory notion of meaning and not meaning what one says at the same time. Irony, metaphor, and other tropes are merely different ways of realizing this possibility from the ones we tend to encounter, on the whole, somewhat more frequently in everyday speech. See in this connection Donald Davidson, "What Metaphors Mean," in *Inquiries into Truth and Interpretation* (Oxford: Clarendon Press, 1984), pp. 245–64.

29. Or, more precisely, to avoid a conscious and overt choice in favor of metaphys-ical dogmatism. As we have seen, neither Fish nor any other skeptic can keep from com-mitting to metaphysical dogmatism in fact.

30. Donald Davidson, "On the Very Idea of a Conceptual Scheme," *Proceedings of the American Philosophical Association* 47 (1973–74): 8.

31. On the "anthropic principle" see, for example, Stephen W. Hawking, *A Brief History of Time: From the Big Bang to Black Holes* (Toronto: Bantam, 1988), pp. 123–25, 145–53.

32. Sincerity is, of course, not the issue here; clarity is. As I have been urging throughout this discussion, skepticism does not represent a real possibility for human

beings under any circumstances, no matter what one may have persuaded oneself of to the contrary.

33. Jane Heal makes the point as follows: "We should not construe the ineluctability of certain judgements as Nature's own conception of herself being printed on our *tabula rasa*. . . . Nature has no conception of herself; we bring to her the concepts we use and they are concepts we have because our interests and way of life are as they are. . . . [W]e have our concepts *because* we have our interests—no interests, no concepts. But this is not to be heard as saying that we choose or devise our concepts in the light of knowledge of our interests. That way of reading things presupposes that we can conceptualize our interests before we have any concepts, which is absurd." See "Pragmatism and Choosing to Believe," in Alan R. Malachowski, ed., *Reading Rorty: Critical Responses to* Philosophy and the Mirror of Nature *(and Beyond)* (Oxford: Blackwell, 1990), p. 112. Heal's essay offers what strikes me as a particularly effective statement of, and argument for, what I will later be calling the *co-originality thesis*. As she puts it on the same page: "[I]f we want to understand why we have the concepts we do . . . , then we must look at *how the whole pattern of our lives fits together*—how making these kinds of judgements in this sort of way is bound up with our caring about the kinds of things we care about and doing the kinds of things we find worth doing" (emphasis added).

With conscious, conceptualized interestedness and purposiveness thus ruled out as originating instances of the process of meaning-formation itself, one might still consider appealing to preconceptual motivations or impulses to explain how this process gets set in motion initially. Two possible candidates for this role would be instinct and subconscious drives. As Herder notes in the *Origin of Language*, however, instinct is a distinctively animal phenomenon. The difference between its workings and those of human intellection is one of kind, not merely degree. It will, accordingly, never be possible to derive the latter from the former. Nor does any help appear to be forthcoming from the realm of the subconscious, or at least none of which anti-foundationalism can make use. For even if one is prepared to grant that coherent sense can be made of the notion of a "subconscious" interest or purpose to begin with (something that strikes me as an unlikely prospect at best), to invoke this as one's ultimate explanation would clearly be tantamount to placing a radically ahistorical, interest-independent element—namely, the very picture of the mind as divided into conscious and subconscious realms—at the foundation of the anti-foundationalist edifice.

34. "Withholding the Missing Portion," in *DWN*, p. 552.

CHAPTER FOUR

1. John R. Searle, "Reiterating the Differences: A Reply to Derrida," *Glyph I* (Baltimore: Johns Hopkins University Press, 1977), p. 203.

2. Richard Rorty, *Philosophy and the Mirror of Nature* (Princeton: Princeton University Press, 1979), p. 32; subsequent references are given in the text.

3. Rorty shares with many contemporary skeptics the belief, noted earlier, that there are close affinities between his views and those of the (again, so-called) "later" Wittgenstein. For Wittgenstein's rejection of the characterization of his thought as "nominalist," see *PI*, § 383.

4. We earlier noted Wittgenstein's observation, "It can't be said of me at all (except perhaps as a joke) that I *know* I am in pain. What is it supposed to mean—except perhaps that I *am* in pain?" (*PI*, § 246). And in the same vein, "It is correct to say 'I know

what you are thinking', and wrong to say 'I know what I am thinking.' (A whole cloud of philosophy condensed into a drop of grammar.)" (*PI*, II, p. 222).

5. For fundamentally similar reasons, though operating, as it were, in the opposite direction, I think it makes no sense to speak of *unconscious* wishes or desires (Rorty's assurance to the contrary notwithstanding that nowadays "*only* philosophers remain perplexed about how one can have" such things [*PMN*, p. 123]). To be told, for instance, that there is active in me a "desire" to kill my father and sleep with my mother, but that at the moment, not having undergone the requisite psychoanalysis, I am merely unaware of that desire—a desire (and this is, of course, crucial to the theory) that with the sole exception of this lack of awareness is otherwise *exactly the same as* what would be active in me were I to speak truthfully the words "I want to kill my father and sleep with my mother"— strikes me as simply incoherent. It seems roughly analogous to suggesting that I might at this moment be truly in agony but merely unaware of that fact.

6. Walter Kaufmann, *Existentialism from Dostoevsky to Sartre* (Cleveland: Meridian, 1956), p. 50. The criticism of academic philosophy as it has too often been practiced in the twentieth century is one of relatively few points on which I find myself in agreement with Rorty. Even this rather modest coincidence in our views ends, however, when it comes to drawing the consequences of that criticism. One way of bringing out this difference is by noting that although Kaufmann's charge clearly had a great deal to be said for it when it was first leveled, over thirty years ago, it would be substantially more difficult (though, unfortunately, by no means yet impossible) to make stick today. As Hilary Putnam, certainly the model of a contemporary analytic philosopher, has noted, "Philosophers are beginning to talk about the great issues again and to feel that something can be said about them, even if there are no grand or ultimate solutions." See "Why Reason Can't Be Naturalized," in K. Baynes et al., ed., *After Philosophy: End or Transformation?* (Cambridge: MIT Press, 1987), pp. 229–30. Putnam follows this observation, significantly, with a reference specifically to *PMN*. He says in part that "if I react to Professor Rorty's book . . . with a certain sharpness, it is because one more 'deflationary' book, one more book telling us that the deep questions aren't deep and the whole enterprise was a mistake, is just what we don't need right now" (ibid., p. 230).

7. "Just try—in a real case—to doubt someone else's fear or pain" (*PI*, § 303).

8. What the situation might be with forms of sentient life *radically* different from those that populate the earth (should there be any such) is, of course, as open a question as what such creatures' concept of experience in general might be, assuming that they had one (or one that we could recognize as one) at all.

9. It is not, of course, as if no one had ever tried to argue for such a conclusion in the case of constitutional law. According to George Will, "Prof. Charles Lawrence of Stanford law school" maintains that notwithstanding the plain wording of the First Amendment, "the real purport and proper effect of the Supreme Court's 1954 school-desegregation decision is to permit, and perhaps to require, sweeping censorship of speech." Specifically, Will reports, Prof. Lawrence holds it to be "constitutional to suppress speech" deemed "racist" (*Durham Morning Herald*, 5 November 1989).

10. This, by the way, has nothing to do with the consideration that different things have been called, for example, "cruel" or "not cruel" by different peoples at different times and in different places. That historical and anthropological truism has always been a favorite of cultural and ethical relativists. The proper response to it, it seems to me, is simply: so what? It is well known, for example, that the Aztecs (or some of them, at any rate) did not regard performing human sacrifice by cutting the hearts out of living victims as excessively cruel, or at least not to an extent that would have rendered the practice morally impermissible. That scarcely shows, however, that it was not in fact cruel to do so.

It merely shows, first, that the Aztecs were capable of systematic cruelty on a rather large scale, and, second, that to the extent this degree of cruelty is morally reprehensible, the Aztecs were morally deficient. It is nothing more than a kind of inverted ethnocentrism to excuse mass human sacrifice by the Aztecs on the grounds, say, that for them it served a "religious" function and so played a central role in fostering "social cohesion," while at the same time condemning the genocidal murderousness of the Nazis or the Khmer Rouge in our own century. Both the Nazis and the Khmer Rouge, after all, had (in some cases, still have) reasons for their brutality just as plausible from their own point of view as any an Aztec high priest could offer to justify his behavior. Martin Hollis, citing "Bernard Williams's distinction between 'thick' and 'thin' concepts in *Ethics and the Limits of Philosophy*," notes: "If Attila the Hun and Vlad the Impaler truly behaved as legend says, then the former was brutal and the latter cruel. This is not a matter of what counted as brutal and cruel either at the time or among those who now describe it so." See "The Poetics of Personhood," in A. Malachowski, ed., *Reading Rorty*, p. 251.

11. Wittgenstein, of course, makes essentially the same point by means of the notion of "family resemblance," some of the implications of which were discussed earlier.

12. Putnam speaks of "meanings as being historic entities in the sense in which persons or nations are historic entities" and thus as "hav[ing] an identity through time but no essence." *See Representation and Reality* (Cambridge: MIT Press, 1988), p. 11.

13. Again, cases such as *Griswold* and *Roe*, mentioned earlier, reflect nothing more than the fact that the Supreme Court cannot be overruled, even when it extends its purview from construing the Constitution to, in effect, amending it, and thereby arrogates to itself a legislative rather than strictly judicial function. Even our political system, brilliantly designed though it is, does not quite embody the ideal of a government solely of laws and not of men; perhaps, in the end, no such thing is truly possible. One is reminded in this connection of an exchange between George C. Scott and the late Peter Sellers in the film *Dr. Strangelove*. Sellers, in the role of the president of the United States, has just been informed by Scott, the chairman of the Joint Chiefs of Staff, that the head of the Strategic Air Command, General Jack D. Ripper, has launched a nuclear attack on the Soviet Union. Sellers is incredulous and says, "I was under the impression that I was the only one authorized to order the use of nuclear weapons." To this Scott replies, "Yes sir, that is correct. You are the only one so authorized. And although I hate to judge before all the facts are in, it is beginning to look as if General Ripper has exceeded his authority."

14. This does not mean, of course, that we should expect to be able to find for all those things that we call good some single, definable property or set of properties that would constitute an answer to the question of "what makes them all good" (*CP*, p. xiii). To accept this formulation of the goal of inquiry as the touchstone of the possbility of doing ethics at all—by which standard, of course, it would plainly not be possible—would be, again, to have allowed ourselves to be taken in by the straw man of (pre-critical) essentialism. Our uses of the term *good*, like those of *true*, are simply much too varied for such a result to be at all likely. (Cf. Michael Clark: "There is no unique way in which language latches on to the world, not because it floats free from it but because in using language we latch on to the world in many different ways"; see "Fact and Fiction," in A. Malachowski, ed., *Reading Rorty*, p. 176). But it scarcely follows from this that we should not try to determine as precisely as possible what those uses are and, where appropriate, distinguish among them. Nor does it mean that we are incapable of giving reasons for those uses and still less that we should not be expected to do so. Nor, finally, does it mean that these will always turn out to be good or satisfactory reasons; some things that we were initially inclined to call "true" or "good" we may, on reflection, decide were not properly so characterized. Differences of opinion will arise here, and not every one of these disagreements

will be finally resolvable. Though we all operate in ultimately the same cognitive and moral universe (by definition, the only one there is), though the overall logic of fact, as of value, is necessarily always and everywhere the same, local cognitive and moral intuitions can and do differ. (Did the defendant act in self-defense in killing the deceased or not? Is it better to preserve our freedom against aggression, even at the cost of massive loss of life, or would it be better simply to surrender to the enemy, thereby avoiding bloodshed?) And sometimes, as a practical matter, in Wittgenstein's famous image, one simply reaches bedrock and the spade is turned. It is my contention, however, that that point is in fact not reached either as quickly or as often as sometimes seems to be supposed. Unbridgeable gulfs between personal *Weltbilder* are not nearly such common phenomena—not even remotely so—as are, for example, conceptual confusions and slips in logic. To these lapses, moreover, may be added such equally human failings as the tendency to try to score debating points off one's conversational "adversary" (rather than pursuing together, in cooperative fashion, a joint inquiry into questions of mutual interest), as well as the psychological obverse of that tendency, the horror at the possibility of having to acknowledge in any given case that one might actually just be *wrong*.

15. "Even those who have followed me this far will want to know how a value-based enterprise of the sort I have described can develop as a science does, repeatedly producing powerful new techniques for prediction and control. To that question, unfortunately, I have no answer at all, but that is only another way of saying that I make no claim to have solved the problem of induction. If science did progress by virtue of some shared and binding algorithm of choice, I would be equally at a loss to explain its success. The lacuna is one I feel acutely, but its presence does not differentiate my position from the tradition." See *The Essential Tension* (Chicago: University of Chicago Press, 1977), pp. 332–33; cited in *PMN*, p. 340. The mistake here, of course, or a large part of it at any rate, is to think of science as "a value-based enterprise" to begin with. In this respect, moreover, Kuhn's position does indeed diverge "from the tradition"—rather dramatically so.

16. No matter at how late a date. As I write this, preparations are nearing completion for a massive experiment to be conducted in outer space, designed to subject Einstein's General Theory of Relativity to by far the most demanding test of its validity yet undertaken—one that by general consent of the scientists involved is capable, depending on the outcome, of leading to a more or less substantial and far-reaching revision of the currently accepted standard model of the universe.

17. It is perhaps worth noting that, of the five definitions of *conversion* given in Webster's Ninth New Collegiate Dictionary, the only one that refers in any way to a change of opinion or belief speaks exclusively of "adoption of religion."

18. Rorty not infrequently indicates his belief (in which he is, of course, far from alone) that specifically the *French* Revolution constituted the great political watershed of the last two centuries by ending the era of feudal absolutism and ushering in the modern age of liberal democracy. See, for example, among numerous such instances in his writings, "Philosophy as Science, as Metaphor, and as Politics," in A. Cohen and M. Dascal, ed., *The Institution of Philosophy: A Discipline in Crisis?* (LaSalle: Open Court, 1989), pp. 22, 27.

19. See Simon Schama, *Citizens: A Chronicle of the French Revolution* (New York: Knopf, 1989).

20. "Though a generation is *sometimes* required to effect the change, scientific communities have again and again been converted to new paradigms. Furthermore, these conversions occur not despite the fact that scientists are human but because they are. Though some scientists, particularly the older and more experienced ones, may resist indefinitely, most of them can be reached in one way or another" (*SSR*, p. 152; emphasis added).

21. The qualification "affecting their *own* lives" is, of course, crucial. We cannot, without doing violence to the procedural basis of the system, decide for ourselves in such a way that we also, in effect, decide for others (as should not really be necessary to add, whether they happen to be born or unborn). In particular, there can be no such thing as a "right," even if a majority of the electorate should seek to vote it into existence, to anything that must be produced or provided to one by someone else; the only exceptions are those cases in which the other person or persons in question have in some way incurred an actual obligation to provide it, as, for example, parents do in conceiving children. Procedurally-based rights are expressions of opportunities and the paths by which they may legitimately be pursued. They are not, because they cannot be, without ceasing to be precisely procedural, guarantees of results. Rorty overlooks this distinction in his analysis of Clifford Geertz's "Case of the Drunken Indian and the Kidney Machine." For Rorty, the fact that a successful claim on society's goods—goods that persons other than oneself have had to produce and must continue to maintain, and, most important, to which individuals no less needy than oneself will not have access to the extent that one does oneself—can be divorced utterly from considerations of personal responsibility for one's own well-being "is not particularly depressing, but rather cheering. It shows our liberal institutions functioning well and smoothly." See "On Ethnocentrism: A Reply to Clifford Geertz," *Michigan Quarterly Review* 25 (1986): 526–27. It seems to me that to the extent this case "shows" anything, it is simply the lack of any intellectually coherent foundation for much so-called "welfare state" policy. As Benjamin Franklin observed, "When the people discover that they can vote themselves money, that will be the end of the Republic."

22. This tendency to a kind of relentless anthropomorphizing of "nature" in characterizing the position to which he is opposed reaches perhaps its most extreme pitch when Rorty imputes to modern science the delusion that its "vocabulary was the one nature had always *wanted* to be described in" (*CP*, p. 193).

CHAPTER FIVE

1. Jean Jacques Rousseau, *Discourse on the Origin of Inequality*, in *The Social Contract and Discourses*, p. 234.

2. Putnam takes a decidedly direct approach to this issue. Addressing the question of Rorty's cultural relativism, he says simply, "I shall count a philosopher as a cultural relativist for our purposes if I have not been able to find anyone who can explain to me why he *isn't* a cultural relativist. Thus I count Richard Rorty as a cultural relativist" ("Why Reason Can't Be Naturalized," p. 228).

3. See, again, *Über Gewissheit/On Certainty*; subsequent references are given in the text.

4. Donald Davidson, "The Method of Truth in Metaphysics," in K. Baynes et al., ed., *After Philosophy*, pp. 166, 168. Davidson's argument here is brilliantly ingenious. I discuss it at greater length in "Strict Constructionism: Davidsonian Realism and the World of Belief," in Reed Way Dasenbrock, ed., *Literary Theory After Davidson* (University Park: Pennsylvania State University Press, forthcoming). Briefly, the argument turns on the impossibility of reconciling an ascription to anyone of fundamental error about how the world is with the existence of the language itself in which such an ascription must be formulated: "Successful communication proves the existence of a shared, and largely true, view of the world" (ibid., p. 168). It follows, moreover, "that in making manifest the large features of our language, we make manifest the large features of reality" (ibid., p. 166). As Davidson notes, this position has also been taken by, among others, Wittgenstein. It is, indeed, an insight to which Wittgenstein seems to have come very early in his career, and

it is one that continues to inform all his subsequent philosophizing, up to and including the late notes collected posthumously in *OC*.

5. As Davidson puts it in "On the Very Idea of a Conceptual Scheme," cited earlier, "In giving up dependence on the concept of an uninterpreted reality, something outside all schemes and science, we do not relinquish the notion of objective truth—quite the contrary. . . . Of course, truth of sentences remains relative to language, but that is as objective as can be" (p. 20).

6. *Critique of Pure Reason*, B xvi.

7. See Jean Paul, *Clavis Fichtiana, Sämtliche Werke: Historisch-kritische Ausgabe*, ed. Eduard Berend (Weimar: Hermann Böhlaus Nachfolger, 1927ff.), 1. Abt., Bd. 9, 459–501.

8. The *Nachtwachen von Bonaventura* appeared in 1804. After many attempts to determine the identity of the author, with numerous candidates for the honor being proposed over the years, the question seems finally to have been resolved in favor of Ernst August Klingemann. See Ruth Haag, "Noch einmal: Der Verfasser der 'Nachtwachen von Bonaventura,'" *Euphorion* 81 (1987): 286–97; cited in Dennis F. Mahoney, *Der Roman der Goethezeit (1774–1829)* (Stuttgart: Metzler, 1988), pp. 119, 121.

9. See, for example, his "Zur Geschichte der Religion und Philosophie in Deutschland" and "Die romantische Schule," both in Heinrich Heine, *Beiträge zur deutschen Ideologie*, intr. Hans Mayer (Frankfurt: Ullstein, 1971).

10. The crucial section of the *Critique* establishing this conclusion is the "Refutation of Idealism," B 274–79.

11. Though not a distinction that in practice Kant himself always remembers to observe, *transcendent* in his idiom refers to what exceeds the limits of any possible experience, while *transcendental* refers to the conditions of possibility of the experience we actually have.

12. See the famous opening lines of the Preface to the First Edition of the *Critique*, A vii.

13. Rorty concludes from the fact of what he calls the "ubiquity of language" (*CP*, xix, xxx) that something like this doctrine is unavoidable. I contend, however, that precisely the "ubiquity of language," properly understood, renders the doctrine of "ubiquity of interpretation" incoherent. Cf. Charles Taylor: "[T]here is a widespread reading of Wittgenstein, which sees him as some kind of refined behaviourist, and hence as a non-realist about inner states. But I think this is an insufficiently radical reading, one which still stays too much within the epistemological picture, which only allows one to alternate between acknowledging some inner life unobservable in principle, and a non-realist reduction of all inner talk to outer behaviour. . . . Wittgenstein can be more fruitfully interpreted as breaking out of this mould altogether. To follow him in overcoming epistemology [in this sense of the term] is to return to an aggressive realism" ("Rorty in the Epistemological Tradition," in A. Malachowski, ed., *Reading Rorty*, p. 265).

14. Taylor notes that "there is one principal line of argument, which Rorty returns to again and again in different forms. . . . This is that the only alternative to his Pragmatism is some belief in a [pre-critical] correspondence theory" ("Rorty in the Epistemological Tradition," p. 268). "And this is why," Taylor says, "I want to claim that Rorty is still partly trapped in the old model. [For my part, I would say still entirely trapped in it.] It is not that he explicitly subscribes to the representational view, and indeed, he often seems to be repudiating it. It is rather that his conception of the alternatives still seem to be commanded by that view. That is, his notion of what it is to reject [pre-critical] representationalism still seems commanded by the doctrine being rejected. So to learn that our thoughts don't correspond to things-in-themselves is to conclude that they don't cor-

respond to anything at all. If transcendent entities don't make them true, then nothing makes them true. These were the only game in the epistemic town, and if they go the place has to be closed down. Rorty seems to be operating within the logic of the old system that linked us to transcendent reality through a screen of representations, even while distancing himself from it. Within this logic, he makes the decisive move of rejecting the transcendent; and then all the non-realist conclusions naturally follow. But they only follow if you make this move while leaving everything else unchanged. . . . But the question is very much whether it makes sense to scrap the transcendent without jettisoning the whole system. Rorty still seems trapped half-way" (ibid., p. 271). In my terminology, not having made the critical turn, he remains squarely within the pre-critical orbit, merely on the skeptical side of it.

15. Alexander Nehamas makes a similar point with regard specifically to the interpretation of texts. Having asserted—to my mind, to be sure, already giving away too much to the skeptical side of the argument—that "the author [of a text] is . . . the product of interpretation, not an object that exists independently in the world" (the familiar pre-critical antinomy is, of course, once more readily discernible here), he addresses the obvious question, "If the author is our product, why not produce anyone we like out of a particular text?" Conceding that "[n]o argument can show that we would be wrong [in principle] to try to revise the history of literature" in this way—and given his analysis to this point, he no longer has any way to avoid making that concession—he nevertheless observes that "in order to show that the author is an arbitrary figure, we would actually have to produce such a revision, as well as a number of others, involving different but equally plausible rearrangements of the canon and even new canons. To say this can always be done is very different from doing it. And only this latter, if it is successful and convincing, can show that the author is arbitrary." See "Writer, Text, Work, Author," in Anthony J. Cascardi, ed., *Literature and the Question of Philosophy* (Baltimore: Johns Hopkins University Press, 1987), pp. 284–85. For a fuller statement of this position, Nehamas refers the reader to his *Nietzsche: Life as Literature*, pp. 62–73.

16. As Wittgenstein says in another well-known and often-cited passage, "[A] wheel that can be turned though nothing else moves with it, is not part of the mechanism" (*PI*, § 271).

17. To anticipate a possible objection: it is, of course, conceivable that someone knows what the name *Titanic* refers to and yet does not know what happened to it. Perhaps the person was absent from class that day; perhaps he has simply forgotten. But no one (or, again, no one who is aware of what he is saying) is going to claim seriously *both* that a ship by this name existed *and* that there is nevertheless not something in particular—regardless of what, on investigation, that may turn out to be—that happened to it. No one, in other words, is going to assert the determinate existence of something and in the same breath deny that at least some properties—whatever they may be—must be definitely predicable of it. For to posit "propertyless determinate existence," which is what this would amount to, would be to commit oneself to a manifest contradiction in terms.

18. Rorty sees "the idealist tradition" as merely "buil[ding] upon Kant" (*CP*, xviii). So far as I can tell, he nowhere evinces a sense for the extent to which post-Kantian Idealism becomes possible at all only by virtue of a fundamental misunderstanding of Kant on the part of his successors.

19. I undertake such an analysis of a text by Herder in my *Herder and the Poetics of Thought: Unity and Diversity in* On Diligence in Several Learned Languages (University Park: Pennsylvania State University Press, 1989).

20. For an extended discussion of this issue as it appears both in the *Tractatus* and in Herder's early work, drawing in part on twentieth-century developments in logic

(Gödel's theorem) and cosmology (Stephen Hawking's "no boundary condition"), see my "The Infinity of Finitude: Criticism, History, and Herder," forthcoming in the *Herder Yearbook*.

21. In his Carus lectures, Hilary Putnam suggests that in fact "almost all of the *Critique of Pure Reason* is compatible with a reading in which one is not at all committed to a Noumenal World, or even . . . to the intelligibility of thoughts about noumena." See *The Many Faces of Realism* (LaSalle: Open Court, 1987), p. 41. Henry Allison takes, in a way, the opposite tack toward the same overall end by arguing instead for a kind of rehabilitation of the notion of the *Ding an sich*. Against what he rightly terms the "persistent" criticism that Kant "has no right to affirm the existence of things in themselves, noumena, or a transcendental object, much less to talk about such things as somehow 'affecting' the mind," he seeks nevertheless, as he says, "to show that talk about things considered as they are in themselves, including the claim that things so considered 'affect us,' does not violate the doctrine of the unknowability of things as they are in themselves." See *Kant's Transcendental Idealism: An Interpretation and Defense* (New Haven: Yale University Press, 1983), p. 237.

22. I have discussed the *Treatise* more extensively on several occasions elsewhere. In addition to *Herder and the Poetics of Thought*, the essays "Herder and the Possibility of Literature: Rationalism and Poetry in Eighteenth-Century Germany" (in Wulf Koepke, ed., *Johann Gottfried Herder: Innovator Through the Ages* [Bonn: Bouvier, 1982], pp. 41–63) and "*Verum est factum*: Critical Realism and the Discourse of Autonomy" (*German Quarterly* 64 [1991]: 149–65) pursue at greater length a number of the issues touched on briefly here.

23. The context does not make entirely clear whether Rorty means to say that this really is the way geometrical theorems are proved; perhaps he is merely adducing the belief in question as one example of the overall view he wishes to attack. In any case, however, it is clear that no "geometrical figure" ever "proves" a theorem or ever could do so. Among other things, if that really were the case, geometry would obviously be a great deal easier than it is, being reducible to nothing more than careful draftsmanship. Theorems are proved by being deduced from axioms or other theorems in accordance with standard rules of inference. Figures illustrate proofs; they do not constitute them.

24. M. H. Abrams, *The Mirror and the Lamp: Romantic Theory and the Critical Tradition* (London: Oxford University Press, 1953).

25. From the vantage point of the present day, the aesthetic optimism of some Romantics, especially in the early years of the movement and particularly in Germany, appears little short of astonishing. Basically secular millenarians, these thinkers and poets were convinced, at least in their more exuberant moments, of the power of poetic art ultimately to bring about both a regeneration of human nature and a transformation of the world into the sort of earthly paradise appropriate to the race of quasi-divinities that that regeneration would bring into being. The consequences of the (inevitable) collapse of that optimism are, of course, still with us today in a host of different forms.

26. Even on the most favorably inclined reading, however, I do not see how anything can save the accompanying assertion that "[t]he question of how we know what conditions [objects] must conform to—how to validate knowledge-claims made from the transcendental standpoint—is discussed [nowhere] in the first *Critique*" (*PMN*, p. 138, n. 12).

27. Robert Paul Wolff bases his disagreement with a certain traditional reading of Kant in part on considerations similar to this one. See *Kant's Theory of Mental Activity: A Commentary on the Transcendental Analytic of the* Critique of Pure Reason (Cambridge: Harvard University Press, 1963; rpt. Gloucester: Peter Smith, 1973), pp. 55–56. Let me

emphasize that I do not wish to be unfair to Rorty. If the point he wants to make against Kant could be sustained, it would certainly not be the first time that a large and impressive body of thought had been shown to rest, at least in significant part, on a rather massive contradiction. And, as far as that goes, it is widely recognized that there are indeed unresolved, and probably unresolvable, problems standing in the way of a reconciliation of every aspect of Kant's "critical" philosophy with every other aspect of it. One particularly acute such problem is the apparently fundamental incompatibility of Kant's epistemology with his ethics; see R. P. Wolff, *The Autonomy of Reason: A Commentary on Kant's Groundwork of the Metaphysic of Morals* (New York: Harper & Row, 1973), pp. 7–8, 11–15. I merely wish to maintain that the particular contradiction of which Rorty wishes to convict Kant here is in fact one that his argument can be shown to have anticipated and so taken the necessary steps to avoid.

28. One of the less attractive features of Rorty's way of presenting his views appears in his reference to "Kant's *self-deceptive* use of [the notion of] 'ground' " as a central element in his argument (*PMN*, p. 151, n. 31; emphasis added). Rorty shares with many contemporary skeptics a tendency to impute to his adversaries both repressed and vaguely (or sometimes not so vaguely) disreputable motives for disagreeing with him or with those whose views he shares. His dismissal of "the charges of 'relativism' and 'irrationalism' once leveled against Dewey" as "mindless defensive reflexes" on the part of the latter's opponents (*PMN*, p. 13), for example, is not nearly the isolated case one might wish it were.

In general, the skeptical hegemony (or near-hegemony) in critical theory in recent years has often seemed to coincide with a notable decline in the level of civility in the exchange of views. It has become more or less routine, for example, for partisans of the skeptical standpoint to accuse their opponents of "nostalgia" for an (imagined) age of wholeness and harmony, "fear" (again, usually "repressed") of contingency and indeterminacy, support for any of a number of structures of "domination" ("Eurocentric," "patriarchal," "capitalistic"), and a variety of other sins as well.

29. Both my reading of the first *Critique* in particular and my understanding of Kant's "critical" philosophy generally are considerably indebted to Wolff's two studies cited above. Of the more recent literature on Kantian epistemology, I have found Allison's *Kant's Transcendental Idealism* an especially valuable source of insight. Subsequent references to these works are given in the text.

30. There seems to me at least a partial analogy here to the distinction drawn by Lotman and Uspensky between cultures oriented primarily toward *expression* (and so to the idea of correct *texts*) and those directed chiefly toward *content* (and in that way to rules for the *production* of texts). See "On the Semiotic Mechanism of Culture," *New Literary History* 9 (1978): 211–32. The distinction implicit in the Kantian notion of a "transcendental" argument is also broadly analogous to that between a politics that directs itself chiefly to the attainment of particular policy *objectives*—certain selected *ends* or *results*—and one geared to securing those modes of *procedure* that permit the most unencumbered pursuit possible of virtually any objectives whatever (save only those whose realization would undo the framework of activity itself). Much political debate, both past and present, although not usually formulated in precisely these terms, in fact turns ultimately on the choice between these two quite different conceptions (or meta-conceptions) of the ideal of justice. In this connection, see in particular Thomas Sowell, *A Conflict of Visions* (New York: Morrow, 1987).

31. Cf. "All the mental entities which had been described [by Kant's predecessors] in static terms on the analogy of pictures before the mind, or shapes abstracted from their material, are seen by Kant to be actually mental functions or activities. Knowledge is an activity, not a state, of the mind" (*KMA*, p. 323).

32. "[Anyone] must grant that he is conscious, if he is to engage in argument at all. Thus Kant's argument at its very deepest level is a dialectical *ad hominem*, designed to force his opponents either to assent to his conclusions or to remain silent" (*AR*, p. 26).

33. Wittgenstein deals with the obvious objection that one might say precisely this while talking in one's sleep in the last of the notes in *OC* (§ 676).

34. Again, as earlier, it is not a matter of conscious hypocrisy here but simply a matter of deep confusion over what one is actually saying and what it entails.

35. The two positions, the skeptical and the relativist, are at bottom one. One principal difficulty with which Rorty grapples throughout his writings is the effort to maintain historical-cultural relativism without being obliged at the same time to embrace skepticism. But because, as I am trying to show, these positions ultimately converge, that effort cannot but be doomed to failure.

36. As Allison in effect notes, the strength of Kant's argument lies ultimately in its demonstration that we would not even be able to *think* of the sorts of question that are at stake in the philosophical controversies with which he is concerned if the conclusions in which the argument issues were not *already* valid. See, for example, the following passage, which can stand for many such in his study: "Kant is not engaged . . . in the misguided project of attempting to 'deduce' the ontological concept by claiming that it is itself a necessary condition for judgment. On the contrary, Kant's goal is to show how the ontological concept arises from the concept which is such a necessary condition" (*KTI*, p. 213).

37. Almost nobody, at any rate. As we saw earlier, Rorty is prepared to assert that it makes perfect sense to suppose that tables might really vanish when no one is looking at them. And if tables, why not trees, too, or even whole forests?

38. Berkeley, of course, is precisely this determined. Most people, however, have seen in that determination simply the *reductio ad absurdum* that his system provides of itself.

39. Charles Altieri, "Wittgenstein on Consciousness and Language: A Challenge to Derridean Theory," *MLN* 91 (1976): 1401.

40. This is presumably what Terry Eagleton means in asserting that "there are no facts that we do not know about." *See Literary Theory: An Introduction* (Minneapolis: University of Minnesota Press, 1983), p. 86. He is surely not taking the absurd position that in order for something to qualify as a fact, it must be known by everyone. Counterexamples are, of course, all too easy to produce. Such a conclusion, if only it were valid, would, for instance, render the Sixth Commandment (or, depending on the religious tradition in which one was raised, the Seventh) practically speaking all but unnecessary. One is reminded here of a cartoon that appeared several years ago, I believe, in *The New Yorker* magazine. The cartoon shows Moses at the foot of Mt. Sinai telling the people gathered there, "Well, there's good news and bad news. I've got Him down to ten. But adultery's still in there."

41. The relationship to which I am referring with the expression "conceptual presence" is, of course, precisely the opposite of the impossible one contemplated by the notorious "metaphysics of presence." It requires someone thoroughly imbued with the precritical outlook to have thought of something like a "metaphysics of presence" in the first place. But—and this is the more important consideration at the moment—it requires someone no less in thrall to that outlook to believe that there is any philosophical mileage to be gotten out of a skeptical assault on the "metaphysics of presence."

42. In the *Tractatus*, for example, he asserts, in a frequently cited passage, that "[l]ogic must look after itself." And from that it follows in turn that "[i]n a certain sense, we cannot make mistakes in logic" (*TLP*, 5.473; cf. *Notebooks, 1914–16*, 22.8.14). For "lan-

guage itself prevents every logical mistake.—What makes logic a priori is the *impossibility* of illogical thought" (*TLP*, 5.4731).

43. David Pears, interestingly, employs this very same image in discussing Wittgenstein: "It is Wittgenstein's later doctrine that outside human thought and speech there are no independent, objective points of support, and meaning and necessity are preserved only in the linguistic processes which embody them. [This is, of course, as we have seen, Wittgenstein's earlier doctrine, too.] They are safe only because the practices gain a certain stability from the rules. But even the rules do not provide a fixed point of reference, because they always allow divergent interpretations. What really gives the practices their stability is that we agree in our interpretations of the rules. [As we saw in the discussion of anti-foundationalism above, what we actually agree in for Wittgenstein is, in the first instance, "form of life," not interpretation.] We could say that this is fortunate, except that this would be like saying that it is fortunate that life on earth tolerates the earth's natural atmosphere. What we ought to say is that there is as much stability as there is." See *Ludwig Wittgenstein* (New York: Viking, 1969), p. 179; cited, interestingly enough, by Rorty in *CP*, pp. 22–23. Rorty follows this passage with a still longer one from the same book, in which Pears offers an outstanding characterization of the "critical" purport of Wittgenstein's philosophy, culminating in the observation: "Wittgenstein's idea is that objectivism, in its only tenable form, collapses into anthropocentrism" (ibid., p. 182). This is in turn very close to one of the ways in which Davidson has sought to express the theory of "critical realism," namely the thesis that "coherence yields correspondence." See "A Coherence Theory of Truth and Knowledge," in E. LePore, ed., *Truth and Interpretation: Perspectives on the Philosophy of Donald Davidson* (Oxford: Blackwell, 1986), p. 307. That Rorty, on the other hand, has simply not caught on to what "critical realism" is about emerges, again, I think, clearly enough from the fact that, as he sees it, Pears merely "ties himself up in paradoxes" (*CP*, p. 23) in his characterization of Wittgenstein's view.

44. Cf. "Instead of a 'pure original unchangeable consciousness,' . . . we have the logical possibility, *which may not even be actualized*, of attaching the bare representation 'I' to all the contents of consciousness" (*KMA*, p. 176). Recognizing the indispensability of a correct grasp of this point to an understanding of Kant's thought at large, Wolff returns to it repeatedly in the course of his commentary (see, e.g., *KMA*, pp. 102, 178, 186, and 301, n. 71). And this is, in turn, merely another way of formulating the central point that "[w]here [both the rationalists and the empiricists among Kant's predecessors] concentrated their attention on the *objects* of awareness, he sought the nature of *awareness* itself" (*KMA*, p. 109; emphasis added). Allison, too, is entirely clear on this crucially important aspect of Kantian theory: "[T]he doctrine of apperception . . . is most properly viewed as a formal model or schema for the analysis of the understanding and its 'logical' activities. Correlatively, the theory of synthesis implied by this doctrine is to be taken as an analytical account of the mode of operation of the model. As such, it is neither a bit of introspective psychology nor an idealistic ontological thesis concerning the manner in which the mind 'creates' the phenomenal world by imposing its forms upon the given sensible data. This modeling function provides the basis for the transcendental status assigned to the principle of apperception and for the claim that all of our representations must conform to its conditions if they are not to be epistemically null" (*KTI*, p. 144).

45. Cf., again, "The work of the philosopher consists in assembling reminders for a particular purpose" (*PI*, § 127).

46. Cf., again, Allison: "[T]o think this thought (that of the identity of the 'I think') *is* [for Kant] to unify the distinct representations in a single consciousness" (*KTI*, p. 142; emphasis added). Allison illustrates the point as follows. Consider, he says, "the simplest possible case: where a subject has two representations, *A* and *B*, each of which is

accompanied by a distinct awareness or 'empirical consciousness.' In other words, there is an 'I think' *A* and an 'I think' *B* pertaining to a single subject. Clearly, in order for the subject of both these thoughts to become reflectively aware of its identity, it must combine A and *B* in a single consciousness. Only by so combining A and *B* can it possibly become aware of the identity of the I that thinks *A* with the I that thinks *B*. It cannot, therefore, apperceive its own identity as a thinking subject without *in the same act* also unifying these representations. Consequently this act does necessarily 'contain' a synthesis. . . . The awareness of the identity of the I that thinks *A* with the I that thinks *B* obviously requires an awareness of both *A* and *B*. This is because the I of the 'I think' has no determinate content, and thus cannot be characterized apart from its representations. Consequently, unless I can become aware of both representations together, I cannot become aware of the identity of the I that thinks the one with the I that thinks the other. As Kant puts it, 'I should have as many and as diverse a self as I have representations of which I am conscious to myself' (B 134). But not only is such an awareness possible only by means of the combination of these representations in one consciousness, it is itself an awareness of the result of their combination. In this sense, then, apperception clearly involves the consciousness of a synthesis or combination of representations" (ibid., pp. 142–43).

47. In a footnote at this point, Wolff refers the reader as well to Norman Kemp Smith's *A Commentary to Kant's 'Critique of Pure Reason,'* 2d ed. (London: Macmillan, 1923), pp. 186–94.

48. Hazard Adams, ed., *Critical Theory Since 1965*, p. 4.

49. I do not mean that I think Kant himself construed the derivation of the Table of Judgments in such terms. I doubt very much that he did. I think he saw himself engaged here in a strictly *logical* analysis of the forms of judgment, and that in his view this had no particular implications for language at all. That, in a way, is precisely the point. For Kant seems not to have regarded intellection as in any fundamental sense a *linguistic* phenomenon to begin with. As I will be arguing in a moment, it was Herder who, at least in the German tradition, took the first decisive steps toward the recognition of that key linkage. With the benefit of hindsight, however, it seems to me that we can nevertheless make out at least a kind of tacit or implicit acknowledgment of this linkage at the foundation of Kant's argument as well. But even if this view of the Metaphysical Deduction is found unpersuasive, the larger point that I am concerned to make at this juncture with regard to the first *Critique* as a whole can still stand, independently of that view. For my claim is simply that Kant needlessly weakens his position by abandoning what is in effect the linguistic standpoint of the Metaphysical Deduction in favor of the "faculty psychology"-vocabulary that thereafter largely dominates the rest of the work. And hence it can still be the case—in my view, clearly is the case—that he would have produced a still more effective argument for "critical realism" than he in fact did if, like Herder and later Wittgenstein, he actually had cast the argument in explicitly linguistic terms throughout. On the possibility of a linguistic interpretation of at least part of Kant's argument—to be sure, a later stage of the argument than the one at hand, the "transcendental schematism" of the categories—see *KTI*, pp. 185–86, where Allison refers to what he calls "schema judgments" as "semantic claims," citing also Robert Butts's characterization of them as "semantic rules."

50. In a footnote here Allison adds: "The clearest expression of this line of thought is Kant's well-known statement concerning the categories: 'If we can prove that by their means alone an object can be thought, this will be sufficient deduction of them, and will justify their objective validity' (A96–97)" (*KTI*, p. 352). At a slightly earlier juncture in his study than the passage from the body of the text last cited, he presents the same point in perhaps somewhat more concrete terms: "Every judgment . . . necessarily makes use of some pregiven concept (or concepts). Of course, it does not follow from the fact that every

judgment presupposes some concept or other that there are some concepts that are presupposed by every judgment. It might be the case that a concept applied (and thus presupposed) in a judgment is itself the product of an antecedent judgment. For example, the judgment 'Socrates is a man' obviously presupposes the concept *man*, which it predicates of the individual Socrates. This concept, however, is itself the product of a prior judgment in which the real definition of 'man' is determined. Nevertheless, it is clear that this process cannot be continued indefinitely. For one thing, we soon arrive at certain very general concepts, such as entity, property, individual, class, and totality, that cannot themselves be regarded as products of prior judgments; for another, these very general concepts can be shown to be necessarily involved in all judgments as conditions of the very possibility of the activity. Although we become explicitly aware of such concepts only by a reflection on the nature of judgment, we become aware of them *as presuppositions* of this activity. Such concepts are the pure concepts of the understanding; they are second-order concepts or rules for the generation of rules. Given Kant's theory of judgment, there must be some such second-order concepts if there are to be any concepts at all" (ibid., pp. 116–17). In a footnote to this passage, Allison adds that "[t]he conception of pure concepts as second-order rules or rules for the formulation of empirical concepts, which are first-order rules, is developed by Robert Paul Wolff in *Kant's Theory of Mental Activity*, pp. 24–25" (ibid., p. 348).

51. It is worth noting at least in passing that Herder also provides a clear counterexample to Rorty's contention that Western philosophy, and specifically the epistemology of the West, has been dominated by an originally Platonic (or Parmenidean) interpretation of knowledge as essentially a form of *vision* (what Rorty, as we have seen, calls the "ocular metaphor"). For Herder is not merely that eighteenth-century thinker who more than any other lays the foundation for the eventual assimilation of theory of knowledge to theory of language. He does so with reference, not to vision, but rather to *hearing* and to *touch* as the primary human senses. (See in this connection, again, my "Herder and the Possibility of Literature: Rationalism and Poetry in Eighteenth-Century Germany.") As Wolff notes, however, Kant, too, "sets himself against the widespread identification of knowing with seeing"; such an identification is incompatible with his conception of the mind as inherently active: "For Kant the principal mistake of this theory would be the description of knowing as passive" (*KMA*, p. 149). The critical turn is directed precisely against this view of the mind as ultimately acted upon rather than acting, a view implicit in both the dogmatic and the skeptical variants of the pre-critical outlook, with their common conception of intellection as a process of reflection rather than of illumination or construction.

52. In a far from uncharacteristic expression of pique, Herder declared upon reading Kant's reviews that he could not reasonably be expected to put up with this sort of thing, for he was after all "now forty years old and no longer sitting on [the latter's] metaphysical school bench."

53. In this connection, see in particular Thomas M. Seebohm, "Der systematische Ort der Herderschen Metakritik," *Kant-Studien* 63 (1972): 59–73. Seebohm was, so far as I know, the first commentator on the *Metacritique* to look beyond Herder's overt polemical intent and recognize the substantive philosophical accomplishment of the work. Among more recent studies seeking to build on this insight, see Karl Menges, " 'Seyn' und 'Daseyn', Sein und Zeit. Zu Herders Theorie des Subjekts," and my "Changing the Subject: Herder and the Reorientation of Philosophy," both in Kurt Mueller-Vollmer, ed., *Herder Today* (Berlin: de Gruyter, 1990).

54. In this way, among other things, Herder also undermines in advance the possibility of yet another distinction that Rorty seeks to draw. "We need to make a distinction," the latter contends, "between the claim that the world is out there and the claim

that truth is out there. To say that the world is out there, that it is not our creation, is to say, with common sense, that most things in space and time are the effects of causes which do not include human mental states. To say that truth is not out there is simply to say that where there are no sentences there is no truth, that sentences are elements of human languages, and that human languages are human creations" (*CIS*, pp. 4–5). The "distinction," however, as Herder shows, cannot be sustained. For apart from language, there is quite literally no "out there" in the first place. The demonstration of that fact is precisely the burden of the specifically Herderian version of the critical turn.

55. Marx, of course, is noted for arguing that consciousness is determined by the concrete particulars of social existence (rather than the latter being determined by the former), and, at least at first glance, this might appear to align him with the general view I am attributing to both Herder and Nietzsche. Marxism, however, is in the end merely a revival of pre-critical dogmatic metaphysics in materialist guise; and the often Byzantine complexity of the various categories of thought and action devised by Marxist exegetes certainly gives away nothing in a priori intricacy to the most ardent faculty psychologist.

56. Hans-Georg Gadamer, *Volk und Geschichte im Denken Herders* (Frankfurt: Klostermann, 1942), p. 6; cited by Wulf Koepke in his Introduction to *Johann Gottfried Herder: Innovator Through the Ages*, p. 1.

57. Charles Taylor, "Overcoming Epistemology," in K. Baynes et al., ed., *After Philosophy*, p. 478.

58. *The Philosophy of Peirce: Selected Writings*, ed. Justus Buchler (London: Kegan Paul, 1940), p. 99; cited in *Of Grammatology* (Baltimore: Johns Hopkins University Press, 1976), p. 49. It is not merely nitpicking, I think, to note that what Derrida here represents as the *beginning* of a sentence ("The science of semiotics . . . ") in fact occurs in Peirce's text within a larger context, following the phrase (with which the sentence in question actually begins), "In consequence of every representamen being thus connected with three things, the ground, the object, and the interpretant." In the two paragraphs immediately preceding this, Peirce has, among other things, explained what he means by the terms *representamen, ground, object,* and *interpretant.* These explanations, however, make it significantly more difficult to suggest with even a remote degree of plausibility that Peirce "goes very far in the direction" of Derrida's own linguistic nihilism.

59. Aram Vartanian, in a penetrating analysis of Derrida's reading of Rousseau's *Confessions,* shows something of the considerable extent to which the entire deconstructionist program derives its support from little more than a cavalier disregard for elementary requirements of scholarly responsibility in the citing of texts. See "Derrida, Rousseau, and the Difference," *Studies in Eighteenth-Century Culture* 19 (1989): 129–51. In reminding ourselves of this, however, a more general issue of critical method needs to be addressed at the same time. For both deconstructionists themselves and those broadly sympathetic to the movement are on the whole prepared to acknowledge that this observation is in fact substantially correct, at least as regards the practice of reading itself to which it refers; the agreement would obviously not extend to the particular way in which I have formulated the observation. They nonetheless deny, however, that it represents any objection either to Derrida's method or to his conclusions. Jonathan Culler, for example, in the opening chapter of *The Pursuit of Signs* (Ithaca: Cornell University Press, 1981), notes that in Derrida's writings "[t]here is no deference to the integrity of the text" (p. 14). The justification for that procedure, in Culler's view, is that "Derrida characteristically concentrates on elements which others find marginal, seeking not to elucidate what a text says but *to reveal an uncanny logic that operates in and across texts, whatever they say*" (pp. 14–15; emphasis added). This claim, however, is plainly inconsistent with the contention that Derrida is wholly indifferent to any sort of textual "integrity." For to have

discovered the alleged "uncanny logic" in question is merely to have redefined the locus of "integrity" as it pertains to texts, not to have abandoned the notion altogether. Indeed, there is no way in which that could be done under any circumstances. For as soon as one acknowledges that one is dealng with a *text* at all (as opposed, say, to random marks on a page), one is implicitly committed to the existence of some principle of coherence of that text (even if masked as a kind of anti-coherence), and so eo ipso to the notion of textual "integrity." As it happens, the example that Culler cites in what he takes to be support of his point is precisely the discussion of Rousseau in *Of Grammatology* that Prof. Vartanian so effectively "deconstructs." To put the point in slightly different terms, Derrida simply wants to have things both ways. He wants to base his argument on an analysis of actual texts, sensing rightly enough that if he does not, he will not be taken seriously by even the most credulous or naive among his readers. To gain entry at all to discussions among those whose business it is to analyze and interpret texts, he must at least appear to be talking about texts in his own right; otherwise he will be dismissed out of hand as someone who is, in Wittgenstein's words, "just gassing." But because no text will actually support the theory he is propounding—that theory being manifestly false—he has no alternative but to talk in reality exclusively about the theory itself. At the same time, however, through occasional citation of words and phrases severed from the contexts in which they actually occur, he seeks to preserve the fiction that he is not merely spinning his theory out of a kind of airy nothing but is rather deriving it from real instances of language use.

60. "Man makes the word, and the word means nothing which the man has not made it mean, and that only to some other man. But since man can think only by means of words or other external symbols, these might turn around and say: You mean nothing which we have not taught you, and then only so far as you address some word as the interpretant of your thought. . . . [T]he word or sign which man uses is the man himself. . . . Thus my language is the sum-total of myself; for the man is the thought" (*CP*, p. xx). Neither Herder nor Wittgenstein, it seems to me, could have expressed the co-originality of man, language, and world any more effectively than Peirce does here. And it is precisely that bedrock co-originality that in turn, as we have seen, renders Rorty's argument, not merely invalid, but actually incoherent, deprived from the outset of any intelligible point of departure.

61. See in this connection Buchler's commentary on the passage in question, in which he notes that Peirce's "earliest statement [of this tripartite schema] is" the following:

> The first would treat of the formal conditions of symbols having meaning, that is, of the reference of symbols in general to their grounds or imputed characters, and this might be called formal grammar; the second, logic, would treat of the formal conditions of the truth of symbols; and the third would treat of the formal conditions of the force of symbols, or their power of appealing to a mind, that is, of their reference in general to interpretants, and this might be called formal rhetoric. (*The Philosophy of Peirce*, p. 379)

This formulation surely makes clear that even what Peirce characterizes in the passage cited by Derrida as *"pure rhetoric"* has in fact nothing to do with the fantasy of endless semiosis entertained by the latter and which he believes he can see anticipated in Peirce's own thinking on language. Rather Peirce is referring to what Charles Morris would later term "pragmatics." In Morris's system, this is the division of semiotics dealing with "the relation of signs to interpreters"—that is, with the question of how language is understood (or otherwise acted upon) in various concrete situations by other language-users. See C. Morris, *Signs, Language, and Behavior* (New York: Prentice-Hall, 1946), pp. 217–18.

62. Derrida's ability systematically to ignore whatever cannot be accommodated to his theory, even though it be staring him directly in the face, is difficult to overstate. Immediately preceding the passage from Peirce under discussion here, he writes in *Of Grammatology:* "It is [for Peirce] a matter of elaborating . . . a formal doctrine of conditions which a discourse must satisfy in order to have a sense, in order to 'mean,' even if it is false or contradictory. The general morphology of that meaning . . . *is independent of all logic of truth*" (pp. 48–49; emphasis added). The passage itself, however, quite obviously says precisely the opposite. Within the "science of semiotics," as Peirce conceives it, the analyses of *meaning* (i.e., the determination of conditions of intelligibility) and of *truth* (the determination of what in principle can and cannot exist in the world) are both inseparable from one another and of exactly equal standing in the overall system. Nor are any momentous conclusions to be drawn from the order in which Peirce happens to present these two aspects of the enterprise in the passage at hand. In his commentary on the passage referred to above (see n. 58), Buchler cites yet another text, in which what Peirce calls "the theory of the conditions of truth" is this time alluded to first, followed then by a reference to "the doctrine of the general conditions of symbols and other signs having the significant character" (*The Philosophy of Peirce*, p. 379).

In the section of *Of Grammatology* under discussion here, Derrida states his view that for him Peirce and Husserl stand at opposite ends of the philosophical spectrum. "The difference between Husserl's and Peirce's phenomenologies," he says, "is fundamental." For while "Peirce goes very far in the direction that I have called the de-construction of. . . . the metaphysics of presence," Husserl's "phenomenology remains . . . —in its 'principle of principles'—the most radical and most critical restoration of the metaphysics of presence." What Derrida never questions, however, is the nature of the philosophical spectrum itself. He is, in other words, wholly uncritical in his acceptance of what I am here calling a pre-critical context of thought. Within that context, to be sure, as we have now seen repeatedly, there are indeed two and only two positions between which one can choose. And thus, for Derrida, everyone is of necessity either a metaphysician of presence or a deconstructor of that metaphysics—in our idiom, either a dogmatist or a skeptic. The principal thesis of this book, however, is that those who, like Derrida, assert the inescapability of the pre-critical context of thought are themselves seriously mistaken. Once we recognize the basic untenability of the assumptions underlying that context, it becomes possible for us to move beyond the stale antinomy of dogmatism and skepticism altogether in the direction of critical realism. And it seems to me this is precisely what Peirce does, along with, among others, Kant, Herder, and Wittgenstein.

63. In like manner, proponents of the view in question often seem to feel that there are important and far-reaching consequences to be derived from the thoroughly mundane fact that linguistic signification is in one sense always *arbitrary.* The fact that the concept "tree," for example, is expressed in English by *tree,* in German by *Baum,* in Latin by *arbor,* and so forth—from which it can be seen that there is no "natural" relationship between any of these terms in particular and the concept "tree"—is frequently taken as the starting point of an argument purporting to demonstrate as its conclusion that there is no such thing as fixed, stable, or determinate meaning under any description. A large part of the reason for this misapprehension seems to be a simple confusion—one that Saussure himself, of course, took explicit pains to avoid—between two senses of *arbitrary:* on the one hand, "conventional" (or "unmotivated"); on the other, "alterable at will." Only in the former sense of the term is linguistic signification properly characterized as "arbitrary"; but only the latter sense can provide any support for a skeptical denial of determinate

meaning. We shall return to this point at greater length in the next chapter, in connection with what I there call the doctrine of radical linguistic voluntarism.

64. There is insofar a certain analogy between a linguistic system and the plate from which a hologram is generated, in contrast to an ordinary photographic negative. If a negative is cut in half and either part of it developed, one gets one half of the original picture; the other half of the information contained in the negative is simply lost. If, however, a holographic plate is cut in half, the images produced from either of the two parts contain all the original hologram, but with the degree of clarity or resolution of the image reduced by a factor of one half.

65. The finite character of the system is, of course, to be distinguished from the fact that with that system it is possible to generate an indefinitely large set of well-formed utterances. That fact is no more remarkable, however, and thus no more in need of special comment, than are the corresponding facts that from a finite set of basic numerical signs (in binary notation, of course, even two will do), together with a few rules of combination and succession, one can go on generating new numbers to infinity, or that with the finite number of notes in the diatonic scale it is possible to create a limitless number of musical compositions.

66. Rorty is, of course, far from alone today in believing that there is anything at all in common between Wittgenstein's views and those of Derrida. See, for example (to mention only two others), Newton Garver's Preface to the English translation of Derrida's *La Voix et le Phénomène* (*Speech and Phenomena and Other Essays on Husserl's Theory of Signs* [Evanston: Northwestern University Press, 1973], pp. ix–xxix) and Henry Staten, *Wittgenstein and Derrida* (Lincoln: University of Nebraska Press, 1984).

67. Russell was referring to Wittgenstein's analysis of meaning as use (in contrast, for example, to the verificationism of the logical positivists), an idea that, although already visible in his earliest work (see, e.g., *TLP*, 3.326–3.328, *passim*), came to assume an ever more prominent role in his thought after his return to philosophy in the late 1920s and 1930s. See, for example, *The Blue and Brown Books*, p. 4. As directed specifically at Wittgenstein, Russell's remark, while attesting to the continued vigor of his wit, nonetheless also reminds us of the extent to which by the years following World War I the development of twentieth-century philosophy had already largely passed him by.

68. In what might be thought of as a kind of previous philosophical incarnation, Rorty, of course, himself once edited and wrote the Introduction to a collection of essays entitled *The Linguistic Turn* (Chicago: University of Chicago Press, 1967).

69. Here and in the following paragraph, see, in particular, Wolff's discussion of Kant's distinction between the "analytical" (or "regressive") and the "synthetic" (or "progressive") modes of argumentation. As Wolff also notes, however, Kant himself frequently allows this crucial distinction to be blurred in the very course of the argument of the first *Critique*. See the Introduction to *KMA*, "Chapter III: The Structure and Method of the Analytic," pp. 44–56; also, in the Introduction to *AR*, "The Structure of Kant's Exposition" and "A Cautionary Word about Reading Kant," pp. 24–30.

70. Another way of characterizing Rorty's basic dilemma is to note that, as with skeptics generally, he simply attacks dogmatism at the wrong end. What bothers him about dogmatism is its apodictic assertion of objectivity. What he goes after, however, is the aspect of apodicity, denying that it is ever possible. In so doing, however, he cannot avoid at the same time tying himself up in the net of self-refutation that such a denial inevitably brings with it. What he needed to do instead was to look at the notion of *objectivity* peculiar to dogmatism and, discovering the flaws in it, seek a new way of conceiving *that* notion. In so doing, however, he would presumably also have recognized the incoherence of skepticism as well (inasmuch as both sides of the pre-critical dichotomy

rest, as seen, on a common misconception) and might in that way have been led eventually to a version of the critical turn.

CHAPTER SIX

1. For an excellent discussion of the flaws in this claim, see Jane Heal, "Pragmatism and Choosing to Believe," in A. Malachowski, ed. *Reading Rorty,* pp. 101–14.

2. Though this notion often seems simply to be taken for granted today, there is to my mind at least some question as to just how "underdetermined by fact" theory really is. Consider the following proposal of Quine's, adopted, as he says, in accordance with a suggestion of Davidson's. Suppose that we have two theories which, although empirically equivalent, are nonetheless logically incompatible with one another. The question is then: "Sind sie dennoch beide wahr? Das Gespenst des Kulturrelativismus beginnt sich zu erheben, wenn wir beide von ihrem jeweiligen Standpunkt aus betrachtet für wahr halten. Das Gespenst läßt sich allerdings verscheuchen. . . . Um einander zu widersprechen, müßten die beiden Formulierungen irgendeinem Satz ø entgegengesetzte Wahrheitswerte zuordnen. Da die Formulierungen empirisch äquivalent sind, muß dieser Satz bestimmte Wörter enthalten, deren Gebrauch nur teilweise empirisch bestimmt ist. Wir können ein solches Wort wählen und es behandeln, als hätten wir es mit zwei verschiedenen Wörtern zu tun, wovon das eine in der einen und das andere in der anderen Theorieformulierung vorkommt. Diesen Schritt kann man dadurch kenntlich machen, daß man in einem Fall die Schreibweise des Wortes ändert. Durch wiederholte Anwendung dieses Verfahrens wird es gelingen, die Theorieformulierungen verträglich zu machen, und wir können dann beide als wahre Beschreibungen ein und derselben Welt mit verschiedenen Terminen betrachten. Damit wäre die Gefahr eines drohenden Wahrheitsrelativismus abgewiesen." See Willard V. O. Quine, "Gegenstand und Beobachtung," in Dieter Henrich, ed., *Kant oder Hegel? Über Formen der Begründung in der Philosophie* (Stuttgart: Klett-Cotta, 1983), p. 418. On the issue of "underdetermination of theory by fact," see also, in the same volume, William H. Newton-Smith, "Trans-theoretical Truth without Transcendent Truth?," pp. 466–78.

3. As with a number of others among the better known items in the poststructuralist idiolect, this one, too, is of Heideggerian provenance. See, for example, the essay "Language," in the collection *Poetry, Language, Thought,* trans. Albert Hofstadter (New York: Harper & Row, 1971), pp. 187–210.

4. Cf. Jane Heal: "There is clearly an absurdity in the idea . . . that I arrive at my beliefs by comparing candidate judgements with the world and putting myself in that cognitive state which I see to have the desirable property of matching the world. This requires me to have access to the world, that is get some beliefs about it, before I fix on my beliefs" ("Pragmatism and Choosing to Believe," p. 108); and further, in a passage seen earlier: "we [do not] choose or devise our concepts in the light of knowledge of our interests. That way of reading things presupposes that we can conceptualize our interests before we have any concepts, which is absurd" (ibid., p. 112).

5. Cf. in this connection Wolff's characterization of Kant's transcendental argument as "at its very deepest level . . . a dialectical *ad hominem,* designed to force his opponents either to assent to his conclusions or to remain silent" (*AR,* p. 26).

6. Cf. David Houghton: "[O]ne thing is clear. A distinction will have to be observed between thinking one has made a valid move in the [language-]game and actually making one" ("Rorty's Talk-About," in A. Malachowski, ed., *Reading Rorty,* p. 163).

7. Thomas McCarthy, Introduction, *The Philosophical Discourse of Modernity: Twelve Lectures*, by Jürgen Habermas, trans. Frederick G. Lawrence (Cambridge: MIT Press, 1987), pp. viii–ix. Later in the same paragraph McCarthy, continuing his gloss of the contemporary skeptical position, effectively brings out the self-contradiction into which that position inevitably lapses. This comes with the assertion that "the epistemological and moral subject has been definitively decentered and the conception of reason linked to it irrevocably desublimated" (p. ix). With the best will in the world, it is difficult to believe completely in the seriousness of someone who is prepared to assert that "*ultimate* foundations in *any* form" have been "*definitively*" and "*irrevocably*" rejected. As we have seen, negative foundationalism is still foundationalism; skepticism, again, is merely dogmatism with a bad conscience.

8. Much of Herder's thinking on these matters is, as noted earlier, anticipated in the work of Vico. That work, however, was to remain all but unknown outside of Vico's own circle in Naples until more than a half-century after his death in 1744. On the dissemination of Vico's ideas throughout the rest of Europe, in particular through the writings of the French historian Michelet, see Isaiah Berlin, *Vico and Herder: Two Studies in the History of Ideas* (New York: Vintage, 1977), pp. xx, 92–93.

9. Herder's specifically linguistic interpretation of the idea of *Denkart* (already enunciated in the early essay *On Diligence in Several Learned Languages*) was, of course, to be taken up and popularized a generation later by Wilhelm von Humboldt with his notion of a unique *Weltanschauung* embodied in the "character" or "spirit" of each national language. In this form the idea is then passed on to the twentieth century, where it once again gains prominence in the work of writers such as Sapir and Whorf.

10. I discuss the point at some length in *Herder and the Poetics of Thought* as one of the central elements of what Herder calls his "human philosophy" (*menschliche Philosophie*). This is a body of thought that, among other things, seeks in its most basic conception to combine philosophy of language and philosophy of history.

11. *Herder and the Poetics of Thought*, p. 143.

12. In Schiller's case, one thinks, for example, of his notions of "grace" and "dignity" and the corresponding aesthetic categories of "beauty" and "sublimity," as well as of his distinction between "naive" and "sentimental" modes of poetry, modes that he associates in turn with the philosophical standpoints of "realism" and "idealism." In each such case, Schiller remains unflagging in his insistence on somehow overcoming the opposition in a higher synthesis, notwithstanding that such a synthesis appears to have been rendered impossible in advance, literally by definition. For a recent discussion of this aspect of Schiller's at once literary and philosophical thought, see Juliet Sychrava, *Schiller to Derrida: Idealism in Aesthetics* (Cambridge: Cambridge University Press, 1989).

13. Much of the traditional literature on Herder simply takes for granted that in fact his thought does remain trapped in irresolvable contradiction in instances such as these. I discuss the issue at greater length in both *Herder and the Poetics of Thought* and "The Infinity of Finitude."

14. Thus there is no objection to Herder's theory of humanity to be derived from pointing out that the human race actually manifests, by virtually any measure that one might choose to apply, at least as much fragmentation as genuine cohesiveness (and by a rather wide margin at that). To see in this an objection would be, again, to have abandoned historical thinking in favor of a conception of the race as essentially static. It would be, in other words, tantamount to leaving out of account the extent to which the reality of human unity is of necessity a *projective* reality, and hence one that in the nature of the case must always be at least to some extent virtual rather than actual (if only because never quite wholly self-aware).

15. Donald Davidson, "On the Very Idea of a Conceptual Scheme," p. 11.

16. Ibid., p. 6.

17. Ibid.

18. The obvious candidate for a counterexample, of course, would appear to be a case like that of Egyptian hieroglyphic prior to the discovery of the Rosetta Stone. The appearance is deceiving, however. Neither hieroglyphic nor any other similar case constitutes a genuine counterexample to the claim in question, as I will try to show below.

19. A suggestion to this effect seems to me at least implicit in Apel's "The Problem of Philosophical Foundations in Light of a Transcendental Pragmatics of Language." See K. Baynes et al., ed., *After Philosophy*, pp. 261–62 and 286, n. 36.

20. Hilary Putnam, *Reason, Truth and History* (Cambridge: Cambridge University Press, 1981), pp. 114–15.

21. Cf. Davidson: "Languages that have evolved in distant times or places may differ extensively in their resources for dealing with one or another range of phenomena. What comes easily in one language may come hard in another, and this difference may echo significant dissimilarities in style and value" ("On the Very Idea of a Conceptual Scheme," p. 6).

22. For what it is worth, by the way, in my view "the worst thing you can do to somebody" (*CIS*, p. 177), Rorty notwithstanding, has nothing, or nothing directly, to do with infliction of pain. The worst thing anyone can do to anyone else, short of actually taking the person's life, is to betray that person, to violate one's solemnly given word. This (as it seems to me, fairly basic) fact of morality was, of course, recognized long ago by Dante, who reserved the deepest circle of his Hell for traitors of all sorts.

23. The other of the two new notions that Rorty introduces in *Contingency, Irony, and Solidarity* is what he terms his "firm distinction between the private and the public" sides of our existence (*CIS*, p. 83, *passim*), between, that is, "our attempt to form a private self-image" and our participation in "politics" (ibid.). In his earlier works, Rorty had run up against what seemed to him a serious problem in explaining how these two aspects of our being might be brought into consonance with one another. The following passage lays out the difficulty as it appeared to him at that point: "[The] moral objection to textualism is also a moral objection to pragmatism's claim that all vocabularies, even that of our own liberal imagination, are temporary historical resting-places. It is also an objection to the literary culture's isolation from common human concerns. It says that people like Nietzsche, Nabokov, Bloom, and Foucault achieve their effects at a moral cost which is too much to pay. . . . [I]t says that the stimulus to the intellectual's private moral imagination, provided by his strong misreadings, by his search for sacred wisdom, is purchased at the price of his separation from his fellow-humans. I think that this moral objection states the really important issue about textualism and about pragmatism. But I have no ready way to dispose of it. . . . To do so would involve a full-scale discussion of the possibility of combining private fulfillment, self-realization, with public morality, a concern for justice" (*CP*, p. 158). Nevertheless, at this earlier stage in his deliberations, Rorty still seemed willing to leave the question open, apparently in the belief, or at least the hope, that a solution might yet be found. In *CIS*, however, as just seen, he renounces the attempt altogether. One mild irony of this worth noting is that with his "firm distinction" between these two (as he now supposes) mutually exclusive realms of our existence, in which we nonetheless somehow manage to participate simultaneously, Rorty in fact reinstates one of the great leitmotifs of precisely that side of the German intellectual tradition from which he is elsewhere most intent on distancing himself. Though a notion that already informs the thought of figures in the Middle Ages such as Meister Eckhart, and one that continues to play a central role, for example, in the work of Luther, it appears perhaps most prominently in

the writings of one of Rorty's "philosophical" archvillains, Kant. This same dichotomy, however, is one that Herder and Schiller, but, again, perhaps most strikingly, one of Rorty's professed heroes of the "anti-philosophical" wars, Hegel, are all persistently intent on finding a way to overcome.

24. Nor is it entirely a matter of indifference that this should be so. As Hilary Putnam notes, it is not merely that Rorty's views are mistaken (indeed, for all the reasons we are seeing here, actually self-contradictory); they are, at least potentially, genuinely harmful. After explaining, in a passage seen earlier, why he regards Rorty as a "cultural relativist," Putnam goes on to say that "[t]here is something that makes cultural relativism a *far more dangerous cultural tendency* than materialism [to which he has referred briefly in the immediately preceding paragraph]. At bottom, there is a *deep irrationalism* to cultural relativism, a denial of the possibility of thinking (as opposed to making noises in counterpoint or in chorus)" ("Why Reason Can't Be Naturalized," p. 229; emphasis added). I find nothing either exaggerated or alarmist in this diagnosis. When anti-intellectualism comes to be embraced by the intellectuals themselves—as Nietzsche, of course, foresaw that it would be in the twentieth century—that can surely not be taken to bode much in the way of good for the future of culture at large.

25. Cited in Putnam, *Representation and Reality* (Cambridge: MIT Press, 1988), p. 9.

26. Cf. Julian Bell: "[Rorty's] philosophy seems to exclude what is commonly meant by experience: getting things wrong, being deceived, learning from mistakes. He seems blind to the possibility that, denied all public and metaphysical elbow-room, his 'privatized self-creation' might be labelled lying to oneself. It does not make for a serviceable account of human life." See "A liberal Utopia" (Review of *Contingency, Irony, and Solidarity*), *Times Literary Supplement* (24–30 November 1989), 1296.

27. As Putnam notes, "[I]t is precisely the mistake of cultural relativism, in its many forms, to ignore the fact that rejecting the concepts which are current in a particular 'culture' at a particular time can be a *reform* and not just a *change*" (*Representation and Reality*, p. 134, n. 14). Or, as he expresses essentially the same point elsewhere: "[T]alk of what is 'right' and 'wrong' in any area only makes sense against the background of an inherited tradition; but . . . traditions themselves can be criticized. . . . On the one hand, there is no notion of reasonableness at all without cultures, practices, procedures; on the other hand, the cultures, practices, procedures we inherit are not an algorithm to be slavishly followed. . . . Reason is, in this sense, both immanent (not to be found outside of concrete language games and institutions) and transcendent (a regulative idea that we use to criticize the conduct of all activities and institutions)" ("Why Reason Can't Be Naturalized," pp. 227–28).

28. Martin Heidegger, *An Introduction to Metaphysics*, trans. Ralph Mannheim (Garden City: Doubleday Anchor, 1961), p. 1.

29. As Wittgenstein observes, "This astonishment [that anything exists] cannot be expressed in the form of a question, and there is no answer to it. Everything which we feel like saying can, a priori, only be nonsense." See "Zu Heidegger," cited in Michael Murray, ed., *Heidegger and Modern Philosophy: Critical Essays* (New Haven: Yale University Press, 1978), p. 80; originally in *Ludwig Wittgenstein und der Wiener Kreis: Gespräche, aufgezeichnet von Friedrich Waismann*, ed. B. F. McGuinness (Frankfurt a. M., 1967), pp. 68–69. Cf. from Wittgenstein's "Lecture on Ethics": "I believe the best way of describing [a certain sort of experience in question at this point] is to say that when I have it I *wonder at the existence of the world*. And then I am inclined to use such phrases as 'how extraordinary that anything should exist' or 'how extraordinary that the world should exist.' . . . And . . . the first thing I have to say is, that the verbal expression which we

give to these experiences is nonsense! If I say 'I wonder at the existence of the world' I am misusing language. . . . To say 'I wonder at such and such being the case' has only sense if I can imagine it not to be the case. . . . [I]t is nonsense to say that I wonder at the existence of the world, because I cannot imagine it not existing"; see *Philosophical Review* 74 (1965): 8–9.

30. On this point, see *Herder and the Poetics of Thought*, pp. 138 ff., *passim*.

31. There is still encountered occasionally the belief that support for skepticism can be found in some of the developments of twentieth-century natural science or mathematical logic. See, for example, Lyotard: "Postmodern science—by concerning itself with such things as undecidables, the limits of precise control, conflicts characterized by incomplete information, '*fracta*,' catastrophes, and pragmatic paradoxes—is theorizing its own evolution as discontinuous, catastrophic, nonrectifiable, and paradoxical. It is changing the meaning of the word *knowledge*, while expressing how such a change can take place. It is producing not the known, but the unknown" (*PMC*, p. 60). That belief, however, is fraught with multiple confusion. The argument for it goes more or less like this: from the fact, for example, that, as quantum mechanics shows, "the *most* we can know of a microparticle is its *partially* defined state—that is, its 'contribution' to an irresolvable ensemble" (Norwood Russell Hanson, "Quantum Mechanics, Philosophical Implications of," *The Encyclopedia of Philosophy*, VII, 43), and hence that "nature is fundamentally indeterministic; that elementary particles . . . do not in any sense that is scientifically respectable and philosophically intelligible have both a precise position and an exact energy" (ibid., 46), it is supposed to follow that the extent of the knowledge we are capable of possessing of such constellations of elementary particles as persons, objects, and the facts in which they participate must be correspondingly limited. Or, more baldly stated, because reality is itself, at bottom, radically indeterminate, certain knowledge of reality must also be ultimately impossible. The latter version of the argument is the easier of the two to deal with. For it commits the obvious fallacy of predicating the properties of *objects* of a propositional attitude (in this case, "knowing that . . .") of that *attitude* itself. This is as if, to take a parallel example, one were to conclude from the fact that a certain fear rests on nothing more than a kind of conceptual confusion (something demonstrated, for example, by Lucretius in "On the Fear of Death") that the phenomenon, or experience, of fear was itself illusory. The argument errs, in other words, in overlooking the fact that precisely the *establishment of indeterminacy*, in accordance with both the theory of quantum mechanics and the body of experimental data supporting that theory, is *itself* a matter of entirely determinate fact. (This is above all the point that Lyotard misses. See again *PMC*, pp. 53ff., especially pp. 58–59.) A similar confusion among what might be called spheres of relevance obtains as well, however, in the case of the first version of the argument. Here it is a matter of the mistake (repeatedly pointed out by Wittgenstein) of lifting the grammar of a given language-game out of the realm in which it is at home and seeking to apply it in another realm, to which, however, it has no connection. To conclude, for example, from the indeterminate nature of elementary particles that the phenomena of everyday life are themselves correspondingly indeterminate (and, in that sense, uncertain) would be analogous to supposing that in conversation with an acquaintance I do not really know to whom I am speaking if I am unable to specify his blood type or whether he dreams in black and white or in color. As Putnam observes, in a passage cited, interestingly enough, by Rorty himself: "[O]ne cannot give an account of why square pegs do not fit into round holes in terms of the elementary particles which constitute the peg and the hole, but nobody [for that reason] finds a perplexing ontological gap between macrostructure and microstructure" (as given by Rorty in *PMN*, p. 26). See Putnam, "Philosophy and Our Mental Life," *Mind, Language and Reality: Philosophical Papers, Vol. 2* (Cambridge:

Cambridge University Press, 1975), pp. 295–97; also *Meaning and the Moral Sciences* (London: Routledge and Kegan Paul, 1978), pp. 42–43.

32. Cf. Charles Taylor: "There are some issues in the long history of Western thought which have been settled. For instance, a science which tried to explain inanimate nature in terms of the realization in different kinds of entity of their corresponding Form has given way to a science which explains by efficient causation, mapped by mathematical formulae. Aristotle on this issue has been buried by Galileo and Newton, and there is no looking back. Certain views are unrecoverable; nobody can even get close to marshalling good grounds for believing them any more" ("Rorty in the Epistemological Tradition," p. 262).

33. Essentially the same dilemma arises again, from a slightly different direction, in his attempt to reduce such notions as "true," "good," and "rational" to what he calls "conversational values." Virtually no one, of course, believes, or ever will believe, that, for example, the word *true* just *means* "whatever happens to win the argument." But "whatever happens to win the argument" is *already* Rorty's sole definition of the truth of *any* assertion, including this one. And thus, on its own terms, it depends for its very validity on a (foredoomed) effort to convince other people to assent to it.

34. Cf. Martin Hollis: "I conclude . . . that Rorty does indeed paint himself into a corner. The poets' 'effort to achieve self-creation by the recognition of contingency' will fail without active spinners of the web [of belief] and will end in tyranny or suffocation without rules to direct the communal conversation of mankind aright. His epistemological behaviourism and his relativism close the way to the promised hermeneutics" ("The Poetics of Personhood," p. 256).

35. As we saw earlier, of course, this position is abandoned in *CIS* in favor of a "pain"-criterion of humanness. As we also noted, however, adopting that criterion in fact deprives us of any basis on which to conceive of human beings as a distinct class at all.

36. Again, so far as I know, Herder first makes the point in explicit fashion (in part, in terms that anticipate even the contemporary vocabulary for discussing these matters): "There is a symbolism common to all people—a great treasure-vault in which is preserved the knowledge belonging to the entire human race. The true philosopher of language, whom, however, I have not yet seen, has the key to this dark vault. When he comes, he will open it, throw light on it, and show us its treasures. That would be the true *semiotics*, something that we now find in name only in the indexes of our philosophical encyclopedias: *a deciphering of the human soul through its language*" (*SWS*, II, 13; emphasis added).

37. Michael Morton, "Life Against Death in Bohemia: The Structure of the Debate in *Der Ackermann aus Böhmen*," *Fifteenth-Century Studies* 9 (1984): 125.

38. On the dating of the epic, see, for example, N. K. Sandars, Introduction, *The Epic of Gilgamesh* (Harmondsworth: Penguin, 1983), pp. 7–8.

39. See, for example, Marshall Brown: "The mind receives *sense impressions* from unknowable 'things in themselves' and reconstructs these impressions into coherent *images*. . . . For Kant, then, the objective world is the *silhouette* on the mind of things in themselves" ("The Logic of Realism: A Hegelian Approach," *PMLA* 96 [1981]: 234; emphasis added). Such a characterization of Kantian epistemology represents him less as the author of the first *Critique* than as a kind of combination of Hume and the Plato of the Allegory of the Cave. Or consider, in the same vein, Wolfgang Iser: "Kant . . . conceiv[ed] the categories of cognition as *heuristic fictions* to be taken *as if* they corresponded to something. This *as if* was, in Kant's view, an indispensable necessity for cognition" ("Fictionalizing: The Anthropological Dimension of Literary Fictions," *New Literary History* 21 [1990]: 940; first emphasis added). Here Kant is represented as merely Vaihinger *avant*

la lettre. Interestingly, however, Iser follows this passage at once with the following nearly correct statement of the true state of affairs: "Necessities without alternatives, however, *must be true,* even if one has to add that such truth will be anthropological rather than epistemological" (ibid.; emphasis added). The essence of the "critical turn," however, is the recognition that this "rather than" is merely a distinction without a difference: "anthropological" truth *is* "epistemological" truth, precisely *because* "[n]ecessities without alternatives . . . must be true."

    40. In the course of this century, and especially in the years since World War II, academic philosophy, particularly in the English-speaking world, has turned dramatically in on itself, becoming programmatically esoteric but thereby also almost completely irrelevant to anyone not actually engaged in it. Virtually no one but another analytic philosopher would so much as have it occur to him to read most of what is produced today by most members of that profession (even assuming—for the most part, counterfactually— that it were presented in such a way that a person unschooled in the mysteries of that discipline could begin to make sense of it at all). As Arthur Danto observes, the bulk of these philosophical papers "are not . . . terribly distinct from one another" in any case ("Philosophy as/and/of Literature," in A. J. Cascardi, ed., *Literature and the Question of Philosophy,* p. 5). Historically, however, as has been noted on more than one occasion, this state of affairs represents something of an anomaly. The "professionalization" of philosophy, or what some have referred to as the "capture" of the field by university departments, is itself a comparatively recent phenomenon, dating only from about the eighteenth century. But that development in itself neither ruled out the possibility of academic "outsiders" continuing to make significant contributions—one thinks, for example, of figures such as Mill, Kierkegaard, and (after his relatively early departure from the university) Nietzsche—nor, more important in the present connection, did it prevent even academic philosophers from becoming actively engaged with, and in some cases even centrally important to, the broader interests and concerns of their societies, as philosophers had traditionally done since antiquity. One need only recall, for example, the degree of influence exerted in their time across almost the entire range of cultural life by professors such as Hegel, Mach, and Dewey.

    If philosophy has managed to reap a harvest of more or less general societal irrelevance from its self-consciously arcane pursuit of problems remote from the ordinary run of human affairs, however, contemporary criticism has done much to accomplish the same (surely rather dubious) feat in what is if anything even more aggressive fashion. The theoretical vocabulary of many contemporary critics itself yields, of course, little or nothing in sheer incomprehensibility from the point of view of most people outside the field (as well as, if we are candid, more than a few inside it as well) to the most recondite technical formulations of analytic philosophers. But if recent philosophy has done no more than show itself largely indifferent to the sorts of questions that nonprofessionals tend to think of as "philosophical" ones—the sorts of basic questions regarding the nature, meaning, and purpose of human existence with which philosophers have been primarily concerned throughout most of the history of the discipline—criticism has often appeared actively hostile to the corresponding concerns of people at large where these intersect with the business of textual analysis. The skeptical denial of such common notions as "fact" and "personhood," as well as of such things as "rational decidability" and "semantic determinacy," in which everyone in fact believes (including critics themselves, regardless of what they may say to the contrary), often has about it a distinctly (not to say disturbingly) misanthropic quality. Even Rorty, as we saw earlier, has difficulty with so thoroughly antihumanist a figure as Foucault, in whose view, for example, the paradigmatic figure in the transition from the "Classical" to the "modern" *episteme* appears to have been of all people the Marquis de Sade; see *The Order of Things: An Archaeology of the Human Sciences* (New York: Vintage, 1973), pp. 208–11. Arthur Danto speaks of what he calls the "frivolous sadism" of the deconstructionist approach to texts ("Philosophy as/and/of Literature," p. 4). And the *Times Literary Supplement* reviewer of Smith's *Contingencies of Value*, interestingly enough, finds in her argument as well a "definite echo" of the Marquis (Bernard Harrison, "Relatively violent," *TLS*, 29 Dec. 1989–4 Jan. 1990, 1446). I do not want to make too much of what is after all only a coincidence (albeit, to my mind, a rather striking one). The larger point with which I am concerned is the chasm that has been permitted to open up between contemporary criticism and ordinary life, something that I think can scarcely fail to be obvious to all. I believe it is over time ultimately destructive of the life of a culture when such a condition is allowed to continue and still more so when it is actively encouraged. It is, in any case, difficult to see how the study of literature in particular, or of culture in any of its other manifestations, or the lives of people at large, whether inside or outside the academy, can be thought to benefit from such a radical split.

41. For an exceptionally candid formulation of this version of the doctrine, see Smith's *CV*, discussed above.

42. This claim is in turn the source of the further one that there are radically different "ways of knowing" peculiar to any group(s) in particular that one might wish to privilege in this way. Thus it becomes possible, for example, to argue (in all apparent seriousness) that there is such a thing as "feminine" science, in accordance with what are alleged to be distinctive modes of cognition peculiar to women. As is hardly necessary to add, of course, this view has found a less than overwhelmingly favorable response among practicing scientists themselves, for whom, whether male or female, reality is the test of doctrine, not the other way around.

43. "On the Very Idea of a Conceptual Scheme," p. 16. As Davidson also notes, however, this "criterion" in fact fails to pick out anything and is insofar merely a kind of pseudo-criterion: "The question whether this is a useful criterion is just the question how well we understand the notion of truth, as applied to language, independent of the notion of translation. The answer is, I think, that we do not understand it independently at all" (ibid., p. 16).

44. On this point, see in particular *PMN*, p. 302, n. 35. Rorty contends that "Davidson . . . misinterprets Kuhn as meaning 'untranslatable' by 'incommensurable'," adding that "[i]t is important for my argument in this book to separate sharply these two notions."

45. "On the Very Idea of a Conceptual Scheme," p. 19.

46. See, for example, *SSR*, in particular chaps. 6 and 7.

CHAPTER SEVEN

1. Like skepticism, dogmatism, too, has over the centuries appeared in a multitude of different guises. Platonic dogmatism is not the same as Cartesian dogmatism, which is not the same as Husserlian dogmatism, and so forth—just as, on the other side of the fence, Pyrrhonian skepticism is not the same as Montaignian skepticism, which is not the same as Humean skepticism, and so forth. But just as it is also possible to discern certain key elements in common in the welter of different versions of skepticism, the same holds true as well—and for essentially the same reason—in the history of dogmatism.

2. The reader will have noticed that this two-stage process parallels the one that Kuhn argues is characteristic of the history of science (as described briefly in the previous

chapter) only in its first half. One principal difference between scientific and nonscientific fields generally—something already recognized, for example, by Kant—is precisely that while the former do develop, if not in simple linear fashion, nonetheless in such a way that over time the body of reasonably secure knowledge actually expands, the latter for the most part do not. And thus pendular, back-and-forth movements tend to characterize their history far more than in the case of the true sciences, as the same questions and problems are returned to over and over again. Hegel's observation that what we learn from history is that we learn nothing from history seems to find particular applicability in this field of human endeavor.

3. See, for example, the essay sometimes regarded as the founding manifesto of poststructuralism, Derrida's "Structure, Sign, and Play in the Discourse of the Human Sciences." The essay first appeared in print in English in Richard Mackrey and Eugenio Donato, ed., *The Languages of Criticism and the Sciences of Man: The Structuralist Controversy* (Baltimore: Johns Hopkins University Press, 1970).

4. On this point, though with a rather different moral drawn from the observation, see also Christopher Norris: "Th[e] belief [that truth (or validity) is beside the point in issues of interpretive judgment, that there is no appeal to standards of right reading, argumentative rigor, etc.]. . . . is virtually an item of faith among modern literary critics. . . . The American New Critics were among the most orthodox in this regard, treating poetry as an utterly distinctive kind of language, hedged about with various doctrinal sanctions amounting to a form of wholesale aesthetic ideology. But there was . . . another aspect to this 'old' New Critical program, one that emphasized the virtue or necessity of rhetorical close-reading, even to the point where such reading subverted its own more doctrinaire claims"; in "Right You Are (If You Think So): Stanley Fish and the Rhetoric of Assent," *Comparative Literature* 42 (1990): 178.

5. Like mannerisms generally throughout the history of arts and letters, moreover, it is also something that readily becomes quite mechanical in application. It has been observed on more than one occasion that just as any reasonably competent graduate student a generation ago could (and almost certainly would) have described a given text as a fabric of paradox, tension, irony, and ambiguity, that student's counterparts today can with fair reliability be counted on to present (or rather, again, "re-present") the same text as, in one way or another, an embodiment of undecidability, failure to achieve closure, and semantic or psychic dislocation. Though the song is a technically intricate one and to that extent not entirely easy to learn, once learned it is all too easy to sing repeatedly, without essential variation, in virtually whatever setting one happens to find oneself.

6. As noted earlier, it has historically proved exceedingly difficult for thinkers to hold on to the "critical" insight. In practice the tendency has always been for it to slide more or less inexorably into one form or another of dogmatism or skepticism superficially similar to it. As Strawson observes: "Metaphysics has a long and distinguished history, and it is consequently unlikely that there are any new truths to be discovered in descriptive metaphysics. But this does not mean that the task of descriptive metaphysics has been, or can be, done once and for all. It has constantly to be done over again" (*Individuals*, p. 10). Or in other words, in a passage from Wittgenstein's *Investigations* seen earlier: "The work of the philosopher consists in assembling reminders for a particular purpose" (*PI*, § 127).

7. Carolyn Porter, "History and Literature: 'After the New Historicism,' " *New Literary History* 21 (1990): 253; subsequent references to this essay are given in the text. Porter's argument can stand for many similar ones in the current literature. For an extended statement of the position in question (in a work to which Porter obviously alludes in the title of her essay), see Frank Lentricchia, *After the New Criticism* (Chicago: University of Chicago Press, 1980).

8. See also Thomas Kuhn, "The Relations between the History and the Philosophy of Science," in *The Essential Tension*, p. 15ff.

9. On this point, see also Edward Pechter: "[T]he histories being recovered [by the new historicists] are themselves transcendental signifieds (or sometimes, perhaps, transcendental ways of signifying) in the sense that their capacity to explain seems independent of many particulars. . . . From this perspective, the new historicists' contextualization is just another form of interpretation. . . . New historicists often privilege their criticism by assuming that their version of history is the thing itself"; in "The New Historicism and Its Discontents: Politicizing Renaissance Drama," *PMLA* 102 (1987): 298.

10. Not always in precisely so many words, of course. Once again, as earlier, where the emphasis was primarily on skeptical aspects of contemporary critical theory, so here as well I am principally interested in singling out key elements of a certain basic outlook informing a significant portion of the work in criticism being done today. For ease of reference, I will continue to use the expression *genuine history* as a kind of shorthand. I am not attempting to present a detailed portrait faithful in all respects to the particulars of any one position, school, or movement. Given the manifold ways in which the outlook in question is reflected in actual critical practice, that would be a difficult task at best in any case. In particular, the sort of relentless fine-tuning of positions that has historically been especially characteristic of those on the (more or less) radical left continues today to generate among those who share the outlook in question a running, many-sided debate over who finally—but, of course, there is no "finally" here—has the politically "correct" standpoint. An example of this phenomenon is the essay by Porter just cited, in which her professed aim is to show how the "new historicism," its own frequently asserted intention to the contrary notwithstanding, nonetheless "serves finally to resecure a formalist agenda and the politics of containment it serves" (*HL*, p. 257). For purposes of the present discussion, however, little if anything of importance is lost by omitting the bulk of these details. For those interested in such details, a very good working bibliography might be assembled from nothing more than the footnotes to several of the articles in a recent edition of *New Literary History*, entitled "New Historicisms, New Histories, and Others." See, in particular, Jonathan Dollimore, "Shakespeare, Cultural Materialism, Feminism and Marxist Humanism," *NLH* 21 (1990): 471–93.

11. This tendency toward, if not convergence, then at any rate a certain notable degree of overlap, between theoretical standpoints that at first glance might appear to have relatively little to do with one another shows up, for example, in Derrida's "textualist" defense of de Man's actions in World War II and Jameson's argument for the political implications of Adorno's notoriously difficult expository style. Just as we are assured by Derrida that de Man's seemingly overtly anti-Semitic writings actually contain a subversive, oppositional subtext whose effect is really to undermine the very regime they appear to be supporting (see "Like the Sound of the Sea Deep within a Shell: Paul de Man's War," trans. Peggy Kamuf, *Critical Inquiry* 14 [1988]: 590–62), so Jameson maintains that "[i]n the language of Adorno . . . density is itself a conduct of intransigence . . . intended to be read in situation, against the cheap facility of what surrounds it, as a warning to the reader of the price he has to pay for genuine thinking" (Preface to *Marxism and Form: Twentieth-Century Dialectical Theories of Literature* [Princeton: Princeton University Press, 1971], p. xiii). For Derrida's estimate of the (in his view, wholly laudable) political implications of deconstruction, see also, for example, "Racism's Last Word," *Critical Inquiry* 12 (1985): 290–99; and "But Beyond . . . (Open Letter to Anne McClintock and Rob Nixon)," *Critical Inquiry* 13 (1986): 155–70.

12. Adriana Méndez Rodenas, " A Journey to the (Literary) Source: The Invention of Origins in Merlin's *Viaje a La Habana*," *New Literary History* 21 (1990): 707.

13. Jerome E. Thornton, "The Paradoxical Journey of the African American in African American Fiction," *New Literary History* 21 (1990): 733; subsequent references are given in the text.

14. The passage cited is from Williams's *Marxism and Literature* (Oxford: Oxford University Press, 1977), p. 123. The echoes of Marcuse's notion of "repressive desublimation," enunciated some thirty years ago, seem clearly audible.

15. Rena Fraden, "Response to Professor Porter," *New Literary History* 21 (1990): 275. Fraden is, as she says, "anguish[ed]" by "the suspicion that no matter how politically correct I try to be—how many voices I am able to bring to the surface which weren't 'there' before because they had been thought to be unimportant or had been actively suppressed—that I am by virtue of my critical power to choose (and limited by my historical blindness) still practicing some version of colonization. I agree that our alternative critical role must be to 'make audible' those other voices, but is it possible to listen to that 'other' without somehow recontaining it in our discourse, academic or otherwise?" (ibid., p. 276). Cf. Johannes Fabian's characterization of what he calls "the anthropologist's dilemma: if writing is part of a system of intellectual and political oppression of the Other, how can we avoid contributing to that oppression if we go on writing?" Fabian notes that "[t]here are those who respond to [this] seemingly radical question with a radical answer; they give up writing about the Other and drop out, if not out of anthropology, then out of ethnography"; see "Presence and Representation: The Other and Anthropological Writing," *Critical Inquiry* 16 (1990): 767. This is not the solution that Fabian himself recommends. Yet accepting as he apparently does that "the premise is correct, namely that given the power relations in this world writing as such is an act of oppression" (ibid.), he has nowhere to turn save to the vague radicalism of slogans such as "power relations must change" and to scarcely less vague notions of "a critique that might have a chance of being truly subversive" and "[a] dialectical conception of writing" toward that end (ibid., p. 768). A large part of my argument here, on the other hand, comes down to the suggestion that one would almost certainly do better instead to question the correctness of the premise itself.

16. Felicity Nussbaum, for example, acknowledges that "a theory of incommensurability" is "crucial to the formation of feminism"; see "The Politics of Difference," *Eighteenth-Century Studies* 23 (1990): 382. Earlier in the same essay she asserts that "feminism and racial equality would seem to require for their political efficacy an assumption of something universal, some nature common to all the members of the group in question" (ibid., p. 380). Certainly the recent history of racial and sexual politics in the United States suggests that such an assumption may well be an aid to "political efficacy" of a sort. I think that Nussbaum is precisely mistaken, however, with regard to the relationship between this assumption and the achievement of "equality." In my view, it serves only to defer, never to hasten, the realization of that goal. As has been frequently observed, the essentialism of gender, race, and the like takes over without alteration the basic structure of the position shared by racist and sexist alike; it merely revalorizes some of the particular elements already postulated within that overall structure. Faced with "opposition" of this sort, however, neither racists nor sexists (unfortunately) need worry unduly about the continued survival of their ideology. The essentialist assumption, moreover, is not entirely free of difficulties even on its own terms. Nussbaum points out that "[a] current crisis in feminist theory . . . is to determine what the category of 'woman' holds in common if we begin with the assumption that gender difference is culturally and historically constructed," and she notes that "[p]arallel debates about racial essentialism . . . have emerged in African-American and ethnic studies" as well. The question in each such case is: "How . . . do we recognize differences within the categories without eliminating the categories themselves?" (ibid.). It seems to me, however, that to ask the

question is already to answer it: inasmuch as these "categories" were never anything other than metaphysical postulates to begin with, and as such served only to obscure the fact that what really matters are the actual relationships of *both* commonality *and* difference between concrete, individual persons, there is no reason to be concerned at the prospect of their "eliminat[ion]" and, indeed, every reason to welcome that development.

17. Richard Levin points out a number of the flaws in this position in "Unthinkable Thoughts in the New Historicizing of English Renaissance Drama," *New Literary History* 21 (1990): 433–47.

18. Edward Said comments in this regard in a way more revealing than he seems to recognize. First making the now common move of attempting to explain the failures of Third World societies and their governments (where such have occurred) exclusively by reference to their "experience of being colonized" and the still lingering effects of that experience, he adds: "And far from being a category that signified supplication and self-pity [!], 'the colonized' has since expanded considerably to include women, subjugated and oppressed classes, national minorities, and even marginalized or incorporated academic subspecialties"; see "Representing the Colonized: Anthropology's Interlocutors," *Critical Inquiry* 15 (1989): 207. As a commentator on Ewa M. Thompson's essay "The Writer in Exile: The Good Years" notes, "We live in an age that adores victims"; see *The Wilson Quarterly* 14/3 (Summer 1990): 132. And in this circumstance the competition to have one-self designated a "victim" is understandably acute. On the psychology of self-imposed "victimization," see also Shelby Steele, "Thinking Beyond Race," in the same number of *The Wilson Quarterly* just cited, as well as his recent *The Content of Our Character: A New Vision of Race in America* (New York: St. Martin's Press, 1990). The weakness of Said's effort at blame shifting with regard to Third World countries, by the way—in general, the twin tropes of complaint and blame are indispensable to the sort of discourse under consideration here—becomes entirely transparent, I think, when one considers the differences in the developmental paths taken by formerly "colonized" Third World nations since gaining independence. For some of them clearly *have* prospered, though, unfortunately, not yet nearly as many as would have been both desirable and possible. What Said and others of similar political persuasion by and large leave out of account in their analyses is the evidently key role played by a given nation's decision to opt for a free-market or a command economy. Predictably, those taking the former course have tended to experience economic growth; those taking the latter have not. In the same article, Said observes that "[t]hese two words, 'difference' and 'otherness,' have by now acquired talismanic properties. Indeed," he says, "it is almost impossible not to be stunned by how magical, even metaphysical they seem." And he goes on to speak of this "fetishization and relentless celebration of 'difference' and 'otherness' . . . as an ominous trend" (ibid., p. 213). This strikes me as a classic case of being right for the wrong reasons. For Said nowhere evinces any awareness of precisely how metaphysically implicated his own, highly politicized position is in its own right. As Robert J. Griffin observes, "Said subscribes to two conflicting epistemologies, a postmodernist one for his political enemies who are enmeshed in a web of historical determinations, and a classical one for himself, whose perspective is consonant with truth. . . . [H]aving . . . begun his argument by claiming 'that there is no point of view, no vantage, no perspective available like an Archimedean principle outside history,' he ends it by ignoring the implications of his own statement in appealing to an unqualified 'truth' "; see "Ideology and Misrepresentation: A Response to Edward Said," *Critical Inquiry* 15 (1989): 624–25.

19. I have dealt above with some of the flaws in the doctrine of the ubiquity of the political, and there will be more to say on the question later in the present chapter. It is worth noting again, however, for purposes of analyzing the claims of "genuine history" in

particular, that that doctrine is in any case logically subsequent to the thesis of radical Otherness. And thus if the latter can be shown to be fatally flawed, as I am contending it can, the former does not arise as an issue in this connection at all. For in this case there is no longer even a theory of "genuine history" to begin with, and hence nothing for the doctrine of the ubiquity of the political to be supporting.

20. Alexander Nehamas, "Who Are 'The Philosophers of the Future'?: A Reading of *Beyond Good and Evil*, in Solomon and Higgins, ed., *Reading Nietzsche*, p. 51; subsequent references are given in the text.

21. Alexander Nehamas, *Nietzsche: Life as Literature* (Cambridge: Harvard University Press, 1985), p. 7; subsequent references are given in the text.

22. Cf. Richard Schacht: "Nietzsche may have linked his proclamation of the 'death of God' with an attack upon the 'soul-hypothesis'; but he did not proceed to an announcement of what Foucault has called 'the death of man' as well, contrary to the efforts of Foucault and his kindred spirits to make Nietzsche out to be the herald of this sequel they themselves proclaim. If one attends at all closely to what he says and undertakes to do in *The Gay Science* and subsequent writings, it should be clear that he instead supposes the 'death of God' and the demise of the clutch of metaphysical hypotheses associated with the God-hypothesis (in particular the soul- and being-hypothesis) to serve rather to prepare the way for what might be called 'the *birth* of man' as a newly significant philosophical notion" ("Nietzsche's *Gay Science*, Or, How to Naturalize Cheerfully," in Solomon and Higgins, ed., *Reading Nietzsche*, pp. 83–84). Schacht notes that "Nietzsche did indeed repudiate the notion of 'man' as a kind of 'eternal truth' very early on"; he adds, however, that "it is of no little significance that he did so very early—and that, having made this point, he then went on to *recast* this notion, devoting a great deal of effort to the investigation of our nature thus reconceived. He evidently was convinced that this notion can and should be rehabilitated—liberated from metaphysical and theological interpretations, and also from its status (made much of by Foucault) as a conceptual correlate of certain disciplines originating earlier in his century—and made the focus of enlightened philosophical inquiry of the sort he commended to his 'new philosophers' and sought himself to undertake" (ibid., p. 84). The distinction between *rejection* of a notion and *reanalysis* of it is, of course, fundamental to sound intellectual history. It is a distinction, however, that Foucault in particular, with his prejudice in favor of supposedly radically discontinuous *epistemes*, is not especially well equipped to make, or even to recognize.

23. Peter Winch, "Understanding a Primitive Society," *American Philosophical Quarterly* 1 (1964): 307–24; rpt. in Bryan Wilson, ed., *Rationality* (New York: Blackwell, 1971).

24. Thomas McCarthy, "Scientific Rationality and the 'Strong Program' in the Sociology of Knowledge," in Ernan McMullin, ed., *Construction and Constraint: The Shaping of Scientific Rationality* (Notre Dame: University of Notre Dame Press, 1988), p. 84; subsequent references are given in the text.

25. Peter Haidu, "The Semiotics of Alterity: A Comparison with Hermeneutics," *New Literary History* 21 (1990): 690; subsequent references are given in the text.

26. See, for example, Frederick Copleston, S. J., *A History of Philosophy, Vol. I: Greece and Rome, Part II* (Garden City: Doubleday Image, 1962), pp. 230–32.

27. There is a long-standing belief cherished by some in academe that it is possible to "radicalize" students, both in relatively large numbers and in a way that takes hold for the rest of their lives, for the purpose of eventually bringing about the sort of sweeping social change envisaged by the political left. The more extreme, not to say slightly fantastic, version of this belief is that as a teacher one is little by little preparing cadres who will one day come forward and play their roles in the great revolution. Framed in at least

slightly more this-worldly terms, the belief takes the form of the supposition that one is contributing to an incremental, though nonetheless pervasive, transformation in basic outlooks on the part of the populace at large. The idea is that society will ultimately find itself subjected by more or less imperceptible degrees to the sort of revolutionary change one desires, without an actual old-style revolution ever being necessary. Neither version of this view, of course, is at all new, and precisely its relatively long history testifies as well as anything could, it seems to me, to its fundamental untenability. There have always been at least a few students in every generation who are (temporarily) "radicalized," and waves of more widespread and broadly based student activism come and go, chiefly influenced by events outside the university and by demographic changes from one generation of students to the next. It is mere self-congratulation to suppose that academics themselves ever play more than a comparatively modest and incidental role in such developments, and it is necessary to overlook a fair amount of history to suppose that the effects of such influence are, in all but a vanishingly small number of cases, ever more than transitory.

28. The familiar complaint of many of its supporters that Marxism cannot really be said to have "failed," inasmuch as it has never really been "tried," has recently been addressed by Scott Arnold. See *Marx's Radical Critique of Capitalist Society: A Reconstruction and Critical Evaluation* (Oxford: Oxford University Press, 1990). As Arnold is able to show, Marxism already fails at the level of theory, even before its practical failures become apparent.

29. In the general euphoria accompanying the collapse of socialism in Eastern Europe and the former Soviet Union, it is too often overlooked, as George Will has noted, that fully a fourth of the world's population—that of China—is not only not better off than it was before the summer of 1989, but has in fact actually seen its situation deteriorate.

30. A claim that seems somewhat puzzling, to be sure, in light of his willingness at the same time to "celebrate [this form of society] as the best polity actualized so far" (*CP*, p. 210).

31. Frederick Turner, "The Meaning of Value: An Economics for the Future," *New Literary History* 21 (1990): 748; subsequent references are given in the text.

32. For an at once entertaining and informative overview of this and similar stratagems, see Dario Fernández-Morera, "Materialist Discourse in Academia During the Age of Late Marxism," *Academic Questions* 4 (Spring 1991): 15–29.

33. The underlying difficulty here goes back at least to the Frankfurt School of the 1920s and 1930s. See the Editors' Introduction to *Habermas: Critical Debates:* "The critical theorists [of the Frankfurt School] were concerned, among other things," to account for "the degeneration of the Russian revolution into Stalinism" (p. 2). The sentence immediately following this one, however, makes all too clear why that effort was doomed to failure from the outset: "While rejecting Marxism-Leninism, the critical theorists nevertheless found in Marx's thought a powerful tool for the analysis of historical events" (ibid.). The initial mistake here was to view Stalinism as a "degeneration" of the Russian revolution in the first place. And that mistake is then only compounded by the supposition that one can reject Marxism-Leninism and still consistently profess oneself a Marxist at all. For Marxism, at least as that doctrine was formulated by Marx and Engels, in fact entails Marxism-Leninism. And Stalinism, in turn, represents the culmination of Marxism-Leninism, merely translating into actual practice the full political logic already inherent in the Bolshevik Revolution. History made no puzzling detours here. Rather it unfolded in wholly predictable fashion, following a pattern of development already firmly established in the founding texts of the movement in question.

34. Michael Ryan, *Marxism and Deconstruction: A Critical Articulation* (Baltimore: Johns Hopkins University Press, 1982), p. xiii. Cited in Robert Markley, "What

Isn't History: The Snares of Demystifying Ideological Criticism," *Critical Inquiry* 15 (1989): 654–55; subsequent references to this essay are given in the text.

35. In addition to Ryan, see also, for example, Laura Brown, "Reading Race and Gender: Jonathan Swift," *Eighteenth-Century Studies* 23 (1990): 426.

36. For the latter, see Felicity Nussbaum, "The Politics of Difference," *Eighteenth-Century Studies* 23 (1990): 377.

37. Consider, as merely one example from among a great many that could be cited, the following passage from Althusser: "[I]deologies, . . . whatever their form (religious, ethical, legal, political), always express *class positions*. . . . [A] theory of ideologies depends in the last resort on the history of social formations, and thus of the modes of production combined in social formations, and of the class struggles which develop in them. . . . [T]he peculiarity of ideology is that it is endowed with a structure and a functioning such as to make it a non-historical reality, i.e. an *omni-historical* reality, in the sense in which that structure and functioning are immutable, present in the same form throughout what we can call history, in the sense in which the *Communist Manifesto* defines history as the history of class struggles, i.e. the history of class societies. . . . If eternal means, not transcendent to all (temporal) history, but omnipresent, trans-historical and therefore immutable in form throughout the extent of history, I shall adopt Freud's expression word for word, and write *ideology is eternal*, exactly like the unconscious." See "Ideology and Ideological State Apparatuses," in *Lenin and Philosophy, and Other Essays*, trans. Ben Brewster (London: New Left Books, 1971); cited in Adams and Searle, ed., *Critical Theory Since 1965*, pp. 239–40. Again, no actual argument is ever presented by Althusser for any of the rather extensive array of assumptions and postulates on which his theory of "ideology" depends.

38. Markley contends further that "to argue that the materialist critique of metaphysics is subsumed within the very modes of thought that it attacks would necessitate working one's way back through Althusser, Bakhtin, Baudrillard, and other twentieth-century Marxists to Marx and Engels and then, presumably, to Vico and Hobbes" (ibid., p. 656). Leaving Vico and Hobbes aside for the moment—again, the concern here is specifically with the metaphysically dogmatic character of contemporary "Marxisms" and their various cognates—we can readily acknowledge that the claim is true enough (at least if one were intent on making a really thorough job of it). But it is also a completely innocuous requirement. What Markley evidently assumes would be an "arduous path of demystification" (ibid.) would in fact be, although doubtless a lengthy process, nonetheless at each stage in particular (as suggested a moment ago in connection with Althusser) a fairly easy, even routine, matter of analysis of argumentative structure.

39. Oscar Kenshur, "Demystifying the Demystifiers: Metaphysical Snares of Ideological Criticism," *Critical Inquiry* 14 (1988): 348–49; subsequent references are given in the text.

40. Oscar Kenshur, "(Avoidable) Snares and Avoidable Muddles," *Critical Inquiry* 15 (1989): 666.

41. Cf. "(Avoidable) Snares and Avoidable Muddles": "[R]ationalism and logocentrism have no eternal political essences, because, like . . . other symbolic structures . . . , they can be put to different political uses in different historical contexts" (p. 659). As I will be suggesting in a moment, however, I think Kenshur stops an important step short in his decoupling effort, when he says: "This is not to say that epistemological claims (or literary styles, or any other symbolic structures) are ideology-free and impervious to ideological analysis, only that the relationship between the epistemological claim or other symbolic structure and the interests that it serves is a contextual one that can change as the historical context changes" (ibid.). The latter half of this statement is surely true in those

cases in which there exists a relationship between epistemology and ideology to be considered at all. The assumption, however, that there is of necessity always and everywhere such a relationship, which is at least tacitly reflected in the statement's first half, is defective on both logical and empirical grounds. Despite that, of course, it nonetheless ranks among the most widely accepted of all the dogmas of contemporary critical theory.

42. Kenshur refers the reader to *Outlines of Pyrrhonism,* in *Sextus Empiricus,* trans. R. G. Bury, 3 vols. (London: W. Heinemann, 1933–49), 1:13, as well as to Richard H. Popkin's *The History of Scepticism from Erasmus to Spinoza,* rev. ed. (Berkeley: University of California Press, 1979).

43. Habermas's reference here is to Axel Honneth, *Kritik der Macht: Reflexionsstufen einer kritischen Gesellschaftstheorie* (Frankfurt a. M.: Suhrkamp, 1985), p. 182.

44. The reference is to Gehlen, *Die Seele im technischen Zeitalter: Sozialpsychologische Probleme in der industriellen Gesellschaft* (Hamburg: Rowohlt, 1957).

45. Jürgen Habermas, *The Philosophical Discourse of Modernity,* p. 287. For Habermas, Foucault's theory of power is, among other things, simply too crude an instrument to deal adequately with the complexities of social reality. In connection with the rise of modern legal codes, for example, he notes that Foucault's "generalization, in terms of the theory of power, . . . hinders [him] from perceiving the phenomenon actually in need of explanation: In the welfare-state democracies of the West, the spread of legal regulation has the structure of a dilemma, because it is the legal means for securing freedom that themselves endanger the freedom of their presumptive beneficiaries. Under the premises of his theory of power, Foucault so levels down the complexity of social modernization that the disturbing paradoxes of this process cannot even become apparent to him" (ibid., pp. 290–91). What we might call, with a nod to Horkheimer and Adorno, the "dialectic of the welfare-state"—that is, its tendency to reduce to permanent dependent status precisely those whom it is designed to liberate from the constraints of material want—is trenchantly analyzed by Charles Murray in *Losing Ground: American Social Policy 1950–1980* (New York: Basic Books, 1984).

46. Martin J. Matusik, "Habermas on Communicative Reason and Performative Contradiction," *New German Critique* Nr. 47 (Spring/Summer 1989): 149; subsequent references are given in the text. For Matusik, by the way, the answer to this question is unequivocally "no." In addition to presenting a cogently argued statement of the position of critical rationality, his notes also include an extensive selection of important sources for further study of this entire topic.

47. The passage from Gadamer is from *Truth and Method* (New York: Crossroad, 1975), p. 432. There is perhaps a mild irony, of course, in citing Gadamer in support of a Habermasian argument. At least in this one respect, however, the positions of the two do appear quite close to one another.

48. Jürgen Habermas, "Towards a Theory of Communicative Competence," *Inquiry* 13 (1970): 372; cited in Matusik, p. 164.

49. In a letter to Ludwig Ficker, Wittgenstein writes of the *Tractatus:* "*The book's point is an ethical one.* I once meant to include in the preface a sentence which is not in fact there now, but which I will write out for you here, because it will perhaps be a key to the work for you. What I meant to write, then, was this: My work consists of two parts: the one presented here plus all that I have *not* written. And *it is precisely this second part that is the important one.* My book draws limits to the sphere of the ethical from the inside as it were, and I am convinced that this is the ONLY rigorous way of drawing those limits. In short, I believe that where *many* others today are just *gassing,* I have managed in my book to put everything firmly into place by being silent about it." See Ludwig Wittgenstein, *Briefe an Ludwig von Ficker,* ed. G. H. von Wright in collaboration with Walter Methlagl,

in *Brenner Studien*, Vol. I (Salzburg: Otto Müller, 1969), p. 35; cited in Allan Janik and Stephen Toulmin, *Wittgenstein's Vienna* (New York: Simon and Schuster, 1973), p. 192.

50. Engelmann continues: "Positivism holds—and this is its essence—that what we can speak about is all that matters in life. *Whereas Wittgenstein passionately believes that all that really matters in human life is precisely what, in his view, we must be silent about.*" See Paul Engelmann, *Letters from Ludwig Wittgenstein, With a Memoir*, ed. B. F. McGuinness, trans. L. Furtmüller (Oxford: Blackwell, 1967), p. 97; cited in *Wittgenstein's Vienna*, p. 220.

51. Announcements of "the end of history" are in general, I think, always at least a bit premature. For a recent, and much commented upon, discussion of this issue as it pertains specifically to competition between different political systems, see Francis Fukuyama, "The End of History?" *The National Interest* Nr. 16 (Summer 1989): 3–18; and, by the same author, "A Reply to My Critics," *The National Interest* Nr. 18 (Winter 1989–90): 21–28.

52. See Charles Altieri, *Act and Quality: A Theory of Literary Meaning and Humanistic Understanding* (Amherst: University of Massachusetts Press, 1981); also "From Expressivist Aesthetics to Expressivist Ethics," in A. J. Cascardi, ed., *Literature and the Question of Philosophy*, pp. 132–66.

53. See his Introduction to the collection *Redrawing the Lines: Analytic Philosophy, Deconstruction, and Literary Theory* (Minneapolis: University of Minnesota Press, 1989), as well as his essays listed in the Bibliography to this volume. In the same vein, see also the forthcoming collection *Literary Theory After Davidson*.

54. See, in particular, *Against Deconstruction* (Princeton: Princeton University Press, 1989) and *Literary Knowledge: Humanistic Inquiry and the Philosophy of Science* (Ithaca: Cornell University Press, 1988), respectively.

55. One consequence that I have sought to draw in my own work of replacing the dogmatic-skeptical paradigm with the standpoint of critical realism involves countering the currently fashionable tendency to view the poets of the age of Romanticism—or, in the case of German literature in particular, the *Goethezeit*—as, in effect, contemporary skeptics *avant la lettre*. In light of the fact that the writers in question did not merely happen to be living at the same time that the theory of critical realism was first being worked out (again, chiefly by Kant and Herder), but in fact in many cases made serious and important contributions in their own right to the development of that theory, the possibility seems prima facie worth pursuing that they might better be read not as skeptics at all, but rather precisely as writers intent on realizing a distinctively new literary idiom, one at once reflective of and itself ringing further changes on this unprecedented turn in philosophical thought. See, again, my "*Verum est factum*: Critical Realism and the Discourse of Autonomy." Claudia Brodsky's *The Imposition of Form: Studies in Narrative Representation and Knowledge* (Princeton: Princeton University Press, 1987) offers a number of valuable suggestions in a similar vein.

56. Donald Davidson, "The Myth of the Subjective," in Michael Krausz, ed., *Relativism: Interpretation and Confrontation* (Notre Dame: University of Notre Dame Press, 1989), pp. 166–67.

57. I discuss this issue briefly as it pertains to both Kant and Herder in "Changing the Subject: Herder and the Reorientation of Philosophy." Davidson's "nonfoundational approach," by the way, is precisely not the same as an *anti*-foundational one. Anti-foundationalism, as seen, is a form of skepticism, denying (depending on exactly how it is formulated in a given context) either the reality or the accessibility of objective fact. Davidson's view, on the other hand, coincides—so far as I can tell, almost exactly—with the

one I am here calling critical realism. See in this regard, again, my forthcoming "Strict Constructionism: Davidsonian Realism and the World of Belief."

58. One thinks in this regard, for example, of M.C. Escher's famous graphic representation of two hands, each holding a pen with which it draws the other. The depiction of such a paradoxical state of affairs is itself unproblematic (apart, obviously, from the level of technical virtuosity required), so long as the field of representation in which the depiction occurs is unambiguously grounded in its own right, as, of course, it is in the case of Escher's drawing. If we imagine the structure of that paradoxical image expanded so as to become coterminous with reality itself, however, then we have, I think, a kind of objective correlative of both the problem of history itself and the sensation of epistemic vertigo that the contemplation of it is easily capable of inducing.

59. The bulk of McCarthy's discussion of the debate occurs at *CTH*, pp. 177–93. See also in this regard Jack Mendelson, "The Habermas-Gadamer Debate," *New German Critique* 18 (1979): 44–73.

60. Cf. Peter Haidu, "The Semiotics of Alterity." Haidu points out that if the goal of "Gadamerian hermeneutics. . . . to integrate the past in the present. . . . has its admirable side, it also presents something of a problem." For example, what does "such a unifying, integrative theory" do about "the fascist period that [Gadamer himself] experienced"? "It is certainly admirable to integrate Racine, Goethe, and Baudelaire in a tradition that constitutes us all as cognitive subjects endowed with a trans-European heritage: Will one easily do so with Ezra Pound and Leni Riefenstahl, to name only very great artists? Will one easily do the same with popular Nazi culture, there where it shades over into Nazi propaganda? Would one not want to leave open the possibility that certain aspects or *Momente* of the 'tradition' are to be rejected, that the postulate of unity, of continuity, of integration, requires certain distinctions that imply differentiations within this 'tradition'? The simple, naive, euphoric valorization of a totalized European culture hardly seems acceptable after the Holocaust, not to mention the Crusades" (pp. 676–77).

61. This at least was the teaching of *Sein und Zeit*, in which the notion of "existentials" was introduced as a central element in the existential analytic of *Dasein*. Following the so-called *Kehre* in Heidegger's thought to *Seinsgeschichte*, the picture, of course, changes somewhat in this regard.

62. Friedrich Schlegel, Review of Herder's *Briefe zu Beförderung der Humanität*, *7. und 8. Sammlung*, *Kritische Friedrich-Schlegel-Ausgabe*, ed. Ernst Behler (Munich: Schöningh, 1959ff.), 1. Abt., Bd. 2, 54.

63. My most recent effort in this regard is an essay entitled "The Infinity of Finitude: Criticism, History, and Herder," to appear in the *Herder Yearbook*.

64. Cf. Herder's exhortation "feel yourself into everything" (*fühle dich in alles hinein*) from *Another Philosophy of History for the Cultivation of Mankind (SWS*, V, 503). For a discussion of both the pivotal role played by this principle in Herder's thought and his full awareness of the other side of the dilemma described here by McCarthy, see again *Herder and the Poetics of Thought*, especially chapter 4.

65. The passages cited by McCarthy here are from Habermas's paper "On Communicative Action" of 1976.

66. In an essay cited earlier, McCarthy, addressing the so-called "strong program" in the sociology of knowledge, notes that the advocates of that program "might . . . propose a division of labor between the sociologist of knowledge who describes and explains belief systems and the humanist or critical theorist who evaluates and criticizes them— that is, between investigators who adopt the objectivizing attitude of the non-involved and those who adopt the performative attitude of participants" ("Scientific Rationality and the

'Strong Program' in the Sociology of Knowledge," p. 89). He further notes, however, that
the response to this proposal was provided a good fifty years ago by "Max Horkheimer and
his colleagues [who] repeatedly argued that this alternative was an illusion, that the social
investigator was unavoidably 'involved' in the object he or she was studying, that the sociologist of knowledge's attitude of above-the-battle neutrality was a prime instance of false
consciousness" (ibid.). No one's position is ever "that of the detached spectator but [rather
always] that of the participating player." We "are implicitly involved in evaluating beliefs
even when [we] are trying merely to describe and explain them. For meaning and validity
are intertwined and both are internally connected with reasons. In interpreting, we cannot but move in the space of reasons. And in coming to understand 'their' beliefs and how
'they' reason about them, the question of whether or not they have come to hold them for
reasons 'we' can accept cannot but play a role in how we proceed" (ibid., pp. 92–93). In a
similar vein, Johannes Fabian, referring to J. Iain Prattis's "Dialectics and Experience in
Fieldwork: The Poetic Dimension," notes that "[t]hroughout [Prattis] defines the problem
as one of overcoming the -emic/-etic distinction—between an inside and an outside view
of other cultures—and the stifling effect it has had on theory and method in anthropology" ("Presence and Representation: The Other and Anthropological Writing," 765). On
the "-emic/-etic distinction," see also Bruno Latour and Steve Woolgar, *Laboratory Life:
The Social Construction of Scientific Facts* (Beverly Hills: Sage Publications, 1979), p. 38.
As any reader of Herder's "On Diligence in Several Learned Languages" knows, however,
the recognition of a need somehow to overcome the apparent gulf between "inside" and
"outside" views is not exactly a new way of formulating "the problem" in question. Fabian's own suggestions in this regard come fairly close, at least in some respects, to the ones
that Herder advanced over two centuries ago, in particular as regards the necessity of reciprocal interaction of the theoretical and practical components of a research program. In
the end, however, as seen earlier, Fabian remains bound within an epistemologically pre-
critical, and thus a fortiori pre-Herderian, context of thought.

     67. Hilary Putnam, "Why Reason Can't Be Naturalized," pp. 227–28; also *Realism
and Reason: Philosophical Papers, Volume 3* (Cambridge: Cambridge University Press,
1983), p. 234.

     68. Thomas McCarthy, "Scientific Rationality and the 'Strong Program' in the So-
ciology of Knowledge," p. 82.

     69. Thomas McCarthy, Introduction, *The Philosophical Discourse of Modern-
ity*, p. x.

BIBLIOGRAPHY

Abbott, Edwin A. *Flatland: A Romance of Many Dimensions*. 6th ed. New York: Dover, 1952.

Abrams, M. H. *The Mirror and the Lamp: Romantic Theory and the Critical Tradition*. London: Oxford University Press, 1953.

———. *Natural Supernaturalism: Tradition and Revolution in Romantic Literature*. New York: Norton, 1971.

———. "How to Do Things with Texts." *Partisan Review* 46 (1979): 566–88.

Adams, Hazard, ed. *Critical Theory Since Plato*. San Diego: Harcourt Brace Jovanovich, 1971.

Adams, Hazard, and Leroy Searle, ed. *Critical Theory Since 1965*. Tallahassee: University Presses of Florida and Florida State University Press, 1986.

Allison, Henry E. *Kant's Transcendental Idealism: An Interpretation and Defense*. New Haven: Yale University Press, 1983.

Althusser, Louis. "Ideology and Ideological State Apparatuses." In *Lenin and Philosophy, and Other Essays*. Translated by Ben Brewster. London: New Left Books, 1971.

Altieri, Charles. "Wittgenstein on Consciousness and Language: A Challenge to Derridean Literary Theory." *MLN* 91 (1976): 1397–1423.

———. *Act and Quality: A Theory of Literary Meaning and Humanistic Understanding*. Amherst: University of Massachusetts Press, 1981.

———. Review of *The Tain of the Mirror: Derrida and the Philosophy of Reflection*, by Rodolphe Gasché. *Comparative Literature Studies* 26 (1989): 376–84.

Amariglio, Jack, Stephen Resnick, and Richard Wolff. "Division and Difference in the 'Discipline' of Economics." *Critical Inquiry* 17 (1990): 108–37.

Apel, Karl-Otto. "Wittgenstein und Heidegger: Die Frage nach dem Sinn von Sein und der Sinnlosigkeitsverdacht gegen alle Metaphysik." *Philosophisches Jahrbuch* 75 (1967): 56–94.

———. "The Problem of Philosophical Foundations in Light of a Transcendental Pragmatics of Language." *Man and World* 8 (1975): 239–75; trans. and rev. rpt. in K. Baynes et al., ed., *After Philosophy*, pp. 250–90.

———— . "Intentions, Conventions, and Reference to Things: Dimensions of Understanding Meaning in Hermeneutics and in Analytic Philosophy of Language." In H. Parret and J. Bouveresse, ed., *Meaning and Understanding*, pp. 79–111. Berlin: de Gruyter, 1981.

Armstrong, D. M. "A moderate skeptic's acknowledgements" (Review of Strawson, *The Secret Connexion: Causation, Realism, and David Hume*). *Times Literary Supplement* (22–28 December 1989), 1425.

Arnold, N. Scott. *Marx's Radical Critique of Capitalist Society: A Reconstruction and Critical Evaluation*. Oxford: Oxford University Press, 1990.

Bachmaier, Peter. *Wittgenstein und Kant: Versuch zum Begriff des Transzendentalen*. Frankfurt: Lang, 1978.

Balch, Stephen H., and Herbert I. London. "The Tenured Left." *Commentary* (October 1986), 41–51.

Barnes, Barry, and David Bloor. "Relativism, Rationalism, and the Sociology of Knowledge." In M. Hollis and S. Lukes, ed., *Rationality and Relativism*. Oxford: Blackwell, 1982.

Baynes, Kenneth, James Bohman, and Thomas McCarthy, ed. *After Philosophy: End or Transformation?* Cambridge: MIT Press, 1987.

Becker, Carl L. *The Heavenly City of the Eighteenth-Century Philosophers*. New Haven: Yale University Press, 1932.

Bedient, Calvin. "Kristeva and Poetry as Shattered Signification." *Critical Inquiry* 16 (1990): 807–29.

Beiser, Frederick C. *The Fate of Reason: German Philosophy from Kant to Fichte*. Cambridge: Harvard University Press, 1987.

Bell, Julian. "A liberal Utopia" (Review of Rorty, *Contingency, Irony, and Solidarity*). *Times Literary Supplement* (24–30 November 1989), 1296.

Benhabib, Seyla. "Epistemologies of Postmodernism: A Rejoinder to Jean-François Lyotard." *New German Critique* 33 (1984): 103–26.

Bensch, Rudolf. *Ludwig Wittgenstein: Die apriorischen und mathematischen Sätze in seinem Spätwerk*. Bonn: Bouvier, 1973.

Berger, Peter L., and Thomas Luckmann. *The Social Construction of Reality: A Treatise in the Sociology of Knowledge*. Garden City: Doubleday, 1966.

Bergmann, Frithjof. "Nietzsche's Critique of Morality." In R. Solomon and K. Higgins, ed., *Reading Nietzsche*, pp. 29–45.

Berlin, Isaiah. *Vico and Herder: Two Studies in the History of Ideas*. New York: Vintage, 1977.

Bernstein, Charles. "Optimism and Critical Excess (Process)." *Critical Inquiry* 16 (1990): 830–56.

Bernstein, Richard J. "Philosophy in the Conversation of Mankind." *The Review of Metaphysics* 33 (1980): 745–75.

———— . *Beyond Objectivism and Relativism: Science, Hermeneutics, and Praxis*. Philadelphia: University of Pennsylvania Press, 1983.

———— , ed. *Habermas and Modernity*. Cambridge: MIT Press, 1985.

———— . "The Rage Against Reason." In E. McMullin, ed., *Construction and Constraint*, pp. 189–222.

Berthoff, Werner. "The Way We Think Now: Protocols for Deprivation." *New Literary History* 7 (1976): 599–617.

Binkley, Timothy. *Wittgenstein's Language*. The Hague: Nijhoff, 1973.

Blumenberg, Hans. *The Legitimacy of the Modern Age*. Translated by Robert M. Wallace. Cambridge: MIT Press, 1983.

Böhler, Dietrich. "Wittgenstein und Augustinus: Transzendentalpragmatische Kritik der Bezeichnungstheorie der Sprache und des methodischen Solipsismus." In A. Eschbach and J. Trabant, ed., *History of Semiotics*, pp. 343–67. Amsterdam: Benjamin, 1983.

Bonnefoy, Yves. "Lifting Our Eyes from the Page." Translated by John Naughton. *Critical Inquiry* 16 (1990): 794–806.

Bork, Robert H. *The Tempting of America: The Political Seduction of the Law.* New York: The Free Press, 1990.

Boyne, Roy. Review of L. D. Kritzmann, ed., *Michel Foucault; Politics, Philosophy, Culture: Interviews and Other Writings 1977–1984;* L. H. Martin, et al., ed., *Technologies of the Self: A Seminar with Michel Foucault;* J. Bernauer, et al., ed., *The Final Foucault. Theory, Culture, and Society* 6 (1989): 471–74.

Brandon, Robert. "Truth and Assertibility." *The Journal of Philosophy* 73 (1976): 137–49.

Brinton, Crane. *The Anatomy of Revolution.* New York: Vintage, 1952.

Brodsky, Claudia. *The Imposition of Form: Studies in Narrative Representation and Knowledge.* Princeton: Princeton University Press, 1987.

Brown, Marshall. "The Logic of Realism: A Hegelian Approach." *PMLA* 96 (1981): 224–41.

Brown, Richard Harvey. "Positivism, Relativism, and Narrative in the Logic of the Historical Sciences." *American Historical Review* 92 (1987): 908–20.

Bruns, Gerald L. "What is Tradition?" *New Literary History* 22 (1991): 1–21.

Carroll, David, ed. *The States of "Theory": History, Art, and Critical Discourse.* New York: Columbia University Press, 1990.

Carroll, Lewis. *Alice's Adventures in Wonderland and Through the Looking-Glass.* New York: Collier, 1962.

Cascardi, Anthony J. "Skepticism and Deconstruction." *Philosophy and Literature* 8 (1984): 1–14.

———, ed. *Literature and the Question of Philosophy.* Baltimore: Johns Hopkins University Press, 1987.

Cassam, Quassim. "Kant, Hume and the bundle theory (Review of Powell, *Kant's Theory of Self-Consciousness*)." *Times Literary Supplement* (18 January 1991), 20.

Cavell, Stanley. "The Availability of Wittgenstein's Later Philosophy." In G. Pitcher, ed., *Wittgenstein: The Philosophical Investigations—A Collection of Critical Essays,* pp. 151–85. Garden City: Doubleday Anchor, 1966.

———. *The Claim of Reason: Wittgenstein, Skepticism, Morality, and Tragedy.* Oxford: Oxford University Press, 1979.

Chatterjee, Ranjit. "Reading Whorf Through Wittgenstein: A Solution to the Linguistic Relativity Problem." *Lingua* 67/1 (Sept. 1985): 37–63.

Clark, Kenneth. *Civilisation: A Personal View.* New York: Harper & Row, 1969.

Close, Anthony. "Centering the De-Centerers: Foucault and *Las Meninas.*" *Philosophy and Literature* 11 (1987): 21–36.

Coleman, James S. "On the Self-Suppression of Academic Freedom." *Academic Questions* 4 (1990–91): 17–22.

Connor, Steven. Review of Wayne C. Booth, *The Company We Keep;* J. Hillis Miller, *The Ethics of Reading;* Barbara Herrnstein Smith, *Contingencies of Value. Modern Language Review* 85 (1990): 891–94.

Copi, Irving M., and Robert W. Beard, ed. *Essays on Wittgenstein's* Tractatus. New York: Hafner, 1973.

Copleston, Frederick, S. J. *A History of Philosophy.* Garden City: Doubleday Image, 1962.

Crews, Frederick. *Skeptical Engagements.* New York: Oxford University Press, 1986.

Culler, Jonathan. *The Pursuit of Signs: Semiotics, Literature, Deconstruction.* Ithaca: Cornell University Press, 1981.

———. *On Deconstruction: Theory and Criticism after Structuralism.* Ithaca: Cornell University Press, 1982.

Danto, Arthur C. "Philosophy as/and/of Literature." In A. J. Cascardi, ed., *Literature and the Question of Philosophy,* pp. 1–23.

———. "Some Remarks on *The Genealogy of Morals.*" In R. Solomon and K. Higgins, ed., *Reading Nietzsche,* pp. 13–28.

Dasenbrock, Reed Way. "Coming to an Understanding of Understanding: Deconstruction, Ordinary Language Philosophy and Contemporary Critical Theory." *The Missouri Review* (1984), 234–45.

——— . "Word-World Relations: The Work of Charles Altieri and Edward Said." *New Orleans Review* (Spring 1985), 92–96.

——— . "Accounting for the Changing Certainties of Interpretive Communities." *MLN* 101 (1986): 1022–41.

——— , ed. *Redrawing the Lines: Analytic Philosophy, Deconstruction, and Literary Theory.* Minneapolis: University of Minnesota Press, 1989.

Davidson, Donald. "On the Very Idea of a Conceptual Scheme." *Proceedings of the American Philosophical Association* 47 (1973–74): 5–20.

——— . "The Method of Truth in Metaphysics." *Midwest Studies in Philosophy* 2 (1977): 244–54.

——— . *Essays on Actions and Events.* Oxford: Clarendon Press, 1980.

——— . "Paradoxes of Irrationality." In R. Wollheim and J. Hopkins, ed., *Philosophical Essays on Freud.* Cambridge: Cambridge University Press, 1982.

——— . *Inquiries into Truth and Interpretation.* Oxford: Clarendon Press, 1984.

——— . "A Nice Derangement of Epitaphs." In R. E. Grandy and R. Warner, ed., *Philosophical Grounds of Rationality: Intentions, Categories, Ends.* Oxford: Clarendon Press, 1986.

——— . "A Coherence Theory of Truth and Knowledge." In E. LePore, ed., *Truth and Interpretation*, pp. 307–19.

——— . "Empirical Content." In E. LePore, ed., *Truth and Interpretation*, pp. 320–32.

——— . "Afterthoughts, 1987." In A. Malachowski, ed., *Reading Rorty*, pp. 134–38.

——— . "The Myth of the Subjective." In M. Krausz, ed., *Relativism*, pp. 159–72.

——— . "The Structure and Content of Truth." *The Journal of Philosophy* 87 (1990): 279–328.

DeLacy, Phillip. "Skepticism in Antiquity." *Dictionary of the History of Ideas*, IV, 234–40.

Deleuze, Gilles. "The Conditions of the Question: What Is Philosophy?" Translated by D. W. Smith and A. I. Davidson. *Critical Inquiry* 17 (1991): 471–78.

De Man, Paul. *Blindness and Insight: Essays in the Rhetoric of Contemporary Criticism.* 2d ed. Minneapolis: University of Minnesota Press, 1983.

Derrida, Jacques. "Structure, Sign, and Play in the Discourse of the Human Sciences." In R. Mackrey and E. Donato, ed., *The Languages of Criticism and the Sciences of Man: The Structuralist Controversy*, pp. 247–65. Baltimore: Johns Hopkins University Press, 1970.

——— . *Speech and Phenomena, And Other Essays on Husserl's Theory of Signs.* Translation and Introduction by David. B. Allison. Preface by Newton Garver. Evanston: Northwestern University Press, 1973.

——— . *Of Grammatology.* Translation and Preface by Gayatri Chakravorty Spivak. Baltimore: Johns Hopkins University Press, 1976.

——— . "Signature Event Context." *Glyph I*, pp. 172–97. Baltimore: Johns Hopkins University Press, 1977.

——— . *Positions.* Translated by Alan Bass. Chicago: University of Chicago Press, 1981.

——— . *Margins of Philosophy.* Translated by Alan Bass. Chicago: University of Chicago Press, 1982.

——— . "Racism's Last Word." *Critical Inquiry* 12 (1985): 290–99.

——— . "But Beyond . . . (Open Letter to Anne McClintock and Rob Nixon)." *Critical Inquiry* 13 (1986): 155–70.

——— . "Like the Sound of the Sea Deep Within a Shell: Paul de Man's War." Translated by Peggy Kamuf. *Critical Inquiry* 14 (1988): 590–652.

Dictionary of the History of Ideas. Ed. Philip P. Wiener. New York: Scribner's, 1973.

Dollimore, Jonathan. "Shakespeare, Cultural Materialism, Feminism, and Marxist Humanism." *New Literary History* 21 (1990): 471–94.

Donoghue, Denis. "Deconstructing Deconstruction." Review of Harold Bloom, et al., *Deconstruction and Criticism*, and Paul de Man, *Allegories of Reading. The New York Review of Books* (12 June 1980), 37–41.

Eagleton, Terry. *Literary Theory: An Introduction.* Oxford: Blackwell, 1983.

Ellis, John M. *The Theory of Literary Criticism: A Logical Analysis*. Berkeley: University of California Press, 1974.

——— . "Wittgensteinian Thinking in Theory of Criticism." *New Literary History* 12 (1981): 437–52.

——— . *Against Deconstruction*. Princeton: Princeton University Press, 1989.

——— . "Doing something different (Review of Fish, *Doing What Comes Naturally*)." *London Review of Books* (27 July 1989): 20–22.

The Encyclopedia of Philosophy. Ed. Paul Edwards. New York: Macmillan, 1967.

Evans, Joseph Claude. *The Metaphysics of Transcendental Subjectivity: Descartes, Kant and W. Sellars*. Amsterdam: Grüner, 1984.

Fabian, Johannes. "Presence and Representation: The Other and Anthropological Writing." *Critical Inquiry* 16 (1990): 753–72.

Fain, Haskell. "Some Comments on Stern's 'Narrative versus Description in Historiography.' " *New Literary History* 21 (1990): 569–74.

Fann, K. T. *Wittgenstein's Conception of Philosophy*. Berkeley: University of California Press, 1971.

Fernández-Morera, Dario. "Materialist Discourse in Academia During the Age of Late Marxism." *Academic Questions* 4/2 (Spring 1991): 15–29.

Feyerabend, Paul. *Against Method*. New York: New Left Books, 1975; rev. ed. London: Verso, 1988.

——— . *Realism, Rationalism, and Scientific Method*. Cambridge: Cambridge University Press, 1981.

Fine, Arthur. "How to Compare Theories: Reference and Change." *Nous* 9 (1975): 17–32.

Fish, Stanley. *Is There a Text in This Class? The Authority of Interpretive Communities*. Cambridge: Harvard University Press, 1980.

——— . *Doing What Comes Naturally: Change, Rhetoric, and the Practice of Theory in Literary and Legal Studies*. Durham: Duke University Press, 1989.

Fleck, Ludwik. *Genesis and Development of a Scientific Fact*. Translated by Fred Bradley and Thaddeus J. Trenn. Chicago: University of Chicago Press, 1979.

Foucault, Michel. *The Order of Things: An Archaeology of the Human Sciences*. New York: Random House, 1970.

——— . "What Is An Author?" in *Language, Counter-Memory, Practice: Selected Essays and Interviews*. Translated by D. F. Bouchard and S. Simon. Edited by D. F. Bouchard. Ithaca: Cornell University Press, 1977.

Fraden, Rena. "Response to Professor Carolyn Porter." *New Literary History* 21 (1990): 273–78.

Frank, Manfred. *What Is Neostructuralism?* Translated by Sabine Wilke and Richard Gray. Minneapolis: University of Minnesota Press, 1989.

Fukuyama, Francis. "The End of History?" *The National Interest* Nr. 16 (Summer 1989): 3–18.

——— . "A Reply to My Critics." *The National Interest* Nr. 18 (Winter 1989–90): 21–28.

Gadamer, Hans-Georg. *Volk und Geschichte im Denken Herders*. Frankfurt: Klostermann, 1942.

——— . *Truth and Method*. New York: Crossroad, 1975.

Gaier, Ulrich. *Herders Sprachphilosophie und Erkenntniskritik*. Stuttgart: Frommann-Holzboog, 1988.

Galison, Peter. "History, Philosophy, and the Central Metaphor." *Science in Context* 2 (1988): 197–212.

——— . "Aufbau/Bauhaus: Logical Positivism and Architectural Modernism." *Critical Inquiry* 16 (1990): 709–52.

Gallagher, Kenneth T. "Rorty on Objectivity, Truth, and Social Consensus." *International Philosophical Quarterly* 24 (1984): 111–24.

Geertz, Clifford. "From the Native's Point of View: On the Nature of Anthropological Understanding." In Rabinow and Sullivan, ed., *Interpretive Social Science: A Reader*, pp. 225–41. Berkeley: University of California Press, 1979.

——— . "History and Anthropology." *New Literary History* 21 (1990): 321–36.

Gehlen, Arnold. *Die Seele im technischen Zeitalter: Sozialpsychologische Probleme in der industriellen Gesellschaft.* Hamburg: Rowohlt, 1957.

Gleick, James. *Chaos: Making a New Science.* New York: Penguin, 1987.

Goodman, Nelson. *Ways of Worldmaking.* Indianapolis: Hackett, 1978.

——— . "Just the Facts, Ma'am!" In M. Krausz, ed., *Relativism,* pp. 80–85.

Graff, Gerald. *Literature Against Itself.* Chicago: University of Chicago Press, 1979.

——— . "Other Voices, Other Rooms: Organizing and Teaching the Humanities Conflict." *New Literary History* 21 (1990): 817–39.

Grene, Marjorie. "Life, Death, and Language: Some Thoughts on Wittgenstein and Derrida." In *Philosophy In and Out of Europe,* pp. 142–54. Berkeley: University of California Press, 1976.

Griffin, Robert J. "Ideology and Misrepresentation: A Response to Edward Said." *Critical Inquiry* 15 (1989): 611–25.

Gutting, Gary. "Michel Foucault and the History of Reason." In E. McMullin, ed., *Construction and Constraint,* pp. 153–88.

Habermas, Jürgen. *Erkenntnis und Interesse.* Frankfurt: Suhrkamp, 1968.

——— . "Vorbereitende Bemerkungen zu einer Theorie der kommunikativen Kompetenz." In *Theorie der Gesellschaft oder Sozialtechnologie.* Frankfurt: Suhrkamp, 1971.

——— . *Legitimation Crisis.* Translated by Thomas McCarthy. Boston: Beacon Press, 1975.

——— . *Communication and the Evolution of Society.* Translated by Thomas McCarthy. Boston: Beacon Press, 1979.

——— . "A Reply to my Critics." In Thompson and Held, ed., *Habermas: Critical Debates,* pp. 219–83.

——— . "Philosophy as Stand-In and Interpreter." In *Moral Consciousness and Communicative Action.* Cambridge: MIT Press, 1987.

——— . *The Philosophical Discourse of Modernity: Twelve Lectures.* Translated by Frederick Lawrence. Introduction by Thomas McCarthy. Cambridge; MIT Press, 1987.

——— . "Remarks on the Discussion." In Van Reijen, et al., "Symposium on Habermas," pp. 127–32.

Hacker, P.M.S. *Insight and Illusion: Wittgenstein on Philosophy and the Metaphysics of Experience.* London: Oxford University Press, 1972.

Hacking, Ian. "Is the End in Sight for Epistemology?" *The Journal of Philosophy* 77 (1980): 579–88.

——— . "Rules, scepticism, proof, Wittgenstein." In I. Hacking, ed., *Exercises in Analysis: Essays by Students of Casimir Lewy,* pp. 113–24. Cambridge: Cambridge University Press, 1985.

——— . "Styles of Scientific Reasoning." In J. Rajchman and C. West, ed., *Post-Analytic Philosophy,* pp. 145–65.

——— . "Two Kinds of 'New Historicism' for Philosophers." *New Literary History* 21 (1990): 343–64.

Haidu, Peter. "The Semiotics of Alterity: A Comparison with Hermeneutics." *New Literary History* 21 (1990): 671–91.

Hanson, Norwood Russell. "Quantum Mechanics, Philosophical Implications of." *The Encyclopedia of Philosophy,* VII, 41–49.

Harpham, Geoffrey Galt. "Constraints, not consequences (Review of Fish, *Doing What Comes Naturally*)." *Times Literary Supplement* (9–15 March 1990), 247.

Harrison, Bernard. "Relatively violent (Review of B. H. Smith, *Contingencies of Value*)." *Times Literary Supplement* (29 December 1989–4 January 1990), 1446.

Hauge, Hans. "The Will to Consensus: Manfred Frank on Derrida." *MLN* 105 (1990): 596–609.

Hawking, Stephen W. *A Brief History of Time: From the Big Bang to Black Holes.* Toronto: Bantam, 1988.

Heal, Jane. "Pragmatism and Choosing to Believe." In A. Malachowski, ed., *Reading Rorty*, pp. 101–14.

Heidegger, Martin. *Being and Time*. Translated by John Macquarrie and Edward Robinson. New York: Harper & Row, 1962.

———. *An Introduction to Metaphysics*. Translated by Ralph Mannheim. Garden City: Doubleday Anchor, 1961.

———. *The Question of Being*. Translation and Introduction by W. Kluback and J. T. Wilde. New Haven: College and University Press, 1958.

———. *On the Way to Language*. Translated by P. D. Hertz. New York: Harper & Row, 1971.

———. *Poetry, Language, Thought*. Translation and Introduction by Albert Hofstadter. New York: Harper & Row, 1971.

Heine, Heinrich. *Beiträge zur deutschen Ideologie*. Introduction by Hans Mayer. Frankfurt: Ullstein, 1971.

Henrich, Dieter, ed. *Kant oder Hegel? Über Formen der Begründung in der Philosophie*. Stuttgart: Klett-Cotta, 1983.

Herder, Johann Gottfried. *Sämtliche Werke*. 33 vols. Edited by Bernhard Suphan. Berlin: Weidmannsche Buchhandlung, 1877–1913; rpt. Hildesheim: Olm, 1967.

———. *Frühe Schriften: 1764–1772*. Edited by Ulrich Gaier. Frankfurt: Deutscher Klassiker Verlag, 1985.

———. *Werke*. 2 vols. Edited by Wolfgang Pross. Munich: Hanser, 1984, 1987.

———. *Ideen zur Philosophie der Geschichte der Menschheit*. Edited by Martin Bollacher. Frankfurt: Deutscher Klassiker Verlag, 1989.

Hiley, David R. *Philosophy in Question: Essays on a Pyrrhonian Theme*. Chicago: University of Chicago Press, 1988.

Hillach, Ansgar. "Sprache, das hypertrophe Gesellschaftsspiel: Über Fritz Mauthner." *Horen* 31 (1986): 24–40.

Hollinger, David A. "Free Enterprise and Free Inquiry: The Emergence of Laissez-Faire Communitarianism in the Ideology of Science in the United States." *New Literary History* 21 (1990): 897–919.

Hollis, Martin. "The Poetics of Personhood." In A. Malachowski, ed., *Reading Rorty*, pp. 244–56.

Holub, Robert C. "*Germanistik* and Theoretical Discourse in the 1980's." *Monatshefte* 80 (1988): 364–76.

Honneth, Axel. *Kritik der Macht: Reflexionsstufen einer kritischen Gesellschaftstheorie*. Frankfurt: Suhrkamp, 1985.

Horton, Robin. "African Traditional Thought and Western Science." In B. Wilson, ed., *Rationality*, pp. 131–71.

Howe, Irving. "The Value of the Canon." *The New Republic* (18 February 1991), 40–47.

Irmscher, Hans Dietrich. "Die geschichtsphilosophische Kontroverse zwischen Kant und Herder." In Bernard Gajek, ed., *Hamann-Kant-Herder: Acta des vierten Internationalen Hamann-Kolloquiums*. Frankfurt: Lang, 1987.

———. "Aneignung und Kritik naturwissenschaftlicher Vorstellungen bei Herder." In J. L. Hibberd and H. B. Nisbet, ed., *Texte, Motive und Gestalten der Goethezeit: Festschrift für Hans Reiss*. Tübingen: Niemeyer, 1989.

Iser, Wolfgang. "Fictionalizing: The Anthropological Dimension of Literary Fiction." *New Literary History* 21 (1990): 939–55.

Jameson, Fredric. *Marxism and Form: Twentieth-Century Dialectical Theories of Literature*. Princeton: Princeton University Press, 1971.

———. *The Prison-House of Language: A Critical Account of Structuralism and Russian Formalism*. Princeton: Princeton University Press, 1972.

Janik, Allan, and Stephen Toulmin. *Wittgenstein's Vienna*. New York: Simon and Schuster, 1973.

Jean Paul. *Sämtliche Werke: Historisch-kritische Ausgabe*. Edited by Eduard Berend. Weimar: Hermann Böhlaus Nachfolger, 1927ff.

Jensen, Henning. "Reid and Wittgenstein on Philosophy and Language." *Philosophical Studies* 36 (1979): 359–76.

Kahn, Victoria. "Habermas, Machiavelli, and the Humanist Critique of Ideology." *PMLA* 105 (1990): 464–76.

Kant, Immanuel. *Critique of Pure Reason*. Translated by Norman Kemp Smith. New York: St. Martin's Press, 1965.

———. *Kritik der reinen Vernunft*. Edited by Raymund Schmidt. Leipzig: Meiner, 1930.

Kaufmann, David. "The Profession of Theory." *PMLA* 105 (1990): 519–30.

Kaufmann, Walter, ed. *Existentialism from Dostoevsky to Sartre*. Cleveland: Meridian, 1956.

Kawin, Bruce. "On Not Having the Last Word: Beckett, Wittgenstein, and the Limits of Language." In P. S. Hawkins and A. H. Schatter, ed., *Ineffability: Naming the Unnamable from Dante to Beckett*, pp. 189–202. New York: AMS Press, 1984.

Kelman, Mark. "Reasonable Evidence of Reasonableness." *Critical Inquiry* 17 (1991): 798–817.

Kenny, Anthony. *Wittgenstein*. Cambridge: Harvard University Press, 1973.

Kenshur, Oscar. "Demystifying the Demystifiers: Metaphysical Snares of Ideological Criticism." *Critical Inquiry* 14 (1988): 335–53.

———. "(Avoidable) Snares and Avoidable Muddles." *Critical Inquiry* 15 (1989): 658–68.

Kim, Jaegwon. "Rorty on the Possibility of Philosophy." *The Journal of Philosophy* 77 (1980): 588–97.

Knodt, Eva. "Dramatic Illusion in the Making of the Past: Shakespeare's Impact on Herder's Philosophy of History." In W. Koepke, ed. *LHE*, pp. 209–23.

———. *"Negative Philosophie" und dialogische Kritik: Zur Struktur poetischer Theorie bei Lessing und Herder*. Tübingen: Niemeyer, 1988.

Koelb, Clayton, and Virgil Lokke, ed. *The Current in Criticism: Essays on the Present and Future of Literary Theory*. West Lafayette: Purdue University Press, 1987.

Koepke, Wulf, ed. *Johann Gottfried Herder: Innovator Through the Ages*. Bonn: Bouvier, 1982.

———. *Johann Gottfried Herder*. Boston: Twayne, 1987.

———, ed. *Johann Gottfried Herder: Language, History, and the Enlightenment* [cited *LHE* elsewhere in bibliography]. Columbia: Camden House, 1990.

Kordig, Carl R. *The Justification of Scientific Change*. Dordrecht: Reidel, 1971.

Koselleck, Reinhart. *Critique and Crisis: Enlightenment and the Pathogenesis of Modern Society*. 1959; trans. Oxford: Berg, 1988.

———. *Futures Past: On the Semantics of Historical Time*. Translated by Keith Tribe. 1979; trans. Cambridge: MIT Press, 1985.

Krausz, Michael, ed. *Relativism: Interpretation and Confrontation*. Notre Dame: University of Notre Dame Press, 1989.

Kristeva, Julia. *Revolution in Poetic Language*. Translated by Margaret Waller. New York: Columbia University Press, 1984.

Kuhn, Thomas S. *The Structure of Scientific Revolutions*. Chicago: University of Chicago Press, 1962.

———. "Postscript—1969." *The Structure of Scientific Revolutions*. 2d ed. Chicago: University of Chicago Press, 1970.

———. *The Essential Tension: Selected Studies in Scientific Tradition and Change*. Chicago: University of Chicago Press, 1977.

Kuzniar, Alice. *Delayed Endings: Nonclosure in Novalis and Hölderlin*. Athens: University of Georgia Press, 1987.

Lacoue-Labarthe, Philippe, and Jean-Luc Nancy. *The Literary Absolute: The Theory of Literature in German Romanticism*. Translated by Philip Barnard and Cheryl Lester. Albany: SUNY Press, 1988.

Lamb, David. "Hegel and Wittgenstein on Language and Sense Certainty." *Clio* 7/2 (1978): 285–301.

Lanham, Richard. *The Motives of Eloquence*. New Haven: Yale University Press, 1976.

Latour, Bruno, and Steve Woolgar. *Laboratory Life: The Social Construction of Scientific Facts*. Beverly Hills: Sage Publications, 1979.

Lefkowitz, Mary R. "Should Women Receive a Separate Education?" *New Literary History* 21 (1990): 799–815.

Lehan, Richard. "The Theoretical Limits of the New Historicism." *New Literary History* 21 (1990): 533–53.

Leinfellner, Elisabeth. "Zur nominalistischen Begründung von Linguistik und Sprachphilosophie: Fritz Mauthner und Ludwig Wittgenstein." *Studium Generale* 22 (1969): 209–51.

Leinfellner, Elisabeth, W. Leinfellner, H. Berghel, and A. Höbner, ed. *Wittgenstein and His Impact on Contemporary Thought*. Vienna: Hölder, Pichler, Tempsky, 1978.

Lentricchia, Frank. *After the New Criticism*. Chicago: University of Chicago Press, 1980.

Lentricchia, Frank, and Thomas McLaughlin, ed. *Critical Terms for Literary Study*. Chicago: University of Chicago Press, 1990.

LePore, Ernest, and Brian P. McLaughlin, ed. *Actions and Events: Perspectives on the Philosophy of Donald Davidson*. Oxford: Blackwell, 1985.

LePore, Ernest, ed. *Truth and Interpretation: Perspectives on the Philosophy of Donald Davidson*. Oxford: Blackwell, 1986.

Leventhal, Robert S. "Semiotic Interpretation and Rhetoric in the German Enlightenment 1740–1760." *Deutsche Vierteljahrsschrift* 60 (1986): 223–48.

——— . "The Parable as Performance: Interpretation, Cultural Transmission and Political Strategy in Lessing's *Nathan der Weise*." *German Quarterly* 61 (1988): 502–27.

——— . "Progression and Particularity: Herder's Critique of Schlözer's Universal History in the Context of the Early Writings." In W. Koepke, ed., *LHE*, pp. 25–46.

Levin, Richard. "The Poetics and Politics of Bardicide." *PMLA* 105 (1990): 491–504.

——— . "Unthinkable Thoughts in the New Historicizing of English Renaissance Drama." *New Literary History* 21 (1990): 433–47.

Livingston, Paisley. *Literary Knowledge: Humanistic Inquiry and the Philosophy of Science*. Ithaca: Cornell University Press, 1988.

Lotman, Yurij, and B. A. Uspensky. "On the Semiotic Mechanism of Culture." *New Literary History* 9 (1978): 211–32.

Love, Nigel. "Transcending Saussure." *Poetics Today* 10 (1989): 793–818.

Lyotard, Jean-François. *The Postmodern Condition: A Report on Knowledge*. Translated by Geoff Bennington and Brian Massumi. Minneapolis: University of Minnesota Press, 1984.

Magnus, Bernd. "The Deification of the Commonplace: *Twilight of the Idols*." In R. Solomon and K. Higgins, ed., *Reading Nietzsche*, pp. 152–81.

——— . "The Use and Abuse of *The Will to Power*." In R. Solomon and K. Higgins, ed., *Reading Nietzsche*, pp. 218–35.

Mahoney, Dennis F. *Der Roman der Goethezeit (1774–1829)*. Stuttgart: Metzler, 1988.

Makkreel, Rudolf A. *Imagination and Interpretation in Kant: The Hermeneutical Import of the* Critique of Judgment. Chicago: University of Chicago Press, 1990.

——— . "Traditional Historicism, Contemporary Interpretations of Historicity, and the History of Philosophy." *New Literary History* 21 (1990): 977–91.

Malachowski, Alan R., ed. *Reading Rorty: Critical Responses to* Philosophy and the Mirror of Nature (*and Beyond*). Oxford: Blackwell, 1990.

Mandel, Ross. "Heidegger and Wittgenstein: A Second Kantian Revolution." In M. Murray, ed., *Heidegger and Modern Philosophy*, pp. 259–70.

Marcuse, Herbert. *One-Dimensional Man: Studies in the Ideology of Advanced Industrial Society*. Boston: Beacon, 1964.

Markley, Robert. "What Isn't History: The Snares of Demystifying Ideological Criticism." *Critical Inquiry* 15 (1989): 647–57.

Marsh, James L. *Post-Cartesian Meditations: An Essay in Dialectical Phenomenology*. New York: Fordham University Press, 1988.

Marx, Werner. *Heidegger and the Tradition*. Translated by Theodore Kisiel and Murray Greene. Evanston: Northwestern University Press, 1971.

Matusik, Martin J. "Habermas on Communicative Reason and Performative Contradiction." *New German Critique* 47 (1989): 143–72.
McCarthy, Thomas. *The Critical Theory of Jürgen Habermas.* Cambridge: MIT Press, 1978.
———— . "Scientific Rationality and the 'Strong Program' in the Sociology of Knowledge." In E. McMullin, ed., *Construction and Constraint*, pp. 75–95.
———— . "Private Irony and Public Decency: Richard Rorty's New Pragmatism." *Critical Inquiry* 16 (1990): 355–70.
———— . "Ironist Theory as a Vocation: A Response to Rorty's Reply." *Critical Inquiry* 16 (1990): 644–55.
McDowell, Gary L. "Rights Without Roots." *The Wilson Quarterly* 25/1 (Winter 1991): 71–79.
McMullin, Ernan, ed. *Construction and Constraint: The Shaping of Scientific Rationality.* Notre Dame: University of Notre Dame Press, 1988.
Mendelson, Jack. "The Habermas-Gadamer Debate." *New German Critique* 18 (1979): 44–73.
Menges, Karl. "Erkenntnis und Sprache: Herder und die Krise der Philosophie im späten achtzehnten Jahrhundert." In W. Koepke, ed., *LHE*, pp. 47–70.
———— . " 'Seyn' und 'Daseyn', Sein und Zeit. Zu Herders Theorie des Subjekts." In K. Mueller-Vollmer, ed., *Herder Today*, pp. 138–57.
Meyer, Hermann. "Schillers philosophische Rhetorik." *Euphorion* 53 (1959): 313–50.
Mitchell, W.J.T., ed. *Against Theory: Literary Studies and the New Pragmatism.* Chicago: University of Chicago Press, 1985.
Morris, Charles. *Signs, Language, and Behavior.* New York: Prentice-Hall, 1946.
Morton, Michael. "Herder and the Possibility of Literature: Rationalism and Poetry in Eighteenth-Century Germany." In W. Koepke, ed., *Johann Gottfried Herder: Innovator Through the Ages*, pp. 41–63.
———— . "Life Against Death in Bohemia: The Structure of the Debate in *Der Ackermann aus Böhmen.*" *Fifteenth-Century Studies* 9 (1984): 125–46.
———— . *Herder and the Poetics of Thought: Unity and Diversity in "On Diligence in Several Learned Languages."* University Park: Pennsylvania State University Press, 1989.
———— . "Changing the Subject: Herder and the Reorientation of Philosophy." In K. Mueller-Vollmer, ed., *Herder Today*, pp. 158–72.
———— . "*Verum est factum:* Critical Realism and the Discourse of Autonomy." *German Quarterly* 64 (1991): 149–65.
———— . "Strict Constructionism: Davidsonian Realism and the World of Belief." In R. W. Dasenbrock, ed., *Literary Theory After Davidson* (University Park: Pennsylvania State University Press, forthcoming).
———— . "The Infinity of Finitude: Criticism, History, and Herder." *Herder Yearbook* (forthcoming).
Mueller-Vollmer, Kurt. "From Sign to Signification: The Herder-Humboldt Controversy." In W. Koepke, ed., *LHE*, pp. 9–24.
———— , ed. *Herder Today.* Berlin: de Gruyter, 1990.
Mulhall, Stephen. "Inside the great mirror (Review of D. Peterson, *Wittgenstein's Early Philosophy: Three Sides of the Mirror;* P. Carruthers, *Tractarian Semantics: Finding Sense in Wittgenstein's "Tractatus"* and *The Metaphysics of the "Tractatus"*)." *Times Literary Supplement* (18 January 1991), 20.
Murphy, Bruce F. "The Exile of Literature: Poetry and the Politics of the Other(s)." *Critical Inquiry* 17 (1990): 162–73.
Murray, Charles. *Losing Ground: American Social Policy 1950–1980.* New York: Basic Books, 1984.
Murray, Michael, ed. *Heidegger and Modern Philosophy: Critical Essays.* New Haven: Yale University Press, 1978.
Nägele, Rainer. *Reading After Freud: Essays on Goethe, Hölderlin, Habermas, Nietzsche, Brecht, Celan, and Freud.* New York: Columbia University Press, 1987.

Nehamas, Alexander. *Nietzsche: Life as Literature*. Cambridge: Harvard University Press, 1985.

——— . "Writer, Text, Work, Author." In A. J. Cascardi, ed., *Literature and the Question of Philosophy*, pp. 265–91.

——— . "Who Are 'The Philosophers of the Future'?: A Reading of *Beyond Good and Evil*." In R. Solomon and K. Higgins, ed., *Reading Nietzsche*, pp. 46–67.

Norris, Christopher. "Philosophy as *Not* Just a 'Kind of Writing': Derrida and the Claim of Reason." In R. W. Dasenbrock, ed., *Redrawing the Lines*, pp. 189–203.

——— . "Right You Are (If You Think So): Stanley Fish and the Rhetoric of Assent." *Comparative Literature* 42 (1990): 144–82.

——— . "Limited Think: How Not to Read Derrida." *Diacritics* 20 (1990): 17–36.

——— . *What's Wrong With Postmodernism: Critical Theory and the Ends of Philosophy*. Baltimore: Johns Hopkins University Press, 1990.

Nussbaum, Felicity. "The Politics of Difference." *Eighteenth-Century Studies* 23 (1990): 375–86.

Pearce, Glenn, and Patrick Maynard, ed. *Conceptual Change*. Dordrecht: Reidel, 1973.

Pears, David. *Ludwig Wittgenstein*. New York: Viking, 1969.

Pechter, Edward. "The New Historicism and Its Discontents: Politicizing Renaissance Drama." *PMLA* 102 (1987): 292–303.

The Philosophy of Peirce: Selected Writings. Edited by Justus Buchler. London: Kegan Paul, 1940.

Penrose, Roger. *The Emperor's New Mind: Concerning Computers, Minds, and the Laws of Physics*. Oxford: Oxford University Press, 1989.

Perkins, David. "Discursive Form Versus the Past in Literary History." *New Literary History* 22 (1991): 359–76.

Petrey, Sandy. *Speech Acts and Literary Theory*. New York: Routledge, 1990.

Popkin, Richard H. "Skepticism." *The Encyclopedia of Philosophy*, VII, 449–61.

——— . "Skepticism in Modern Thought." *Dictionary of the History of Ideas*, IV, 240–51.

——— . *The History of Scepticism from Erasmus to Spinoza*. Rev. ed. Berkeley: University of California Press, 1979.

Porter, Carolyn. "History and Literature: 'After the New Historicism.' " *New Literary History* 21 (1990): 253–72.

Posy, Carl. "Dancing to the Antinomy: A Proposal for Transcendental Idealism." *American Philosophical Quarterly* 20 (1983): 81–94.

Pradhan, Shekhar. "Minimalist Semantics: Davidson and Derrida on Meaning, Use, and Convention." *Diacritics* 16 (1986): 66–77.

Prattis, J. Iain. "Dialectics and Experience in Fieldwork: The Poetic Dimension." In Prattis, ed., *Reflections: The Anthropological Muse*, pp. 266–83. Washington, D.C.: American Anthropological Association, 1985.

Putnam, Hilary. *Mind, Language and Reality*. Cambridge: Cambridge University Press, 1975.

——— . "Literature, Science, and Reflection." *New Literary History* 7 (1976): 483–91.

——— . *Meaning and the Moral Sciences*. London: Routledge and Kegan Paul, 1978.

——— . *Reason, Truth and History*. Cambridge: Cambridge University Press, 1981.

——— . "Why Reason Can't Be Naturalized." *Synthese* 52 (1982): 1–23.

——— . *Realism and Reason*. Cambridge: Cambridge University Press, 1983.

——— . "On Truth." In L. Cauman, et al., ed., *How Many Questions? Essays in Honor of Sidney Morgenbesser*. Indianapolis: Hackett, 1983.

——— . "After Empiricism." In J. Rajchman and C. West, ed., *Post-Analytic Philosophy*, pp. 20–30.

——— . "A Comparison of Something with Something Else." *New Literary History* 17 (1985): 61–79.

——— . *The Many Faces of Realism*. LaSalle: Open Court, 1987.

——— . *Representation and Reality*. Cambridge: MIT Press, 1988.

——— . "Truth and Convention: On Davidson's Refutation of Conceptual Relativism." In M. Krausz, ed., *Relativism*, pp. 173–81.

————. *Realism with a Human Face.* Edited by James Conant. Cambridge: Harvard University Press, 1990.

Rader, Ralph W. "Fact, Theory, and Literary Explanation." *Critical Inquiry* 1 (1974): 245–72.

————. "Explaining Our Literary Understanding: A Response to Jay Schleusener and Stanley Fish." *Critical Inquiry* 1 (1975): 901–11.

Rajchman, John, and Cornel West, ed. *Post-Analytic Philosophy.* New York: Columbia University Press, 1985.

Rapaport, Herman. *Heidegger and Derrida: Reflections on Time and Language.* Lincoln: University of Nebraska Press, 1989.

Ravitch, Diane. "Multiculturalism: E Pluribus Plures." *The American Scholar* (Summer 1990): 337–54.

Rawls, John. "A Kantian Conception of Equality." In J. Rajchman and C. West, ed., *Post-Analytic Philosophy,* pp. 201–13.

Rée, Jonathan. "Funny Voices: Stories, Punctuation, and Personal Identity." *New Literary History* 21 (1990): 1039–58.

Reeves, Charles Eric. "Wittgenstein, Rules, and Literary Language." *Neophilologus* 67/1 (January 1983): 15–20.

Riffaterre, Michael. "Fear of Theory." *New Literary History* 21 (1990): 921–38.

Rodenas, Adrian Méndez. "A Journey to the (Literary) Source: The Invention of Origins in Merlin's *Viaje a La Habana.*" *New Literary History* 21 (1990): 707–32,

Rohrmoser, Günther. "Zum Problem der ästhetischen Versöhnung: Schiller und Hegel." *Euphorion* 53 (1959): 351–66.

Rorty, Richard, ed. *The Linguistic Turn: Recent Essays in Philosophical Method.* Chicago: University of Chicago Press, 1967.

Rorty, Richard. "Criteria and Necessity." *Nous* 7 (1973): 313–29.

————. *Philosophy and the Mirror of Nature.* Princeton: Princeton University Press, 1979.

————. *Consequences of Pragmatism (Essays: 1972–1980).* Minneapolis: University of Minnesota Press, 1982.

————. "Deconstruction and Circumvention." *Critical Inquiry* 11 (1984): 1–23.

Rorty, Richard, J. B. Schneewind, and Quentin Skinner, ed. *Philosophy in History: Essays on the Historiography of Philosophy.* Cambridge: Cambridge University Press, 1984.

Rorty, Richard. "The Historiography of Philosophy: Four Genres." In Rorty, et al., ed., *Philosophy in History,* pp. 49–75.

————. "Solidarity or Objectivity?" In J. Rajchman and C. West, ed., *Post-Analytic Philosophy,* pp. 3–19.

————. "Beyond Realism and Anti-Realism." In L. Nagel and R. Heinrich, ed., *Wo steht die Analytische Philosophie heute?,* pp. 103–15. Vienna: Oldenbourg, 1986.

————. "The Contingency of Language." *London Review of Books* (17 April 1986), 3–6.

————. "On Ethnocentrism: A Reply to Clifford Geertz." *Michigan Quarterly Review* 25 (1986): 525–34.

————. "Pragmatism, Davidson and Truth." In E. LePore, ed., *Truth and Interpretation,* pp. 333–55.

————. "The Higher Nominalism in a Nutshell: A Reply to Henry Staten." *Critical Inquiry* 12 (1986): 462–66.

————. "Unfamiliar Noises: Hesse and Davidson on Metaphor." *Proceedings of the Aristotelian Society,* Supp. vol. 61 (1987): 283–96.

————. "The Priority of Democracy to Philosophy." In M. D. Peterson and R. C. Vaughan, ed., *The Virginia Statute for Religious Freedom.* Cambridge: Cambridge University Press, 1988.

————. "Is Natural Science a Natural Kind?" In E. McMullin, ed., *Construction and Constraint,* pp. 49–74.

————. *Contingency, Irony, and Solidarity.* Cambridge: Cambridge University Press, 1989.

————. "Philosophy as Science, as Metaphor, and as Politics." In A. Cohen and M. Dascal, ed., *The Institution of Philosophy: A Discipline in Crisis?*, pp. 13–33. LaSalle: Open Court, 1989.

————. "Two Meanings of 'Logocentrism': A Reply to Norris." In R. W. Dasenbrock, ed., *Redrawing the Lines*, pp. 204–16.

————. "Truth and Freedom: A Reply to Thomas McCarthy." *Critical Inquiry* 16 (1990): 633–43.

Rosen, Stanley. "The Limits of Interpretation." In A. J. Cascardi, ed., *Literature and the Question of Philosophy*, pp. 210–41.

Rouse, Joseph. *Knowledge and Power: Toward a Political Philosophy of Science*. Ithaca: Cornell University Press, 1987.

Ryan, Michael. *Marxism and Deconstruction: A Critical Articulation*. Baltimore: Johns Hopkins University Press, 1982.

Ryle, Gilbert, C. Lewy, and K. R. Popper. "Symposium: Why Are the Calculuses of Logic and Arithmetic Applicable to Reality?" *Logic and Reality (Proceedings of the Aristotelian Society, Supp. vol. 20)*, pp. 20–60. London: Harrison and Sons, 1946.

Said, Edward. "Representing the Colonized: Anthropology's Interlocutors." *Critical Inquiry* 15 (1989): 205–25.

Sanders, N. K. "Introduction." *The Epic of Gilgamesh*. Harmondsworth: Penguin, 1983.

Sauder, Gerhard, ed. *Johann Gottfried Herder: 1744–1803*. Hamburg: Meiner, 1987.

Sayce, Olive. "Das Problem der Vieldeutigkeit in Schillers ästhetischer Terminologie." *Jahrbuch der deutschen Schillergesellschaft* 6 (1962): 149–77.

Schacht, Richard. "Nietzsche's *Gay Science*, Or, How to Naturalize Cheerfully." In R. Solomon and K. Higgins, ed., *Reading Nietzsche*, pp. 68–86.

Schalkwyk, D. J. "A social theory of language: Ludwig Wittgenstein and the current theoretical debate." *Journal of literary studies/Tydskrif vir literatuurwetenskap* 1/2 (April 1985): 43–58.

Schama, Simon. *Citizens: A Chronicle of the French Revolution*. New York: Knopf, 1989.

Scheffler, Israel. *Science and Subjectivity*. Indianapolis: Bobbs-Merrill, 1967.

Kritische Friedrich-Schlegel-Ausgabe. Edited by Ernst Behler. Munich: Schöningh, 1959ff.

Scholes, Robert. "Deconstruction and Communication." *Critical Inquiry* 14 (1988): 278–95.

Schwyzer, Hubert. "Thought and Reality: The Metaphysics of Kant and Wittgenstein." *Philosophical Quarterly* 23 (1973): 193–206.

Searle, John R. "What Is A Speech Act?" In Max Black, ed., *Philosophy in America: Essays*. Ithaca: Cornell University Press, 1965.

————. *Speech Acts: An Essay in the Philosophy of Language*. Cambridge: Cambridge University Press, 1969.

————. "The Logical Status of Fictional Discourse." *New Literary History* 6 (1975): 319–32.

————. "Reiterating the Differences: A Reply to Derrida." *Glyph I*, pp. 198–208. Baltimore: Johns Hopkins University Press, 1977.

————. *Expression and Meaning: Studies in the Theory of Speech Acts*. Cambridge: Cambridge University Press, 1979.

————. "The Word Turned Upside Down (Review of J. Culler, *On Deconstruction*)." *The New York Review of Books* (27 October 1983), 74–79.

————. "The Storm Over the University." *The New York Review of Books* (6 December 1990), 34–42.

Searle, John R., Gerald Graff, Barbara Herrnstein Smith, and George Levine. " 'The Storm Over the University': An Exchange." *The New York Review of Books* (14 February 1991), 48–50.

Seebohm, Thomas M. "Der systematische Ort der Herderschen Metakritik." *Kant-Studien* 63 (1972): 59–73.

Sextus Empiricus. Translated by R. G. Bury. London: W. Heinemann, 1933–49.

Shapiro, Gary. "The Writing on the Wall: *The Antichrist* and the Semiotics of History." In R. Solomon and K. Higgins, ed., *Reading Nietzsche*, pp. 192–217.

Shusterman, Richard. "Postmodernism and the Aesthetic Turn." *Poetics Today* 10 (1989): 605–22.

Siegel, Fred. "The Cult of Multiculturalism." *The New Republic* (18 February 1991), 34–40.

Skinner, Quentin. "The End of Philosophy? (Review of R. Rorty, *Philosophy and the Mirror of Nature*)." *The New York Review of Books* (19 March 1981), 46–48.

Smart, J.J.C. "How to Turn the *Tractatus* Wittgenstein into (Almost) Donald Davidson." In E. LePore, ed., *Truth and Interpretation*, pp. 92–100.

Smith, Barbara Herrnstein. *On the Margins of Discourse: The Relation of Literature to Language*. Chicago: University of Chicago Press, 1978.

———. *Contingencies of Value: Alternative Perspectives for Critical Theory*. Cambridge: Harvard University Press, 1988.

Smith, Norman Kemp. *A Commentary to Kant's 'Critique of Pure Reason.'* 2d ed. London: Macmillan, 1923.

Soll, Ivan. "Reflections on Recurrence." In R. Solomon, ed., *Nietzsche*, Modern Studies in Philosophy. Garden City: Doubleday, 1973.

———. "Pessimism and the Tragic View of Life: Reconsiderations of Nietzsche's *Birth of Tragedy*." In R. Solomon and K. Higgins, ed., *Reading Nietzsche*, pp. 104–31.

Solomon, Robert C., and Kathleen M. Higgins, ed. *Reading Nietzsche*. New York: Oxford University Press, 1988.

Sowell, Thomas. *A Conflict of Visions*. New York: Morrow, 1987.

———. *Preferential Policies: An International Perspective*. New York: Morrow, 1990.

Specht, E. K. "Wittgenstein und das Problem des 'A Priori'." *Revue Internationale de Philosophie* 88–89 (1969): 167–78.

Spivak, Gayatri Chakravorty. "The Making of Americans, the Teaching of English, and the Future of Culture Studies." *New Literary History* 21 (1990): 781–98.

Staten, Henry. *Wittgenstein and Derrida*. Lincoln: University of Nebraska Press, 1984.

Stecker, Robert. "Apparent, Implied, and Postulated Authors." *Philosophy and Literature* 11 (1987): 258–71.

Steele, Shelby. "Thinking Beyond Race." *The Wilson Quarterly* 14/3 (Summer 1990): 62–68.

———. *The Content of Our Character: A New Vision of Race in America*. New York: St. Martin's Press, 1990.

Stenius, Erik. *Wittgenstein's Tractatus: A Critical Exposition of Its Main Lines of Thought*. Ithaca: Cornell University Press, 1964.

Stern, Laurent. "Narrative versus Description in Historiography." *New Literary History* 21 (1990): 555–68.

Stout, Jeffrey. "What Is the Meaning of a Text?" *New Literary History* 14 (1982): 1–12.

Strawson, P. F. *Individuals: An Essay in Descriptive Metaphysics*. London: Methuen, 1959.

———. *The Bounds of Sense: An Essay on Kant's* Critique of Pure Reason. London: Methuen, 1966.

Sturrock, John. "Writing Between the Lines: The Language of Translation." *New Literary History* 21 (1990): 993–1013.

Suppe, Frederick, ed. *The Structure of Scientific Theories*. Urbana: University of Illinois Press, 1974.

Sychrava, Juliet. *Schiller to Derrida: Idealism in Aesthetics*. Cambridge: Cambridge University Press, 1989.

Tanning, Dorothee, et al. "Deconstruction: An Exchange." *The New York Review of Books* (4 December 1980), 57–58.

Taylor, Charles. "Philosophy and Its History." In R. Rorty, et al., ed. *Philosophy in History*, pp. 17–30.

———. "Overcoming Epistemology." In K. Baynes, et al., ed., *After Philosophy*, pp. 464–88.

———. "Rorty in the Epistemological Tradition." In A. Malachowski, ed., *Reading Rorty*, pp. 257–75.

Thompson, John B., and David Held, ed. *Habermas: Critical Debates.* Cambridge: MIT Press, 1982.

Thornton, Jerome E. "The Paradoxical Journey of the African American in African American Fiction." *New Literary History* 21 (1990): 733–46.

Toulmin, Stephen. *Human Understanding.* Princeton: Princeton University Press, 1972.

———. "The Construal of Reality: Criticism in Modern and Postmodern Science." *Critical Inquiry* 9 (1982): 93–111.

Turner, Frederick. "The Meaning of Value: An Economics for the Future." *New Literary History* 21 (1990): 747–62.

Ueding, Gert. *Schillers Rhetorik: Idealistische Wirkungsästhetik und rhetorische Tradition.* Tübingen: Niemeyer, 1971.

Uhlig, Ludwig. "Georg Forster und Herder." *Euphorion* 84 (1990): 339–66.

Van Reijen, Willem, et al. "Symposium on Habermas." *Theory, Culture, and Society* 7/4 (November 1990): 91–125.

Vartanian, Aram. "Derrida, Rousseau, and the Difference." *Studies in Eighteenth-Century Culture* 19 (1989): 129–51.

Vermazen, Bruce, and Merrill B. Hintikka, ed. *Essays on Davidson: Actions and Events.* Oxford: Clarendon Press, 1985.

Vesey, Godfrey, ed. *Understanding Wittgenstein.* Ithaca: Cornell University Press, 1974.

Von Molnár, Géza. *Romantic Vision, Ethical Context: Novalis and Artistic Autonomy.* Minneapolis: University of Minnesota Press, 1987.

Walters, Michael. "In the life of the postmodern (Review of Sarup, *An Introductory Guide to Post-structuralism and Postmodernism*, et al.)." *Times Literary Supplement* (22–28 December 1989), 1419–20.

Weissberg, Liliane. "Language's Wound: Herder, Philoctetes, and the Origin of Speech." *MLN* 104 (1989): 548–79.

Wheeler, Samuel C., III. "Indeterminacy of French Interpretation: Derrida and Davidson." In E. LePore, ed., *Truth and Interpretation*, pp. 477–94.

———. "The Extension of Deconstruction." *The Monist* 69 (1986): 3–21.

———. "Wittgenstein as Conservative Deconstructor." *New Literary History* 19 (1988): 239–58.

White, Hayden. *Metahistory: The Historical Imagination in Nineteenth-Century Europe.* Baltimore: Johns Hopkins University Press, 1973.

———. *Tropics of Discourse: Essays in Cultural Criticism.* Baltimore: Johns Hopkins University Press, 1978.

Whorf, Benjamin Lee. *Language, Thought, and Reality: Selected Writings of Benjamin Lee Whorf.* Edited by John B. Carroll. Cambridge: MIT Press, 1956.

Williams, Bernard. *Ethics and the Limits of Philosophy.* Cambridge: Harvard University Press, 1985.

Williams, Raymond. *Marxism and Literature.* Oxford: Oxford University Press, 1977.

Wilson, Bryan R., ed. *Rationality.* New York: Blackwell, 1970.

Winch, Peter. "Understanding a Primitive Society." *American Philosophical Quarterly* 1 (1964): 307–24.

———, ed. *Studies in the Philosophy of Wittgenstein.* London: Routledge and Kegan Paul, 1969.

Winspur, Steven. "Wittgenstein's Semiotic Investigations." *American Journal of Semiotics* 3/2 (1984): 33–57.

Wisdom, John, J. L. Austin, and A. J. Ayer. "Symposium: Other Minds." *Logic and Reality (Proceedings of the Aristotelian Society, Supp. vol. 20)*, pp. 122–97. London: Harrison and Sons, 1946.

Wittgenstein, Ludwig. *Notebooks, 1914–1916.* Edited by G. H. von Wright and G.E.M. Anscombe. Translated by G. E. M. Anscombe. New York: Harper & Row, 1969.

———. *Tractatus Logico-Philosophicus.* Translated by D. F. Pears and B. F. McGuinness. 2d ed. London: Routledge and Kegan Paul, 1972.

————. "Lecture on Ethics." *Philosophical Review* 74 (1965): 3–12.
————. *The Blue and Brown Books: Preliminary Studies for the "Philosophical Investigations."* New York: Harper & Row, 1965.
————. *Philosophical Investigations.* Translated by G.E.M. Anscombe. 3rd ed. New York: Macmillan, 1958.
————. *Zettel.* Edited by G. E. M. Anscombe and G. H. von Wright. Translated by G. E. M. Anscombe. Oxford: Blackwell, 1967.
————. *Über Gewißheit/On Certainty.* Edited by G. E. M. Anscombe and G. H. von Wright. Translated by Denis Paul and G. E. M. Anscombe. New York: Harper & Row, 1972.
Wittgenstein and Literary Theory. New Literary History 19/2 (Winter 1988).
Wohlfahrt, Günter. "Grammatik und Ästhetik: Zum Verhältnis von Sprache und ästhetischer Erfahrung bei Wittgenstein." *DVLG* 57/3 (September 1983): 399–414.
Wolff, Robert Paul. *Kant's Theory of Mental Activity: A Commentary on the Transcendental Analytic of the* Critique of Pure Reason. Cambridge: Harvard University Press, 1963; rpt. Gloucester: Peter Smith, 1973.
————. *The Autonomy of Reason: A Commentary on Kant's* Groundwork of the Metaphysic of Morals. New York: Harper & Row, 1973.
Wuchterl, Kurt, and Adolf Hübner. *Ludwig Wittgenstein in Selbstzeugnissen und Bilddokumenten.* Reinbek: Rowohlt, 1979.
Yeakey, Carol Camp. "Social Change Through the Humanities: An Essay on the Politics of Literacy and Culture in American Society." *New Literary History* 21 (1990): 841–62.

INDEX

343